D0914379

The United States and
International Markets

New York University
Center for International Studies
Studies in Peaceful Change

Why Federations Fail: An Inquiry into the Requisites for Successful Federalism, Thomas M. Franck, Gisbert H. Flanz, Herbert J. Spiro, and Frank N. Trager (New York: New York University Press), 1968

A Free Trade Association, Thomas M. Franck and Edward Weisband, eds. (New York: New York University Press), 1968

Comparative Constitutional Process, Thomas M. Franck (New York: Praeger; London: Sweet and Maxwell), 1968

The Structure of Impartiality, Thomas M. Franck (New York: Macmillan), 1968

Agents of Change: A Close Look at the Peace Corps, David Hapgood and Meridan Bennet (Boston: Little, Brown), 1968

Law, Reason and Justice: Essays in Legal Philosophy, Graham B. Hughes (New York: New York University Press), 1969

Czechoslovakia: Intervention and Impact, I. William Zartman, ed. (New York: New York University Press), 1970

Sierra Leone: An Experiment in Democracy in an African Nation, Gershon Collier (New York: New York University Press), 1970

Microstates and Micronesia: Problems of America's Pacific Islands and Other Minute Territories, Stanley A. de Smith (New York: New York University Press), 1970

International Business Negotiations: A Study in India, Ashok Kapoor (New York: New York University Press), 1970

Foreign Capital for Economic Development: A Korean Case Study, Seung Hee Kim (New York: Praeger), 1970

The Politics of Trade Negotiations between Africa and the European Economic Community: The Weak Confront the Strong, I. William Zartman (Princeton, New Jersey: Princeton University Press), 1971

Word Politics: Verbal Strategy Among the Superpowers, Thomas M. Franck, Edward Weisband (New York: Oxford University Press), 1972.

The United States and International Markets

Commercial Policy Options in an Age of Controls

Studies in Peaceful Change
Prepared under the Auspices of
The Center for International Studies
New York University

Edited by
Robert G. Hawkins
and
Ingo Walter
Graduate School of Business
Administration
New York University

Lexington Books
D.C. Heath and Company
Lexington, Massachusetts
Toronto   London

Hawkins, Robert G
      The United States and International Markets
      (Studies in peaceful change)

Hawkins, Robert G
  The United States and International Markets
  (Studies in peaceful change)
  Includes bibliographical references.
  1. Tariff—Addresses, essays, lectures.
  2. Commercial policy—Addresses, essays, lectures.
  3. United States—Commercial policy—Addresses, essays, lectures.
I. Walter, Ingo, joint author. II. Title. III. Series.
HF1713.H38   382'.0973   72-3548
ISBN 0-669-84020-3

HF
1713
.H38

Table of Contents

List of Figures

List of Tables

Foreword

This volume is ideally suited for the "Studies in Peaceful Change" series of the Center for International Studies of New York University. The studies in this series are directed toward the analysis and exploration of avenues of peaceful social change in the international context. The international trade issues confronting the world economy represent a serious potential danger to the continued stability of international commercial relations. In analyzing these issues and their underlying causes, and in indicating the possible results of alternative policy changes, the studies in this volume provide a more sound basis for sensible "peaceful change."

In the postwar period, there has been a marked trend toward liberal international economic relations—tariffs have been reduced, currency convertability has been restored and extended, foreign investment has grown rapidly, and international travel, transportation, and communications have undergone a veritable revolution. Among the results have been a growing interpenetration and interdependence among national economies, as foreign trade and foreign investment have grown much more rapidly than national production and income. The rapid expansion of international economic relations has paralled a deemphasis of and increasing frustration with international military, strategic, and political matters. The result has been that trade, investment, and finance have recently been of preeminent concern in international diplomacy.

The focus of attention on international trade matters, dramatized by President Nixon's New Economic Policy of August 1971, is one result of a major shift over the last two decades in the structure of the international economy. This has been manifest in a loss of markets and a persistant balance-of-payments problem for the United States. Additionally, a growing use of nontariff barriers to trade and a reemergence of protectionist—as well as nationalist—sentiment suggest the "end of an era" of trade liberalization.

What, then, are the prospects for international trade policy in the 1970s? This volume, in identifying the domestic interest groups in commercial policy, how these interests have been translated into particular structures of tariff and nontariff barriers to trade, and into business practices to restrict competition, provides considerable insight into how the world reached its present state. Moreover, it goes further by addressing the question of what is to come. It assesses the playoff which nations must face under trade and investment liberalization. This playoff involves the costs of economic transition which would result from the further opening of the domestic economy to foreign competition and the potential benefits from improved allocation of national and international resources. This playoff is obvious, and is currently in a state of flux with respect to a number of particular issues examined in this volume. These include trade policy in agricultural commodities, treatment of exports from developing countries, trade policy aspects of foreign production by American firms, and U.S. policy with respect to East-West trade.

On these and other issues, such as the predictability of the efforts of trade liberalization, new and original insights are provided. Hopefully, as international confrontation on these problems evolves into negotiation, the understanding of positions and results of alternative outcomes will be enriched by these studies.

Thomas M. Franck
Director
Center for International Studies
New York University

Preface

Each of the essays in this volume is intended to address a major problem in international commercial policy facing the United States in the decade ahead. They focus on the structure of barriers to international market access among the industrial countries, which to a large extent shape the policy options that are open to the United States in the face of changing international alignments.

The first section of the book attempts to discern the main trends in international trade policy that seem to be forming and which will condition the course of future events, including the available options for the United States. Recognizing the importance that must be attributed to domestic forces in the formation of international trade policy, a politico-economic decision model is developed which is designed to explain the way these forces operate.

Four chapters are specifically devoted to barriers to international market access, since the existing structure of commercial distortions defines where we are now and how difficult it will be to progress in the future. The structure of tariffs is examined in detail, as is the operation and application of nontariff obstacles to international trade, with emphasis on the principal developed market-economy countries that account for the bulk of world commerce. No less important, private distortions of competitive conditions and governmental attempts to deal with them are also examined.

The second half of the book deals with several specific aspects of the trade-policy issue. To what extent do the economic structures of the industrial countries determine the benefits of mutual trade liberalization and, by inference, the costs of increased trade restrictions? What may happen to United States trade flows if trade among the industrial countries undergoes significant further liberalization? To what extent are economies of large-scale production important as a determinant of the "dynamic" benefits of trade liberalization?

Finally, several specific issues are addressed: the problem of agricultural trade, of especial interest to the United States; trade preferences for the developing countries, as part of system of trade discrimination that has existed for centuries; and the American position in East-West trade.

The book makes few predictions, except to indicate quite clearly that the future course of commercial relations between nations will be considerably more diffuse than it has been in the past. It does, however, examine many of the major issues that need to be considered in making predictions—in summing up and netting out the pressures toward and away from freer trade and in assessing the significance of the parameters that determine the response of the system.

The editors would like to express their thanks to the New York University Center for International Studies, under whose auspices much of the volume was prepared, and to Harry H. Bell, Ernest H. Preeg and Thomas A. Wolf, who took the time to contribute essays in their respective areas of expertise. Miss Kathy Alamo, Miss Nora O'Connor, and Miss Lee Silman contributed the typing services in their usual cheerful ways.

Robert G. Hawkins
Ingo Walter

The United States and
International Markets

1

Trends in International Commercial Policy— Implications for the United States

The Editors

The late 1960s marked the end of an era of trade liberalization which had its roots in the Great Depression of the 1930s. Although interrupted by World War II and the ensuing reconstruction period, the principle of free trade as an imperative of global economic progress was generally accepted—even if it was not always implemented forcefully, directly, or multilaterally.

For almost thirty years, United States commercial policy likewise focused on trade liberalization, beginning with the Reciprocal Trade Agreements Act of 1934 and ending with the Trade Expansion Act of 1962. More often than not, the United States provided the initiative in international commercial diplomacy, in its role as the world's largest single trader. The United States not only fostered freer trade policies where it was a participant, but also actively encouraged closer economic ties among groups of countries in various parts of the world as being fundamentally in the American national interest.

That era in international economic policy has apparently ended and world trade now faces a set of new realities. The rules of the game have changed, and a new set of principles is being learned and implemented. International trade policy in the future will be much more diffuse, and it may not be unusual to see significant liberalization of commercial relations proceeding *simultaneously* with the creation of new barriers to international commerce. Progress in multilateral negotiations may parallel increasing restrictions applied by national governments. There is no longer a powerful and consistent underlying theme—such as the principle of nondiscrimination—and this by itself ensures the emergence of trends that may not be mutually consistent and indeed may be contradictory. Several such trends may be identified in an attempt to discern the shape of things to come.

Shifting Economic Influence

The United States is no longer the world's largest trading region. The European Economic Community has usurped this position, and the gap will widen considerably once EEC enlargement has been completed. Perhaps less pronounced, but equally important, U.S. economic leverage based on other indicators such as national income and population has also declined in relative

1

terms. And yet the diminution of U.S. influence in world trade has not kept pace with these ongoing shifts in realities.

Several reasons may be cited. First, the EEC has been unable thus far to take the initiative in international trade negotiations. In part, this is due to the nature of the Community's internal decision-making mechanism. In part, it may be attributed to its preoccupation with the integration process itself, accentuated by a major expansion in membership in the 1970s. An additional factor is that the Community members often do not have a complete harmony of interests on trade issues. The community thus *reacts*; it does not act as a mover and shaker on the global economic scene. It frequently checks intiatives originating elsewhere; it seldom contributes important initiatives of its own except in bilateral arrangements with nonmembers, as will be seen below.

Second, the shift in relative economic and commercial strength away from the United States has not been paralleled by a corresponding shift in relative political strength. The EEC is not a political union, nor will it be one for years to come. There has been a notable unwillingness or inability on the part of other Western industrial countries to build their defense commitments in proportion to their economic strength, with the result that military reliance on the United States continues largely undiminished. Consequently, the U.S. role in international relations exceeds that justified on economic grounds alone.

Third, despite a persistent balance-of-payments problem, restrictions on some capital outflows, and the 1971 devaluation and inconvertibility of the dollar, the United States remains the major financial center of the world and the principal long-term creditor country. The link between international commercial and international financial matters ensures that the preeminant role of the United States as a supplier of world capital and financial services will spill over onto its role in commercial policy negotiations. While one might anticipate a gradual decline in the relative importance of the United States, as other capital markets grow and become internationalized, this will take considerable time.

Lastly, the United States remains far less dependent on international trade than do the other industrial countries. The export market plays a relatively minor role as a determinant of U.S. income and employment, while dependence on imported raw materials and other inputs remains comparatively low. Relative invulnerability of this nature, although diminishing in certain sectors, is important in the determination of leverage and freedom of action in international commercial policy. The U.S. market, on the other hand—in part because of the relatively free access accorded to imports—plays a major role in the economies of its trading partners, and this serves as a further underpinning of the American position in international commercial relations.

In short, the U.S. relative position in the world economy is indeed diminishing, as well it should. And yet its preeminence in international economic policy matters remains. No longer do American initiatives and proposals receive uncritical acceptance, and this is probably all to the good. But it is far too early to view the United States as simply a coequal partner in the game of world trade. Its commercial-policy options are perhaps constrained and conditioned by these trends but its responsibilities are enhanced.

Economic Regionalism

No less important than the pervasive shifts in the underlying economic parameters is a fundamental change in the climate of trade-policy formation, from globalism to regionalism. The "most-favored-nation" principle of nondiscrimination embodied in the U.S. Reciprocal Trade Agreements Acts and later in the General Agreement on Tariffs and Trade (GATT) is today honored more in the breech than in practice. Already in the early 1950s, the European Coal and Steel Community (ECSC) represented an agreement by a group of industrial countries to provide free access to their national markets for each other's products in a specific economic sector, and toward the end of that decade this was extended to substantially all industrial products in the Rome Treaty creating the European Economic Community.

While legal under Article XX of the GATT, these arrangements greatly eroded the principle of nondiscrimination. Yet they were tolerated, even encouraged, on the grounds that effective regional economic integration in Europe would, in the final analysis, benefit nonmembers and members alike in spite of possibly troublesome interim trade adjustments. The European Free Trade Association (EFTA) followed as a somewhat looser, essentially defensive, arrangement among non-EEC Western European countries—as did a host of emulative experiments in developing countries, most of which were doomed to failure.

The United States participated in none of these arrangements. Its lone foray with economic regionalism remains the Canadian-U.S. Automotive Agreement, negotiated in 1965, providing for regional free trade in automobiles and parts. American strategy concentrated instead on broadbased trade liberalization, producing a series of successful multilateral negotiations which ended with the Kennedy Round of 1964-67. The U.S. defense against economic regionalism in Europe was thus a powerful offense pressing for liberalization on a broader basis, anticipating that the trade-discriminatory effects of the EEC and EFTA would be minimized by bringing down trade barriers in general.

The Kennedy Round agreements on tariffs, implemented during 1968-72, represented a major success under which average tariff rates on industrial products were reduced by about one-third. Nevertheless, it gradually became clear that the regional approach to trade liberalization was proving to be an even greater success. And with the increasing inward orientation of the EEC, the success of its enlargement to encompass fully the United Kingdom, Denmark, Norway, and Ireland; and its bilateral arrangements with the other EFTA members as well as a variety of developing countries, which give preferential access to each other's markets, and with additional special trade relationships with various other developed and developing economies, the potential costs to the United States of the regional approach in Europe grew and became more visible in relation to the potential benefits. Disenchantment followed, and the vigorous American support of the EEC ebbed in the late 1960s and changed into a serious scepticism in the early 1970s.

Defenders of the EEC point to the fact that U.S. exports to the Community have grown rapidly, that massive and highly profitable American investments in Europe are in large measure based on the emergence of a sizeable and unified regional market, and that the U.S.-EEC trade balance has always been heavily in favor of the United States. But such arguments are unconvincing. The real question is what *would have happened* had alternative policies been followed by the EEC in place of aggressive commercial regionalism. No one can argue that the EEC damaged American trade absolutely, but it has become clear that U.S. exports have been harmed by its extending regional preferences. And there is increasing concern with an apparent internal dynamic characterizing the Community which seemingly impedes liberalization of trade relations between the EEC and the rest of the world.

The new American position on regionalism has been stated forcefully, in retrospect perhaps belatedly, with little apparent effect. Proposals have been made for broader free-trade areas, e.g., encompassing an Atlantic Community or even all of the industrial market-economy countries. Efforts have been made to encourage acceptance of more liberal alternatives in EEC policies, particularly with respect to agriculture and special trade agreements with nonmember states. Protests have been made in the GATT, OECD and other international forums, all with a notable lack of success, regarding the fundamental issues involved. The momentum of economic regionalism thus threatens to divide the world economy into major economic blocs, a result which all parties specifically decried during the early years of the EEC.

There are clearly two lines of defense for nonparticipants against growing economic regionalism centered in Western Europe. One is *defensive regionalism*, perhaps with a North-South American bloc centered on the United States, and/or a Pacific Basin bloc centered on Japan—a "tripolarization" of the non-Communist world. Relatively free trade would be pursued within each bloc, and trade discrimination leveled against outsiders. The political and economic consequences of such an arrangement have not been fully explored, but they certainly call for a great deal of caution in pursuing this route.

The second alternative is the vigorous promotion of new and ambitious *multilateral trade negotiations*. To the extent that trade barriers can be reduced or eliminated on a broad basis, the challenge of economic regionalism in the trade sphere will be correspondingly lessened. In particular, the total elimination over a specified adjustment period of all tariffs on industrial products would make a major contribution toward this end. Both politically and economically, an integrated world trading system is clearly preferable to a multipolar one.

East-West Economic Ties

Apprehension about developments in Europe and a deteriorating trade balance, together with an increasing recognition of the role of trade in promoting an East-West political détente, all figured in a relaxation of U.S. restrictions on trade with the Socialist countries of Eastern Europe and Asia in the late 1960s and early 1970s. It became amply clear, as some economists had been saying for years, that many U.S. trade controls had very little adverse impact on the belligerence of actual or potential American adversaries.

First, the Eastern Socialist states gradually developed their own supply capabilities for many of the restricted products which the United States refused to export. Second, the industrial countries of Western Europe and Japan obligingly provided a wide range of goods which U.S. suppliers were prohibited from exporting, in spite of periodic American counterpressure and restrictions imposed on the trading activities of subsidiaries of U.S. firms located abroad. Third, the strategic importance of many of the restricted products was often being undermined, necessitating a substantive revision of policy in this area. Finally, it became increasingly clear that trade liberalization is a major component of global harmony, and that a desired relaxation of East-West tensions would in part have to build on a corresponding liberalization of commercial arrangements.

Intense European and Japanese activity in trade with the Socialist countries, including construction of major industrial facilities and long-term supply contracts, served to hasten a major reassessment of U.S. policy in this area during the early years of the Nixon administration. This included an easing of many of the existing export restrictions and a unilateral elimination of the embargo on U.S. imports from the Peoples Republic of China. Liberalization was extended significantly in connection with the President's visits to Peking and Moscow, including high-level trade negotiations with the Soviet Union, although a comprehensive commercial treaty proved more elusive than originally expected.

Apart from its political significance, the liberalization of East-West trade constitutes an important option for the United States in the trade-policy sphere. It clearly represents a diversification of American interest, and a hedge against the possibly adverse consequences of regionalism. At the same time, it may provide access to a new market for U.S. exports heretofore largely untapped, thereby helping to counter a significant adverse shift in the balance of trade.

Nevertheless a great many questions remain. What is the size of the Eastern European and Chinese markets for U.S. exports? Can the United States compete effectively? What products can the Socialist countries, in time, realistically supply to the markets of the West and in what volume? How will trade relations with the East be carried out? What products will remain legitimately under restrictions? How will the vagaries of international politics affect the orderly conduct of trade? Only time will clarify these issues. The fact remains, nevertheless, that the pursuit of expanded trade relations with the Socialist countries of Eastern Europe and Asia will represent an important objective of United States commercial policy in the coming decade.

Balance-of-Payments Adjustment and Trade Policy

Yet another determinant of trends in commercial policy is its organic interrelationship with developments in the area of international monetary policy. Every barrier to free international competition represents—by virtue of the fact that it distorts product prices between national markets—a *de facto* alteration in the effective rate of exchange between national currencies.

Under the international monetary arrangements that have existed since World War II, exchange rates have been relatively rigid and—given macroeconomic policies geared to divergent national needs—periodic payments disequilibria were endemic to the system. Restoration of balance in external payments required the application of potentially costly measures affecting domestic economic activity and/or significant shifts in currency parities, both moves being distasteful and politically sensitive, accelerated by massive intercountry flows of short-term funds for speculative reasons. Imperfections in the payments adjustment mechanism and limited available policy options prompted periodic use of commercial policy actions as tools of international monetary adjustment.

One of the major factors tending to minimize pressures for the use of restrictive trade practices for balance-of-payments purposes during the decades of the 1950s and 1960s was the large and consistent U.S. external deficit. This, together with the foreign desire to accumulate dollar balances as part of their international reserves (at least to the mid-1960s), made it possible for most advanced countries to run, on average, external surpluses and thus build up their international reserves. This effectively removed the balance-of-payments argument for trade restrictions among a large group of countries for a substantial period of time.

At the same time the United States, following its general commitment to principles of freer trade, avoided any *major* commercial policy actions in response to its growing external deficits until August, 1971. Over the same period, however, exchange rates had also remained relatively fixed, and so the sizeable American deficit and the ensuing currency speculation inevitably led to a recasting of the monetary system.

This is not to suggest that payments difficulties never led individual countries to resist or retrench from freer trade in the 1950s and 1960s. Rarely, as in the case of Germany in 1967, was unilateral trade *liberalization* used explicitly to countervail a troublesome balance of payment surplus and to ease the pressure of domestic inflation through increased competition from imports. More common were increases in trade barriers to depress imports in the case of payments deficits and losses in international reserves. Major examples include the general imposition of import quotas by France in 1968, prior import deposits by the United Kingdom in 1967-69, and a surcharge on import duties by the United States in 1971. But, these reversals were certainly less frequent than would have been the case if international payments difficulties had been experienced by more countries, more often.

Perhaps less dramatic but more important is the fact that international monetary turmoil automatically provides a fertile environment for pressures for increased trade barriers that always emanate from protectionist interests. This occurred in the late 1960s, as the U.S. deficit became undesirably large and its adjustment proved elusive. The monetary system was challenged in such an environment, and trade distortions were likely to proliferate.

The reform of the system, being worked out in the first half of the 1970s, surely will provide for more frequent exchange rate changes and quicker adjustments for external imbalances. The situation of the 1950s and 1960s, in which one "center" country runs large and consistent deficits and the rest of the world runs average surpluses without an effective means of adjustment, should be remedied. To the extent that the particular structure of international payments just described was conducive to restrictive trade policies, its replacement by a system which provides quicker, more effective, and more automatic adjustment to external payments crises will be beneficial.

Improvements in the international monetary adjustment mechanism may thus favor more liberal commercial relations between nations. Commercial policy responses tend to be used when there is no effective—or less costly—alternative. In the 1950s and 1960s, they did not have to be used. In the new monetary environment, adjustment must occur, and exchange rate variations are likely to be a more usable and effective alternative to trade-restriction. While monetary reform does not mean automatic trade liberalization, it will, however, mitigate a significant obstruction and provide a viable substitute. There is also ample reason for caution; nothing will bring about the massive imposition of trade-inhibiting policies and resultant economic disintegration faster than international monetary collapse.

The inexorable interconnection between international trade and monetary problems naturally extends into the negotiation sphere as well. There is ample evidence that major trade and monetary negotiations will henceforth be closely linked. American pressures for international monetary reform in 1971 and 1972 were closely tied to freer access for U.S. products to foreign markets, and a return of the international monetary system to reasonable normality was clearly linked to progress on the trade front. And this is as it should be. Although trade negotiations in the 1970s may take place in forums distinct from those for monetary negotiations, it is clear that they will be closely connected. On the other hand, once a viable monetary system is devised—based on meaningful and orderly exchange-rate flexibility—the monetary sector will once again become less important in the formation of international commercial policy.

Market-Sharing, Disruption, and Adjustment

With tariff levels bound by regional and multilateral agreements, and the more obvious nontariff barriers subject to increasing scrutiny, the periodic exposure of individual sectors of national economies to serious import competition has become a source of concern in a number of industrial countries. In particular, continuous structural change in national economies forces corresponding shifts in international competitive advantage and trade flows, and these in turn require significant internal economic adjustments to meet the new international market conditions.

Often the required structural adjustments are gradual, and indistinguishable from similar responses attributable to domestic economic growth and change. Sometimes however they develop rapidly, with a sudden and highly visible impact. Domestic competitive advantage stagnates or declines while foreign supply capabilities expand. Imports of the product in question reach growth rates of 10, 15, even 25 percent per annum. Domestic absorption may grow, but if a mature and standardized product is involved, much of the import growth will be at the expense of domestic suppliers. Profits decline, jobs are lost, plants close, and pressures to "do something" mount, in the face of substantial and highly visible adjustment costs to be borne by the import-competing sector.

The result, frequently, is to declare the affected product to be "sensitive," and to seek an accommodation with the relevant suppliers designed to ease the pressure from imports. The approach may be unilateral, requesting self-restraint of export-expansion in the form of "voluntary" restrictions. Administration of the restrictions is left up to the government of the exporting country, but it is made clear that stronger measures are indeed available if cooperation is not forthcoming. The goal is a share of the local market not exceeding that attained currently, or in a recent base year. Imports may be permitted to grow, but normally not at a rate exceeding overall growth of the national market.

Market-sharing, or administrative throttling of imports has, in a dynamic context, the same effects as a fixed import quota in a static context. Such arrangements are also extended on a multilateral level, joining together all or most major importers and suppliers of certain sensitive products, and seeking "orderly marketing" on a global scale. The United States has imposed such arrangements unilaterally on trading partners in the case of steel, woolens, and synthetic textiles, to cite the most prominent examples. The major multinational market-sharing scheme is the Long-Term Arrangement on Cotton Textiles (LTA), first implemented in 1962 under the auspices of the GATT, and encompassing virtually all major markets and suppliers in this particular product group.

The evidence seems to point to a further extension of explicit and implicit market-sharing arrangements in the 1970s, together with antidisruptive measures at the national level to place ceilings on import growth. Regardless of whether the plight of the domestic industry is attributable to foreign competition, imports represent an easy target, and this renders them highly vulnerable to this type of solution. It is therefore not unreasonable to expect a gradual widening of multilateral market-sharing agreements to encompass noncotton textiles, shoes, and electronic products, for example. Should that fail, national efforts to develop individual market-sharing agreements on a bilateral basis may well become more sought-after.

The classic prescription for trade shifts induced by international structural change is, of course, to carry out responsive adjustment in the domestic economy—shifting resources out of low-productivity, internationally uncompetitive lines into sectors where their use is more efficient and competitive on world markets. Since the benefits of reallocation accrue to the economy as a whole, it is the economy as a whole that should pay their costs, and not the impacted sectors alone. This principle of equity in a dynamic economy requiring constant structural change thus calls for *adjustment assistance* financed out of general tax revenues. The case must be made more forcefully that adjustment assistance is inherently preferable to and more equitable than import-restriction, from the standpoint of the national economic welfare. If this view wins out, U.S. economic structure and trade flows in the 1980s may be quite different from that which exists today—even to the extent that import controls may become obsolete—at significantly higher levels of real income. If it does not, the gap between actual and potential efficiency in the use of productive resources will grow substantially in the coming decades.

The Developing Countries

An important potential breakthrough in trade policy towards the developing countries occurred in 1971, when a Generalized System of Preferences (GSP) was implemented by the EEC, Japan, and several other industrial countries. After long negotiations in the United Nations Conference on Trade and Development (UNCTAD) and the Organization for Economic Cooperation and Development (OECD), special trade concessions for developing countries were accepted in principle by the developed countries. The horizontal equity embodied in nondiscrimination (each supplier nation treated equally) was thereby recognized as being unfair to developing countries, which are hardly "equal" in competitive terms. By according special trade concessions to developing economies, the GSP provides an element of vertical equity (unequals treated unequally) intended specifically to benefit them.

In principle, the developed market-economy countries committed themselves to admit a wide variety of manufactures from developing countries on a generally tariff-free or preferential basis—*without* demanding reciprocity from the beneficiaries. Generally excluded from the products covered were agricultural commodities and a varying range of "sensitive" goods. Unfortunately, the latter encompass many of the goods in which the developing countries have a current or near-term competitive advantage. Furthermore, many of the preference offers—including those of the EEC and Japan—incorporated extremely tight "ceilings" on the level of imports to which preferences are extended. This means, in general, that if a developing country actually *succeeds* in taking advantage of the preferences by substantially increasing its exports of a given product, the preference is automatically withdrawn. To compound the irony, since the ceilings are predetermined and thus predicted by importers, even the marginal customs revenues that would otherwise go to the LDCs may—given effective competition among suppliers—go instead to the importers in the preference-granting nations.

Although conceptually sound, the generalized preferences as finally implemented may be of little value. The net benefits to the developing countries will be marginal at best, and their efforts to achieve liberalization have been directed toward the restrictive features of the GSP offers that have been implemented. Unhappily, the United States has failed to implement its own, much more liberal, preference offer—due mainly to an extremely protectionist mood in the Congress—and hence little pressure can be brought by the United States to bear on the more restrictive features of the EEC and Japanese systems. Moreover, the prospect for broad-scale trade liberalization among industrial countries promises to make the preferences redundant, since the scope for preference margins would be narrowed with reduced or eliminated tariffs.

Developing countries' trade problems are no less serious in the area of nontariff distortions, particularly the kind of market-sharing arrangements noted in the previous section. First, the kinds of products in which the developing countries have, or expect to have, an international competitive advantage are very often considered "sensitive" in the advanced countries. They are standard, light manufactures with a high labor content, and hence highly susceptible to measures aimed at preventing market disruption. Second, quantitative import controls are usually administered on the basis of historical supplier relationships, and the traditionally small market shares of developing countries relegate them to a virtually permanent status as marginal suppliers. Certainly the rapid rates of export growth which they require to become viable competitors in world markets is thus precluded.

At a time of shrinking foreign-aid commitments and general disenchantment with traditional resource transfers, the prescription of "trade, not aid" seems ever more appropriate to the LDCs. And yet it seems that, at least for manufactures and semimanufactures, the failure of generalized preferences and the spectre of increasing regionalization of trade among advanced countries offer little basis for optimism among the developing economies.

Agriculture

Nowhere has international commercial policy failed as dramatically as in trade in agricultural commodities. The ultimate reason is that agriculture is a "problem" sector in virtually every country—rich or poor. As a result, each nation has devised separate internal policies to deal with this "problem" sector; ranging from price support schemes, to direct subsidies, to government marketing boards for various feed grains. Since each nation has developed its own set of policies to deal with its own unique agricultural problems, there is great difficulty in securing *international* agreement to liberalize trade. Almost any proposal conflicts with some nation's vital national interests in its own agricultural policy. Yet agriculture is of primary importance because a large percentage of actual and potential international trade is in agricultural products.

The problem of "disruption" of domestic markets is far more serious in agriculture than it normally is for external competition in manufactures. In agriculture, the production period is longer, and supply and demand elasticities lower, than in manufacturing. National agricultural policies have been devised to mitigate, slow down, and suppress the adverse social effects of the structural change from agrarian societies to industrial and urban societies. In short, to accomplish substantial changes in trade policy in agricultural products, it is necessary that one or more nations change their *national* farm policies.

In general this institutional difficulty in liberalizing trade in agricultural commodities has worked to the disadvantage of the national suppliers who are most efficient. The greatest effective protection is most often found in the net importing countries, as they perpetuate their own, less efficient suppliers and prolong the retrenchment process.

Not only do the less efficient suppliers (such as the EEC) often relegate imports to the status of filling the gap between domestic supply and domestic demand at the support price, but the high support price itself stimulates internal oversupply which is sometimes thrown on world markets as a convenient way to dispose of unwanted surpluses. In such cases, the interests of the efficient agricultural suppliers—developed or developing—tend to coincide, but the coalitions change depending upon the particular product under consideration.

If the existing policy posture can generally be characterized as promoting free market-access for industrial goods while special considerations make a similar policy impossible for agricultural goods, countries which have a substantial competitive advantage in agricultural goods have little leverage and suffer a sizable burden in the international commercial policy sphere. One of their alternatives, of course, is to impose (or retain) substantial restrictions in imports of manufactures. Fortunately, nations cannot be divided up so neatly into manufactures and agricultural producers, and such sharp distinctions in policy interests seldom develop. All the same, it must be expected that a large proportion of effort in the area of commercial policy will focus on the agricultural sector in the future.

Competitive Structures, Multinational
Corporations, and Environmental Issues

Efforts to promote trade liberalization only ensure that the most efficient suppliers can compete in the international marketplace. They do not by themselves ensure that such suppliers indeed will compete. Private arrangements for the division of markets among suppliers—whether regionally or globally— impede the gains to be derived from international specialization just as effectively as do tariffs and other governmentally-imposed trade distortions. The tendency toward restrictive business practices in international trade cannot be underrated, and can easily develop into the kinds of massive international cartels that existed during the interwar period. This results in serious distortions of competitive conditions which would maximize individual and collective profits of participating suppliers.

The problem is that antitrust regulations differ materially among nations, and this impedes effective action against trade-restraining arrangements that transcend national political frontiers. At the same time, the competition for exports contributes pressure for business—government partnerships which may lead to reduced competition. Export credit—guarantee schemes proliferate; increasing proportions of export financing are provided by government agencies; profits derived from export sales are tax-sheltered; government-financed trade representation is increasingly common; government-induced mergers to encourage larger and fewer firms to compete for export sales are frequently in the news; and so forth. The danger in such business-government partnerships is that they contribute powerfully to restraint of competition. Once governments and "national interests" become involved in normal commercial rivalry, it is difficult to prevent the eventual emergence of cartels—e.g., the International Air Transport Association.

A second important question for the future of commercial policy concerns the growth of the multinational corporation (MNC). Implementing production and marketing logistics on a global scale, the MNC has become involved in political controversies ranging from the export of jobs, extraterritoriality of business decision-making, and national ownerships of local resources, to tax evasion and economic imperialism. To a growing extent, trade is concentrated in intermediate products manufactured worldwide for assembly in still other locations and for distribution in diverse markets. The MNC is sensitive to commercial-policy changes, and can shift production and marketing decisions as conditions for national market-access change.

One result is that policy governing international investment is now closely related to policy governing international trade. When trade policy shifts, the MNC responds; when national governments are blocked from achieving their ends through trade policy, they can impose controls over investment flows and/or MNC operations. A nation's leverage in international commercial diplomacy is no longer determined largely by its trade position, but also by its role as a host or source country for international investment. Actions in the trade sphere can easily lead to reactions in the investment sphere.

Thus trade and investment policy in the future will be closely linked. Just as a set of rules for international trade have prevailed through the GATT, another set of rules governing international investments and the operations of multinational firms may be forthcoming, regardless of the currently slow progress.

Another major issue which is emerging in most countries, and which will affect future commercial policy decisions and negotiations, is that of environmental standards and control. Different nations are developing and will develop different norms, priorities, and policies governing pollution and consumer protection. So long as these differ substantially between nations—notwithstanding vigorous efforts at harmonization and coordination in various international organizations—nations may react in the trade policy arena to avoid penalizing their domestic industries as a result of their own environmental policies. Certainly interregional experience in the United States has shown that, even in the presence of strong national government, differences tend to be a durable, but hopefully transitional, phenomena. In the absence of supranational authority in this area, it is to be expected that some of the environmental control issues will be deflected into the arena of trade policy.

In that context, national economic structures will be changed as greater or fewer resources are required to achieve the environmental targets. Some nations, with higher standards, will require greater application of resources, thus losing their international competitive advantage in some lines while capturing new advantages in other lines of production.

As it becomes clear that differing costs are incurred by different national producers to meet the disparate environmental control standards, nations will be tempted to use countervailing import duties on products produced in nations with easier pollution control regulations than exist domestically, and also to offer export subsidies to local industries to equalize costs of exports to nations with lower pollution control standards. This will likely become an issue for debate in trade policy negotiations in the coming decade.

More directly, trade restrictions on certain products which are considered pollutants, directly or indirectly, can be expected. Also, products (and processes) designed to control pollution and the environment will be thrown on the international market, with important trade pattern implications. The location of production activities by MNCs are also likely to be affected by issues of national differences of the costs of pollution control. This may become an important issue between the developed and developing countries.

This new area of problems in international commercial policy is yet to be carefully analyzed but will be a complicating factor in the commercial policy debate of the 1970s.

Retrenchment from MFN

One of the important indications emerging from this discussion is that the world, and belatedly the United States, is turning away from the concept of "most-favored-nation" (MFN) treatment in trade policy, and toward the concept of "fair competition." Fair competition is a concept which embraces not only the "unequal treatment of unequals" (developed vs. developing countries), but also recognizes that many governmental inducements to exports are as "unfair" as import restrictions. Specific sectors in different countries which are competitive should be allowed to compete freely; bilateral (or multilateral) market access agreements in specific commodities are necessary; and trade with Communist countries must almost by definition involve specific, unique, and nonuniversal agreements on a bilateral basis.

If it is in fact the case that pragmatic considerations with respect to trade policy matters replace such past overriding principles as "freer trade is better" and "MFN is better than discriminatory trade policy," one can look forward to a more heterogeneous and narrowly focused set of trade practices in the future. While this seems to be in the offing, it is certainly true that some overall guiding concept is needed. This may well turn out to be the concept of "fair competition" because it incorporates both factors relating to restricting imports and factors concerning artificial export stimulus. It may also be able to encompass the need to avoid dramatic domestic market disruptions as a result of very rapid technological change in the international market. Thus "fair trade" considerations might sanction quotas on imports when imports captured more than X percent of additional share of a national market but would not guarantee any particular share, over the long run, to a particular national supplier. It might also sanction subsidies for exports to overcome NTBs in importing countries, or outlaw the NTBs themselves. While this may be the sensible, and hopefully logical, end of the current evolution in international trade policy, the source of the problems is not widely understood.

The issues outlined above are considered in substantial detail in the following chapters. Each has a significant bearing on the general posture of international trade policy and on the policy options open to the United States in the next decade. Our purpose is not to provide forecasts of what will happen, or judgments as to what should happen, but rather to provide a relatively thorough analysis of where we are (and why) and where we have been, with respect to trade barriers, industrial structures, and trade policy options. This is an effort to provide a sounder base upon which to make judgments about the future course of international trade policy and the results of alternative courses of action rather than to critically evaluate past policies.

2

How Trade Policy is Made: A Politico-Economic Decision System

Ingo Walter

One of the principal questions that invariably arises in discussions of international economic relations focuses on the nature of the political decision process. Clearly, national policy positions differ materially from one another at any given point in time, and these differences may or may not be resolved using appropriate international machinery existing for that purpose—resulting in a movement either toward or away from the free exchange of goods, services, and productive factors. Conflict resolution among governments has been thoroughly explored, both in a broad-based multilateral context and within regional economic groupings.[1] What is less well understood is how the perceived national policy positions come about in the first place. That is, what kinds of factors determine the particular policy stance that a nation brings to the bargaining table? Only when these questions have been answered with a reasonable degree of clarity is it possible to forecast, with a modicum of success, future configurations in international economic policy and to identify the causative forces underlying current problems.

This chapter attempts to elucidate the realities of trade-policy formation at the national level, in terms of the interplay of countervailing economic and political pressures. It reviews the factors underlying a nation's commercial policy and proposes a politico-economic decision model designed to explain how a national position on trade policy is established. In the process, it examines the behavior of affected interest groups within a society and the political transformation of these interests at the national level—within existing institutions—either into direct policy action undertaken unilaterally or into a national policy position subject to international conciliation. The basic model is intended to be operationally useful for analysis, regardless of the economic or political organization of the nation under consideration, although it will become evident shortly that major differences in the relative importance of the various inputs into the decision process will necessarily differ among countries.

Introduction

Economists generally begin discussions of commercial relations between national economies with a very simple premise: Given effective competition in national

17

markets for goods, services and the factors of production, as well as rapid and essentially costless adjustment to changing conditions within the national economic system, only essentially unrestricted international trade and productive-factor movements can maximize world economic welfare. If the relevant welfare criterion is defined as world real income per capita, and if the necessary assumptions are approximately fulfilled, the case for unrestricted international trade can be rigorously established. Unrestricted access to national markets thus represents a policy prescription that will yield maximum world output of goods and services, based on the benefits of international specialization and division of labor, and hence satisfy the welfare criterion adopted. Free international trade amounts to an economic imperative: if the assumptions are satisfied and the welfare norms accepted there can be no other first—best solution in the trade-policy sphere.

Yet even the most cursory examination of international commercial relations, from the rise of the modern national state to the present, indicates that the free-trade imperative has never attained preeminence from a policy standpoint. Tariffs, quotas, export controls, as well as a wide variety of paratariff and nontariff trade distortions have always existed and will continue to exist in the future. There are several reasons for the failure of the free-trade norm in the practical world of international economic relations.

First, the critical assumptions underlying the free-trade position do not survive in the cold light of the facts. Labor and capital are *not* fully mobile within national economies, and the cost of adjusting to shifts in trade flows is substantial, often slow, and indeed may be prohibitive under certain conditions. Moreover, competition is far from perfect, both among producers and among suppliers of productive factors. Such violations of the necessary conditions upon which the free-trade position is built may justify the maintenance of commercial barriers even if a welfare criterion based on world per capita real income is accepted.

But the definition of world welfare is itself at issue. Most economists will readily acknowledge that it is *social* welfare which needs to be maximized. Economic welfare forms a major part of social welfare, and to this extent it is important. Concern with the level of real income must be tempered by a parallel concern with its distribution, its effects on environmental quality, and a variety of social, political and philosophical parameters must likewise be incorporated in the equation. Free trade may not follow from the implicit global social-welfare function thus derived, and significant departures from free market access may be justified on these grounds.

Third, the case for free trade is based on a static analytical framework, under which total emphasis is placed upon efficiency in the allocation of existing productive resources on a transnational scale. The world has a fixed quantum of resources and useful knowledge at a given point in time, and the goal is to utilize these endowments as efficiently as possible to maximize current output and income. But no economy is static; economic change is all-pervasive, even among the least-developed of the developing economies. Again, whereas free international trade may well facilitate economic efficiency on a global level, significant departures from free trade may be required to maximize the rate of economic and social advance. Future income is not independent of current income.

Finally, and perhaps most important, the commercial-policy conditions that serve to maximize world welfare—however defined, either in a static or dynamic context—do not necessarily maximize national welfare or group welfare within the national political collectivity. The fact is that trade policy is indeed formed at the *national* level, and the elements that feed into the determination of a country's trade-policy position are primarily national in origin. These pressures are both economic and noneconomic, and may severely compromise the case for free international trade, or the case for a commercial policy that would satisfy normative assessments with respect to economic or social welfare requirements on a global scale.

Departures from Liberal Trade:
Maximizing National Social Welfare

An important rationale for the imposition of trade distortions by national governments may be found in efforts to maximize the social welfare of the national collectivity, given domestic and international social, economic and political conditions as they evolve over time. We may regard this as an essentially *nonbiased* element underlying the imposition of national commercial barriers. The relevant factors do not systematically favor or oppose freer international trade; they may weigh in one direction or the other in response to shifts in the underlying variables. It is possible to identify the salient national welfare objectives under eight main headings, generally along the following lines.

Terms of Trade. Under certain conditions, a nation may be able to improve it material well-being by imposing restrictions on its exports or imports *if* such action/would tend to cause a decline in the prices of products it buys from other countries and/or rise in the prices of products it sells abroad. If foreign countries do not somehow retaliate, such measures tend to improve the terms under which exports exchange for imports in the international marketplace and hence improve the aggregate level of real income of the economy. Such gains can *only* be achieved at the expense of the economic welfare of trading partners. Other countries, however, may be able to attain offsetting gains at the expense of the home country. It is also well known that the extent of barriers to access to the national market in part determines a country's strength in such bargaining with trading partners, and hence such restrictions partially govern its ability to secure trade concessions in return for liberalization of its own barriers. The terms-of-trade basis for barriers to free international commerce—if perceived by national political decision-makers as defensible grounds for the implementation of restrictions—thus reduces to a matter of intercountry bargaining.

Balance of Trade. International financial factors may exert an important influence on a nation's trade policy. Balance of payments deficits tend to bring pressures for trade restrictions designed to cut expenditures on imports and for incentives to increase export earnings. Whether this rationale for trade distortions is invoked depends on the state of and prevailing shifts in the balance of payments, the adequacy of international reserves, the availability and political feasibility of alternative adjustment techniques and rules of behavior imposed by international agreements, as well as probable reactions on the part of other nations.

Trade distortions, in that they affect prices inside the economy in relation to those obtained in the international marketplace, represent in a very real sense alterations in the value of a nation's currency—departures from equilibrium exchange rates. Conversely, changes in the value of the national currency may have significant implications for national commercial policy.

Hence questions of international trade policy and international monetary policy are closely linked. A national government which is subject to serious balance-of-payments difficulties and a deteriorating international reserve position under essentially fixed exchange rates is thus highly susceptible to pressures for increased national trade restrictions as an *ad hoc* technique of international monetary adjustment. Clearly, a balance of payments deficit is more likely to move a country toward increased protectionism in its commercial policy and is less likely to promote agreement on trade liberalization than a balanced payments position or a payments surplus.

Competitive Distortions. Trade policy may be used to help counter distortions that may prevail within the national economy; for example, to offset market control exercised by monopolistic industries or suppliers of productive factors. To the extent that trade barriers serve to reallocate production from areas where such distortions are serious to areas where they are not so troublesome—and this reallocation is considered to yield greater benefits to the society than the foregone benefit of freer trade lost due to the barriers themselves—a net gain may be obtained by the nation as a whole.

Unemployed Resources. A national economy operating at unacceptably low levels of capacity-utilization may seek to alleviate unemployment of productive resources by means of trade-policy techniques. Restrictions on imports and export incentives tend to *switch* national expenditure patterns from goods and services produced abroad to those produced at home, thereby strengthening aggregate demand and helping to absorb idle resources in productive employment. Again, reductions in imports and/or artificial stimulation of exports means—by definition—that foreign economies must be selling fewer goods and services abroad and/or spending more on imports. If these economies are likewise subject to unused productive capacity and idle resources, such developments will be adverse to their own interests and countermoves in the trade-policy field may be expected.

Conversely, a country undergoing inflationary pressures may work toward a moderation of price-level increases through selective reductions in its trade restrictions. The increased expenditures on imports reduce the effective demand for home-produced goods and subject domestic suppliers to a stiffening of foreign price and quality competition. In either case, the prevailing state of the domestic economy will determine the direction of this particular force in national trade-policy formation.

Growth. Under certain conditions a country may be willing to forego significant gains attributable to unhindered international exchanges of goods and services if this sacrifice promises even greater long-range benefits. In general, a liberal trade policy can be relied upon to "clean out" the lagging and increasingly noncompetitive producing units and sectors of an economy through import competition. This frees productive factors for more efficient use in other parts of the economy and thereby promotes economic advance. On the other hand, the growth of important emerging industries or the economic survival of regional development zones may militate in favor of increased restriction of imports. A national government may justifiably wish to protect an emerging industry from low-cost foreign imports until such time as that industry becomes internationally competitive. Or it may decide to protect a group of such industries to promote diversification and growth through substitution of home-produced goods for imports. An assessment that the "gains from growth" outweigh the "gains from trade" in any given instance may underlie the application of appropriate obstacles to trade, with the cautionary note that such a policy can easily be carried to excess.

Fiscal Considerations. Certain types of distortions of international trade produce substantial revenues. Tariffs, import levies and surcharges, license fees, and export taxes are some examples. National states, particularly those with unreliable or underdeveloped internal fiscal systems, frequently find it desirable to levy charges bearing on international exchanges of goods and services—thereby unavoidably distorting competitive conditions and intercountry trade flows.

Although confined primarily to developing countries, this commercial-policy-based source of revenue is sporadically employed by developed nations as well.

Social and Environmental Arguments. On occasion, national social considerations are raised in defense of restrictions imposed on international trade—restrictions intended to ensure the attainment of politically accepted goals relating to income distribution or to the quality of life. For example, heavy tariffs may be applied to imports of alcoholic beverages or tobacco products in order to reduce consumption levels. Quantitative restrictions or import surcharges may be applied to products deemed harmful to the consumer, or damaging to the environment, or to products processed abroad under less rigorous environmental standards than exist at home. Concern for environmental management and consumer protection has accentuated these issues in recent years. Export controls may also be imposed on certain raw materials for ecological reasons or to conserve natural resources. Or particular subgroups of society may depend on trade restrictions to maintain income parity with accepted standards of living. Generally, trade policy is only one of many paths to the realization of such social goals, and it frequently represents a decidedly inferior alternative.

Politico-Military Arguments. Trade policy is a major component of a nation's foreign economic policy, and hence is frequently employed in the pursuit of general foreign-policy goals. Trade concessions, in the form of reduced tariffs or other import restrictions, may be accorded to certain foreign countries for political reasons, and the withholding or withdrawal of such concessions may be similarly employed. Economic assistance to developing areas, for instance, may favor liberalized import controls, particularly as regards tropical and subtropical agricultural commodities, raw materials, semimanufactures, and manufactured goods of particular export interest to them.[2] On the export side as well, trade controls may be used to deny access to certain products to foreign countries. In spite of its frequent ineffectiveness in obtaining major political objectives, trade policy as a tool of economic warfare continues to be in widespread use.[3]

Following another line of reasoning, trade restrictions may be employed to protect against import competition certain domestic industries whose output is ostensibly critical for the national defense. The importance of such industries in a national emergency is deemed sufficient to more than offset the annual costs incurred—in terms of the induced inefficiencies and the trade gains foregone—in insuring their survival. Such costs and foregone gains are considered in a very real sense an "insurance premium" that should be added to the cost of the national defense.[4] National security considerations usually show up on the protectionist side of the ledger, although they may on occasion support freer trade.

All of the foregoing reasons for the existence of distortions of international trade have a single underlying theme: the pursuit of national economic, political, and social goals. The positions presented do not explicitly favor groups within a nation. Whether one or more of such factors affecting trade policy gains the forefront in a particular nation at a particular time depends on factors operating within the national and international environment. None of them is an inherent constant force biased against freer trade, regardless of other factors in a nation's situation. Their weights may shift in accordance with shifts in the underlying economic, political, or social conditions.

Group Interests: The Biased Factors

There is another complex of elements which underlies the national trade-policy position that has very little to do with maximizing the welfare of the collectivity. These elements are based on the material self-interest of specific groups in an economy. Their focus is on the concepts of protection and market access, and on the distribution of real income among groups within that economy—generally with little regard for the impact of their action on the economic well-being of the national entity as a whole. Such forces—see Table 2-1—may be reduced to two basic interest groups.[5]

The first of these—which we may call the *protection–biased sector*—advocates high levels of trade restriction in order to shield itself from foreign competition. The second group—the *trade-biased sector*—for equally compelling reasons of self-interest, demands low trade barriers. It strives to obtain low-cost imports, ensure maximum access to foreign markets, or to secure favorable policy actions on the part of foreign governments. The political process serves to resolve this conflict, and the existing national trade-policy position reflects this internal resolution, set agains the essentially *nonbiased* considerations based on the national interest as delineated above. The final mix of commercial policies that results represents the bilateral and multilateral conciliation of differing national trade-policy positions on an international level. As the product of extended internal and external conflict-resolution and constantly shifting economic and noneconomic conditions, the resultant commercial policy naturally cannot satisfy both the protection-biased and trade-biased groups at home (or abroad) and this gives rise to an observed, constant pressure for change in that policy.[6]

Arguments for freer trade generally do not take into account the preexistence of relatively inefficient and internationally uncompetitive domestic producers, nor the continued survival of such suppliers as a result of barriers that would have to be dismantled in any move toward more liberal trade. This would affect the vital economic interests of such producers, their employees, managements, suppliers, dependent municipalities and regions, and other groups. These forces will naturally resist freer trade as it affects their industry, and use their political power to prevent it. Since the benefits of freer trade may *on net* outweigh the damage it does to import-competing interests, it stands to reason that those groups in society that gain from liberalized trade could somehow compensate those groups suffering damage—and still be ahead.

However, the damaged groups may be hurt to such a degree that the harm is irreparable. A firm may cease to exist. A job classification or skill may be eliminated. A town may lose all of its industry and a region may suffer serious economic depression. As a result, those damaged may feel that no amount of adjustment assistance or compensation is sufficient to offset their losses. Whether or not just compensation would in fact be impossible, it is the attitude that is important and renders resistance to freer trade extremely vociferous in the political arena.

Table 2-1

Pressures and Feedbacks in the Formation of National Trade Policy

The Trade-Biased Sector	Intersectoral Conflicts of Interest	The Protection-Biased Sector
Exporting firms.	Multiproduct firms.	Import-competing firms.
Multinational business.	Multicraft and industrial labor	Linked suppliers.
Linked suppliers.	organizations.	Labor & investors tied to
Labor & investors tied	Import-using import-competing firms.	PB Sector.
to TB Sector.		Other.
Consumer interests.		
Importers, distributors.		
Retail outlets.		
Other.		

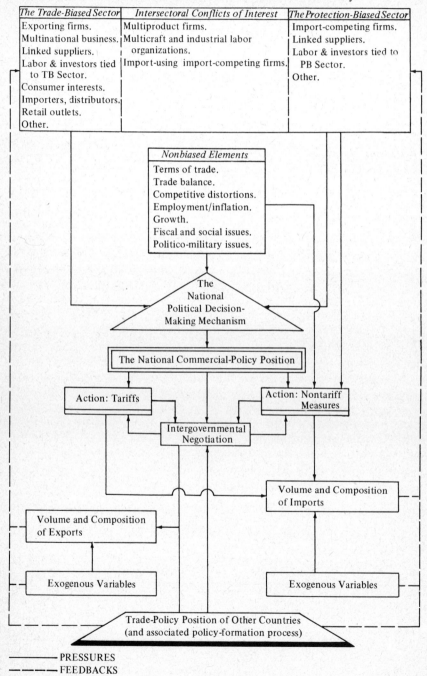

————— PRESSURES

— — — — FEEDBACKS

Moreover, even if it were possible to compensate the injured, there exists no effective economic or political mechanism to capture from those groups benefited just enough real income to effect equitable reparations or to defray fully the cost of transfers to new employments. Both comprise highly diverse groups, with the benefits and costs attributable to freer trade distributed unevenly within these groups. In addition, the benefits of trade liberalization do not necessarily accrue to the economy during the same time period as the damages that must be absorbed. And those benefited by freer trade would in addition be expected to resist a removal of some of their gains for compensation purposes.

In short, the difficulty of intergroup and interpersonal comparisons of gains and losses in material welfare attributable to freer trade renders virtually impossible not only effective compensation on a national scale but also a system of taxation and transfers which would make such a system feasible. In practice, therefore, the conflict between the gainers and losers from freer trade is inevitable in a system of commercial relations between national states.

Finally, it should be noted that the conflict between protection-biased and trade-biased interest groups tends to be characteristic of *any* political collectivity, regardless of its form of economic or social organization—although the basic model is best suited to explaining the trade-policy behavior of developed market-economy countries. In "mixed" economies, the same kind of conflict tends to prevail, although the greater the degree of control by the government the greater will be the weight of the nonbiased forces as decision inputs. At the other end of the scale, under total central planning one would expect the trade-biased and protection-biased forces to drop out of the model altogether, with all trade-policy decisions based on purely national considerations and the requisite adjustments imposed upon the affected groups by government fiat. But studies of international trade under central planning tend to refute this argument, with pressures in one direction or the other constantly emanating from managers and technocrats throughout the planning structure.[7] Similarly, in developing countries strongly influenced by economic planning, we would expect the nonbiased forces to have considerably more influence—particularly those based on economic growth considerations—but these hardly lead to the demise of the model as a whole.

Composition and Behavior of the Protection–Biased Sector

Domestic production units actually or potentially in competition with foreign suppliers for sales in the home market form the core of the protection-biased sector and generally stand in opposition to a more liberal trade policy. They would prefer to see national trade barriers become more restrictive as regards those products which they themselves supply. Around this core are grouped the labor unions and the owners of cooperant productive factors employed by these firms, other enterprises supplying the import-competing suppliers with raw materials and components, businesses producing complementary products, as well as the political representatives of the regions and communities affected (see Table 2-1). All tend to support increased trade restrictions. Indeed, if the latter acted in a manner other than to oppose trade liberalization, they would be neglecting their responsibilities to their respective constituencies.

Certain enterprises may be unable to enter a line of import-competing production because their initial costs are too high, so that they are merely potential producers, excluded from the market by the low import-price of the product. Should increased trade restrictions be introduced, (a) the inframarginal producers would suddenly find that they are earning substantially increased profits at larger volumes of output and higher prices; (b) the marginal producers would find that they are now operating at a profit and are in a position to expand, and (c) those producers who formerly had been excluded from the production of the import-competing lines find that the new price is sufficiently high that they can enter production and operate at viable profit levels. In particular, newer industries whose current productivity is low but which expect in the future to increase the level of operating efficiency will make a vigorous effort to secure temporary shielding via trade restrictions.

At the other end of the scale, old and declining industries tend to be both more vigorous and more successful in their efforts to obtain protection. Dated management structures and techniques, obsolete technology and capital facilities, archaic work rules, and many other factors may have reduced productivity to such an extent that the enterprise is no longer able to compete effectively against similar industries established more recently in other countries. These often tend to be relatively slow-growing sectors, tied to increases in population or similar long-term facets of the economy, with standard middle-range technologies widely available abroad.

As national economies develop, the very new "front-edge" industries and those at the "back-edge" of the industrial spectrum tend to form the vanguard of protection-biased interest: The former have not yet attained a competitive advantage in international trade, and the latter are gradually losing it. Political strength is attained if the front-edge and back-edge industrial groups comprise a very major part of the national economic structure, powerful in relation to those highly efficient and export-oriented industries that have developed a technical or productive advantage in world markets. There is thus the prospect that back-edge industries in the more advanced countries will be able to secure sufficient protection to prevent these same—but more efficient—industries from prospering in other nations, thereby impeding the development of that industry on an international scale and neutralizing the beneficial growth effects of the international transfers of technology.

The "scavenging-effect" of international trade, if not impeded, may have a broad positive impact on growth. Economic development is always an uneven process, and one of the major symptoms of this unevenness is the continual emergence of front-edge and back-edge industries of the kind just described. Imports serve an important role in the growth process by efficiently cleaning out particularly the back-edge industries—supplanting their production with that of foreign suppliers possessing an international competitive advantage—and releasing the productive resources employed by these industries for use in other sectors of the economy, including the front-edge and exporting industries. The induced shift in resources from less efficient to more efficient employments is clearly beneficial from the standpoint of growth, and represents an important and dynamic function performed by imports. To the extent that trade is impeded through tariffs or other restrictions, of course, this scavenging function is likewise impeded, with a corresponding negative implication for growth.

The economic health and well-being of many communities and regions is closely linked to the prosperity of one or more domestic firms or industries engaged in competition with imports. This is particularly true of single-industry communities or in political jurisdictions where only a few enterprises dominate the area. National legislatures elected predominately on a local basis are influenced by community pressures emanating from the economic position and prospects of producers operating in their constituencies. Even in countries in which the national legislature does not specifically determine current trade policy, it is often able to exercise great influence over executive authority or administrative practice. Local pressure may be brought to bear in a variety of other ways, making itself felt via alternative routes.

Pressure for increased trade barriers may not, however, originate with the import-competing suppliers themselves. Recent years have seen the rapid expansion of multinational business—the operation of business enterprises on a global scale, allocating production, financing, and trade in accordance with transboundary logistical planning within the corporate entity. Faced with increased competition from importers, they frequently fail to follow the classic policy response outlined here. Rather, they may close down domestic plants and shift production to foreign affilitates or suppliers for subsequent captive-importation into the home market. The import-competing firm thus *fails* to seek the predicted commercial-policy relief; indeed, it adopts the views of the trade-biased sector. But the damaging effects on workers, suppliers, and localities are the same—if less obviously attributable to trade-related factors—and the battle for increased barriers to imports must be taken up directly by organized labor, regions and localities, frequently against the interests of the producers themselves. This is the origin of the "export of jobs" challenge facing the multinational firms.

It should perhaps be added that organized labor tends to have its own internal drive in this direction as a result of the diminution of membership attributable to such developments; in an era of rapid structural change in the direction of a predominantly "service-oriented" economy, industrial unions are particularly sensitive to this issue.

The protection-biased sector is in an inherently strong political position because the possibilities of gain or loss attributable to trade-policy shifts are both immediate and direct. For them, increased trade barriers would seem to result in an obvious output expansion, increased employment and higher profits manifested in regional or local prosperity, and a general gain in real income of all concerned. Conversely, they can argue that a reduction in trade barriers will inevitably result in a direct loss in their share of the market, a reduction in output and employment, idle capacity, and generally harmful effects upon their region of the country. Many of the industries so involved also maintain that their demise would compromise the security of the nation.

This is the kind of short-run economic pressure to which representatives in national governing bodies tend to respond. However, political bodies sometimes take a considerable period of time in responding with concrete action. Furthermore, since direct trade policy is, at any one time, but one of many public-policy questions before the national decision-making organs, offsetting coalitions of interests may make it appear that commercial policy responds to pressures other than the causal economic forces and resulting political alliances described here. Such clouding of the process almost inevitably will be temporary.

Composition and Behavior of the
Trade-Biased Sector

The opposing force—the trade-biased sector—is concerned with (a) access to foreign markets for exports, (b) the domestic availability and price of imported goods and services, and (c) foreign reactions that increased protectionism at home will tend to result in the imposition of more restrictive trade barriers abroad and in a narrowing of their markets.[a] At the same time, they are fully aware that they cannot widen their access to foreign markets through reduced foreign trade restrictions without simultaneously-negotiated domestic trade concessions. This places the export suppliers squarely on the side of trade liberalization.[8] Again, the factors of production used in the export-oriented industries, associated labor groups, firms supplying that industry with raw materials and intermediate inputs, and the representatives of export-dependent local and regional political jurisdictions join in opposing increased protection and in favoring generally freer trade.

[a]This narrowing may come in two ways. Foreign countries may retaliate against increases in national trade restrictions by raising their own barriers to imports from abroad. But even if this does not occur, they may be forced to curtail imports administratively if their export earnings of foreign exchange fall to levels insufficient to sustain previous import levels.

Export-oriented producers and linked interest groups are aided in their efforts by consumer-interest groups, importers, distributors, retailers, and final users of imported goods and services, who likewise support trade liberalization from the standpoint of costs, prices, product choices, and sales volumes. Not least important are business firms, financial institutions and individuals with substantial investments abroad—including multinational corporations—realizing full well that foreign retaliation against national restrictive trade policy measures may manifest itself as investment controls detrimental to their interests. Multinational corporations are particularly concerned with free access for their foreign subsidiaries to raw materials, components and capital goods, and to the domestic market for "captive" imports of final goods. Together, these domestic interest-groups combine to make up a respectable force diametrically opposed to the protection-biased sector.

Consumer groups, insofar as they can organize for political action, inherently tend to promote a liberal national commercial policy. Trade barriers do impose losses on consumers. Some, who would have purchased a given product at a lower price, are squeezed out of the market. Those remaining in the market pay higher prices for the product, thus reducing their real incomes and their ability to purchase other products, and have a narrower range of products to choose from. In the case of tariffs, the loss in consumer welfare is to a limited extent offset by revenues collected by the government. If this revenue were distributed to consumers of the protected product in the *same* proportion in which they would have purchased the item, then a part of the loss in consumer welfare might be recovered; but even this would represent only a partial recompense.

Consumers until very recently have been the least effective members of the trade-biased sector. This should not be taken to mean that the loss or gain in consumer satisfaction resulting from a trade-policy shift is not very substantial indeed. The consumers often most heavily affected by trade barriers belong to low-income groups which depend on low-cost imports to maximize their severely limited purchasing power, and this contributes to the frequent "regressive" nature of import restrictions.

But consumers are in many cases unable to translate even strong feelings into political action. They have not been well organized, and speak as individuals to government officials. Only in some rare instances has the consumer's fundamental interest in trade policy been articulated.[9] Nor have recently-expanded efforts by governments to protect and promote the welfare of the consumer— particularly in the United States—been implemented with great measure of success as regards the nation's commercial policy, although the unfolding "consumerism" movement may well change all this.[10]

Part of the difficulty derives from the fact that consumers almost always identify with producing interests as well. They may be members of trade unions, employees of businesses, owners of capital, or owners of land. They may come from easily-identified parts of the country where other interests may predominate, and their interests as producers may well be damaged by vigorous promotion of their interests as consumers. Moreover, the loss in consumer welfare resulting from increased trade barriers is difficult to identify in practice. With rare exceptions, import controls represent only a small portion of the price of the final product, and since imports themselves normally constitute a relatively small part of total consumption, per capita consumer real income may be little affected in any apparent way.

The general state of the economy plays an important role as well. Under conditions of rapid economic growth and high employment, consumers often seem to refuse to be agitated about the marginal losses in real income attributed to trade barriers. During periods even of very gradual inflation, price increases due to more restrictive trade barriers cannot be separated from the generally rising prices of goods and services in the economy and therefore attract little notice.

Closely allied to the consumers are importers, distributors, and retailers of foreign-made goods, whose welfare is very directly linked to the flow of these products into the national market. For example, in many countries large retail chains, discount houses and mail-order concerns tend to draw a major share of their low-priced consumer durables, textile products, footwear, toys and various other standard items from foreign sources, and they are highly active in opposing trade restrictions or supporting liberalization. For obvious reasons, this sector tends to be particularly vociferous in its advocacy of liberal trade, and can usually be counted upon to represent the basic interests of consumers.

Consumers and importer-distributors join the export sector in the political trade-policy alignment. Exporters are anxious to promote minimum import barriers, so that foreigners will be able to finance the purchase of their export-goods and foreign reciprocal trade concessions can be secured; they realize full well that national trade-barrier increases may trigger retaliatory increase in restrictions abroad. There are also domestic producers who are potential exporters, if foreign trade barriers can be reduced or eliminated on a reciprocal basis within a bargaining context. They are in the forefront of the forces promoting general lowering of trade obstacles and tend to include some of the more vigorous and expanding industries in the economy: those in which new technology is being applied, new products are being introduced, and imaginative management techniques employed.

Business firms investing in foreign production facilities also generally support freer trade. As noted earlier, they may be interested in supplying foreign affiliates from the home country with raw materials, intermediates or finished products, in serving the domestic market or other countries from foreign bases, or in maintaining a favorable investment climate abroad. Hence trade policy represents a factor influencing international investment patterns, while motivations centering around international direct-investment flows simultaneously influence the formation of the national trade policy.

Support for a more liberal trade policy also may be expected from those domestic firms who find it advantageous to buy inputs from abroad, either raw materials or components. The interest of such firms lies in buying inputs as cheaply as possible. Import-using firms may well be in the import-competing sector, which makes their stand on trade policy equivocal: If generally higher trade barriers are applied, their own output will be protected and prices are likely to rise. But at the same time, the cost of imported inputs will rise, which will have a negative impact on output and profits.

Export interests often experience difficulty in translating their economic interests into effective political action. Since these interests generally represent vigorous, growing, and independent elements in the national economy, they are frequently tardy in demanding improved access to foreign markets, and often fail to see the immediacy of the relationship between the freedom of imports and the volume of their exports. Furthermore, they suffer no direct damage as a result of increased import restrictions: Any damage constitutes a possible *foregone gain*, something that they would have had in the absence of import barriers, or if trade barriers were reduced. But an economic loss is not recorded or reflected in layoffs, cuts in output, or reduced profits.

Productive factors employed in the export sector likewise are not always aware that their interests are being damaged by import restrictions. Labor legislation and tax measures have tended to represent a major focal point of organized labor's political actions, while interests of investors have often been absorbed by antitrust and other regulatory policies and by general fiscal and monetary issues. Agricultural groups in the export sector are frequently relieved of pressure through government support and export-subsidy programs which permit them to be relatively less concerned about domestic import policies than they otherwise might be.

In the absence of any apparent direct damage or visible social impact, it is difficult for the export sector to generate very much interest or sympathy from the community at large or from the relevant political forces. Political leadership would be quite concerned if exporters were able to prove that their interests had indeed been harmed by a shift in the national trade policy. But they frequently cannot do this. They must argue simply that they are indeed being hurt by the existence of domestic trade barriers, and that they would be in a better economic position if these were reduced. Only in areas where the government exercises controls over exports has this particular interest group been able to perceive a more direct link between trade restrictions and its own welfare.

Aside from purely domestic interest groups favoring liberal trade policies, foreign exporting interests through their respective governments and through their own influence-generating tactics are often found to be active in the formation of the national trade policy. Efforts directed toward opinion leaders and public policy makers are coupled with unmistakable foreign official statements concerning the possible consequences of a more restrictive trade-policy position. This contributes credibility to foreign exporters' fears of market losses and materially serves to strengthen their arguments.

The Political Transformation

The foregoing discussion has attempted to sort out the basic forces tending to determine the national trade-policy position. Two sets of group interests confront each other in the political arena, the trade-biased and the protection-biased sectors. A third set of essentially nonbiased forces focused on the national interest (e.g., balance of payments, employment, national security) may swing the balance in one direction or the other, and may be adopted by either group to support its own position. Once the basic economic structure and political decision machinery of a nation are fully understood, therefore, it would not appear to be difficult to forecast the impact on the national trade-policy position of any of a host of shifts in the underlying economic and noneconomic variables.

We have pointed out that the alliance of forces for and against trade liberalization is not quite as simple as this, nor are the groupings as discrete, indicated by the intersectoral conflicts depicted in Table 2-1. Individuals are both consumers and producers; this would pose a conflict of interest as regards trade policy for a household whose head is employed in an import-competing industry. Business firms, especially multiproduct enterprises and conglomerates, may have among their operating divisions some which are decidedly export-oriented and others falling into the import-competing group, while labor unions may have individual locals that identify their own interests fundamentally with one sector or the other. Such considerations and internal conflicts may render a company or union decision for or against freer trade extremely difficult, unless it can precisely target its influence in a discretionary manner in accordance with the needs of its various interest subgroups. On a somewhat broader scale, trade and industry associations, political representatives, and others may face no less severe internal decision problems in reaching a coherent and defensible position with regard to the national commercial policy.

All of the economic interest groups discussed here must operate within a domestic political structure that has heretofore been assumed essentially neutral with respect to trade policy. In this way a trade policy can be derived which presumably may best promote the interests of the collectivity. Unfortunately, the process of translating the economic interests into political influence is at best highly uncertain. Conflicting economic interests must be translated into conflicting political interests, and conflicting political interests must in turn be resolved in the light of prevailing nonbiased factors according to accepted procedures.

There would appear to be four major links in the process of trade-policy formation. They exist: (1) between the underlying national and international economic and political developments and the attitude toward trade policy of domestic interest groups; (2) between the economic power of the interest groups and their political influence; (3) between the attitudes of individual political decision-makers and the resultant trade-policy actions; and (4) between the enabling legislation or other political action and trade-policy implementation. Because of uncertainty, error, time-lags, and misinterpretation at each stage, it is therefore rather unlikely that the national trade-policy position in practice reflects very accurately the underlying political and economic considerations.

Structural and competitive conditions at home and abroad undergo continuous change. When such change takes place, the economic groups affected by international trade must reevaluate their positions. In some cases, a group that has favored a liberal trade policy in the past may find that under the new conditions a somewhat more restrictive commercial policy is better suited to its needs. When this is the case, the economic influence of that group may help to shift the political balance. The new political alignment may be successful in changing trade-policy legislation, and that legislation may lead to actual changes in the degree of protection. Thus a change in a nation's commercial policy tends to result from a change in economic structure via the four linkages noted above and is triggered by information feedbacks from trade trends. The commercial policy-stance of major countries such as the United States has tended to move in waves, as the confluence of forces on one side or the other have gathered sufficient strength over a period of time to effect a reversal in the prevailing trend of the nation's trade policy. Historically, swings toward liberalization tend to occur over relatively extended periods of time, while swings toward protection tend to be much more abrupt and short-term in character, often occurring in an atmosphere of crisis.[11]

Aside from changes in the underlying economic conditions, national trade policy may also change because of a shift in any one of the linkages themselves, such as: (a) increasing or decreasing political influence of a given interest group; (b) a different path of influence open to an interest group; (c) a revised interpretation of its best interests by such a group; (d) a new attitude as to what constitutes the national interest in the international economic and political arena; (e) new trade-policy devices becoming available to certain groups, and so forth. These changes may arise even without a causal economic change.

Finally, it has already been pointed out that the political weight of opposing economic interests is hardly symmetrical as between the trade-biased and protection-biased interests. Because the beneficial effects of trade liberalization are often difficult to perceive, relatively long periods of time are generally required for the trade-biased sector to assert its full efforts in behalf of lower restrictions to imports. In fact, a rather substantial swing of nonbiased forces in the direction of freer trade, sometimes accompanied by extreme political agitation, has often been required to turn the balance in the direction of freer trade. By way of contrast, the protection-biased interests, actually or potentially facing damage from imports, have generally been able to assert themselves without much outside assistance on the basis of short-term economic exigencies.

As a result of asymmetry in the influence of opposing groups and considerations related to the national interest, the observed national position on trade policy may not emerge from the political decision-making process in accordance with the balance of economic forces. With this kind of slippage, the resultant outcome with regard to the nature, magnitude, and even the direction of change in the national commercial policy may be at odds with the expectations. This is particularly true in countries where the formation of trade policy is in large measure a legislative prerogative.

Access to the Instruments of Trade Policy

Once a national trade-policy position has been established along the lines indicated, it must be implemented. This involves the intensified application or liberalization of the techniques of international trade policy: tariff and nontariff obstacles to the free international mobility of goods and services. In part, the devices chosen depend on the pressures brought to bear during the course of the decision-making process just described. A particular protective device may be specified by elements in the protection-biased sector and be accepted in the course of the political transformation process. Or trade-policy devices other than those specified may be substituted in the bargaining process, either because they are less onerous than the former or because the danger of foreign repercussions is deemed to be less serious.

The output of the national decision-making process will be either to raise or to lower restrictions to trade, or to leave them unchanged. If the political balance weighs in favor of liberalization, a mandate is normally created for international negotiations designed to bring this about under the proviso that the bargaining outcome be as favorable as possible to the protection-biased sector. When damage is quite obviously unavoidable, provision may be made for tax-financed adjustment assistance for injured industries and linked economic groups—a case of compensation by the gainers (the general public) of the losers from freer trade. The nation will then enter into negotiations for the reciprocal liberalization of tariffs or nontariff barriers as an exercise in multinational bargaining within a predetermined institutional framework. Under certain conditions, bilateral liberalization, sectoral or regional free-trade arrangements or even unilateral liberalization may also result.

But suppose the political balance weighs in favor of increased trade restriction. The policy mix chosen will reflect the specific demands of the protection-biased sector as modified in the political decision-making process according to the influence of the opposition and nonbiased estimates of the least-cost course of action. Specific account must be taken of the likelihood of foreign trade-policy reactions and of damage to import-using groups, and the trade-policy techniques adopted will reflect these assessments. Once a course of action and mix of trade-policy devices is decided upon, application of the relevant measures is often unilateral.

However, the availability of access to the instruments of trade policy, like the political weight of protection-biased and trade-biased arguments, is not symmetrical as between the two interest groups—as indicated in Table 2-1. Whereas the trade-biased interests must expose themselves to the entire political decision-making mechansim in the case of tariffs (see Chapter 3), it is often possible for the protection-biased interests to short-circuit this process by resorting to certain nontariff measures (see Chapters 4 and 5). Such restrictions are applied by a wide variety of governmental units, often with little apparent coordination, central direction or even awareness on the part of national decision-making units. Alternatively, private restraints of international competition may be applied (see Chapter 6). Consequently, it is possible for individual protection-seeking forces to avail themselves of measures imposed under these conditions and thereby translate their interests into policy action without exposing themselves to public debate and scrutiny as well as to the opposing forces in the political arena.

Once a national trade-policy position has been established and implemented, it must be exposed to corresponding forces operating in other national economies and emerging as foreign trade-policy positions. The latter will often influence the domestic decision-making process and may be considered in this respect together with the nonbiased forces. If the foreign political outcome is such that an important trading partner applies, or is about to apply, nonnegligible trade restrictions, this fact weighs in the domestic decision process in favor of the protection-biased sector. In some instances, retaliation may be mandatory as a result of preexisting legal provisions designed to protect the trade-biased sector by discouraging unilateral restrictive action abroad. Conversely, foreign tendencies toward freer trade will be reflected in the national debate on the side of the trade-biased sector; a "climate" of trade liberalization may exist which adds momentum to any initiatives toward freer trade. Hence the national trade policy position is not formed in a vacuum. Rather, it is influenced by corresponding forces operating abroad, just as it affects the commercial policy stance of foreign countries. In general, therefore, the flavor of the interdependence tends to produce mutual reinforcement of prevailing tendencies internationally.

The national trade-policy position, once established, emerges in the international arena to face corresponding positions formed abroad and to be subjected to conciliation efforts bilaterally or under the auspices of established international institutions. A trade-biased policy position, if reflected abroad, will tend to produce international consultation leading to a general reduction of international trade barriers. The degree of this liberalization will depend upon the relative strength of the trade-biased forces in the participating countries, as mirrored in the respective national commercial-policy positions and the negotiating mandates accorded representatives in the relevant international fora. A protection-biased policy position, on the other hand, is more likely to result in isolated and bilateral measures, dealing with specific products and applied to individual nations, unless the protectionist tendency is extremely strong.

Conclusion: Trade-Policy Norms and Realities

This chapter provides a setting for what follows by attempting to come to grips with the realities of international trade-policy formation as a political amalgam of group and national interests. The national trade-policy position emerges as the logical result of an interplay of forces between two broad interest groups, each of which possesses substantial economic and political power and each of which defends a commercial-policy stance fundamentally tailored to relatively narrow group interests. This basic conflict is acted out against the backdrop of nonbiased economic and political considerations addressed to the national interest; at any given point in time, these may work in favor of either one of the internal protagonists.

The political power of the trade-biased and protection-biased groups, as well as the political significance of the various considerations making up the nonbiased elements, constantly undergo change as a result of fundamental shifts in economic structure, aggregate demand and employment, economic policy, politico-military developments, and other factors emerging both at home and abroad. Perception of their own interests and access to the techniques of commercial policy tends to be somewhat asymmetrical as between the two internal interest groups. The underlying shifts in economic and noneconomic conditions lead to corresponding shifts in trade-policy pressures, with eventual alterations in the national trade-policy position itself. This position is subsequently set against those of other nations in the international arena with the final result being the actual alteration of the techniques of commercial policy—tariffs and paratariff barriers as well as nontariff distortions and private restrictions with a view toward controlling the intercountry flow of goods and services in terms of its direction, volume or product composition.

It should be clear by now that the actual formation of international trade policy, and hence the pattern of distortions and restrictions to intercountry trade that exist, have relatively little to do with the free-trade norm stated at the beginning. Controls have always existed and will continue to exist. Free trade is simply not the outcome of the decision process described. And even if this were the case for a given country—either because of the overwhelming force of the trade-biased group or because the appropriate nonbiased configuration at the national level has prevailed—this might not be the case for its trading partners, and a defensive structure of controls might be considered mandatory.

If one rejects the free-trade norm on the ground of its untenable assumptions and omission of welfare considerations other than the maximization of real income and output on a worldwide scale, what is the alternative? Clearly, the structure of distortions to free international trade should maximize world social welfare. This should combine maximum possible real per capita incomes and rates of national economic advance with consideration of the "equitable" distribution of income, minimization of the risk of military conflagration, resistance to national economic and political crises, alleviation of social and environmental costs, and a host of similar inputs.

Almost certainly, the trade policies prescribed according to such a normative function would differ from the free-trade position. And, the gap between trade policy reality and that required by a subjectively-defined social-welfare norm is surely wide, as is the gap between reality and free trade. The latter possesses an historical intellectual force, and practical importance, giving it an honored place in the national trade-policy debate. But agreement on the definition and composition of world social welfare—however slow—may gradually endow it with similar, and complementing, influence in national debates on trade policy.

Notes

1. See for example: Ernest H. Preeg, *Traders and Diplomats*, (Washington, D.C.: Brookings Institution, 1969); W. Michael Evans, *The Kennedy Road in American Trade Policy: Twilight of the GATT* (Cambridge: Harvard University Press, 1971); and Thomas B. Curtis and John Robert Vastine, Jr., *The Kennedy Round and the Future of American Trade* (New York: Frederick A. Praeger, 1971). Within regional economic groups, see Leon N. Lindberg, *The Political Dynamics of European Economic Integration* (Stanford: Stanford University Press, 1963).

2. For a good account of the arguments involved, see John Pincus, *Trade, Aid, and Development* (New York: McGraw-Hill for the Council on Foreign Relations, 1967), and his "Trade Preferences for Underdeveloped Countries" in Subcommittee on Foreign Economic Policy, Joint Economic Committee, 90th Cong., 1st Sess. (Washington, D.C.: GPO, 1967), as well as Harry G. Johnson, *Economic Policies Toward Less Developed Countries*, (Washington, D.C.: Brookings Institution, 1966).

3. See Chapter 14. Also Thomas A. Wolf, "The Quantitative Impact of Liberalization of United States Unilateral Restrictions on Trade with the Socialist Countries of Eastern Europe," State Department External Research Study XR/RECS-3, February 16, 1972.

4. Cf., Kaj Areskoug, "U.S. Oil Import Quotas and National Income," *Southern Economic Journal*, January 1971.

5. This discussion is based in part on earlier work by this author and Robert Loring Allen, *The Formation of United States Trade Policy: Retrospect and Prospect* (New York: New York University Institute of Finance, 1970).

6. There are various possible strategies for the resolution of these external and internal conflicts. For an interesting set of alternative strategies for the

post-Kennedy era, see Richard N. Cooper, "Trade Liberalization Among Developed Countries," in *The Future of U.S. Foreign Trade Policy*, Hearings before the Subcommittee on Foreign Trade Policy, Joint Economic Committee, 90th Cong., 1st sess. (Washington, D.C.: GPO, 1967). See also Ernest H. Preeg, op. cit., and Kenneth W. Dam, *The GATT: Law and International Economic Organization* (Chicago: University of Chicago Press, 1970).

7. See Frederick Pryor, *The Communist Foreign Trade System* (Cambridge: MIT Press, 1963).

8. For an enumeration of some of the gains, see Peter B. Kenen, "The Strategy of Trade Liberalization" in Subcommittee on Foreign Economic Policy, Joint Economic Committee, 87th Cong., 1st Sess., in *United States Commercial Policy—A Program for the 1960s*, (Washington, D.C.: GPO, 1961).

9. For an exception see "The High Cost of Quotas," *Consumer Reports*, March 1969.

10. See, for example, testimony by Betty Furness in Committee on Ways and Means, U.S. House of Representatives, 90th Cong., 2nd sess., *Foreign Trade and Tariff Proposals* (Washington, D.C.: GPO, 1968) pp. 649 ff and 662 ff.

11. An historical verification of this cyclical tendency in the degree of protectionism in the United States is contained in Allen and Walter's *Formation of the United States Trade Policy*.

3

Tariffs and Tariff Structures: An International Comparison

Robert G. Hawkins

Tariffs have traditionally been the principle tool of commercial policy. For the advanced countries, however, the relative importance of tariffs in overall commercial policy has receded in the postwar period. This is the result of a combination of the lowering of tariffs by international negotiation and the growing utilization of nontariff barriers to trade, such as quotas. The spread of nontariff barriers will be dealt with in the following chapters.

This chapter describes the structure of tariff protection among the major industrial countries. The analysis is confined to a subset of advanced countries, because comparable data on tariff averages by commodity group are not generally available and are totally lacking for developing countries.[1] Constructing such data from national tariff schedules is simply too cumbersome a task to be warranted.

Two types of comparative tariff averages are used, and the country coverage of each is dictated by data availability. The first is a cross-country comparison of averages of nominal tariff rates by commodity group. The second attempts to reflect more fully the structure of the tariff rates and calculates "effective rates of protection" of value added for four countries for various commodity groups. In each case, tariffs are the only element considered. Implicit protection by nontariff barriers, excise taxes, or artificial exchange rates are not examined.

The Setting

The reduction in tariff rates by the advanced, Western economies over the past thirty years has been dramatic. Tariffs were at an historical high in the early stages of the great depression, with the Hawley-Smoot Tariff of the United States—embodying the highest rates in U.S. history—in the vanguard. In a complete reversal of policy, the United States again led the way by the passage of the Trade Agreements Act of 1934. This gave the president power to negotiate reciprocal trade agreements for lower tariffs, with the avowed intent to expand exports and increase domestic employment to ameliorate the effects of the depression. This basic act was repeatedly renewed until the passage of the

The computational and programming assistance of Robert F. Haskell and N. Hill White is gratefully acknowledged.

Trade Expansion Act of 1962. Over the period of the Trade Agreements Act, it is estimated that the average tariff on dutiable imports of the United States fell from 57 to about 12 percent.[2]

During the postwar period, international trade negotiations for the reduction or elimination of barriers have been carried out under the auspices and rules of the General Agreement on Tariffs and Trade (GATT). Six such multilateral negotiations have occurred. The last, and most important, known as the "Kennedy Round" of negotiations, was carried out over the period 1963 to 1967. The motivation for the Kennedy Round came from the major new U.S. trade policy initiative embodied in the Trade Expansion Act of 1962. This act gave the president the power to negotiate tariff reductions of 50 percent, across the board rather than on the item by item basis which had been the practice in earlier negotiations. It also provided a new Office of Special Representative for Trade Negotiations in the White House to plan, coordinate, and execute future trade negotiations. Provision was made for adjustment assistance to workers and firms displaced by imports as a result of tariff reductions and thus provided an alternative to the protectionist "escape clause" under which the United States could withdraw tariff concessions, should increased imports harm the domestic industry. A final major provision granted the president authority to *eliminate* tariffs on items for which the United States and the EEC accounted for 80 percent of world trade. This provision would have been meaningful only if the United Kingdom, which had applied for EEC membership in 1961, had been admitted. But, the United Kingdom application for membership met with a French veto, and the U.S. incentive for widened community membership proved for naught.

The GATT is a loosely structured organization, with questionable legal status, which has informally acquired the role originally planned for the World Trade Organization under the Havana Charter in the immediate postwar period.[3] It has, however, provided a viable forum for trade negotiations and consultations with and among its members on trade issues. The GATT shares with the trade policy of the United States the principle of nondiscrimination under which tariff concessions granted to one country are automatically extended to other countries to which the "most-favored-nation" policy applies. Another general principle is that member nations are to avoid the use of physical restrictions on imports (quotas) and other nontariff barriers, to the extent possible, since tariffs maintain reliance on the price system, even if only in a limited way. While the GATT system has had, overall, a large measure of success in the postwar period in fostering reductions in tariffs and minimizing the erection of new trade barriers, rather substantial erosion of its general principles has occurred. It may well be that the GATT or the principles must yield as the trade policy issues change and old problems are solved.

From the very beginning, GATT has violated the principle of nondiscrimination, as the preferential trading arrangements between the colonial countries and their excolonies—mainly the Commonwealth Preference System—were allowed to remain.[4] Thereafter, the principle has been further eroded. The first derogations were sanctioned under the GATT articles which permit discriminatory arrangements among members which eliminate barriers on "substantially all of the trade" between participants. Thus the formation of the EEC and EFTA was permitted under these rules, even though free trade in agricultural products was specifically excluded from EFTA's objectives. Other regional integration schemes, such as the Latin American Free Trade Area, the Central American Common Market, the Andean Group, and numerous others are additional, sanctioned departures from most-favored-nation policy, although relatively less important than the major European schemes. The latest breech of the principle involves the free trade area in industrial products between the enlarged EEC and the remaining members of EFTA, negotiated in 1972.

A different kind of erosion of the nondiscrimination principle is the Canadian-U.S. Automotive Agreement which established free trade in cars and parts in North America. This agreement, covering a specific and narrowly defined industry, was an approved "exception" to the articles of the GATT. It was similar, with respect to tariff policy, to the European Coal and Steel Community formed in the early 1950s, and like it, was designed to achieve the full rationalization of production in an industry which was already highly integrated across national boundaries.

The system of *generalized*, unilateral *tariff preferences* extended by some developed countries (the EEC, Japan, and some members of EFTA) to exports of a selected list of manufactured goods from developing countries, constitutes another departure from the most-favored-nation treatment.[5] While this breach may be justified as a means of furthering economic development, and as a partial redress of the colonial preference systems and the special trading arrangements set up by the EEC with certain developing countries, it is an additional element tending to make nondiscrimination a principle which is out of phase with realities.

With respect to the principle of "using tariffs only," and avoiding quantitative controls on trade, the GATT also has seen major failures in recent years. The most sticky problem in this area is with agricultural trade.[6] While tariffs have been lowered on a sustained basis in the postwar period, those on agricultural goods have hardly been touched, while quotas, marketing boards, the EEC variable levy system, and other distortive policies have been added or extended. The inability of GATT to provide a framework within which to effectively attack barriers to agricultural trade suggests more about the reasons for the barriers than about the shortcomings of GATT. Barriers to trade in agricultural commodities are a reflection of and protection for national agriculture policies, including systems of price supports, governmental stockpiling of commodities, and the like. Unless it directly addresses the harmonization of national agriculture policies, no mechanism for negotiating trade barriers is likely to be successful in agriculture.

But proliferation of nontariff distortions to trade is not limited to those covering agricultural goods. Quotas; bilateral agreements limiting export of textiles, steel, and other commodities; quotas on petroleum imports; and international commodity agreements are all examples of the growing exceptions to the exclusive use of tariffs. In most of these cases, the GATT framework has not been a very useful one in avoiding or eliminating such restrictions; often it has simply been bypassed.

Thus the GATT system which served well the international trading community for twenty years as a mechanism for the reduction of tariffs has gradually seen two of its major principles assaulted, and faces new trade problems far less tractible than tariffs. The popularity of regional trading blocs and other forms of discriminatory trading relations, the intransigence of the problems in agricultural trade, and the growing recourse to quantitative controls and other NTBs on international trade are ample reason to suppose that the GATT system will change or, barring that, will be displaced by new forums for trade negotiations.

International Comparisons of Nominal Tariff Rates

The Kennedy Round of trade negotiations of 1963-67 was the most successful in the postwar period, except in the area of agricultural trade. Average tariffs on manufactures (calculated on almost any basis) were reduced by slightly more than one-third by the advanced countries, to be instituted in five installments over the period 1968 to 1972. This agreement followed on a roughly 10 percent reduction of tariffs as a result of the "Dillon Round" of GATT negotiations of 1961. As a result, tariff rates are currently at a forty-year low for the industrial countries.

This section presents comparisons of nominal tariff rates among ten industrial countries for which consistent data are available. Calculating meaningful tariff rates for cross-country comparisons is a difficult task. The average rates calculated are sensitive to the weights, or relative importance, attached to the individual tariff items in obtaining the average.[7]

One method is to use an unweighted average of the individual tariff rates, thereby implicitly assigning equal weights to the individual items. The difficulty with unweighted averages is that equal importance is assigned to a tariff on a commodity for which there is little actual or potential trade (e.g., fly paper) as to the tariff on a very important import commodity (e.g., passenger cars). Tariff categories are made by legislators, and often without reference to actual or potential trade in a particular item.

Another method of weighting is by the relative importance of the commodity in the overall imports of the country in question. This measure has a downward bias because high tariffs which tend to restrict the volume of imports receive a lower weight as a result. The ideal measure would be an average weighted by the imports which *would occur* if there were no tariffs applied. This would avoid the downward bias of "own-imports" weights and the uncertain bias of unweighted averages. A proxy sometimes used for the "potential import" volume is the relative importance of the item in world trade, or the trade of some relevant group of countries. Such a measure will be among those used in this section.

Tariff averages were calculated for nine individual countries and for the EEC common external tariff, on the basis of the three weighting schemes described above. Average tariffs for 55 two-digit commodity groups according to the Standard International Trade Classification for each country are shown in the appendix to this chapter. The "world trade weighted" averages use the relative importance of the item in the combined imports of all ten regions—constituting almost all of the advanced, industrial countries except Canada.

The country averages for all commodities under the three weighting methods are shown in Table 3-1. The sensitivity of the overall average to different weighting schemes is clearly illustrated. For example, the U.S. average tariff ranges from 10.6 on an unweighted basis to 5.6 percent when the items are weighted by U.S. imports.

Regardless of the weighting scheme used, a few generalizations are possible from the table. First, overall tariff averages are relatively low (12 percent or less) for each country. This, of course, masks the dispersion of individual items about the mean, where very high tariffs may exist on particular categories and no tariffs on others.

The United States has been accused of having more disparities among tariffs

Table 3-1

Average Tariffs on All Commodities, Based on Various Weights for Individual Commodities, Selected Countries, Post-Kennedy Round (1972)

	Unweighted	Weighted by Country's Own Imports	Weighted by the Imports of Industrial Regions
U.S.	10.6%	5.6%	6.0%
U.K.	11.6	8.0	9.1
EEC (CXT)	8.9	5.4	7.0
Japan	10.3	6.7	9.6
Austria	12.0	11.2	11.4
Denmark	6.5	4.1	3.6
Norway	8.2	4.0	4.4
Sweden	5.5	4.8	3.2
Canada[a]	7.7	—	—

[a]The Canadian tariff rate is unavailable on the same basis; the unweighted average shown is not completely comparable with the rates for other countries.

than is true of the United Kingdom and EEC.[8] This is borne out by the averages in the appendix with reference to nonagricultural commodity groups. For example, the United States had six commodity groups with average (world-trade weighted) tariffs in excess of 15 percent, the United Kingdom had two, the EEC had three, and Japan four. However when tariffs on agricultural commodities are also considered, the picture changes considerably. The United States had no two-digit commodity groups in agricultural products with average tariffs above 15 percent, the United Kingdom had one, but the EEC had four, and Japan four. Thus, taking into consideration only tariffs, there seems to be no strong evidence that any one or two countries have widely dispersed tariffs relative to others, when the full range of commodities is considered rather than those on manufactured goods alone.

Using the unweighted and world-trade weighted averages, it appears that Austria and Japan are relatively high-tariff countries, while the Scandinavian countries are relatively low-tariff nations. The United Kingdom has averages above the United States and EEC, while the latter two countries switch relative positions depending on which average is used. The average for Canada, being on a different basis than that for the other countries, cannot be directly compared, but suggests that Canada is among the relatively low-tariff countries.

The distribution of tariff rates among broad types of commodities shows a relatively consistent pattern across countries. Fully manufactured goods tend to have substantially higher tariffs than semimanufactured goods. This can be seen from Table 3-2, which shows simple averages for three broad commodity groups of the world-trade-weighted averages for two-digit commodity divisions in this chapter's appendix. Data for the four large countries are shown.

While the pattern of relatively low rates for semimanufactures and higher rates for fully manufactured goods are consistent across all four regions, such is not the case for primary commodities. For the United States and United

Table 3-2
Tariff Averages by Broad Commodity Groups, Selected Countries[a]

	Primary Commodities	Semimanufactured Goods	Manufactured Goods
United States	6.6%	6.9%	10.2%
United Kingdom	5.6	6.0	10.7
EEC	12.1	5.5	9.5
Japan	15.6	7.4	12.1

[a]Primary commodities are SITC division 0 to 4, and 68; Semimanufactures are SITC divisions 5 and 6 (except 68); and manufactures are SITC 7 and 8. Averages shown here are the simple means of the rates for SITC two-digit divisions, the latter weighted by imports of the ten countries.

Source: Calculated from data in appendix to Chapter 3.

Kingdom, primary commodities have a lower average tariff than either of the manufactured goods categories, at 6.6 and 5.6 percent respectively. However for the EEC (12.1 percent) and Japan (15.6 percent), the average rate on primary commodities exceeds significantly the rate on either category of manufactured goods. This occurs because of the very high rates which these two regions apply to tobacco, beverages, and certain agricultural commodities compared to the rates applied by the United States and United Kingdom. It should also be reiterated that quotas and other nontariff distortions have a much higher incidence in the primary commodity divisions than in manufactured goods, and therefore the average tariff rate on primary commodities is not a very good index of overall protection.[9]

An additional method of summarizing the similarity or dissimilarity of one nation's tariff structure with that of another nation is to observe the simple correlation coefficient between the tariffs on the fifty-five commodity divisions for the two countries. Since the means of the tariff rates on all commodities do not vary widely among countries, a low correlation coefficient would indicate that one country's high tariff commodity groups were not the same as the high tariff groups of the other country. On the other hand, a very high positive correlation would indicate a close correspondence of tariff rates by commodity division; conversely, a high negative correlation would show that one country's high tariffs were matched by the other country's low tariffs.

Correlation coefficients between the tariff rates by SITC two-digit commodity group for the pairs of countries for which data is available are shown in the matrix in Table 3-3. The U.S. tariff structure is not especially similar to that of any other country, being closest to those of Norway and Sweden. Likewise,

Table 3-3
Correlation Matrix of National Tariff Rates, SITC Two-Digit Commodity Divisions[a]

	U.K.	EEC	Japan	Austria	Denmark	Finland	Norway	Sweden	Switzerland
United States	.33	.32	.18	.29	.38	.32	.50	.49	.24
United Kingdom		.32	.08	.59	.10	.15	−.07	.09	.71
EEC			.91	.80	.59	.77	.41	.25	.64
Japan				.69	.54	.71	.29	.20	.53
Austria					.57	.61	.26	.34	.69
Denmark						.47	.56	.75	.29
Finland							.36	.17	.36
Norway								.56	.05
Sweden									-0-

[a]Tariff averages for SITC divisions were weighted by combined imports of the ten regions.
Source: Calculated from data in appendix to chapter 3.

the structure for the United Kingdom is relatively unique, being most closely matched by the tariff rates in Switzerland and Austria.

On the other hand, Japan and the EEC appear to have very similar tariff structures, with a correlation coefficient of 0.91, the highest for any pair examined. Indeed, fairly strong similarities are evidenced among the structures for the EEC, Japan, Austria, and Finland. Slightly lower, but still strong similarities are found among the tariff rates of Denmark, Norway and Sweden.

While only a few of the coefficients indicate a tight correspondence of the commodity structures of protection among the advanced countries, it is noteworthy that in almost every case the correlations are positive, suggesting at least broad similarity. Only one pair of countries—the United Kingdom and Norway—had a negative correlation between their tariff rates, and one pair—Sweden and Switzerland—had zero correlation. The positive coefficients among the majority of countries is indicative of a basic conformity in structures.

This is consistent with the picture presented in Table 3-2 and also with casual observation of the data in the appendix table—that tariffs tend to be higher on products requiring greater amounts of processing and lower on raw material or semiprocessed inputs. There are clearly some exceptions, especially in agricultural commodities, but this broad picture is fairly consistent among the advanced countries shown. Within the fully manufactured goods categories, however, a few commodity groups are almost universally heavily protected—clothing, footwear, and miscellaneous mineral manufactures. These, of course, are the industries at the low end of the competitive scale for the advanced countries, and industries of export potential for developing countries.[10] They also are relatively labor-intensive, and it has been found that the height of nominal tariff rates are significantly correlated with the labor intensity of the industry in the advanced countries. Unfortunately, progress toward reducing tariffs in these categories has been less than dramatic in recent rounds of trade negotiations.

**International Comparison of Effective Rates
of Protection from Tariffs**

A major shortcoming in the use of nominal tariff rates as indexes of protection, even from tariffs alone, is that they ignore the impact of tariffs on inputs into the production process, and thereby implicitly treat all imported items as consumer goods. The theory of effective protection attempts to take into account the impact on the production process of tariffs on imports of the output goods as well as tariffs on inputs.[11] While effective protective rates have been calculated for numerous individual countries, little attempt, with the notable exception of Balassa, has been made to estimate a consistent set of effective rates across country for purposes of comparison.[12] This section provides such estimates for the United States, United Kingdom, EEC, and Japan.

The effective rate of protection measures the proportion of value added by an industry which depends on the overall tariff structure. In symbols,

$$Z_j = \frac{V_j' - V_j}{V_j},$$

(3-1)

where V_j' is actual value added with tariffs on imported output goods and on imported inputs and V_j is the value which *would have been* added by the industry without tariffs, i.e., value added at world prices. Actual value added per unit of output can bé defined as $V_j' = P_j - \sum A_{ij}$, where P_j is the sales price per unit and A_{ij} is the input coefficient for good i into product j. Tariffs are assumed to be included in the price of outputs and inputs. Value added at world prices (i.e., without tariffs) cannot be observed, of course, and must be estimated. An approximate estimate of value added in the absence of tariffs is

$$V_j = \frac{P_j}{1+t_j} - \sum \left(\frac{A_{ij}}{1+t_i} \right).$$

(3.2)

Substituting into Equation (3.1), the formula for the effective rate of protection becomes[13]

$$Z_j = \frac{\left[1 - \sum A_{ij} \right] - \left[\frac{1}{(1+t_j)} - \sum \frac{A_{ij}}{(1+t_i)} \right]}{\frac{1}{1+t_j} - \sum \frac{A_{ij}}{(1+t_i)}},$$

(3.3)

where P in the earlier expressions is assumed to be 1. This is the basic formula used in the calculations below. The input coefficients (A_{ij}) are adjusted to reflect distortions in their measurement as a result of tariffs on input goods. And $1/1 + t_j$ reflects the proportion by which the domestic price is raised by tariffs on the output goods. The estimate is thus of the proportion of value added, at world prices, which is a result of the overall tariff structure. It will be noted that if the tariffs on inputs are equal to that on output, the effective rate will be identical to the nominal rate. If the nominal rate on the output good exceeds the weighted average tariff on inputs, the effective rate will be higher than the nominal rate, and vice versa.

In applying this theory for an international comparison, a number of critical assumptions are necessary, both including and in addition to those appertaining when the theory is used for a single country estimate. First, the input coefficients (A_{ij}) are assumed fixed and unchanging if tariffs on inputs were removed. This is tantamount to assuming no elasticity of substitution between material inputs, or between material and direct inputs. This is clearly unrealistic, and to the extent that some substitutability is present, the estimates are biased away from the nominal rate on the output good.[14]

Second, in making cross-country comparisons, an assumption must be made as to whether production functions are identical across country, so that A_{ij}'s are the same in each case, or whether different production conditions exist. Reasonable arguments can be made for each case, but the pragmatic problem of a lack of comparably defined input-output industries for the various countries dictated the solution. It is thus assumed that input coefficients are identical across countries.

A third assumption is that protection from tariffs is independent of protection from other barriers. Put differently, effective tariff estimates for an industry in a country without nontariff distortions are made on the same basis as such estimates for another country which may have numerous—and inter-related—NTBs. Curing this difficulty lies far beyond the scope of the chapter.

It will be seen from Equation (3-2) that two basic kinds of data are required for the calculations of effective rates of protection from tariffs: nominal tariff rates (t_i's and t_j's) and input coefficients (A_{ij}'s). Both sets of data must have the same industry definitions.

For the input coefficients, it was decided to use the U.S. input-output coefficients from the U.S. Department of Commerce as the A_{ij}'s for all four countries. The coefficients employed were for 1961, the latest available at the time of computation.[15] It was believed that the large, tariff-free U.S. market would likely be less distorted and more closely approximate free-trade production conditions in all regions. In addition, the coefficients used were the most recent available for any of the four countries, and it is clearly desirable to use the latest, so as to capture the newest technical relationships possible. The results still must be qualified because of the age of the coefficients.

For tariff averages by input-output industry, the United Nations Conference on Trade and Development tariff sample was used. The tariff rates used in the previous section of this chapter, while covering the universe of commodities, was available only on the SITC (Standard International Trade Classification) product group basis, and it was not feasible to reclassify individual tariffs to an input-output (or SIC) industry basis. The UNCTAD sample was available on an SIC basis and was thus used. The sample covers 200 items in all product classes. The sample items accounted for 60 percent or more of total trade in 1964 of the countries under study here.[16] The chance that any particular item would be chosen for inclusion in the tariff sample was weighted according to its importance in OECD imports. The averages from the sample are thus implicitly weighted by OECD imports. While the sample is a fairly inclusive one, it does introduce some sample bias, as will be seen below, in comparison with tariff averages derived earlier from the universe. This bias, however, is not thought to be serious in the comparison across country for effective protection rates by individual industry.

Since the input coefficients were for 1961, the tariff rates used to adjust the coefficients to "free trade" values were the pre-Kennedy Round tariff rates. On this basis, effective rates of protection from tariffs were calculated based on the pre- and post-Kennedy Round nominal tariffs from the sample. The results of the post-Kennedy Round calculations for the United States, United Kingdom, Japan, and the EEC are shown in Table 3-4 for U.S. input-output industries. Nominal tariff rates on the output goods, from the same tariff sample, are shown for purposes of comparison.

For all four countries, the majority of the industries show the effective rate to be higher than the nominal rate, confirming the notion that products with higher degrees of processing enjoy greater protection than that on the inputs. On the other hand, a sizable minority of product groups show lower effective rates, and in a few cases—especially primary commodities with low nominal rates—the effective rate is negative. This implies that the tariff structure imposes an implicit tax on the industry, and that its competitive position would improve if all tariffs were removed.[17]

Casual observation of the table suggests that the effective tariff estimates are highly correlated with the nominal rates on the import good for each of the countries. This was confirmed by the fact that the simple correlation coefficient was 0.94 or above between the nominal and effective rate estimates for all four countries. This closeness was less marked in the pre-Kennedy Round rates, indicating that across the board nominal tariff rate reductions bring the nominal and effective tariff rates into closer alignment.

Casual observation also indicates that a number of industries are heavily protected by all four regions. Tobacco manufacturing (15); fabrics, yarn, and thread (except Japan) (16); apparel (18); and miscellaneous textile products (17) all stand out as examples. The high correlation between protection and labor-intensity of the industry thus seems to be even more pronounced with effective rates than with nominal rates.

The United Kingdom, Japan, and the EEC protect relatively heavily containers and boxes (25); radio, T.V. and communication equipment (56); electronic computers (57); and motor vehicles (59)—all industries on which the effective tariff rate is relatively low in the United States. The United States, on the other hand, has a relatively high effective rate on rubber and miscellaneous plastic products (32) (as does the United Kingdom), and scientific instruments (62). It can also be noted that Japan has an effective tariff rate in a number of manufacturing industries significantly higher than the rates in the other three countries—e.g., engines and turbines (43), service industry machines (52), and aircraft (61).

As with the nominal tariffs covering the universe of goods, the similarity of effective rate structures as measured by simple correlation coefficients between effective rates is highest between Japanese and EEC effective rates (the correlation coefficient is 0.92). Also, as before, the United Kingdom has little similarity with the EEC (0.49) and even less with Japan (0.25). The United

Table 3-4
Effective (E) and Nominal (N) Rates of Protection from Tariffs, Post-Kennedy Round Rates for Various Countries (%)

U.S. Input-Output Number and Description		U.S.	U.K.	Japan	EEC
1. Livestock Products	E	9.5	−5.2	−35.9	−9.7
	N	9.6	0.0	2.5	0.0
2. Other Agriculture Products	E	10.0	5.7	66.8	8.7
	N	9.7	5.4	55.2	7.8
3. Forest and Fish Products	E	−2.8	− .4	− 1.3	−1.6
	N	0.0	.8	5.0	.3
5. Iron Ore Mining	E	−.4	− .7	− .8	− .5
	N	.3	0.0	0.0	0.0
6. Nonferrous Ore Mining	E	2.7	−1.7	−1.8	−1.2
	N	3.5	0.0	0.0	0.0
7. Coal Mining	E	−1.4	−1.6	−1.8	2.7
	N	0.0	0.0	0.0	3.3
8. Crude Petroleum	E	3.2	4.8	11.9	− .3
	N	3.4	5.0	11.9	.1
9. Stone and Clay Mining	E	−2.2	3.9	− .2	−2.0
	N	0.0	4.8	1.8	0.0
10. Chemical Mineral Mining	E	−1.1	−1.4	4.4	− .9
	N	0.0	0.0	5.0	0.0
14. Food Products	E	10.8	8.6	35.0	23.4
	N	9.9	6.0	25.4	17.1
15. Tobacco Manufacturing	E	81.2	22.7	489.4	125.4
	N	59.4	17.7	355.0	90.0
16. Fabrics, Yarn, and Thread	E	36.1	22.8	−5.1	17.2
	N	24.8	16.5	8.9	13.4
17. Miscellaneous Textile Goods	E	8.1	17.2	13.3	15.3
	N	11.6	15.0	11.7	13.1
18. Apparel	E	35.9	28.4	23.7	17.2
	N	30.0	23.0	17.8	15.2
19. Misc. Fabricated Textile Products	E	23.4	27.1	43.8	29.8
	N	22.0	20.0	22.0	19.0
20. Lumber Products	E	.2	2.2	3.1	3.9
	N	1.3	2.8	5.5	4.0
22. Household Furniture	E	3.0	9.2	9.9	8.0
	N	5.7	10.0	10.0	8.5
24. Paper & Allied Products	E	− .1	5.0	6.2	7.5
	N	1.9	5.7	7.0	7.5
25. Paperboard Containers & Boxes	E	9.8	17.5	18.3	22.0
	N	6.3	12.0	13.0	15.0
26. Printing & Publishing	E	4.7	6.5	.9	4.6
	N	4.4	6.5	2.5	5.3
27. Chemicals & Products	E	12.9	11.2	10.6	6.0
	N	10.7	9.3	10.6	5.9
28. Plastics	E	10.9	10.2	7.4	10.2
	N	10.2	9.6	8.9	8.4

Table 3-4 (cont.)

U.S. Input-Output Number and Description		U.S.	U.K.	Japan	EEC
29. Drugs, Cosmetics	E	.4	4.2	11.6	5.6
	N	3.1	5.8	11.7	6.5
30. Paints and Products	E	.2	5.9	9.3	7.4
	N	4.8	7.5	10.0	7.5
31. Petroleum Refining	E	4.5	−6.6	17.1	10.4
	N	4.2	.3	14.0	4.9
32. Rubber & Misc. Plastic Products	E	21.5	25.6	13.1	12.5
	N	17.5	20.0	11.9	11.3
33. Leather Tanning	E	4.1	12.6	6.8	4.5
	N	4.8	12.0	7.5	5.0
34. Footwear & Leather Products	E	2.5	3.7	29.4	8.0
	N	5.0	7.5	21.3	7.8
35. Glass and Glass Products	E	7.9	11.0	13.3	9.5
	N	7.1	10.6	12.6	9.5
36. Stone and Clay Products	E	10.6	5.3	6.9	9.8
	N	9.3	5.7	6.9	8.7
37. Primary Iron and Steel	E	5.1	11.7	8.6	6.4
	N	5.0	10.0	7.9	5.9
38. Primary Nonferrous Metals	E	3.6	2.9	11.4	3.1
	N	4.2	3.6	9.8	3.4
39. Metal Containers	E	2.3	10.1	6.3	5.4
	N	4.1	10.0	7.5	6.0
40. Fabricated Metal Products	E	5.0	11.3	6.2	7.9
	N	5.4	10.0	7.5	7.0
41. Screw Machine Products	E	9.3	12.6	8.4	10.8
	N	7.8	11.0	8.7	9.0
42. Other Fabricated Metal Products	E	11.6	9.4	8.3	7.4
	N	9.1	9.1	8.5	6.9
43. Engines and Turbines	E	4.5	11.5	18.7	8.7
	N	5.0	10.4	14.7	8.0
44. Farm Machinery	E	−5.0	7.0	9.3	12.0
	N	0.0	8.4	9.5	10.0
45. Construction Machines	E	6.6	6.8	6.2	3.9
	N	6.4	7.9	7.5	5.2
46. Materials Handling Machines	E	1.1	8.5	10.9	7.1
	N	4.1	9.0	10.0	7.0
47. Metal Working Machines	E	5.3	8.2	10.0	6.7
	N	5.6	8.5	10.0	7.0
48. Special Industrial Machines	E	4.4	7.9	6.9	5.8
	N	5.3	8.3	7.8	6.1
49. General Industrial Machines	E	5.5	6.8	10.6	6.5
	N	5.9	7.7	10.0	6.6
51. Office Machines, Computers	E	9.2	9.6	10.0	8.2
	N	9.0	9.8	10.0	8.2
52. Service Industry Machines	E	1.6	5.8	14.1	2.5
	N	4.8	7.5	11.2	5.0

Table 3-4 (cont.)

U.S. Input-Output Number and Description		U.S.	U.K.	Japan	EEC
53. Electric Transmission Equipment	E	14.6	9.6	6.2	7.6
	N	11.7	9.3	7.5	7.4
54. Household Appliances	E	4.2	5.3	5.9	6.8
	N	6.1	7.5	7.5	7.0
55. Electric Lighting	E	6.7	7.0	8.4	5.9
	N	7.0	8.0	8.7	6.5
56. Radio, TV & Communication Equipment	E	5.9	17.3	19.8	14.6
	N	6.9	15.0	16.2	12.8
57. Electronic Computers	E	9.6	15.0	12.2	13.8
	N	9.0	13.3	11.7	12.0
58. Miscellaneous Electric Equipment	E	3.3	14.8	5.5	8.4
	N	5.2	12.5	7.5	8.0
59. Motor Vehicles	E	−.1	13.4	21.5	18.5
	N	3.4	12.4	16.4	13.9
60. Aircraft and Parts	E	2.5	6.5	15.3	5.0
	N	3.8	7.5	14.0	5.8
61. Other Transport Equipment	E	7.4	9.8	7.3	5.6
	N	6.7	9.5	8.1	6.1
62. Scientific and Electronic Instruments	E	15.6	13.0	8.7	6.8
	N	13.1	12.0	9.3	7.3
63. Optical & Photo Equipment	E	7.2	9.9	12.8	9.6
	N	7.4	9.6	12.0	9.0
64. Miscellaneous Manufactures	E	14.8	13.8	8.2	6.6
	N	12.5	12.4	8.9	7.2

Note: E denotes Effective Rate of Tariff Protection of Value Added; N is the nominal tariff rate on the output goods of the industry.

States structure is more like the EEC's (0.81) than Japan's (0.73) or the United Kingdom's (0.63). This structure of similarity is almost identical to that found with nominal rates.

To facilitate a summary comparison of effective and nominal rates between the four regions, and also to illustrate the impact of Kennedy Round tariff cuts on each, a simple unweighted average of the input-output industry rates are shown in Table 3-5. It can be readily seen that the reductions as a result of the Kennedy Round were substantial, both in terms of nominal rates and effective rates. Reductions were at least one-third in every case, except Japan's nominal rate, and the percentage of reductions in the effective rates were greater for all three countries. This tends to reflect the concentration of the Kennedy Round cuts in manufactures—i.e., outputs of the production process—rather than semimanufactures or primary commodities—i.e., inputs to the process.

The average rates under the effective protection measure are significantly

Table 3-5
Nominal and Effective Protection Rates from Tariffs: Means of Input-Output Industry Rates, Four Regions

	Nominal Tariff Rates (%)		Effective Tariff Rates (%)	
	Pre-Kennedy Round	Post-Kennedy Round	Pre-Kennedy Round	Post-Kennedy Round
United States	12.3	8.0	19.9	12.9
United Kingdom	14.0	8.8	23.1	14.4
Japan	22.4	16.6	37.6	28.0
EEC (Common External Tariff)	14.7	8.8	25.9	15.3

Source: Calculated from Table 3-4.

higher, both pre- and post-Kennedy Round, than under nominal measures. Japan, for example, by these calculations, has an average effective protection rate over 80 percent higher than her average nominal rate. The rates for the other countries are at least 50 percent higher than nominal rates.

The cross-country comparisons yield a different picture in this table than was true earlier using the universe of tariff rates. Japan is still the highest tariff country of any, including effective rates of protection. But whereas the EEC was a relatively low tariff country in Table 3-1, it appears equal to or higher than the United States and United Kingdom, using the UNCTAD sample of tariffs. The EEC appears also to have a higher effective tariff rate than either the United States or United Kingdom. While a part of this difference is surely the result of using a sample rather than the universe, the differences are not large, and the general picture is fairly consistent in both comparisons. Certainly the sample appears sufficiently reliable for the product group comparisons among countries.

Summary

Over the past thirty years, tariffs imposed by advanced countries have undergone a substantial decline. This was climaxed by the Kennedy Round of tariff negotiations in the mid-1960s, which accomplished a one-third reduction in tariffs on manufactured goods. In the meantime, the main principles of GATT—nondiscrimination and "tariffs only"—have increasingly been undermined by the proliferation and expansion of regional (i.e., discriminatory) trading blocs; by a growing use of nontariff barriers, and by bilateral free trade by specific industry (the Canadian-U.S. Automotive Agreement), and by preferential trading arrangements (unilateral preferences schemes for imports of selected manufactures from developing countries). These cumulative pressures, together with the intractability of the problem of foreign trade in agricultural commodities, have and will continue to test the viability of the GATT as the main forum for international trade discussions and negotiations. The GATT must change to accommodate the new environment or ever more of the vital issues in trade policy will be resolved outside its context.

With the culmination of the Kennedy Round, it was concluded that nominal tariff rates, on average for all products, were relatively low historically. Depending on the method of averaging, the average tariff on all products fell within the 5-15 percent range for the major industrial countries. Japan and Austria are relatively high tariff countries; Denmark, Norway, and Sweden are relatively low tariff countries, with the United Kingdom, United States and EEC holding a middle ground as ranked from highest to lowest in that order. Comparisons of the commodity structure of average tariffs showed the EEC and Japan to be very similar, the United Kingdom (MFN rate) not to be very similar to other advanced countries, with the other countries enjoying broad, but not close similarity. Labor-intensity of the commodity was found to be positively correlated with the height of the nominal tariff rates.

Using a different procedure and different tariff averages, effective rates of tariff protection were calculated for four regions. The results were broadly consistent with the findings of the earlier procedure. However, effective tariff rates were substantially higher than nominal rates, although the structure of the nominal rates and effective rates were quite close for each region after the implementation of the Kennedy Round cuts. Effective rates also tend to be high in labor-intensive manufacturing. Japan again was estimated to have the highest effective rates, but the levels of average effective tariffs in the United States, United Kingdom, and EEC were close, but not the same as had been estimated using the universe of nominal rates. More precise international comparisons must await better data.

Notes

1. For an exception, see Harry H. Bell.

2. Not all of this decline was a result of actual reductions of ad valorem tariffs. About half of the decline, it has been observed, was a result of increase in prices of imports on which a specific duty (i.e., flat absolute duty) was applied. See Ernest Preeg, *Traders and Diplomats* (Washington, D.C., Brookings Institution, 1969), p. 15. See also Robert L. Allen and Ingo Walter, *The Formation of United States Trade Policy: Retrospect and Prospect* (New York: New York University Institute of Finance, 1971).

3. Gerard Curzon, *Multilateral Commercial Diplomacy* (London: J. Joseph, 1965).

4. See Chapters 12 and 13.

5. Ibid.

6. See Chapter 11.

7. For an extensive discussion of the pros and cons of different averaging systems, see Preeg, *Traders and Diplomats*, Chapters 13-15.

8. Ibid., pp. 60ff.

9. See Chapter 5.

10. For more on this issue, see for example Harry G. Johnson, *Economic Policies Toward Developing Countries* (Washington, D.C.: Brookings Institution, 1967), Chapter 3.

11. Major contributions to the theory of effective tariff rates can be found in C.L. Barber, "Canadian Tariff Policy," *Canadian Journal of Economics and Political Science* (November 1955), pp. 513-30; Harry G. Johnson, "The Theory of Tariff Structure with Special Reference to Trade and Development," *Trade and Development* (Geneva, 1965); W.M. Corden, "The Structure of a Tariff System and the Effective Protective Rate," *Journal of Political Economy,* June

1966; and Bela Balassa, "Tariff Protection in Industrial Countries: An Evaluation," *Journal of Political Economy*, December 1965. For a comprehensive treatment of various issues, see the papers presented at a GATT conference in H. Grubel and H. Johnson, eds., *Effective Tariff Protection* (Geneva, 1971).

12. Balassa, "Tariff Protection," and "The Effects of the Kennedy Round on the Exports of Processed Goods from Developing Areas," United Nations Conference on Trade and Development, Document TD/69, 15 February 1968.

13. This is a variation of the formula used by Corden in his "Structure of a Tariff System"; Balassa, "Tariff Protection"; and H.G. Grubel and H.G. Johnson, "Nominal Tariffs, Indirect Taxes, and Effective Rates of Protection: The Common Market Countries in 1959," *Economic Journal* (December 1967), pp. 761-77.

14. For a part of the debate on this assumption, see W.P. Travis, "The Effective Rate of Protection and the Question of Labor Protection in the U.S.," *Journal of Political Economy* (May-June 1968), pp. 444-48; and J.C. Leith, "Substitution and Supply Elasticity in Calculating the Effective Protection Rate," *Quarterly Journal of Economics* (November 1968), pp. 588-94.

15. U.S. Department of Commerce, *Input-Output Transactions: 1961*, Staff Working Paper No. 16, July 1968, Table 3.

16. For a detailed description of the sample and its coverage, see "Illustrative Tariff Profiles of Selected Developed Countries: Kennedy Round—part III and appendix," UNCTAD Research Memorandum No. 13/14, 18 December 1967.

17. In no case did the calculations yield negative value added at world prices. Such instances confuse the interpretation of the estimates. See Stephen E. Guisinger, "Negative Value Added and the Theory of Effective Protection," *Quarterly Journal of Economics* (August 1969), pp. 415-33.

Nominal Tariff Averages by SITC Division—Ten Regions, Post-Kennedy Round Rates (1972), by Three Different Weighting Bases

SITC Division	Type of Tariff Average[a]	United States	United Kingdom	EEC Common External Tariff	Japan	Austria	Denmark	Finland	Norway	Sweden	Switzerland
01 Live Animals	A	8.2	9.8	16.9	16.0	23.3	3.3	86.4	26.2	2.1	6.9
	B	2.5	3.8	3.7	1.3	4.0	3.3	9.1	3.7	1.2	2.3
	C	2.1	3.1	6.5	5.8	7.1	3.9	5.4	5.5	0.9	3.6
02 Meat and Meat Preparation	A	12.2	7.8	16.8	29.0	19.8	10.1	55.0	29.5	0.8	19.7
	B	11.7	3.6	20.4	34.1	21.2	0.9	79.7	30.8	0.5	14.3
	C	10.2	7.8	20.7	23.1	27.3	2.5	33.0	19.5	0.5	3.7
03 Milk Products and Eggs	A	4.0	9.4	13.2	9.8	24.9	1.7	17.3	3.3	1.1	5.1
	B	1.5	6.6	12.6	6.5	5.2	.9	6.7	2.2	0.7	4.1
	C	1.9	7.8	13.7	8.9	33.4	3.1	7.3	4.6	0.3	4.3
04 Fish and Fish Preparations	A	16.5	5.6	20.3	15.3	16.2	5.1	26.7	16.0	6.4	9.3
	B	2.7	5.5	17.3	7.2	7.3	5.3	4.8	10.0	3.6	8.4
	C	5.0	5.0	20.2	13.2	14.3	5.7	17.1	12.1	2.7	8.8
05 Cereals and Cereal Preparations	A	12.6	8.3	15.9	18.2	13.0	10.2	32.7	18.7	7.1	13.7
	B	8.7	7.0	15.0	41.9	8.6	5.0	20.4	3.9	4.0	11.4
	C	11.3	6.4	15.5	25.8	11.0	6.0	30.1	6.5	4.6	14.0
06 Sugar, Syrup, and Honey	A	7.8	33.8	38.1	52.6	30.3	12.2	68.7	18.2	4.4	32.7
	B	9.2	3.0	66.4	142.4	29.5	14.8	84.5	12.5	.5	62.6
	C	9.1	1.0	71.3	128.3	49.5	16.6	83.2	13.2	.3	61.3
07 Coffee, Cocoa, Tea, and Spices	A	3.5	3.5	19.2	16.2	18.7	4.5	21.9	8.2	2.8	10.5
	B	0.2	2.2	9.5	8.5	16.7	21.0	15.7	.2	4.4	9.3
	C	0.3	1.7	10.0	2.8	17.7	19.3	14.3	.4	4.1	12.5
08 Feed Grains and Preparations	A	1.6	6.9	4.8	0.9	2.5	-0-	28.4	1.1	-0-	3.4
	B	.7	8.5	1.8	1.6	.5	-0-	51.4	-0-	-0-	1.0
	C	4.1	8.3	2.7	1.0	1.5	-0-	32.0	0.1	-0-	.7
09 Miscellaneous Food Preparations	A	9.1	16.2	19.2	26.4	20.5	8.3	29.8	15.9	6.0	15.5
	B	7.9	27.3	19.0	22.2	22.1	8.2	45.8	2.1	6.0	25.3
	C	7.5	125.9	24.9	38.7	37.3	10.0	54.0	4.8	5.2	17.5

Appendix to Chapter 3 (cont)

SITC Division	Type of Tariff Average[a]	United States	United Kingdom	EEC Common External Tariff	Japan	Austria	Denmark	Finland	Norway	Sweden	Switzerland
11 Beverages	A	19.3	96.5	55.2	58.8	50.7	23.3	77.2	3.3	21.8	20.7
	B	9.6	87.5	37.7	73.5	66.2	16.3	68.3	0.1	11.0	29.8
	C	10.3	311.2	41.2	73.4	70.2	16.5	67.1	1.0	11.1	19.6
12 Tobacco and Tobacco Manufactures	A	19.6	552.8	48.6	–0–	132.6	34.2	69.7	35.2	15.9	59.2
	B	28.5	892.6	22.9	–0–	72.6	5.7	5.7	8.9	5.5	75.6
	C	18.5	884.7	23.7	–0–	51.7	3.1	10.8	2.8	2.0	75.8
21 Hides, Skins, and Furskins	A	5.7	8.2	4.5	11.0	5.0	5.0	10.9	8.3	3.4	3.9
	B	1.6	3.8	1.0	1.2	3.0	3.9	7.7	4.7	2.4	2.3
	C	1.6	3.3	1.5	5.1	1.5	1.8	5.9	2.9	1.5	0.7
22 Oil Seeds and Nuts	A	3.4	5.2	3.6	2.1	4.6	–0–	5.2	7.0	–0–	1.4
	B	3.5	3.6	0.6	4.6	5.3	–0–	0.1	0.1	–0–	0.4
	C	3.7	3.1	0.7	4.4	2.2	–0–	0.6	0.5	–0–	0.2
23 Crude Rubber	A	7.7	9.1	5.9	5.4	12.4	6.5	12.2	9.4	6.0	2.9
	B	1.3	5.6	2.1	0.2	8.5	2.2	9.0	5.0	4.0	2.5
	C	2.2	3.7	2.2	2.1	5.7	1.4	5.2	2.5	2.3	1.0
24 Wood, Lumber, and Cork	A	8.0	4.5	7.0	5.9	7.2	1.3	3.0	3.4	1.2	5.7
	B	3.5	2.1	1.0	0.1	2.7	0.7	0.4	0.3	0.7	4.9
	C	1.6	3.2	2.5	2.8	3.8	0.8	1.0	1.2	0.6	6.2
25 Pulp and Waste Paper	A	–0–	5.0	1.2	4.2	3.6	–0–	–0–	–0–	–0–	4.0
	B	–0–	–0–	2.5	4.5	4.3	–0–	–0–	–0–	–0–	3.6
	C	–0–	0.3	2.4	4.9	5.3	–0–	–0–	–0–	–0–	4.4
26 Textile Fibers and Wastes	A	16.8	10.0	8.7	7.7	10.4	6.6	17.4	11.6	9.9	7.3
	B	15.5	3.3	1.7	0.7	5.9	5.6	8.0	6.5	6.7	3.8
	C	12.1	2.9	2.5	2.5	2.2	1.6	3.0	2.3	2.2	1.9
27 & 56 Crude Fertilizers & Minerals, & Manufactured Fertilizers	A	3.4	4.4	3.7	1.7	3.0	0.4	1.0	0.4	0.7	3.9
	B	2.3	1.8	0.2	3.7	1.9	0.1	0.4	–0–	–0–	10.2
	C	2.4	2.1	1.2	3.2	3.3	0.1	0.3	0.1	0.1	4.3

28 Metalliferous Ores and Metal Scrap	A	4.8	-0-	0.1	1.3	-0-	-0-	-0-	-0-	-0-	6.4
	B	1.3	-0-	-0-	0.3	-0-	-0-	-0-	-0-	-0-	15.3
	C	1.3	-0-	-0-	0.3	-0-	-0-	-0-	-0-	-0-	0.1
29 Crude Animal and Vegetable Minerals	A	2.9	7.2	4.0	4.2	3.5	2.5	2.9	2.7	1.9	2.8
	B	2.0	5.8	1.0	6.4	3.5	1.9	2.0	2.3	4.7	2.5
	C	2.9	4.7	2.3	3.5	2.5	2.0	1.6	1.7	0.9	1.7
32 Coal & Coke	A	10.6	7.3	6.5	8.5	14.5	5.5	5.7	5.8	3.3	3.7
	B	23.3	10.7	8.4	10.0	6.8	4.4	4.1	4.2	3.5	2.9
	C	19.4	11.5	8.3	10.4	7.1	2.3	3.8	3.1	1.9	2.6
33-35 Petroleum, Petroleum Products, and Gas	A	3.1	3.6	1.5	6.9	5.6	0.4	4.7	0.6	0.2	16.5
	B	3.4	4.1	-0-	16.8	6.7	0.1	1.8	0.1	0.0	46.5
	C	3.2	1.1	0.1	10.9	13.6	-0-	0.6	-0-	0.1	19.2
41 Animal Oils and Fats	A	6.8	7.7	8.9	10.1	9.1	3.1	63.2	11.8	0.2	6.2
	B	7.4	5.5	12.1	5.7	5.8	10.8	56.6	1.6	0.1	5.6
	C	8.5	7.4	12.7	8.4	16.1	0.8	64.6	13.1	0.1	4.1
42-43 Fixed & Processed Animal & Vegetable Oils, & Fats, and Waxes	A	7.0	7.7	7.5	9.1	5.0	4.4	42.3	3.3	0.3	6.8
	B	5.4	4.8	7.4	4.3	1.0	1.1	55.0	0.4	0.1	6.2
	C	8.8	8.8	8.3	6.5	7.7	1.5	46.5	3.3	0.1	4.1
51 Chemical elements & Compounds	A	7.7	8.3	6.6	8.7	6.5	0.6	2.4	3.9	3.4	1.9
	B	4.6	9.2	6.3	7.1	2.3	0.3	0.8	1.3	2.9	1.0
	C	6.1	8.9	6.5	8.3	3.2	0.3	1.6	4.6	3.8	1.0
52 Mineral Tar & Crude Chemicals from Coal, Petroleum & Natural Gas	A	4.8	4.2	3.0	7.3	8.1	0.5	3.8	2.8	1.1	10.6
	B	3.4	1.5	-0-	16.3	6.5	0.1	1.7	0.1	-0-	44.4
	C	3.1	1.1	0.1	10.6	13.2	-0-	0.6	-0-	0.1	18.7
53 Dyeing, Tanning and Coloring Materials	A	18.9	8.7	6.1	5.2	7.8	5.3	12.1	9.7	7.8	5.8
	B	20.0	2.8	1.6	1.0	5.8	6.8	10.7	6.7	8.3	3.9
	C	16.9	3.0	2.4	2.5	2.0	1.8	3.3	2.6	2.4	2.1

Appendix to Chapter 3 (cont)

SITC Division	Type of Tariff Average[a]	United States	United Kingdom	EEC Common External Tariff	Japan	Austria	Denmark	Finland	Norway	Sweden	Switzerland
54 Medicinal & Pharmaceutical Products	A	9.9	7.7	8.0	9.4	9.0	1.0	1.2	3.2	3.5	2.8
	B	6.5	9.6	6.8	9.4	2.0	0.3	0.1	2.7	2.0	1.4
	C	7.3	7.7	7.1	9.5	2.5	0.3	0.1	2.9	2.6	1.3
55 Essential Oils and Perfume Materials	A	5.0	7.4	5.5	9.2	10.0	6.2	18.6	10.4	5.3	5.7
	B	4.0	4.1	4.9	10.2	9.5	6.5	8.6	12.9	4.1	3.4
	C	4.2	5.2	4.8	10.9	6.0	3.9	5.2	8.6	2.1	3.0
57 Explosives & Pyrotecnic Products	A	9.3	9.1	7.1	9.1	12.6	2.8	13.0	4.3	2.5	4.0
	B	15.6	22.6	8.1	10.7	10.5	2.0	5.1	4.1	1.9	8.9
	C	12.2	3.6	7.8	12.9	11.4	3.2	12.7	5.1	2.8	5.6
58 Plastic Materials & Artificial Resins	A	9.6	8.0	8.7	12.1	10.4	8.4	7.0	14.6	9.0	3.5
	B	9.2	8.9	9.8	12.9	9.1	7.9	2.8	15.4	9.6	3.4
	C	8.6	9.0	10.0	12.7	10.1	8.1	4.8	15.0	9.5	3.3
59 Chemical Products, n.e.s.	A	8.7	6.8	8.6	11.5	15.5	2.1	15.2	12.9	1.9	5.3
	B	5.1	5.3	7.2	7.1	11.0	1.8	12.3	13.7	4.0	2.6
	C	7.1	5.5	7.4	7.7	10.1	1.1	6.3	13.5	3.0	2.9
61 Leather, Leather Manufactures n.e.s., and Dressed Furskins	A	10.4	10.0	6.0	10.9	7.9	8.4	11.8	12.7	5.9	4.8
	B	7.0	6.4	1.3	1.6	4.8	6.0	7.8	9.7	4.6	4.5
	C	4.1	5.2	2.8	5.2	3.7	4.1	6.9	5.4	2.8	1.9
62 Rubber Manufactures, n.e.s.	A	7.7	9.1	5.9	5.4	12.4	6.5	12.2	9.4	6.0	2.9
	B	1.3	5.6	2.1	0.2	8.5	2.2	9.0	5.0	4.0	2.5
	C	2.2	3.7	2.2	2.1	5.7	1.4	5.2	2.5	2.3	1.0
63 Wood & Cork Manufactures	A	6.1	5.6	5.3	4.4	7.0	2.6	2.0	2.5	1.0	7.3
	B	3.5	2.1	0.6	0.1	2.5	6.7	0.3	0.3	0.7	4.9
	C	1.5	3.2	2.3	2.7	3.7	0.8	0.9	1.2	0.6	6.2
64 Paper, Paperboard & Manufactures thereof	A	5.7	13.0	11.4	9.3	16.1	6.8	8.5	5.3	3.0	14.3
	B	0.4	13.3	10.0	8.3	17.5	6.2	8.4	3.8	3.1	13.8
	C	0.9	12.3	9.8	8.6	13.8	2.7	5.8	3.1	2.3	16.9

65 Textile Yarn, Fabrics and Madeup Articles	A	16.5	16.2	10.8	9.7	20.0	9.3	25.7	13.8	11.2	10.3
	B	9.6	6.5	3.4	0.2	14.9	8.1	9.6	11.6	9.3	5.6
	C	8.2	6.2	4.8	3.3	9.1	3.7	8.9	5.3	4.4	5.0
66 Nonmetallic Mineral Manufactures, n.e.s.	A	12.5	9.9	8.6	8.5	15.4	4.4	14.8	5.7	4.6	7.3
	B	19.0	9.2	8.7	9.5	15.8	7.9	14.6	7.9	7.0	7.4
	C	15.3	8.9	9.8	8.7	17.4	6.9	23.6	9.0	7.5	7.5
67 Iron & Steel	A	7.4	10.4	6.3	9.0	9.3	3.8	6.7	4.0	5.2	6.4
	B	5.7	10.2	5.9	2.5	7.8	1.3	5.8	1.4	4.9	4.3
	C	5.1	9.9	6.0	6.8	7.2	1.7	5.6	1.9	4.1	3.6
68 Nonferrous Metals	A	8.6	7.7	5.7	9.2	11.2	3.3	3.1	2.9	2.3	4.8
	B	3.3	1.6	1.9	4.2	4.2	2.6	2.4	1.1	1.0	4.4
	C	5.3	1.8	2.8	4.0	2.8	1.0	0.4	0.6	0.7	5.9
69 Manufactures of Metal, n.e.s.	A	11.0	10.1	7.4	10.7	12.7	4.6	5.7	9.0	4.6	4.5
	B	6.2	5.4	3.4	4.4	8.2	1.8	5.6	3.5	3.5	3.5
	C	6.8	6.8	4.5	5.7	6.8	1.6	3.5	3.1	2.9	2.5
71 Machinery, other than Electric	A	6.5	8.1	0.6	9.0	10.5	5.0	7.2	6.7	4.8	2.8
	B	4.5	8.3	6.5	10.4	11.4	4.3	7.2	6.3	4.8	2.6
	C	5.5	8.2	6.5	9.8	11.1	4.3	6.9	6.4	4.8	2.7
72 Electrical Machinery Apparatus & Appliances	A	8.3	10.4	8.4	9.9	16.8	8.0	0.1	7.2	6.1	3.6
	B	7.6	11.9	9.2	9.3	21.0	7.2	11.5	6.4	6.5	3.7
	C	7.3	11.7	9.3	10.0	23.2	7.2	11.2	7.6	6.9	3.6
73 Transport Equipment	A	7.2	8.3	6.7	6.2	10.8	1.7	4.9	4.9	3.6	4.3
	B	3.5	9.4	8.9	12.0	17.9	2.9	6.6	2.3	8.1	11.7
	C	3.7	9.0	10.3	14.9	14.3	3.0	5.5	6.2	6.8	10.4
81 Sanitary, Plumbing Heating & Lighting Fixtures & Fittings	A	14.1	10.5	9.4	8.6	13.0	4.9	17.6	6.6	5.8	7.9
	B	11.4	9.9	7.1	2.8	10.8	3.2	7.2	3.2	5.8	5.5
	C	9.0	9.7	7.5	7.2	9.9	3.6	12.2	4.3	5.6	5.0
82 Furniture	A	11.2	12.0	7.6	12.0	16.3	7.3	9.7	7.7	7.8	9.3
	B	7.4	10.1	8.4	10.6	20.4	6.4	8.1	7.2	5.0	9.7
	C	7.4	10.2	8.4	10.6	21.0	5.9	8.2	6.9	5.1	9.5
83 Travel goods, Handbags, & similar articles	A	16.7	12.7	8.7	13.3	13.4	12.9	14.4	17.3	8.5	6.0
	B	17.0	14.1	8.9	12.8	15.7	14.8	15.1	18.5	8.8	6.9
	C	16.5	14.6	9.3	12.0	15.2	15.4	14.3	18.0	8.8	6.9

Appendix to Chapter 3 (cont)

SITC Division	Type of Tariff Average[a]	United States	United Kingdom	EEC Common External Tariff	Japan	Austria	Denmark	Finland	Norway	Sweden	Switzerland
84 Clothing	A	18.8	16.4	10.3	13.5	16.7	14.4	24.4	16.9	11.2	9.2
	B	22.1	17.4	14.5	14.9	17.1	17.6	24.6	20.3	14.1	11.1
	C	22.1	17.7	14.6	16.1	15.0	18.0	31.7	20.1	13.7	11.6
85 Footwear	A	8.9	11.7	11.7	17.7	21.4	17.5	15.0	17.7	12.2	8.8
	B	10.5	8.5	14.1	24.6	22.9	21.5	16.9	19.3	13.8	9.1
	C	10.4	8.9	14.4	22.1	25.3	21.9	16.7	18.9	13.7	10.4
86 Professional, Scientific & controlling instruments, Photographic & optical goods; Watches & Clocks	A	14.7	11.1	8.4	14.3	5.2	1.6	6.4	4.4	3.1	5.8
	B	14.8	11.4	8.5	11.6	7.2	2.7	6.6	5.4	4.1	2.5
	C	12.7	11.0	8.9	12.0	7.5	2.8	6.5	5.7	4.0	2.5
89 Miscellaneous manufactured articles, n.e.s.	A	8.2	9.2	6.0	7.1	10.0	4.3	6.2	4.8	3.0	4.7
	B	6.2	5.0	4.7	6.7	7.9	5.6	8.3	7.0	4.4	3.0
	C	7.2	6.4	5.4	6.3	7.3	4.3	5.6	3.9	2.8	3.4

[a]For each SITC division (2 digit), three "average" tariff rates are shown. The weighting basis for each is as follows:

A—unweighted tariff average; i.e., each item on the (BTN) tariff schedule receives equal weight regardless of importance in total trade.

B—"Own-Import weighted tariff average"; i.e., the tariff on each item is weighted by the item's importance in the total imports of the country in 1964.

C—"Advanced Country-Imported Weighted Tariff Averages," i.e., each national tariff rate is weighted according to the importance of that item in the imports of all 10 regions shown in 1964.

Source: General Agreement on Tariffs and Trade and U.S. Office of Special Trade Representative.

4

Barriers to International Competition: The Nature of Nontariff Distortions

Ingo Walter

The preceding chapter has been concerned primarily with tariffs as impediments to international competition and market access. Little has been said about the role of *nontariff barriers* (NTBs), which likewise serve to distort international trade. Certainly, estimates of the direct and indirect effects of trade liberalization on participating economies—whether in a regional or global context—based only on tariff removal, would be severely lacking in validity if nontariff barriers continued to restrict trade among affected countries, or were raised so as to regain some of the lost tariff protection. Consequently, it is necessary to determine whether nontariff barriers are in fact important and, if so, how programs designed to bring about their elimination may be incorporated into future trade-policy developments.

In this chapter, an attempt will be made to delineate the operation of NTBs on a theoretical level and to classify them in a systematic manner useful for subsequent analysis. In the following chapter, the extent to which NTBs affect the trade of the industrial and developing countries will be examined.

Recent years have seen a great deal of dialogue on the importance of nontariff barriers to international trade. Particularly after the successful conclusion of the Kennedy Round of tariff negotiations and its final implementation in 1972, attention has increasingly focused on other factors thought to restrict trade. The charge has been made that nontariff barriers and "market-sharing" arrangements have been used both overtly and covertly by certain countries to offset either wholly or partially the tariff reductions of postwar multinational trade negotiations. Whether or not this in fact is the case, it is nevertheless clear that the relative actual and potential importance of nontariff restrictions and "orderly marketing" arrangements have risen as tariff levels have fallen, and that they will receive far greater attention in future trade discussions.

From an analytical point of view, nontariff barriers to trade comprise one of the most perplexing subjects in the study of international commercial policy.[1] Professional forays into the area have, for the most part, ended in little more than descriptive surveys of the kinds of restrictions thought to exist in various countries. Even the task of identification and classification is often extremely difficult.[2] Aside from problems related to the multiplicity of types, variability, and intent of nontariff restrictions to trade, the major difficulty inheres in their measurement. In the case of tariffs, each individual customs duty represents an explicit burden on imports and is expressed as a number, which may be compared, manipulated and combined with others in a variety of ways in order to develop acceptable and theoretically defensible estimates of protection. This is not true of nontariff barriers, which rarely exist in such explicit form. And even when they do—as in the case of quantitative import restrictions—the incidence may vary greatly from one time period to the next.

How Nontariff Barriers Work

In the broadest sense, *nontariff barriers* to international trade may be said to encompass all private and governmental policies and practices that serve to distort the volume, commodity-composition, or direction of trade in goods and services.[3] Clearly, this represents a weak operational definition. It hinges upon a fine judgment as to what is "distortive" of trade and what is not.

In their day-to-day operations, businessmen influence the volume and pattern of international trade in a wide variety of ways on both the supply and the demand side of the economic equation. Lower production costs and prices or increased product differentiation and advertising may, for example, serve to reduce imports when practiced by import-competing suppliers, and to increase sales abroad when implemented by exporting firms. Yet it would be nonsensical to classify such measures as nontariff barriers and to point to their "distortive" impact—even when practiced by large multinational corporations. At the same time, business firms—acting alone, in groups, or in concert with governments— often engage in practices which clearly do fall under the heading of nontariff barriers. Similarly, national governments and individual governmental units at various levels may apply a wide variety of measures which can and do affect trade, sometimes as a remote side-effect of the primary purpose of the specific policy action.

Economists have contributed to the confusion surrounding NTBs by largely ignoring the problem of intent of nontariff restrictions to trade. They have tended simply to group nontariff policies and practices thought to affect international trade in a functional manner, more or less as: (1) quantitative controls on imports and exports, including state-trading; (2) government procurement policies; (3) customs procedures; (4) antidumping legislation and practices; (5) border tax adjustments; and (6) miscellaneous internal policies that affect trade.[4] Yet the intent of individual restrictions is perhaps the governing element from a definitional standpoint, because it determines when a given device is being used specifically as a tool of commercial policy, as opposed to instances where the existing trade-effects of the device are merely ancillary to some other purpose. Moreover, programs directed at the elimination of nontariff barriers are more easily implemented when the restrictions are classified by their intent.

Nontariff barriers to imports may work in several ways, each of which may or may not be important in any specific instance. *Import-directed* NTBs tend to result in higher prices of imports and import-competing goods, or to reduce the supply of goods available by: (a) imposing significant costs on foreign exporters or domestic importers; (b) limiting the volume of imports permitted; (c) imposing conditions of high uncertainty and risk on domestic importers or foreign exporters, to which they respond by limiting the volume of trade; or (d) a combination of the above.

Export-directed NTBs may artificially stimulate foreign sales by lowering or removing costs that would otherwise have to be borne by exporters. This permits lower export prices and enhances domestic suppliers' competitiveness in world markets relative to their foreign counterparts. For foreign consumers or users, such measures will—if successful—bring about reduced prices and increased supplies of the commodities in question. Export-directed nontariff barriers may also be aimed at impeding sales abroad, particularly of primary commodities, when it is desired to increase value-added at home or to avoid resource depletion.

Nontariff barriers to trade must be viewed within the context of commercial policy in general, since they represent tools applied in pursuit of standard commerical-policy goals. This includes the protection of domestic suppliers of import-competing goods and services, stimulation of exports, improvement of the terms of trade, improvement of the balance of trade and hence the balance of payments, redistribution of income in favor of productive factors employed in import-competing industries, and so forth. It also includes macro-policy goals concerned with the maintenance of high employment, price-level stability, and satisfactory rates of economic growth. Nontariff barriers thus are applied for essentially the same objectives as are tariffs. Indeed, it will be argued in the following chapter that NTBs often represent the more flexible and effective devices in pursuit of these ends, although the economic costs associated with their implementation may on occasion be inordinately high.

It is a simple matter to illustrate the operation of either export or import-directed NTBs—both the quantitative and cost-imposing types—by means of standard, partial-equilibrium diagrams used by economists to explain the workings of international commercial policy.

Figure 4-1, for example, represents the derivation of a price-maintenance quota. Curves S_d and D_d depict a country's respective supply of and demand for a particular commodity. Curve S_f represents the foreign supply, which for simplicity is assumed to be perfectly elastic at price P_3. In order to assure domestic suppliers a larger market and a higher price, an import quota of Q_3Q_4 is set, which results in an equilibrium price P_1. Should the domestic supply curve shift to the right, threatening to lower the price of the commodity if the original quota were maintained, the country simply reduces the import quota by an amount equal to the horizontal distance between curves D_d and $S_d + A_1$. It

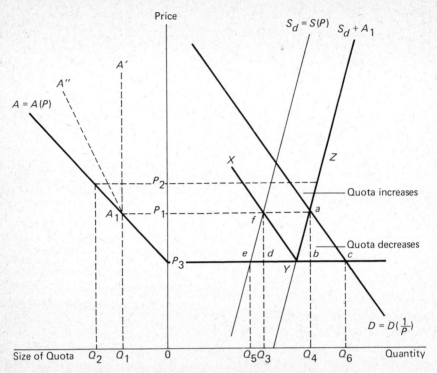

Figure 4-1. The Effects of a Price-Maintenance Quota.

thereby ensures maintenance of price P_1. Similarly, reductions in domestic demand can likewise be offset by similar quota adjustments, and the desired price can therefore be maintained.

On the other hand, reductions in domestic supply or increases in demand may be offset by quota increases in order to maintain price P_1. In any event, the quota necessary to ensure price P_1 will be equal to the horizontal distance between XY and YZ at each hypothetical price level. This produces curve A in the second quadrant of the diagram which relates the size of the quota necessary for the maintenance of price P_1 to different hypothetical price levels that would result if the quota remained unchanged: increases in demand and reductions in domestic supply will tend to result in increased quota size, while increases in domestic supply and reductions in demand will have the opposite effect. Changes in foreign supply price will have no effect on quota size. Finally, should the government decide to permit price to drift upward in response to a strengthening of domestic demand or a fall in supply, it can fail to increase the size of the quota, or increase it at a slower rate than depicted by curve A in Figure 4-1—for example, along curve A' or some curve A'' lying between A and A'.

Using this partial-equilibrium analysis, a number of inferences can be drawn.[5] By reducing the volume of imports from $Q_5 - Q_6$ to $Q_3 - Q_4$ at price P_1—or some similar price-maintenance quota if the domestic supply or demand curve were to shift—domestic output is larger (by $Q_5 - Q_3$) and consumption smaller (by $Q_6 Q_4$) than before. In the process of expanding their output, domestic suppliers must draw resources at higher cost from other parts of the economy, for an efficiency loss of *efd*: the *protective effect* of a quota. At the same time, consumers reduce their purchases of the affected product by $Q_6 Q_4$ and redirect their expenditures to other goods for a net satisfaction loss of *bac*: the *consumption effect* of a quota. These two effects are the net "cost" of the quota to the economy, and constitute a part of the total $P_3 P_1 ac$ loss in consumer surplus attending the quantitative import restriction. The remainder of this consumer-surplus loss is transferred to domestic producers ($P_3 P_1 fe$) and importers (*dfab*) as a result of the higher prices they are now able to command for the protected commodity: the *redistribution effect* of a quota.

The production effect of a quantitative restriction will be greater the more elastic is the domestic supply of the affected commodity, while the consumption effect will be greater the more elastic is the domestic demand for the product in question. At the same time, the redistribution effect in favor of the importers will be greater the less elastic are both the supply of and demand for the product, while the redistribution effect in favor of domestic suppliers will vary inversely with their own supply elasticity. Finally, given a perfectly elastic foreign supply function, there will be no impact on the terms of trade *unless* the foreigners also control the imports, garnering a part of *dfab* for themselves and hence causing an effective increase in import prices from a terms-of-trade standpoint.

In Figure 4-2, the operation of import-directed NTBs of the cost-imposing type is illustrated. Using the same notation as above, S_f is the foreign supply at price P_1, which may include a tariff levied by the importing country if such a tariff exists. At that price, imports would be $Q_1 Q_4$, with domestic suppliers turning out quantity OQ_1 of the commodity. In order to reduce the price competitiveness of imports without raising the tariff level, the country may impose a nontariff charge of $P_1 P_2$ which, as we shall see later, can take a wide variety of forms. This change shifts import supply S_f to $S_f + C$, thereby reducing the amount consumed from OQ_4 to OQ_3, increasing the quantity supplied domestically from OQ_1 to OQ_2, and forcing a reduction of imports from $Q_1 Q_4$ to $Q_2 Q_3$.

Again, a variety of inferences can be drawn. As in the case of quantitative import restrictions, the total loss of consumer surplus is represented by the area $P_1 efg$ in the diagram. Of this, an amount $P_1 gcb$ goes to domestic suppliers as a result of price increases attending the heightened degree of protection in the form of increased producer surplus. Again, there are real losses to the economy in the form of deleterious production effects and consumption effects, represented by the areas *abc* and *def*, respectively. Likewise, there is a positive

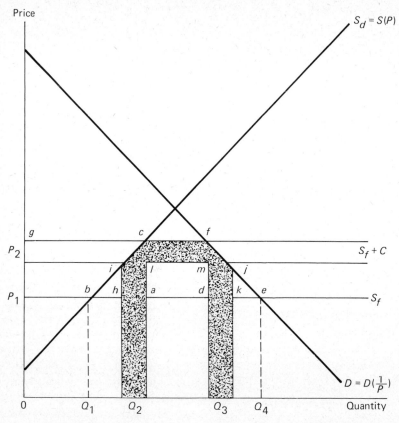

Figure 4–2. The Impact of Cost-Imposing Nontariff Barriers.

balance of payments effect due to the reduced expenditures on imports ($Q_4edQ_3 + Q_1baQ_2$). But what about the area *acfd* which in the case of quotas represents increased profits garnered by domestic importers or foreign exporters? This depends on the nature of the cost-imposing NTB itself.

If the NTB represents safety requirements or other standards which apply equally to imports and import-competing goods, there may be no impact on trade at all: the foreign supply function and the domestic supply function shift upward by exactly the same amount, leaving the volume of imports Q_2Q_3 the same. In such a case, there may be no protective, redistribution, or balance of payments effects, although there is a consumption effect due to the higher price, and a worsening of the terms-of-trade since import prices have gone up. On the other hand, if such cost-increasing requirements are applied only to imports, the area *acfd* represents the total cost of fulfilling them for the volume of imports

$Q_2 - Q_3$. Such costs do not have to be met by import-competing goods produced locally. Hence the real "cost" of such a nontariff barrier may be represented by the areas *abc* + *def* + *acfd* i.e., (*bcfe*) of which *acfd* is a cost which does not exist in the case of tariffs or quantitative import restrictions. Such a cost will also exist if these kinds of standards are applied both to imports and import-competing goods, but weigh more heavily on the former. In either case, the terms of trade effects may be positive or negative. If the required additional processing is done within the importing country and foreigners lower their prices to offset these costs, the terms of trade of the home country may improve. On the other hand, if the additional processing required is accomplished in the exporting country, the home country's terms of trade may worsen as import prices rise.

Yet another important point is that the NTB-cost, imposed in the manner outlined above, may assume a set figure or it may be subject to discretionary variation by those charged with implementing it. This is the case in Figure 4-2, where variation of *C* may produce substantial uncertainty as to the ultimate amount of imports. Assuming for the moment that domestic suppliers do not react to this uncertainty, it is evident that the real cost of the NTB varies substantially—in this instance between *bcfe* and *bih* + *almd* + *kje*—as do the prospective balance of payments, income-redistribution, terms-of-trade, consumption and protective effects. Additionally, the foreign exporters may respond by reducing their shipments, preferring instead to concentrate on markets not subject to such risks.

At the same time, the effects of uncertainty on the part of domestic suppliers may also be of some significance, at least on a theoretical level. On the surface, it would appear that domestic suppliers would be subject to increased uncertainty about the amount they will be able to sell on the home market (OQ_2) and what price they can obtain (P_2). In response to this, they may cut back supply (shift *Sd* to the left) and actually bring about *increased* imports: they shift productive resources into products not subject to such uncertainty. On the other hand, if the variable NTB charge is used to maintain a relatively constant volume of imports, the uncertainty of domestic suppliers might actually be reduced and, by a shifting of the supply function (S_d) to the right, a larger than expected reduction in imports may result. In the former case, the income-redistribution effect of the cost-imposing NTB (area $P_1 bcg$) will be reduced and in the latter case it will be increased. Unless the changed degree of uncertainty alters the *shape* of the domestic supply function, all the effects of cost-imposing NTBs remain the same.

On the export side, the operation of NTBs is equally straightforward, as illustrated in Figure 4-3. If we have a national supply function S_d, domestic demand D_d, foreign demand D_f, and total demand $D = (D_d + D_f)$, the equilibrium price will be P_2 and output will be OQ_6, of which OQ_1 will be sold at home and OQ_4 will be exported. Subsidies to the export industry will tend to

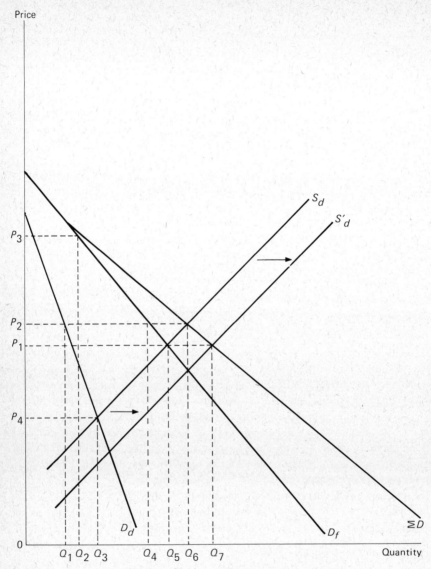

Figure 4–3. The Impact of Subsidies and Quotas on Exports.

lower final costs and permit exporters to offer larger amounts of product to both domestic and foreign buyers at any given price: a shift in the supply function to the right.

A shift of S_d to S'_d will cause the equilibrium price to fall from P_2 to P_1, and quantities sold at home and abroad will tend to rise (by $Q_1 Q_2$ and $Q_4 Q_5$, respectively). The extent to which exports will rise as a result depends on the price-elasticity of domestic and foreign demand: the larger the latter relative to the former, the greater will be the resultant stimulus to exports. On the other hand, if the domestic elasticity of demand is large relative to that prevailing abroad, exports would be affected relatively little.

While the kind of production subsidization just described is nondiscriminatory with respect to sales to domestic or foreign customers, it is also possible that subsidization may be applied exclusively to products destined for export. In that case, export prices alone will tend to fall and foreign sales will rise, while domestic prices may in fact increase as larger quantities are siphoned off into exports. However, this sort of price-discrimination between goods sold at home and abroad is possible only if subsequent reimportation of the commodity is prevented and if the price-elasticity of demand for the product is different in the domestic and foreign markets.

An export quota or other quantitative restriction, on the other hand, tends to cause the domestic price of the affected commodity to fall, while the export price tends to rise. In terms of Figure 4-3, suppose an export quota of OQ_2 is established. The price of exports would rise to P_3. Suppliers would satisfy the domestic market with sales OQ_3 at price P_4, and export OQ_2 under the quota for total output of $OQ_2 + OQ_3$. This represents a rise in export prices, a reduction in quantity exported, a fall in domestic prices and a rise in the quantity demanded domestically. If the purpose of the export quota is to increase domestic value-added, we would expect D_d to begin shifting to the right, as a result of increases in exports of products using this particular commodity as an input. Export quotas fail to attain their goal, however, if alternative sources of supply or substitute commodities can be developed by foreign purchasers. As will become evident later, quantitative export restrictions may also be imposed on a country by its leading partners, who desire to reduce their imports but are unwilling to use tariffs or import-directed nontariff barriers for this purpose.

One final point requires emphasis. Unlike tariffs, nontariff barriers are associated with substantial uncertainty, which imposes an increased risk on exporters and importers alike. They may be varied substantially from one period of time to the next—even when import-destined goods are already in transit—and are often subject to wide administrative discretion. To the extent that importers and those involved in the importing country's distribution network, as well as foreign exporters, are risk-averters, the impact of NTBs on the volume of trade may in fact be many times that implied by the associated costs themselves. Foreign exporters may shift sales to domestic markets or export markets in countries that do not impose NTBs, even in the face of lower but more certain prices. Wholesalers and retailers may shift their purchases to domestic suppliers— in spite of their higher prices—rather than face substantial uncertainty about the final prices or availability of imports.

Nontariff barriers, then, tend to operate primarily through: (a) subsidies to

import-competing suppliers, (b) costs imposed on imports, (c) quantitative restrictions on imports, (d) cost-reducing subsidies to export suppliers, and
(e) quantitative restrictions on exports. There are a wide variety of NTBs which
may be identified, all of which work in one or more of these ways.[a]

Nontariff Barriers and Effective Protection

The impact of nontariff barriers on the effective rate of protection is not
difficult to determine in theory, or empirically, if the tariff-equivalents of NTBs
can be calculated. It is clear that increased nontariff restriction on final-good
imports will increase effective protection of the affected industries. At the same
time, such NTB-increases on imports of intermediate goods and raw materials
will raise their cost to final-goods producers, thereby reducing the effective
protection accorded the latter. In terms of value-added domestically, increased
NTBs on final goods will serve to increase it, while increased NTBs on imports
into that industry will reduce it.

If we define the effective protective rate of duty (Z_j) as:

$$Z_j = \frac{v'_j - v_j}{v_j} \, ,$$

where v'_j is the value-added per dollar of output by domestic final-goods
producers with protection and v_j represents the corresponding domestic value-
added per dollar of output without protection. Clearly, increased NTBs on
final-goods production will tend to widen the spread between v'_j and v_j, while
increased NTB-protection of intermediates or raw materials will reduce it.

The effective protective rate may be expressed in terms of the nominal tariff
rates applying to both final-goods and intermediate/raw materials industries as
follows:[6]

$$Z_j = \frac{t_j - \sum_{i=1}^{n} A_{ij} t_i}{v_j} \tag{4.1}$$

---

[a]An element which may additionally differentiate nontariff barriers to trade from tariffs is
the mechanism involved in translating demands for protection by industries, their suppliers,
and the affected productive factors into actual restrictions. There is considerable evidence to
suggest that for many countries the political process governing the application of NTBs is
less cumbersome and more direct than for tariffs. Moreover, different governmental units
are often involved in according to tariff and nontariff protection. This point has already
been indicated in Chapter 2.

Here t_j represents the nominal tariff applying to imports of the final good, t_i stands for the nominal tariff imposed on each good that serves as an input for the final good, and A_{ij} the value of each input's contribution to every dollar of final-goods output. Again it is clear that, the higher t_j and the lower t_i, the higher the effective rate of protection accorded domestic suppliers of the final good j.

If it is possible to compute the tariff-equivalents of nontariff restrictions on imports of final goods (n_j) and inputs (n_i), it is a simple matter to incorporate these into the above formulation of the effective rate of protection. Cost-imposing NTBs would be represented in terms of their ad valorem values, while the price-effect of quantitative barriers would be similarly stated using appropriate elasticity values. The same would be true of the trade-retarding effects of uncertainty attributable to all kinds of NTBs, as reflected in resulting price differentials expressed, in turn, as ad valorem values:

$$Z_j^* = \frac{t_j + n_j - \sum a_{ij}(t_i + n_i)}{v_j}$$

For example, the incorporation of excise taxes in the above formulation of effective-protection rates was attempted by Harry G. Johnson and Herbert G. Grubel.[7] Using the following formulation in place of Equation (4.1) above:

$$Z_j = \frac{v_j'}{\dfrac{s_j'}{1+t_j} - \displaystyle\sum_{i=1}^{n} \dfrac{m_{i,j}'}{1+t_i}} - 1 \quad,$$

where s_j' represents the sales value of the final-goods industry's output and $m_{i,j}'$ stands for the value of a given intermediate input i into final goods output, excise taxes imposed on the final-goods industry (e_j) and on each intermediate-goods industry (e_i) were simply incorporated as follows:

$$Z_j^* = \frac{v_j'}{\dfrac{s_j'}{(1+t_j)(1+e_j)} - \displaystyle\sum_{i=1}^{n} \dfrac{m_{i,j}'}{(1+t_i)(1+e_i)}} - 1 \quad.$$

The authors conclude that the use of excise taxes by the EEC countries significantly reduce the effective protection accorded final-goods producers as opposed to the case without excise taxes.

The effective-protection analysis of nontariff barriers can be presented quite simply by using geometry, as is done in Figure 4-4. Diagram (A) represents the

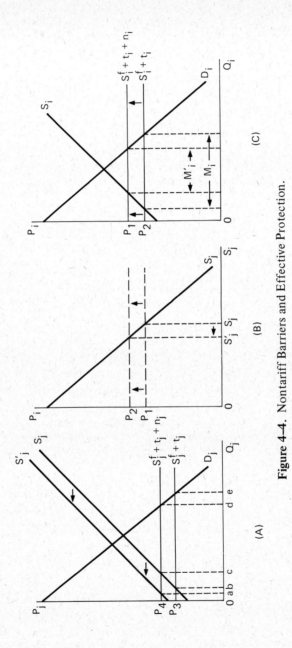

Figure 4–4. Nontariff Barriers and Effective Protection.

partial-equilibrium analysis for final-goods industry j. The imposition of NTBs in the amount n_j on that industry alone reduces imports from be to cd and raises the price of the commodity from P_3 to P_4. What if, on the other hand, an increase in NTBs only on intermediate-goods imports were imposed? In diagram (D) imports of i would be cut from M_i to M'_i, thus raising the price from P_1 to P_2. This, in turn, would cut back supplies of final-good j from S_j to S'_j according to diagram (B), represented as a leftward shift in the industry supply function from S_j to S'_j in diagram (A). Everything else unchanged, the increased cost of inputs due to the new NTBs on intermediate goods would eliminate domestic production altogether in this particular example, with imports of j increasing from be to Oe.

Suppose, on the other hand, NTBs of n_j and n_i were imposed simultaneously. The supply-reducing impact of higher-cost intermediates—as described above, would still be felt by industry j. But this time it would be combined with increased final-goods protection, so that imports of j in this example would change from be to ad. Note that two contradictory effects: increased nontariff barriers on intermediate-goods imports tend to increase imports of the final goods, while increased nontariff barriers on final-goods tend to decrease them. This likewise may be represented graphically in terms of Figure 4-5. Diagram (A) represents imports of j as an inverse function of the rate of nontariff protection of the final-goods industry, while diagram (B) represents imports of j as a direct function of the rate of nontariff protection of the intermediate-goods industry.

Increases in nontariff protection of both industries thus may increase or decrease imports of the final good, depending on, (a) the elasticities of demand for and supply of the final good, and (b) the elasticity of the S_j function in Figure 4-4.

Classification of Nontariff Barriers

Having surveyed the operation of nontariff barriers on a theoretical level, it is necessary at this point to classify the kinds of NTBs known to exist into coherent groups useful for subsequent analysis and application to policy questions.

As noted above, it is useful to group nontariff barriers by intent.[8] This is because there are a large number of distortions to trade which are generally considered NTBs, but which are applied without the specific purpose of impeding imports or artificially stimulating exports. This has certain implications for their impact on trade as well as for attempts at their liberalization. Accordingly, we shall use the following three classifications.

Type I—Measures designed primarily to protect domestic industry from import competition, to restrict exports, or to strengthen domestic industry in competing with imports or competing for export markets. These are subclassified into import-directed and export-directed groups.

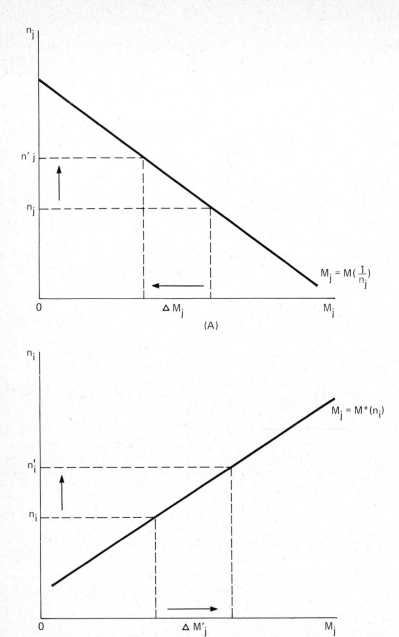

Figure 4–5. Final-Goods Imports as a Function of NTB's on Final Goods and Intermediates.

Type II—Trade-distortive policies and practices which are imposed primarily with the intent of dealing with nontrade-related problems, but which are periodically and purposely employed for trade-restrictive reasons.

Type III—Policies and practices applied exclusively for nontrade-related reasons, but which unavoidably serve to distort international competitive conditions and hence affect trade.

Type I Restrictions: Import-Directed

There are about a dozen NTBs that can be distinguished as belonging to the Type I classification, those implemented with the specific intent of impeding imports or stimulating exports in a manner distortive of trade. This category also includes measures designed to restrict the exports of trading partners for the purpose of protecting domestic industry.

1. *Quantitative restrictions:* Quotas, and discretionary licensing imposed on imports. Also, quotas and licensing designed to restrict exports, including "voluntary export restrictions" to which a nation may submit either under pressure from trading partners desiring to reduce their own imports of the commodity in question, or as part of a multinational agreement.

2. *Variable levies:* Essentially ad valorem import surcharges which may be varied according to conditions prevailing on the domestic market, including tariff-quotas.[b] Variable levies are applied most often to imports of agricultural commodities, in order to ensure that the domestic price of farm produce remains within a range specified under national agricultural policies. A two-fold protective effect may be felt, as a result of (a) the levy itself and (b) increased uncertainty among foreign suppliers and traders as to their ability to compete in the protected market.

   It may be argued that any administrative prerogative to raise tariffs in an *ad hoc* manner for whatever reason represents a form of variable levy. Escape-clause and "national security" provisions for increased tariff protection are two examples of this. In the case of the United States, two additional examples are provisions under the Tariff Act of 1930 which permit tariff increases in order to "equalize costs of production" and offset "unfair acts" on the part of foreign exporters.[9]

3. *Supplementary charges:* Lump-sum specific charges on imports, as opposed to the ad valorem charges, usually associated with variable levies. The impact on costs and uncertainty is essentially the same as under variable levies.

[b]Tariff quotas represent variable tariffs, the levels being contingent on import volume. For example, a country may impose an ad valorem tariff of 10 percent on the first 1000 units imported, 20 percent on the next 1000 units, and 50 percent on all imports over 2000 units.

4. *Minimum import prices:* Often applied, in connection with variable levies or supplementary charges, to imports of agricultural commodities. A minimum import price is fixed which will not disrupt the domestic market. Foreign suppliers must offer their commodities for import at or above this price. Otherwise, a supplementary charge or variable levy will be applied so that the c.i.f. import price equals the established minimum and domestic suppliers are safeguarded. Minimum import prices may also be applied in conjunction with state-trading practices—outlined below— and quantitative import controls.

5. *Conditional imports:* Application of a system similar to that employed under minimum import prices to quantitative import restrictions. Quantitative barriers are set according to the state of the domestic market, with imports freely permitted under certain conditions and severely restricted under other circumstances. Generally, conditional imports are again characteristic of trade in agricultural commodities, with the size of the domestic harvest acting as the determining variable. Once more, there is a two-fold restrictive effect operating through a quantitative limitation of imports and increased uncertainty.

6. *Import calendars:* Usually implemented in connection with quantitative restrictions—and sometimes with supplementary charges and variable levies—on imports of agricultural commodities. Typically, imports are restricted from the time a domestic crop is harvested until all of it has been consumed. They are relatively free from restriction during the remainder of the year.

7. *Mixing, milling and domestic-content regulations:* Restrictive of trade by specifying the domestically-produced content of all products of a certain type permitted to be offered for sale in the importing country. Such regulations may serve as a trade barrier in terms of both reducing the imported content allowed and raising the cost of the product due to the necessity of further processing within the importing country.

8. *Discriminatory government purchasing:* Discrimination in purchases for government account of goods and services in favor of domestic suppliers. Whereas there may at times be sound reasons—with regard to quality and service—for domestic purchases by national and state-local government and quasi-governmental units, restricted bidding and other "buy domestic" practices and legislation, as well as domestic-content regulations imposed on government contractors and subcontractors, clearly represent intentional import restrictions. This includes "tying" foreign-aid credits and grants to purchases in the donor country.[10]

9. *Buy-domestic extensions:* Government action designed to coerce the general public or nationalized, government-regulated, or government-influenced industries or business firms to purchase import-competing goods or services in preference to imports. This distortion may apply

both to goods already in existence as well as goods to be produced in the future which require long production lead-times and a major public or private capital commitment.

10. *Subsidies:* Direct government subsidization of import-competing suppliers through tax rebates, credits, and so forth.

11. *Antidumping measures:* Practices and attendant legislation designed to impede "dumped" imports, except when used against predatory dumping by foreign suppliers. These are generally implemented in the form of quantitative import restrictions or import surcharges, but may also involve government subsidization of import-competing suppliers.[11]

12. *State trading:* Practices associated with state trading insofar as they are distortive of trade and designed to protect import-competing suppliers.

Type I Restrictions: Export-Directed

Certain Type I nontariff restrictions are specifically aimed at promoting or restraining *exports.* These are probably of substantially less overall significance in terms of their distortive impact on trade than are nontariff barriers intended to protect domestic suppliers from import competition.

1. *Subsidies:* Direct government subsidization of exports by means of rebates, resale arrangements, and so forth.

2. *Export-credit-insurance subsidization:* Actuarily unsound export credit insurance schemes that have historically operated with deficits covered by the government.

3. *Dumping:* Pricing practices of a predatory or disruptive nature specifically designed to disturb foreign markets, whether or not engaged in with overt or covert government support.[12]

4. *State trading:* Subsidization of exports under the guise of state trading, as practiced by government export monopolies.

5. *Quantitative export restrictions:* Designed to impede exports of certain commodities in order to increase domestic value-added, preserve domestic resources, avoid disruption of foreign markets, prevent the export of defense-related technology, or for related reasons. Restriction may take the form of quotas or discretionary licensing of exports.

6. *Export charges:* Purpose similar to that of quantitative export restrictions. Normally applied to exports of primary commodities only.

Type II Restrictions

More numerous than those policies and practices specifically aimed at affecting imports or exports are measures employed as trade barriers collaterally with their primary intent of dealing with other economic, social or political problems. Such measures can operate either on the import or export side; often they affect both imports and exports simultaneously.

1. *Customs valuation:* Discriminatory or arbitrary procedures designed to raise the dutiable value of imported commodities in order to increase the real tariff burden borne by these commodities. Valuation procedures may or may not be intentionally protective. U.S. application of "American Selling Price" valuation to imports of benzenoid chemicals, and variations in valuation of bulk and bottled spirits, are examples in this category.[13]

2. *Customs classification:* Discrimination by customs authorities in classifying imports in terms of low-tariff and high-tariff categories. This factor may be especially important when significant discretion is allowed the individual customs agents in the classification process.

3. *Border tax adjustments:* Applied in connection with national indirect tax systems. Tax rebates on exports granted by a country may be overcompensated or undercompensated by countervailing duties levied by the importing nation. Border tax adjustments based on the "origin" or "destination" principle may be turned into implicit export subsidies by means of increased rebates, or into implicit import surcharges by means of increased countervailing duties.[14]

4. *Mark-of-origin regulations:* May be imposed in a discriminatory manner on imports, thereby increasing costs. Variability in such regulations may additionally serve to increase uncertainty on the part of importers and hence retard trade.

   Mark-of-origin regulations may be used as a protectionist device if they require that the country of origin be noted on the imported commodity in a particularly striking or obtrusive manner. Under certain conditions, the importer, wholesaler, or retailer may simply find the goods unsaleable and will terminate his purchases. In the United States, the Federal Trade Commission is charged with preventing deceptive practices with respect to origin marking, and there certainly are differences among those involved as to what is "obtrusive" and hence trade-retarding, and what is not.

5. *Marketing standards:* Advertising and marketing regulations which are used to discriminate against imports.[15] For example, a product may not be advertised and sold as "beer" in Germany unless it is of a stipulated composition of ingredients, and a number of countries forbid the inclusion of corn oil in food products sold under commonly accepted generic names.

6. *Safety requirements:* Application of legitimate safety requirements in such a way as to be discriminatory against imports. Especially vulnerable

to such restrictions are imports of transportation services on public carriers, automotive vehicles, gas cylinders and other pressure vessels, and industrial machinery. Safety regulations may require inspection and approval by agencies which only operate within the importing country, so that an import may not be approved even after the transportation costs have been incurred, thereby raising the risk so high as to effectively exclude foreign-made products.

7. *Health requirements:* Regulations concerning the sanitary characteristics of imports of food and nonfood items when applied in a manner clearly discriminatory against imports. Such restrictions impose costs on importers through service fees, additional processing required before sale, or long inspection delays. They may also result in substantial uncertainty on the part of importers.

8. *Internal transport charges:* Discriminatory charges on transportation of commodities within countries, with preferences granted to selected export or import-competing industries by nationalized, government-regulated, or government-influenced common carriers.

9. *Customs procedures:* Cost-imposing border-clearance procedures, especially those applied at the customs frontier itself such as appraisal and duty determination. This includes customs-clearance practices aimed at imposing costs and increasing uncertainty through harassment and undue delay.

10. *Use taxes:* Imposed on imported commodities in a discriminatory manner. This restriction may be important when applied to automotive motor vehicles based on horsepower, weight, or piston displacement. Generally, such taxes are levied on a highly progressive basis, with most import-competing products falling at the low end and imported goods falling at the high end of the tax-rate scale.

11. *Advance deposits:* Cash deposits required in advance of importation for duties, variable levies or other import charges anticipated to be incurred by the imported product. Advance deposits may also be based on the value of the imports themselves. Such restrictions impose an interest cost which falls on the importer. They are especially significant when the required deposits exceed substantially the amount of the charges payable or are fixed at a high percentage of the value of imports.

12. *Exchange restrictions:* These may be applied primarily for balance-of-payments reasons, but may be used specifically to protect import-competing industries or, in the case of multiple exchange rates, also to stimulate exports.

13. *Media restrictions:* Limitations on the amount of foreign content permitted in imported and locally-published newspapers, books and magazines, or in motion picture films and television and radio programs. Such policies restrict trade in sales or rentals in the affected communications media.

14. *Government entrepreneurship:* Production of import-competing and export goods that would not be supplied without government initiative. This may hold special significance if it involves the formation of government-sponsored consortia and is applied in connection with "by domestic" programs in procurement by the government or government-influenced business firms.

15. *Government financing:* Low-cost financing provided or guaranteed by the government of investments in physical plant and equipment or research and development, to be employed in the production of import-competing or export goods.

16. *Trade agreements:* Bilateral or multilateral in nature, which operate to the complete or partial exclusion of competitive suppliers in certain countries. These include long-term delivery contracts, bulk-purchase agreements, buffer stocks, and bilateral or multilateral commodity agreements.

17. *Monetary restrictions:* Exchange controls, multiple exchange rates and other devices, applied for balance of payments reasons, which affect imports and protect import-competing suppliers or serve to stimulate or retard exports. Such restrictions may be applied with specific protective intent, apart from their primary purpose on the monetary side.

Type III Restrictions

Most of the NTBs falling under the third classification may be considered ancillary effects of policies and measures applied substantially without regard to their probable impact on imports or exports. Nevertheless, some of these may have an important bearing on trade flows, even if the protective intent is absent.

1. *Variation in tariff classification and valuation:* The existence of different tariff classification systems (e.g., TSUS versus BTN) or valuation systems (e.g., c.i.f. versus f.o.b.), may have an effect on costs by reducing efficiency in trade below what it would be under consistent systems.

2. *Variation in indirect tax systems:* If it can be shown that variations of direct taxes imposed on business firms bear on their ability to reinvest earnings, and this affects price and quality of tradeable goods, such variations have an impact on future international competitiveness, via their effect on current business investment in physical plant and in research and development. So far, there is no conclusive evidence of this, although it cannot be dismissed out of hand—nor can similar variations in direct taxes falling on individuals.[16]

3. *Variation in depreciation methods:* There are significant intercountry differences in permissible methods of depreciation for tax purposes.

These affect the cash flow of business firms and may influence the quality and productivity of capital equipment employed in production. There may be a connection between this and the long-term price and quality competitiveness of export and import-competing suppliers.[17]

4. *Variation in weights and measures:* International differences in electrical standards, measuring systems, driving practices, and so forth, affect production costs, product quality, and international competitiveness. Such differences may not be maintained for restrictive purposes, but increased standardization would serve to facilitate both imports and exports of most industrial countries.

5. *Variation in national consumption patterns and related governmental policies:* As influenced by government policies and practices, differences in national cultural, social, and dietary patterns affect tastes and the composition of consumer purchases. This category may include a broad range of actions including income-distribution policies, antismoking campaigns, and so on. Especially important may be sumptuary laws and regulations designed to affect consumption of certain products, particularly alcoholic beverages, for social, moral, religious, or other reasons.

6. *Variation in social charges:* Differences in social security systems and health-insurance schemes in terms of their burden on producers, coverage, and method of application.

7. *Variation in economic policies:* Imports and exports are influenced by national monetary and fiscal policies in terms of their impact on interest cost and credit availability, tax rates and incidence, and aggregate demand. Also of importance may be regional development policies affecting export and import-competing industries.

8. *Government-sponsored R&D:* Government-financed, subsidized, or otherwise materially-supported research and development programs affecting export or import-competing goods. This includes spillovers from R&D expenditures not necessarily related to production of tradeable commodities, particularly with regard to the defense and aerospace areas.

9. *Government-induced scale-effects:* Impact of massive government procurement of military or other goods and services on the cost and quality of export and import-competing commodities. This effect will make itself felt via economies of scale achieved in this manner by the affected industries.

10. *Direct defense spillovers:* Closely related to the two preceding categories—but included here as a separate category—is the cost-reducing impact of government defense-related development contracts and subsequent production of nondefense versions of the same or similar products by export or import-competing industries. Also included is the use of government-owned plant and equipment for production of tradeable goods and services.

11. *Transfer costs:* Docking and port delays and congestion, pilferage and other security lapses, longshoremen's strikes, dockside bribery, inadequate port and warehousing facilities for imports, high dock charges, and so forth, as well as "smuggling duties" for the procurement of licenses. All of these affect costs, either directly or indirectly, as in the case of increased insurance charges. They may also affect delivery times, merchandise quality, and other factors influencing competitiveness. All are to some degree subject to government regulation.

12. *International cartels:* International, government-sanctioned private market-sharing or price-fixing agreements,[18] with respect to trade in goods and services supplied by the participating firms.[c] There may also be important secondary effects, as in the case of the International Air Transport Association (IATA) and the various shipping conferences. Such service cartels, with or without government participation, may grant discriminatory shipping rates in the process of maximizing collective profits. Such discrimination may be applied randomly, but may nevertheless bear disproportionately on the exports of certain countries.[d]

Table 4-1 indicates the distribution of nontariff barriers by type among the nineteen developed market economy countries, using the classification system developed above and the data presented in the following chapter. It is clear that Type I measures are generally the most common among those that have been identified.

The character of nontariff distortions of international trade, as a complex and multifaceted matrix of governmental measures affecting international competitiveness and market access, immediately raises the question of their actual importance as impediments to world trade. Although the difficulties of measurement and analysis should be quite evident, some attempts to come to grips with this issue are presented in the following chapter.

---

[c]A good example of this occurred in December of 1968 in the shipbuilding industry. Changing conditions in the competition for the construction of large-size tankships between Europe and Japan were beginning to shift in favor of Europe. In response to this, European and Japanese shipbuilders began to work toward a market-sharing and price-fixing agreement, rather than continue to compete with one another. The following quotation of the president of a major Japanese shipbuilding company is illustrative: "We don't deny the principle of free competition, but in the past few years, because of cut-throat competition between Europe and Japan, the price has come down to an *unreasonable* level, so we would like to recover. What we are seeking isn't to fix a price for each contract, but to set a reasonable price level; more or less an understanding." (italics supplied) See *The Wall Street Journal*, January 2, 1969, p. 24. See also Chapter 6.

[d]Early in 1969, for example, all of the shipping companies comprising the Atlantic & Gulf Coast-West Coast-South America Conference agreed to raise shipping charges between the United States and Latin American by 7½ to 10 percent due to a longshoremen's strike. This indicates the concerted action such shipping conferences are able to take.

Table 4-1
Distribution of Identifiable Nontariff-Barriers by Type (Percentage)

Country	Type I	Type II	Type III
North American Group:			
United States	66	29	5
Canada	73	27	–
U.K.–Ireland			
United Kingdom	75	23	2
Republic of Ireland	93	7	–
Nordic Group:			
Denmark	74	23	3
Norway	90	2	4
Sweden	73	19	8
Finland	55	45	–
Continental EFTA Group:			
Austria	93	7	–
Switzerland	98	2	–
Portugal	96	4	–
Eastern Group:			
Japan	99	1	–
Australia	19	81	–
New Zealand	87	13	–
EEC Group:			
Common External	100	–	–
Belgium-Luxembourg	95	5	–
France	86	13	1
Germany	83	17	–
Italy	91	8	1
Netherlands	83	15	2

Source: Table 5-1.

Notes

1. For one of the pioneering studies in the field, see Percy Bidwell, *The Invisible Tariff: A Study of the Control of Imports into the United States* (New York: Council on Foreign Relations, 1939). Another early study is J. Grunzel, *International Protectionism* (London: Oxford University Press, 1916).

2. See, for example, William B. Kelly, Jr., "Nontariff Barriers," and Douglas Dosser, "Fiscal and Social Barriers to Economic Integration in the Atlantic Area" in Bela Balassa, ed., *Studies in Trade Liberalization* (Baltimore: Johns Hopkins Press, 1967); Hans Liesner, *Atlantic Harmonization: Making Free Trade Work* (London: Atlantic Trade Study, 1968); International Chamber of Commerce, *Non-Tariff Obstacles to Trade* (Paris: ICC, 1969); Gerard and Victoria Curzon, *Hidden Barriers to International Trade* (London: Trade Policy Research

Centre, 1970); and Harald B. Malmgren, *Trade Wars or Trade Negotiations?* (Washington, D.C.: Atlantic Council, 1970).

3. Part of this chapter relies heavily on the author's "Nontariff Barriers and the Free-Trade Area Option," *Banca Nazionale del Lavoro Quarterly Review*, March 1969.

4. See Kelly's "Nontariff Barriers," and Robert E. Baldwin, "Nontariff Barriers: A Brief Survey," in U.S. Senate, Committee on Finance, *Compendium of Papers on Legislative Oversight Review of U.S. Trade Policies* (Washington, D.C.: GPO, 1968).

5. See Charles P. Kindleberger, *International Economics*, 4th ed. (Homewood, Ill.: Richard D. Irwin, 1968), Chapter 8, or Ingo Walter, *International Economics: Theory and Policy* (New York: Ronald Press, 1968), Chapter 8.

6. See W.M. Corden, "The Structure of a Tariff System and the Effective Protective Rate," *Journal of Political Economy*, June 1966; G. Basevi, "The U.S. Tariff Structure: Estimates of Effective Protection of U.S. Industries and Industrial Labor," *Review of Economics and Statistics*, May 1966; and H.G. Johnson, "The Theory of Tariff Structure" in *Trade and Development* (Geneva: Librairie Droz, 1965).

7. H.G. Grubel and H.G. Johnson, "Nominal Tariffs, Indirect Taxes, and Effective Rates of Protection: The Common Market Countries, 1959," *Economic Journal*, December 1967.

8. An earlier version of this classification system may be found in Walter's "Nontariff Barriers and the Free-Trade Area Option," (see n. 3) and subsequently in United Nations Conference on Trade and Development, *Liberalization of Tariff and Non-Tariff Barriers* (Geneva: UNCTAD Documents TD/B/C.2/R.1 and Add. 1, 1969).

9. The relevant U.S. provisions have been embodied in the following: (a) Escape clause, Trade Expansion Act of 1962, Sections 301b and 351; (b) National security, ibid., Section 232, (c) Cost equalization, Tariff Act of 1930, as amended, Section 336; (d) Unfair acts, ibid., Section 337. The effect of the last two provisions is probably minor and would appear to operate largely through the trade-retarding effects of uncertainty.

10. See, for example, Organization for Economic Cooperation and Development: *Government Purchasing* (Paris: OECD, 1966).

11. For some applications, see A. Mastropasqua, *Le Marché Commun et la Défense Contre le Dumping* (Rome: G. Pastine, 1965). See also General Agreement on Tariffs and Trade, *Anti-Dumping and Countervailing Duties* (Geneva: GATT, 1958).

12. Unfortunately, no recent study of dumping exists. The classic work is Jacob Viner, *Dumping* (Chicago: University of Chicago Press, 1923).

13. See, for instance, H. Grubel and H.G. Johnson, "Nominal Tariff Rates and United States Valuation Practices," *Review of Economics and Statistics*, August 1967.

14. For a good review, see Stanley S. Surrey, "The Wonderful World of Taxes," *Columbia Journal of World Business*, May-June 1968.

15. An interesting case in point is the marketing standard applied to imported tomatoes by the U.S. Department of Agriculture in January of 1969. At the request of import-competing Florida suppliers, USDA ruled that green tomatoes sold in the U.S. must be at least 2 9/32" and ripe tomatoes at least 2 17/32" in diameter. Although they apply to both U.S.-grown and imported tomatoes, only about 15 percent of the American crop is affected while the regulations affect over half of the Mexican crop—Mexico is the chief supplier of tomato imports. The resulting rise in U.S. retail tomato prices is estimated to be well over 50 percent. See *The Wall Street Journal*, March 4, 1969.

16. See Stanley S. Surrey's "World of Taxes," and his "Implications of Tax Harmonization in the European Common Market," statement of the National Industrial Conference Board as reprinted in Committee on Ways and Means, U.S. House of Representatives, 90th Cong., 2nd sess., *Foreign Trade and Tariff Proposals* (Washington, D.C.: GPO, pp. 56-66). See also Douglas Dosser, "Fiscal and Social Barriers to Economic Integration in the Atlantic Area" in Bela Balassa, ed., *Studies in Trade Liberalization* (Baltimore: Johns Hopkins Press, 1967), and Carl S. Shoup ed., *Fiscal Harmonization in Common Markets*, vols. I and II (New York: Columbia University Press, 1966). Also of interest is EEC Commission, *Report of the Fiscal and Financial Committee*—the "Neumark Report"—(Brussels: EEC, 1963), and Organization for Economic Cooperation and Development, *Report on Border Tax Adjustments* (Paris: OECD, 1964).

17. See M. Kryzaniak and Richard A. Musgrave, *The Shifting of the Corporation Income Tax* (Baltimore: Johns Hopkins Press, 1963), and Challis A. Hall, "Direct Shifting of the Corporation Income Tax in Manufacturing," American Economic Review, *Papers and Proceedings*, May 1964.

18. See, for example, Pierre Wack, *Die Anforderungen an ein Unternehmen und Seine Chancen im Gemeinsamen Markt* (Baden-Baden: Lutzeyer, 1961).

5

Barriers to International Competition: The Application and Liberalization of Nontariff Distortions

Ingo Walter

This chapter investigates the application of nontariff distortions by the developed, market-economy countries, including an assessment of their bearing on the exports of developing countries. It employs those available techniques which seem to be of use in analyzing this complex issue. The discussion is intended to show that NTBs are indeed important impediments to international trade. Hence the rationale for their elimination or liberalization—in general or within the confines of regional trade blocs—rests on the same theoretical foundation as does the case for tariff reduction.

Presumably, the gains in terms of improved international resource allocation, increased real incomes, and favorable effects on the rate of economic growth of the affected economies more than offset the inevitable structural readjustments attending the reduction of nontariff barriers which shield domestic suppliers from import competition. It is also useful to determine whether the creation of regional economic blocs represent an effective means of liberalizing NTBs and whether this constitutes an important offset to the deleterious aspects of global economic polarization.

Factors Governing Nontariff Measures

Regardless of the intentions to mitigate the distortive effects of nontariff barriers, it is doubtful that all such distortions can be eliminated, particularly those classified in the previous chapter as Type II and Type III barriers. Apart from the evident difficulties in defining and identifying all such restrictions, and with their close connection with purely domestic programs, in many cases it is patently impossible to develop defensible estimates of their economic impact and to put forward a sound argument for their elimination. Indeed, the number of more or less subtle Type II and Type III NTBs that combine to affect internal commerce in such advanced free-trade areas as the EEC and even the United States testifies to the difficulties involved in eliminating all NTBs to international trade.

States, regions, municipalities and other governmental and quasi-governmental units within a country all apply measures which restrict interregional imports and stimulate the development of regional industries and hence regional exports as well. Even within regional economic blocs these political jurisdictions naturally continue to exist. In addition, within such free-trade zones, the national political jurisdiction provides another potential source of NTBs that may not play a role in purely interregional trade.

In the United States, authority for the reduction of tariffs on a negotiated basis is granted to the executive branch of government by the legislative branch, subject to periodic renewal. This is also true in some of the other industrial countries in Europe and elsewhere, although they frequently give the executive far greater flexibility of action. This negotiating authority has been successfully used to reduce tariffs very substantially during the past two decades, within the framework of the GATT.

But the authority to negotiate simultaneously the reduction of nontariff barriers either has not been included in the powers granted the national executives or it has not been grasped by them. Consequently, nontariff restrictions have remained largely outside the realm of past multilateral trade talks. And even when they have been brought in—as was the American Selling Price system of customs valuation in the Kennedy Round—the negotiators did not in the end have the authority to agree to and implement their liberalization. Because the reduction of many of the most important NTBs is frequently a legislative matter, and is closely tied to sensitive domestic programs, it becomes inordinately difficult.

This is one reason for the deflection of the efforts of protectionist interest from tariff to nontariff barriers. The structure of tariff barriers is based on a complex and intricate set of multinational agreements and, even though temporary relief may be provided, tariffs cannot be increased even temporarily without running the danger of significant and adverse reaction on the part of other countries. Consequently, tariffs may not provide import-competing suppliers with a reliable source of relief—in any event, a very substantial case for protection would have to be made before any reaction would be forthcoming. It would appear, therefore, that a much more direct path for protectionist pressure is through the legislative branch of government and those administrative agencies responsible for implementing a wide variety of regulations and standards that affect the commodities in question.[a] Whether pressure for increased protection is exerted through one or the other of these channels, the vehicle for translating it into action will almost certainly be the nontariff barrier.[1] Because institutional resistance to increased protection via nontariff restrictions may still be less than resistance to increases in tariff levels, the activities of import-competing groups designed to obtain relief from foreign competition have increasingly been centered there.

---

[a]In the United States, national agencies possessing real or potential power to impose various kinds of NTBs are the Departments of Defense, Agriculture, Interior, Transportation, State, and Commerce, the Federal Trade Commission, Federal Communications Commission, Federal Maritime Commission, Interstate Commerce Commission, National Aeronautics and Space Administration, Small Business Administration and Tariff Commission, in addition to direct recourse to the Congress.

This has been particularly true in the United States in the period since the Kennedy Round. The import-competitors themselves—notably the chemical, steel, footwear, textile, petroleum and dairy industries—have worked either to raise nontariff barriers or to keep them from being reduced. An additional element favoring more restrictive NTBs are balance-of-payments considerations, which in the case of the United States, France, and the United Kingdom have been of substantial importance. Again because of the rigidities and commitments existing in the case of tariffs, balance-of-payments pressures have likewise tended to be shunted onto nontariff barriers. In the case of the United States, the measures have involved import surcharges and export tax exemptions or rebates—to offset border tax adjustments used abroad and allegedly harmful to U.S. exports and import-competing industries. In the case of France, temporary quotas were imposed on a wide variety of commodities after the crisis of May 1968, even on the exports of its EEC partners, and the United Kingdom has resorted to such measures as advance-deposit requirements during payments crises.

The present state of affairs, then, is that: (a) declining tariff levels among industrial countries are rendering nontariff barriers relatively more important as impediments to trade; (b) at the same time, there are obvious incentives for import-competitors to recoup some of the lost tariff protection by working to raise nontariff barriers, either through the national legislature or through appropriate administrative agencies; and (c) the increasing rigidity of tariffs cause NTBs to be a logical alternative for securing increased protection.

Another aspect of this question appears to be becoming relatively more important. This is the use of the threat of increased nontariff barriers or other sanctions to force major suppliers of imports to self-limit their exports or increase their imports from abroad. If a country desires to restrict imports of a given commodity, it may approach the major exporting countries and request them to cut back on their sales to customers in the home country. This may be done either on a bilateral or unilateral basis. In either case, the importing country must have sufficient economic, political, or military leverage, relative to that of the exporting country, to force the latter to accede to its wishes. There are of course a wide variety of determinants of such leverage, such as the importance of the importing country to the exporter's market, the vulnerability of the importing country to retaliation, the value of military alliances, the international political climate, and so forth.

Self-limiting export agreements have been applied in steel, cutlery, meat, and other products, and have had a particular impact on Japan and other Asian countries. Moreover, this device may find universal use in the future under explicit or implicit "market-sharing" schemes. The United States has also forced some of its allies to limit their trading with Communist countries and, at the same time, foreign firms using material imports originating in selected countries are restricted in exporting to the United States. Closely related are pressures on foreign countries to join or work towards international agreements to set up quantitative barriers to trade, such as the Long-Term Cotton Textile Agreement negotiated under the GATT in 1962.

In short, nontariff barriers are important, and appear to be becoming even more so as a component of international commercial policy. It has been stated that the "commercial policy vacuum" in the late 1960s and early 1970s, lacking new moves in the direction of freer trade, represented an environment especially conducive to the success of protectionist interests.[2] To some extent this unwelcome success has already materialized, and there is little doubt that much of it is manifested in the area of nontariff barriers.

The Product Coverage of Nontariff Restrictions

One indicator of the overall application or pervasiveness of nontariff measures applied to imports by the industrial countries is their coverage in relation to all traded commodities.[3] Using an inventory of nontariff restrictions developed for that purpose, the incidence of NTB-use is represented in Table 5-1 for the United States, Canada, the EEC and EFTA member countries, Portugal, Finland, Ireland, Japan, Australia, and New Zealand: the nineteen market-economy industrial countries.[4] Each of the figures (A_j) in the table represents the percentage of individual products within the applicable SITC two-digit commodity group subject to identifiable, import-directed Type I or Type II nontariff measures.

$$A_j = \frac{N_r}{\sum N_j} \times 100 ,$$

where N_r represents the number of commodities subject to NTBs within a given two-digit SITC class, and $\sum N_j$ represents the total number of individual commodities included in that class.

Only nontariff restrictions applied in a discretionary manner to individual commodities are included. The index thus does not reflect such measures as discriminatory purchasing for national or state-local public account, undercompensating or overcompensating border tax adjustments, or similar measures which apply to substantially all products.[5] Furthermore, in the case of the EEC countries, the data for each member-nation represents those common external nontariff restrictions that have been applied by the community—primarily in the case of agricultural commodities—as well as those applied by the individual member-country itself. Finally, no data were available for NTBs covering Irish or Finnish farm imports, while New Zealand's application of import licensing to all industrial goods made it impossible to consider that country.

It would appear that those commodity groups most susceptible to the

Table 5-1
Coverage of Nontariff Import Barriers (Percentage of Commodities Covered by NTB's within Each Commodity Group)[a]

SITC	Commodity Group	U.S.	Canada	U.K.	Japan	Belg.-Lux.	France	Germany	Italy	Netherlands	Denmark	Finland	Norway	Sweden	Austria	Switzerland	Portugal	Ireland	Australia	New Zealand	Mean (all countries)
00	Live animals	17	17	–	50	67	50	50	50	50	50	n	17	83	50	67	–	n[b]	100	100	48
01	Meat	25	8	17	42	58	58	50	50	50	58	n	33	58	75	33	25	n	75	17	43
02	Dairy	50	50	67	67	67	67	67	67	67	50	n	67	100	83	50	33	n	33	17	59
03	Fish	25	–	–	100	–	–	–	–	–	25	n	–	50	–	–	25	n	–	–	13
04	Cereals	14	26	50	79	93	93	100	93	93	71	n	71	77	71	57	64	n	36	21	65
05	Fruit	–	–	27	59	27	27	45	27	18	23	n	54	27	50	23	4	n	32	27	28
06	Sugar	33	–	17	67	67	67	67	67	67	100	n	17	67	67	–	17	n	33	–	44
07	Coffee, tea, cocoa, spices	–	–	–	30	30	10	20	10	20	10	n	10	10	–	–	–	n	–	–	8
08	Feeds	–	33	40	40	60	20	60	60	60	60	n	80	40	20	60	–	n	33	40	32
09	Misc. food preps.	–	–	–	67	67	100	100	67	67	100	n	100	100	33	67	–	–	33	–	51
11	Beverages	20	20	20	60	40	40	80	40	40	60	20	80	40	20	60	–	–	25	25	34
12	Tobacco	33	–	25	50	93	50	25	50	–	–	25	–	25	50	–	25	25	25	25	23
21	Hides and skins	12	–	–	–	–	–	–	–	–	–	–	–	–	–	–	–	–	–	–	1
22	Oil, seeds, nuts and kernels	11	–	–	22	–	–	–	9	–	–	–	–	11	–	11	–	–	44	67	9
23	Crude rubber	–	–	–	–	–	–	–	–	–	–	–	–	–	–	–	–	–	–	–	0
24	Wood and cork	–	27	9	9	–	–	–	–	–	–	–	–	–	–	–	–	–	–	–	3
25	Pulp and waste paper	–	–	–	–	–	–	–	–	–	–	–	–	–	–	–	–	–	–	–	0

Table 5-1 (cont.)

SITC	Commodity Group	U.S.	Canada	U.K.	Japan	Belg.Lux.	France	Germany	Italy	Netherlands	Denmark	Finland	Norway	Sweden	Austria	Switzerland	Portugal	Ireland	Australia	New Zealand	Mean (all countries)
26	Textile fibers	8	–	–	–	–	–	–	–	–	–	–	–	4	–	–	31	–	15	4	4
27	Crude minerals and fertilizers	–	–	–	21	–	–	–	10	–	–	–	–	–	5	–	–	–	–	–	2
28	Metal ores and scrap	–	–	–	–	–	–	–	–	–	–	–	–	–	–	–	–	–	–	–	0
29	Misc. crude animal/vegetable materials	–	20	20	–	20	40	20	10	10	20	–	10	–	20	10	–	–	20	50	11
32	Coal, coke and briquettes	–	–	100	60	60	20	20	10	10	20	20	10	–	20	10	–	–	20	A[c]18	11
33	Petroleum	25	–	–	12	60	12	–	–	–	–	–	–	–	20	–	–	–	–	A7	7
34	Gas	–	–	–	–	37	50	50	–	–	–	38	–	–	–	–	–	–	–	A3	3
35	Electric energy	–	–	–	–	100	100	–	–	–	–	–	–	–	–	–	–	–	–	A6	6
41	Animal oils and fats	50	50	–	42	8	50	–	–	–	–	–	–	–	–	–	–	–	–	A11	11
42	Fixed vegetable oils and fats	–	–	–	–	8	8	8	8	8	8	–	–	–	–	17	17	–	–	A7	7
43	Processed oils and fats, waxes	25	25	–	–	–	–	–	25	8	8	–	–	–	–	–	–	–	–	A4	4
51	Chemical elements and compounds	41	–	–	14	9	–	8	18	17	–	67	–	–	4	–	–	–	–	A6	6
52	Tar and crude derivatives	–	–	–	–	–	–	–	–	–	–	–	–	–	–	–	–	–	–	A4	4
53	Dyes	75	–	–	–	–	–	–	–	–	–	–	–	–	–	–	–	–	–	A4	4
54	Medicinal and Pharmaceutical	63	–	–	14	14	14	–	–	14	–	–	14	–	14	–	–	–	–	A8	8
55	Perfumes, cleaners, toiletries	17	–	–	17	–	–	–	–	–	–	–	17	17	–	–	17	–	–	A4	4
56	Manufactured fertilizers	100	–	–	–	25	25	–	–	25	25	25	–	–	–	–	–	25	–	A13	13
57	Explosives	–	–	–	–	25	–	25	–	–	–	–	–	–	–	–	25	–	–	A4	4

Code	Commodity	1	2	3	4	5	6	7	8	9	10	11	12	13	14	15	16	17	18	
58	Plastics	100	–	–	–	–	–	–	–	–	–	–	–	–	–	–	–	–	–	A 6
59	Misc. chemicals	60	–	20	20	20	20	20	20	20	–	–	20	20	20	–	20	–	–	A 14
61	Leather and manufactures	–	–	56	–	–	–	–	–	–	–	–	–	–	–	–	60	–	–	A 3
62	Rubber manufactures	20	–	–	–	–	–	–	–	–	–	20	–	–	–	–	–	–	–	A 6
63	Wood and cork manufactures	10	–	–	–	–	8	–	–	–	–	–	–	–	–	–	–	–	–	A 1
64	Paper and paperboard manufactures	–	–	–	–	–	–	–	–	–	–	–	–	–	–	–	–	–	–	A 0
65	Textile manufactures	14	3	5	11	11	16	3	8	–	3	16	5	11	8	13	–	–	–	A 7
66	Nonmetallic mineral manufactures	3	–	6	–	6	12	3	–	–	–	–	–	9	3	5	–	–	–	A 2
67	Iron and steel	74	26	6	6	–	3	8	–	16	–	–	3	5	3	3	–	–	–	A 6
68	Nonferrous metals	–	–	–	–	6	–	–	11	–	–	–	–	–	–	–	6	–	6	A 2
69	Misc. metal manufactures	12	–	–	–	–	–	–	–	11	–	–	–	–	–	–	–	–	–	A 1
71	Nonelectric machinery	8	12	30	3	–	–	–	–	–	–	–	–	–	–	3	–	6	6	A 3
72	Electric machinery	78	–	29	6	6	–	–	–	–	–	–	–	–	18	18	–	6	6	A 8
73	Transport equipment	24	8	16	8	8	8	20	4	–	–	8	8	8	8	28	–	12	12	A 10
81	Construction equipment	100	–	–	–	–	–	–	–	–	–	–	–	–	–	–	–	–	4	A 6
82	Furniture	–	–	–	–	–	–	–	–	·	–	–	–	–	–	–	–	–	–	A 0
83	Travel goods & accessories	–	–	100	–	–	–	–	–	–	–	–	–	–	–	–	–	–	–	A 6
84	Clothing	57	–	–	–	29	–	–	–	–	100	14	14	14	14	14	–	14	14	A 7
85	Footwear	25	–	–	–	–	7	7	–	–	–	–	–	–	–	–	100	–	–	A 13
86	Precision instruments	–	7	7	7	7	7	–	–	–	–	–	–	7	7	7	–	7	7	A 4
89	Misc. manufactures	14	3	3	3	3	3	–	–	–	3	14	14	3	3	3	–	7	7	A 3
	Total imports	27	7	10	34	19	17	16	13	19	11	n	14	14	10	12	17[d]	n	9	A 16

[a]Data: See text for sources of the nontariff-barrier inventory.

[b]Not available.

[c]New Zealand applies automatic import licensing to most manufactured goods, with preferences granted to Commonwealth suppliers.

[d]Specific commodities covered by NTB's 62% of all dutiable imports subject to bilateral or multilateral quotas.

application of nontariff measures are concentrated in the agricultural sector, particularly dairy products, cereal grains and prepared foods, with live animals and meats, sugar, feeds, and beverages also subject to a heavy incidence of NTB use. Most countries evidently employ nontariff restrictions extensively to protect domestic agricultural markets. These represent primarily quantitative import barriers and variable or lump-sum import charges which constitute an integral part of the national or regional agricultural support program—for example, the variable levy system in the EEC—although such measures as restrictive health and marketing standards are also used extensively.

In the industrial-goods category, fossil fuels and their derivatives, transport equipment, textiles, chemicals, fertilizers, and vegetable fats and oils appear to be most frequently subject to nontariff measures. It is evident that NTBs are applied to industrial goods much more irregularly than on agricultural commodities, and represent a much wider variety of types of restrictions.

Among the various countries, the heaviest incidence of NTB-use appears in the case of Japan, which employs such restrictions to impede imports of a variety of manufactured product groups in addition to the standard agricultural nontariff applications—generally in the form of discretionary licensing. New Zealand automatically licenses imports of all industrial products. Other countries applying NTBs to a comparatively wide range of products are the United States, Portugal, the Netherlands, France, Germany and Belgium-Luxembourg, while those nations with the smallest product coverage of NTBs are Australia, Canada, and the United Kingdom. These data include only nontariff measures applied in a nondiscriminatory manner with respect to country of origin to all imports into a customs area and do not encompass measures such as "voluntary" export quotas or embargoes imposed on products originating in selected individual nations.

The Import-Coverage of Nontariff Measures

A second way to assess the importance of specific Type I and Type II nontariff measures in the import makeup of the various industrial countries is to estimate the proportion of total imports in each commodity group which are subject to NTBs. That is:

$$B_j = \frac{\sum_{i=1}^{n} M_r}{M_j} \times 100 \, ,$$

where M_r represents the value of a nation's imports of each commodity subject to NTBs and M_j represents the value of total imports in SITC commodity group

j. The values of B_j thus indicate the imports actually entering an economy under NTBs in relation to total imports for each country and commodity class. Although this cannot be considered a measure of restrictiveness, it does show the volume of trade subject to NTBs and its importance relative to total trade. These data are presented in Table 5-2.

Approximately 18 percent of all imports of the industrial countries under consideration here entered under nontariff measures in 1967. This amounted to about $24.7 billion. Again, agricultural imports are most heavily subject to NTBs, with over half the value of all imports entering the industrial economies in the case of live animals and meats, cereals, sugar, beverages, tobacco, and food preparations under such measures. In the industrial-goods sector, fossil fuels, transport equipment as well as chemicals and pharmaceuticals stand out as being subject to NTBs in above-average measure.

In terms of individual countries or customs areas, about a third of all imports in 1967 entered under specific nontariff measures in the case of Japan, Belgium-Luxembourg, the United States and Portugal, with Australia, Sweden, Denmark and Canada evidencing the smallest proportions.

An alternative to weighting the coverage of national nontariff measures by each country's own imports would be to use as weights instead some other set of trade figures less biased by that country's nontariff measures. One alternative would be to use OECD data which represent the combined imports of all of the countries under consideration here except Finland, Australia and New Zealand, plus Yugoslavia, Turkey, Greece, Iceland, and Spain. Assuming that the commodity structure of OECD imports is broadly representative of the general importance of the various products in world trade, a weighted NTB-coverage index can be developed such as the following:

$$C_j = \frac{\sum_{i=1}^{n} M_{r:w}}{M_{j:w}} \times 100.$$

That is, for each country and SITC two-digit commodity group j, the OECD-import-weighted index of NTB incidence (C_j) represents the sum of OECD imports of those products to which NTBs are applied ($M_{r:w}$) by that country relative to total OECD imports in that commodity group ($M_{r:w}$). These data are presented in Table 5-3.

If the imports of each market-economy industrial country had the same commodity composition as OECD imports in general, somewhat under a third of all imports would be covered by nontariff measures. Again, the weighted coverage in the agricultural sector is most notable, with a mean rate of 41.6 percent, compared with 8.9 percent for industrial goods.

There are significant differences among the various countries in terms of the

Table 5-2
Percentage of 1967 Imports Subject to Nontariff Restrictions[a]

SITC	Commodity Group	U.S.	Canada	U.K.	Japan	Belg.-Lux.	France	Germany	Italy	Netherlands	Denmark	Finland	Norway	Sweden	Austria	Switzerland	Portugal	Ireland	Australia	New Zealand	Mean (all countries)
00	Live animals	n	100	—	49	97	49	98	88	81	11	n	100	69	96	98	—	n[b]	[n,b]100	100	71
01	Meat	60	64	34	22	85	67	89	94	68	80	n	93	100	97	98	100	n	18	88	67
02	Dairy	97	69	77	42	100	100	100	100	100	2	n	100	100	76	50	81	n	—	—	70
03	Fish	19	—	—	100	—	—	—	—	—	16	n	—	56	—	—	99	n	—	—	17
04	Cereals	2	—	95	99	100	99	100	100	100	91	n	100	49	77	85	94	n	—	82	75
05	Fruit	—	—	28	52	44	63	67	86	43	91	n	43	35	56	46	62	n	37	56	48
06	Sugar	89	—	99	30	83	98	100	54	61	100	n	6	62	19	—	75	n	—	—	52
07	Coffee, tea, cocoa, spices	—	—	—	46	73	7	73	1	44	76	n	4	1	—	—	—	n	—	—	19
08	Feeds	—	—	100	51	79	100	69	75	80	4	n	13	100	100	65	—	n	—	—	49
09	Misc. food preps.	—	4	—	50	95	100	100	92	93	100	n	100	100	17	95	—	n	—	—	56
11	Beverages	79	96	26	96	100	100	98	92	93	99	97	99	99	66	90	—	n	—	96	71
12	Tobacco	5	—	2	100	—	—	—	100	—	—	3	—	60	100	—	—	18	72	96	40
21	Hides and skins	60	—	—	—	—	—	—	—	—	—	—	—	—	—	—	—	—	—	—	3
22	Oil, seeds, nuts and kernels	1	—	—	67	—	—	—	—	—	—	—	—	9	—	100	—	—	9	—	10
23	Crude rubber	—	—	—	—	—	—	—	1	—	—	—	—	—	—	—	—	—	—	—	0
24	Wood and cork	—	37	—	—	—	—	—	—	—	—	—	—	—	—	—	—	—	—	—	2
25	Pulp and waste paper	—	—	—	—	—	—	—	—	—	—	—	—	—	—	—	—	—	—	—	0

26	Textile fibers	67	–	–	–	–	–	–	–	–	–	–	6	–	82	–	21	2	9
27	Crude minerals and fertilizers	–	–	27	–	–	–	–	17	–	–	–	–	–	–	–	–	–	2
28	Metal ores and scrap	–	–	–	–	–	–	–	–	–	–	–	–	–	–	–	–	–	0
29	Misc. crude animal/vegetable materials	–	–	–	15	45	49	3	2	16	–	26	–	22	–	23	61	14
32	Coal, coke and briquettes	–	100	100	95	70	100	–	–	–	–	–	12	–	–	–	A[c]38
33	Petroleum	100	–	19	100	10	–	–	–	100	60	–	–	–	–	–	A	16
34	Gas	–	–	–	–	25	–	–	–	–	60	–	–	–	–	–	A	1
35	Electric energy	–	–	–	–	100	–	–	–	–	–	–	–	–	–	–	A	6
41	Animal oils and fats	74	71	–	–	65	44	–	–	–	–	–	9	–	–	–	A	14
42	Fixed vegetable oils and fats	–	–	9	2	10	2	66	1	2	–	–	3	100	–	–	A	11
43	Processed oils and fats, waxes	49	–	–	–	–	–	56	–	–	–	–	–	–	–	–	A	6
51	Chemical elements and compounds	49	–	96	67	–	24	97	–	–	–	9	–	–	–	–	A	19
52	Tar and crude derivatives	–	–	–	–	–	–	–	100	–	–	–	–	–	–	–	A	6
53	Dyes	81	–	–	–	–	–	–	–	–	–	–	–	–	–	–	A	5
54	Medicinal and pharmaceutical	38	–	100	23	100	–	3	–	100	–	3	–	11	–	–	A	20
55	Perfumes, cleaners, toiletries	19	–	74	–	–	–	–	–	32	–	–	30	–	–	–	A	9
56	Manufactured fertilizers	100	–	68	7	–	100	–	100	–	–	–	18	–	–	A	22
57	Explosives	–	–	–	100	100	–	–	–	100	–	–	100	–	–	A	17
58	Plastics	100	–	–	–	–	–	–	–	–	–	–	–	–	–	–	A	6
59	Misc. chemicals	38	–	23	19	11	18	14	14	–	19	11	8	–	11	–	A	10
61	Leather and manufactures	–	–	93	–	–	–	–	–	–	–	–	–	–	–	–	A	5
62	Rubber manufactures	95	–	–	–	–	–	–	–	58	–	–	100	–	–	A	14
63	Wood and cork manufactures	–	–	–	–	–	–	–	–	–	–	–	–	–	–	–	A	0
64	Paper and paperboard manufactures	–	–	–	18	–	–	–	–	–	–	–	–	–	–	–	A	1
65	Textile manufactures	25	19	45	70	69	18	23	12	–	33	25	30	1	–	A	24
66	Nonmetallic mineral manufactures	3	–	79	16	–	–	–	–	–	–	5	–	3	–	A	6
67	Iron and steel	73	80	–	–	–	–	–	–	8	–	–	13	–	A	9
68	Nonferrous metals	–	–	–	–	–	–	–	–	–	–	–	30	17	A	3

Table 5-2 (cont.)

SITC	Commodity Group	U.S.	Canada	U.K.	Japan	Belg.-Lux.	France	Germany	Italy	Netherlands	Denmark	Finland	Norway	Sweden	Austria	Switzerland	Portugal	Ireland	Australia	New Zealand	Mean (all countries)
69	Misc. metal manufactures	1	—	—	—	—	—	—	—	—	—	—	—	—	—	—	—	—	—	A	0
71	Nonelectric machinery	1	27	—	72	—	3	—	—	—	—	—	—	—	—	—	2	—	11	A	5
72	Electric machinery	72	—	—	58	—	15	—	—	—	—	—	—	—	—	—	37	2	—	A	12
73	Transport equipment	73	39	39	65	75	59	70	65	12	—	39	88	35	—	68	76	10	1	A	45
81	Construction equipment	100	—	—	—	—	—	—	—	—	—	—	—	—	—	—	—	—	—	A	6
82	Furniture	—	—	—	—	—	—	—	—	—	—	—	—	—	—	—	—	—	—	A	0
83	Travel goods & accessories	—	—	—	—	—	—	—	—	—	—	—	—	—	—	—	—	—	—	A	0
84	Clothing	92	—	—	—	—	—	51	—	—	—	—	—	3	—	93	—	—	100	A	19
85	Footwear	16	—	—	35	5	16	—	3	—	—	—	100	—	—	—	—	100	—	A	12
86	Precision instruments	—	—	3	3	2	2	—	3	—	—	15	—	—	24	—	53	—	62	A	11
89	Misc. manufactures	10	13	—	3	30	2	—	19	14	—	—	—	26	—	—	—	2	—	A	4
	Total imports	39	11	13	32	30	20	26	19	14	7	7	9	12	12	12	33d	n	4	A	18

aData: See text for source of the nontariff-barrier inventory; trade data—U.N. Trade Statistics, *Series D, Trade by Commodities* (New York: U.N., 1968).

bNot available.

cNew Zealand applied automatic import licensing to most manufactured goods, with preferences granted to Commonwealth suppliers.

dSpecific commodities covered by NTB's: 62% of all dutiable imports subject to bilateral or multilateral quotas.

																				A	
58	Plastics	100	–	–	–	–	–	–	–	–	–	–	–	20	20	20	–	20	–	A	6
59	Misc. chemicals	74	–	–	20	20	20	20	20	–	–	–	–	20	20	20	–	20	–	A	15
61	Leather and manufactures	63	–	–	79	–	–	–	–	–	61	–	–	–	–	–	100	–	–	A	4
62	Rubber manufactures	63	–	–	–	–	–	–	–	–	–	–	–	–	–	–	100	–	–	A	12
63	Wood and cork manufactures	4	–	–	–	10	–	–	–	–	–	–	–	–	–	–	–	–	–	A	1
64	Paper and paperboard manufactures	–	–	–	–	–	–	–	–	–	–	–	–	–	–	–	–	–	–	A	0
65	Textile manufactures	18	14	19	36	60	73	14	27	14	–	30	–	24	27	29	3	11	–	A	22
66	Nonmetallic mineral manufactures	5	–	49	49	–	12	–	–	–	–	–	–	49	–	–	11	13	–	A	7
67	Iron and steel	84	–	87	1	–	–	–	–	–	9	–	–	–	–	–	13	7	17	A	10
68	Nonferrous metals	–	–	87	–	–	–	–	–	–	9	–	–	–	–	–	7	17	–	A	2
69	Misc. metal manufactures	17	–	1	–	–	–	–	–	–	–	–	–	–	–	–	1	–	7	A	1
71	Nonelectric machinery	1	–	65	65	4	–	–	–	–	–	–	–	–	1	–	1	–	7	A	5
72	Electric machinery	86	27	58	58	25	–	–	–	–	–	–	–	–	49	–	49	–	–	A	14
73	Transport equipment	68	50	13	87	64	55	55	65	13	44	52	43	48	74	22	74	22	1	A	42
81	Construction equipment	100	–	–	–	–	–	–	–	–	–	–	–	–	–	–	–	–	–	A	6
82	Furniture	–	–	–	–	–	–	–	–	–	–	–	–	–	–	–	–	–	–	A	0
83	Travel goods & accessories	–	–	–	–	–	–	–	–	–	–	–	–	–	–	–	–	–	–	A	0
84	Clothing	94	–	–	–	–	49	–	–	–	–	–	2	–	98	98	–	–	98	A	19
85	Footwear	21	–	–	–	–	–	–	–	–	100	100	–	–	–	–	100	–	–	A	22
86	Precision instruments	–	2	28	–	20	–	2	2	3	3	–	22	16	63	63	–	–	2	A	8
89	Misc. manufactures	20	5	2	2	3	3	3	–	3	–	–	22	–	–	–	5	–	5	A	4
	Total imports	39	15	20	52	39	31	30	24	21	26	n	24	26	38	23	28[d]	n	25	A	29

[a]Data: See text for sources of the nontariff-barrier inventory. Trade data: OECD, *Trade by Commodity: Imports* (Paris: OECD, 1968).

[b]Not available.

[c]New Zealand applies automatic import licensing to most manufactured goods, with preferences granted to Commonwealth suppliers.

[d]Specific commodities covered by NTB's are 62% of all dutiable imports subject to bilateral or multilateral quotas.

commodity-coverage, application to imports, and OECD-import-weighted coverage of nontariff measures given in Tables 5-2, 5-3, and 5-4, respectively. For example, in the case of Japan 34 percent of all importable products appear to be covered by NTBs, yet when this is weighted by OECD imports the figure rises to 52 percent; at the same time, 32 percent of all imports actually entered the country under nontariff measures in 1967. Similar comparisons may be drawn for the other countries under consideration here.

One possible indicator of the "restrictiveness" of nontariff measures, at a highly aggregative level, might be the percentage of actual imports entering a given country under NTBs relative to the percentage of OECD imports covered by that country's NTBs. This necessitates the admittedly heroic assumption that each country's import mix without NTBs would parallel that of the OECD as a whole—a questionable proposition. If, for example, 90 percent of OECD imports are covered by a nation's NTBs, yet the country's own imports under those NTBs only amount to 10 percent of its total commodity purchases from abroad,

Table 5-4
Ratios of NTB-Coverage Indexes

	(1) Percentage Commodity Coverage of NTBs (A_j)[a]	(2) Percentage Imports Subject to NTBs (B_j)	(3) Percentage OECD-Import Weighted Coverage of NTBS (C_j)	(4) $B_j \div A_j$	(5) $B_j \div C_j$
U.S.	27	39	39	1.44	1.00
Canada	7	11	15	1.57	0.73
U.K.	10	13	20	1.30	0.65
Japan	34	32	52	0.94	0.61
Belg.-Lux.	19	30	39	1.58	0.77
France	17	20	31	1.18	0.65
Germany	16	26	30	1.63	0.87
Italy	13	19	24	1.46	0.79
Netherlands	19	14	21	0.74	0.67
Denmark	11	7	26	0.64	0.27
Norway	14	9	24	0.64	0.38
Sweden	14	12	26	0.86	0.46
Austria	10	12	38	1.20	0.32
Switzerland	12	12	23	1.00	0.52
Portugal	17	33	28	1.94	1.18
Australia	9	4	25	0.44	0.16
Mean	16	18	29	1.13	0.62

Data: Tables 5-1, 5-2, and 5-3.
[a]See footnote[a] to Table 5-2.

there exists some connotation of restrictiveness if the OECD-coverage measure is granted at least minimal validity as a proxy for what would have occurred. That is, a value of 1 or higher would indicate no apparent restrictiveness, but values substantially lower than one would carry some restrictiveness connotation.

These figures are presented in column 5 of Table 5-4. Note that the smallest values are attained in the case of Australia, Austria, Denmark, and Norway, while the higest overall values characterized Portugal, the United States, Italy, and Canada. In general, the own-import-weighted coverage of NTBs is about half of that weighted by OECD imports, raising the suspicion that nontariff measures are, indeed, restrictive of trade. Finally, column 4 of that table indicates the concentration of actual imports in those commodity categories subject to NTBs—i.e., the value of B_j relative to the value of A_j.

Comparison of NTB Profiles and Tariff Rates

It is apparent, from the data presented in the previous section, that the NTB profiles of the industrial countries are comparatively similar to one another in many instances. That is, the same "sensitive" product categories are subject to nontariff obstacles in several of the industrial economies. If this is true, and the similar pattern of tariff rates found in Chapter 3, then the respective tariff and nontariff profiles should bear some similarity to one another.

Column A of Table 5-5 presents the weighted mean NTB factors applied to manufactures and semimanufactures for Canada, the United States, Japan, EEC, Finland, Denmark, Norway, Sweden, Switzerland, Austria, and the United Kingdom.[6] These data indicate quite clearly the product groups particularly intensively subject to NTBs and those which are relatively infrequent targets of such obstacles. For comparison purposes, column B of Table 5-5 presents weighted mean nominal tariff rates for the same product groups, again using combined imports as weights.

Since the weighting process applies only within product classes and not between them, it is possible to determine whether the indicated tariff and NTB factors are significantly correlated. The computed coefficient of correlation as between the tariff and nontariff factors is 0.54, which is significant at the 0.95 level of confidence and rejects the null-hypothesis that the two factors are unrelated. The inference is that product groups which tend to be subject to a relatively high degree of nominal tariff protection—as measured by 1972 post-Kennedy Round averages—are also relatively strongly susceptible to the application of NTBs.

While this relationship appears to exist when the combined nominal tariff and nontariff distributions of all eleven customs-areas are considered, we find substantial variations in the tariff/nontariff correlation among the individual countries under examination. Table 5-6 presents the corresponding coefficients

Table 5-5
Relation of Tariff Rates and NTB Factors Across Product Groups

SITC	Product Group	A Weighted Mean NTB Factor[a]	B Weighted Mean Tariff[b]	C Tariff-NTB Correlation Coefficient[c]
Ex 01	Processed meat	78.79	4.39	0.30
Ex 03	Processed fish	40.00	8.52	0.12
Ex 04	Cereal products	32.84	10.40	0.61
Ex 05	Prepared fruit products	55.80	13.10	0.55
Ex 06	Sugar confectionary, syrups	43.63	43.37	0.46
Ex 07	Processed coffee, tea, cocoa	27.94	8.30	0.26
Ex 09	Miscellaneous prepared foods	46.51	32.59	0.53
Ex 11	Beverages	79.07	34.16	0.17
Ex 12	Processed tobacco	73.87	107.30	0.79
Ex 23	Synthetic and reclaimed rubber	0.16	2.85	0.01
Ex 24	Sawn and shaped wood and cork	3.62	2.14	0.33
Ex 25	Pulp and waste paper	0.00	1.57	0.00
Ex 26	Textile fibers	0.00	3.46	0.00
Ex 33	Petroleum products	33.79	4.88	0.12
Ex 34	Gas	1.82	4.88	−0.17
Ex 35	Electric energy	1.82	4.88	−0.17
Ex 43	Processed oils, fats, waxes	14.48	8.87	0.20
Ex 51	Chemical elements and compounds	20.64	4.66	0.52
Ex 52	Tar and crude derivatives	10.73	4.63	−0.09
Ex 53	Dyes	10.85	4.13	0.86
Ex 54	Medicinal and pharmaceutical products	38.93	4.44	0.38
Ex 55	Perfumes, cleaners, toiletries	10.64	5.63	0.01
Ex 56	Manufactured fertilizers	24.43	1.01	−0.09
Ex 57	Explosives	1.82	7.72	0.03
Ex 58	Plastics	13.21	8.73	0.21
Ex 59	Miscellaneous chemicals	22.73	6.73	0.47
Ex 61	Leather and leather manufactures	8.59	4.82	0.21
Ex 62	Rubber manufactures	14.86	3.48	0.50
Ex 63	Wood and cork manufactures	5.51	2.83	−0.08
Ex 64	Paper and paperboard manufactures	2.93	7.79	0.17
Ex 65	Textile manufactures	25.74	6.80	−0.08
Ex 66	Nonmetallic mineral manufactures	3.50	11.24	0.04
Ex 67	Iron and steel products	22.56	5.49	0.41
Ex 68	Nonferrous metal manufactures	2.35	3.10	0.05
Ex 69	Miscellaneous metal manufactures	6.31	4.98	0.58
Ex 71	Nonelectric machinery	6.30	6.56	0.34
Ex 72	Electric machinery	54.31	10.09	−0.17

Table 5-5 (cont.)

SITC	Product Group	A Weighted Mean NTB Factor[a]	B Weighted Mean Tariff[b]	C Tariff-NTB Correlation Coefficient[c]
Ex 73	Transport equipment	32.73	8.45	0.38
Ex 81	Construction equipment	12.81	7.73	0.36
Ex 82	Furniture	0.00	9.84	0.00
Ex 83	Travel goods and accessories	0.00	13.12	−0.37
Ex 84	Clothing	68.75	17.87	0.18
Ex 85	Footwear	29.09	16.52	0.17
Ex 86	Precision instruments	8.56	7.82	0.18
Ex 89	Miscellaneous manufactures	6.70	5.60	0.25

[a]Frequency of NTB-applications within each product group, weighted by OECD imports of the affected products, relative to total OECD imports of that product group, averaged over the eleven DMECs under consideration.

[b]Post-Kennedy Round tariff rates weighted by OECD imports and averaged over eleven DMECs under consideration.

[c]Correlation between weighted mean tariff rates and NTB factors for eleven DMECs under consideration. At the 0.95 level of confidence, the critical value of r as between the tariff and non-tariff factors is 0.52.

Data: Ingo Walter and Jae W. Chung, "The Pattern of Non-Tariff Obstacles to International Market Access," *Weltwirtschaftliches Archiv*, Bd. 108 (1972).

Table 5-6
Correlation of Tariff and NTB Factors Across Customs Areas

Country	Coefficient of Correlation, Tariff vs. NTB Factor for 45 Product Groups[a]
Austria	0.05
Canada	0.38
Denmark	0.33
EEC	0.25
Finland	0.19
Japan	0.09
Norway	0.32
Sweden	0.42
Switzerland	0.18
United Kingdom	0.04
United States	0.06

[a]The critical value of r for rejection of null-hypothesis at 0.95 level of confidence is 0.25.

Data: Walter and Chung, "Pattern of Non-Tariff Obstacles."

of correlation between nominal tariff averages and NTB incidence factors at the SITC two-digit product level for the United States, Canada, Japan, the EEC (common external NTBs only) and the EFTA countries (except Portugal). For Canada, Denmark, the EEC, Norway, and Sweden, the results are statistically significant, and this indicates that a tariff-NTB link does indeed appear on a national level, although with notable cross-national variations in degree.

A parallel question is whether there also exists a high degree of correlation between tariffs and NTBs across countries for the individual manufactured and semimanufactured product groups specified. That is, for any given product group, are countries or customs areas which impose high nominal tariffs also characterized by a high rate of NTB incidence, or does an inverse pattern (or no pattern at all) emerge as between the two sets of obstacles to market access? The correlation coefficients presented in column C of Table 5-5 as between (unweighted) tariff averages and NTB-incidence rates for forty-five product groups indicate that a significant positive relationship appears to obtain in the case of processed cereals, prepared fruit products, miscellaneous prepared foods, processed tobacco, chemical elements and compounds, dyes, and miscellaneous metal manufactures.[b] For these groups of manufactures and semimanufactures there seems to be some evidence that levels of nominal tariff protection and NTB-incidence are positively linked; for all other groups the correlation is not statistically significant.

Chapter 3 has already brought out the fact that tariff structures among the industrial countries contain substantial similarities, and the same pattern has emerged for nontariff measures in the foregoing analysis. These similarities in tariff profiles were shown in Table 3-3, which found a positive and significant correlation between the nominal tariff rates by commodity group of the pairs of industrial countries.

According to the analysis presented earlier, a similar commonality should emerge in cross-national comparisons of NTB-incidence rates, when likewise considered in the framework of a correlation matrix. These results are presented, for the fifteen industrial countries under consideration, in Table 5-7. In this instance the EEC members are shown separately in order to discern the degree of similarity of the national NTB profiles among member countries.

Once more a distinct commonality in the distribution of nontariff obstacles among manufactures and semimanufactures is evident, although with somewhat greater variation than in the case of tariffs. The product-distribution of U.S. nontariff measures is similar to those of Canada, Sweden, the United Kingdom, and the Netherlands, while the structure of Japanese NTBs resembles those of

---

[b]The correspondence is very strong ($r = 0.61$ to 0.86) for cereal products, processed tobacco and dyes, somewhat less striking ($r = 0.40$ to 0.59) for prepared fruit products, sugar confectionary, syrups, miscellaneous prepared foods, chemical elements and compounds, miscellaneous chemicals, rubber manufactures, iron and steel products, and miscellaneous metal manufactures, and of little or no significance for the remainder of the product groups.

Switzerland, and Italy only. The British nontariff profile falls much closer to the common denominator, as indicated by statistically significant coefficients of correlation with respect to all of the other industrial countries except Finland and Japan. Within the EEC the degree of commonality is even more evident, with the respective NTB profiles evidencing considerable similarity as between all pairs of member countries.

Nontariff Barriers and Exports of Developing Countries

One of the results of the kind of analysis presented in the previous section is that NTBs appear to bear particularly heavily on "sensitive" products—those products in which the advanced industrial countries are gradually losing in international competitiveness, generally characterized by a high degree of labor intensity in manufacture. This implies that exports of manufactures and semimanufactures from developing countries, also predominantly labor-intensive, should be especially vulnerable to NTBs preventing access to the industrial markets of the world. To this must be added the possibility that certain kinds of NTBs, including many of those classified as Type II, pose particular difficulties for suppliers in the developing world.[7]

The basis for the latter argument includes the following:[8] (a) the affected suppliers often are relatively less able operationally to cope with such obstacles than their competitors in advanced countries, while their capability of affecting the requisite adjustments is notably more limited; (b) more generally, alternative production possibilities tend to be restricted, or essentially nonexistent, for the developing economy; (c) from an informational standpoint, developing countries often do not have sufficient resources to determine precisely the nature of existing nontariff measures and the mechanics of their administration, resulting in faulty and costly supply responses, a high degree of uncertainty, and a corresponding dampening of the export effort; (d) in certain product areas, extraordinarily rigorous standards and procedures may be applied to imports from developing countries, particularly with respect to health and quality controls implemented as part of a concerted national policy or at the discretion of the officials involved; and (e) as in the case of past tariff liberalization efforts, the interests of developing countries have tended to assume a secondary role in ongoing intergovernmental attempts to deal with nontariff obstacles.

Of the thirty-eight more or less distinct types of NTBs identified in the previous chapter, at least seventeen would appear to be capable of exerting at least a marginally heavier impact on developing-country suppliers. But perhaps more persuasive is the first argument: that *by their very nature* manufactured and semimanufactured products from developing countries tend to run into heavier nontariff obstacles to market access in the industrial countries.

In 1968, the developed-market economy countries imported approximately

Table 5-7
Correlation of Rates of Nontariff Barrier Incidence as between Pairs of Industrial Countries[a]

	United States	Austria	Canada	Denmark	Finland	Japan	Norway
United States	1.00						
Austria	0.20	1.00					
Canada	0.79	0.59	1.00				
Denmark	0.21	0.69	0.61	1.00			
Finland	−0.01	0.04	0.07	0.37	1.00		
Japan	0.13	0.05	−0.01	0.19	0.20	1.00	
Norway	0.19	0.66	0.56	0.90	0.29	0.18	1.00
Sweden	0.30	0.74	0.72·	0.85	0.08	0.00	0.75
Switzerland	−0.03	0.32	0.15	0.51	0.61	0.27	0.45
United Kingdom	0.77	0.54	0.85	0.52	−0.07	−0.04	0.58
France	0.23	0.60	0.54	0.75	0.28	0.15	0.86
Germany	0.21	0.76	0.59	0.76	0.07	0.07	0.84
Italy	0.05	0.21	0.10	0.23	−0.02	0.30	0.40
Netherlands	0.29	0.79	0.63	0.68	−0.10	0.08	0.74
Belgium-Luxembourg	0.19	0.17	0.50	0.59	−0.04	0.06	0.75

[a]Simple correlation coefficients as between countries indicated of nontariff barrier incidence rates calculated at an SITC two-digit level of aggregation. Incidence rates represent an index of frequency of NTB application on the part of a given country within a specified SITC two-digit product group. Correlation coefficients exceeding 0.35 are significant at the 0.99 level of confidence; those exceeding 0.25 are significant at the 0.95 level of confidence. Applicable multiple correlation coefficient, United States versus fourteen remaining countries, is 0.980.

$128 billion in manufactures and semimanufactures, of which about 28 percent ($36 billion) were subject to known NTBs. In the same year, 33 percent of the $21 billion of manufactured and semimanufactured imports from developing countries entered under such obstacles. Put another way, the developing countries' share of manufactured and semimanufactured imports of the developed countries in 1968 was 16.5 percent, but their share of imports subject to NTBs was 20.9 percent. Acceptance of the earlier proposition that certain NTBs on individual products or product groups bear disproportionately on developing-country suppliers and hence tend to bias downward their actual market share would mean that the hypothetical latter figure is even larger relative to the former. But even assuming the imposition of nontariff measures had no effect on relative import shares, it would appear that product groups for which developing countries hold a relatively large share of developed-country imports are also characterized by a comparatively intensive application of NTBs—and hence that imports from developing countries do indeed tend to be somewhat more heavily subject to such measures than do developed-country imports in general. Table

		United					
Sweden	Switzerland	Kingdom	France[b]	Germany[b]	Italy[b]	Netherlands	Belgium-Luxembourg
1.00							
0.28	1.00						
0.62	0.11	1.00					
0.73	0.41	0.63	1.00				
0.77	0.39	0.72	0.86	1.00			
0.18	0.18	0.26	0.45	0.43	1.00		
0.83	0.18	0.71	0.78	0.89	0.38	1.00	
0.67	0.26	0.58	0.75	0.78	0.43	0.85	1.00

[b]EEC member countries' NTB-incidence rates represent a composite of national and common external and nontariff obstacles. Correlation coefficients for EEC external NTBs only and nontariff incidence rates of other countries are: U.S. (0.13), Austria (0.62), Canada (0.45), Denmark (0.84), Finland (0.39), Japan (0.35), Norway (0.91), Sweden (0.61), Switzerland (0.62) and the United Kingdom (0.49) with the same critical values as above.

Data: Walter and Chung, "Pattern of Non-Tariff Obstacles."

5-8 indicates, however, that there are substantial variations in the figures among the individual markets, and what seems to be true in the aggregate hold for only half of the individual industrial countries under consideration.

It is also interesting to note that the intensity of application of NTBs appears to correspond at least ordinally to the degree of competitive advantage the developing countries are deemed to possess in the production of manufactures and semimanufactures for the international market. Table 5-9 ranks products by calculated LDC competitive position and indicates the extent of NTB application by all developed market-economy countries combined.[9] The sixty product groups represent categories where some comparative advantage is thought to exist; of the sixty-three remaining manufactured product groups at this level of aggregation to which no foreseeable LDC advantage is ascribed, only fifteen evidenced susceptibility to NTBs. When the NTB factors are also ranked, the correlation (Spearman) coefficient between the two rankings is 0.2317, which is statistically significant at the 0.95 level of confidence. Hence one concludes that those manufactured and semimanufactured product groups for

Table 5-8
1968 Imports from Developed Countries Subject to NTBs: Manufactures and Semimanufactures

Imports of:	Share of Developing Countries in Total Imports (%)	Share of Developing Countries in Imports Subject to NTBs (%)
U.S.	18.6	23.5
Canada	6.8	3.5
Australia	12.5	7.9
New Zealand	10.8	2.0
Japan	43.2	58.4
U.K.	22.9	13.9
Norway	7.5	2.2
Sweden	9.1	6.2
Denmark	7.2	4.7
Finland	2.7	6.8
Austria	3.0	3.5
Switzerland	5.5	13.1
EEC (from nonmember)	7.5	13.7
Belgium-Luxembourg	15.0	27.6
France	17.9	37.9
F.R. Germany	17.0	6.9
Italy	25.0	4.3
Netherlands	11.7	4.3
Total	16.5	20.9

Data: Classification of nontariff barriers by application of products grouped by SITC five-digit identification, see UNCTAD's *Liberalization of Tariff and Non-Tariff Barriers,* annex II. Trade data: U.N. Statistical Papers, Series D, *Commodity Trade Statistics* (New York: U.N., 1969); and OECD Statistical Papers, Series C, *Foreign Trade Statistics* (Paris, OECD, 1969). Definition of manufactures and semimanufactures, see UNCTAD document TD/B/C.2/3 of 2 July 1965. Source: Ingo Walter, "Non-tariff Barriers and the Export Performance of Developing Countries," *American Economic Review,* Papers and Proceedings, May 1971.

which a relatively strong LDC competitive position exists for the developing countries also tend to be the ones most heavily subject to nontariff applications—assuming adequate reliability in the measurement techniques employed.

These conclusions are reinforced by the relationships that appear to exist between the pattern of NTBs and the pattern of products on which the industrial countries in 1970 offered the developing countries preferential access to their national markets by reducing or eliminating tariffs on their exports (see Chapter 13).[10] Since those products considered to be sensitive in the advanced countries appear to be subject to a high incidence of NTBs, we would expect these same products to be excluded from the preference offers.

Table 5-9
Manufactures and Semimanufactures of Export Interest to Developing Countries: Competitiveness and Nontariff Barriers

SITC No.	Product Description	Competitive Position[e]	NTB Factor
841	Clothing	19.0	71.1
657	Carpets	18.0	25.0
243	Chaped wood	16.3	15.0
899	Other products[a]	16.0	8.3
831	Travel goods	13.9	0.0
653	Woven noncotton fabrics[b]	13.2	60.3
032	Preserved fish	12.8	37.5
897	Jewelry	12.5	25.0
632	Wood products	12.5	2.7
651	Yarn and thread	12.4	19.4
656	Bags, sacks, linens	12.2	24.3
053	Preserved fruit	12.2	47.5
055	Preserved vegetables	12.2	46.3
894	Toys and sporting goods	11.8	6.7
532	Tanning and dying extracts	11.5	2.5
655	Special textile fabrics[c]	10.0	15.6
663	Mineral manufactures	9.3	0.1
851	Footwear	9.2	17.5
652	Woven cotton	7.8	117.1
099	Other food products	7.6	21.3
052	Dried fruit	7.5	23.5
892	Printed matter	7.5	5.0
893	Plastic products	7.5	5.0
631	Veneers and plywood	6.6	0.8
611	Leather	6.6	3.3
697	Household metal products	6.5	1.9
698	Other metal products	6.4	1.5
561	Manufactured fertilizers	5.9	23.0
812	Light and sanitary fittings	5.7	8.8
662	Clay producta	5.7	4.4
013	Preserved meats	5.2	78.0
012	Dried and salted meats	5.2	97.5
724	Telecommunications apparatus	4.9	42.0
599	Other chemicals	4.7	10.5
431	Oils, fats and waxes	4.7	7.1
696	Cutlery	4.5	2.1

Table 5-9 (cont.)

SITC No.	Product Description	Competitive Position[e]	NTB Factor
665	Glassware	4.1	1.7
551	Essential oils	4.0	5.0
821	Furniture	3.5	0.0
521	Tar, etc. from coal	3.4	6.7
072.3	Cocoa butter	3.2	15.0
073	Chocolate	3.2	34.7
071.3	Coffee extracts	3.0	44.6
661	Lime, cement, etc.	2.8	0.0
541	Medicinal products	2.8	55.5
861	Scientific instruments	2.7	4.8
641	Paper and paperboard	2.3	4.7
513	Inorganic chemicals, oxides	2.3	10.8
514	Other inorganic chemicals	2.3	10.5
629	Rubber products	2.2	10.2
251	Pulp and waste paper	2.0	0.0
266	Synthetic fibers	2.0	4.3
678	Iron, steel tubes & pipes	1.7	23.0
512	Organic chemicals	1.6	18.2
671	Pig iron	1.4	0.0
673	Iron and steel bars	0.1	30.0
674	Iron & steel plates, sheets	0.1	30.0
533	Pigments, paints, varnishes[d]	< 0.1	4.3
642	Art. of paper, pulp, paperboard[d]	< 0.1	0.0
712	Agric. machinery, implements[d]	< 0.1	0.7

[a]Mainly basketwork, brooms, umbrellas, buttons, artificial flowers, and wigs of human hair.
[b]Primarily jute fabrics.
[c]Mainly cordage, rope, and twine.
[d]Categories where a longer-range competitive advantage may exist but not yet evident in the calculations.
[e]There are sixty-three additional categories of products at this level of aggregation for which developing countries are not deemed to possess a comparative advantage under existing conditions and hence do not appear in this listing; of these, fifteen are subject to NTBs and the remainder (forty-eight) are not.

Data: Estimates of competitive position: UNCTAD, *The Performance of Developing Countries as Exporters of Manufactures to the Developed Market Economy Countries*, Doc. TD/B/C.2/91, 22 December 1969. Estimates of the NTB factor calculated from data assembled by the author and published in UNCTAD, *Liberalization of Tariff and Non-Tariff Barriers*. Doc. TD/B/C.2/R.1, 10 December 1969, Annex II, averaged (unweighted) over products included under indicated SITC category.

Source: Ingo Walter, "Developing Countries."

If we thus find, for the major preference-granting areas, a significantly high negative correlation between the product-coverage pattern of preference offers and the corresponding NTB profiles, it is further probable that the preexisting nontariff measures will not compromise the expected trade-creating effects of the preferential tariff reductions. If, on the other hand, a significantly high positive NTB-preference correlation is found—indicating that precisely those product-groups covered by the preferences are also most heavily subject to NTBs—the beneficiary countries should be aware that nontariff obstacles may in the aggregate endanger the anticipated benefits deriving from the preferences.

Table 5-10 presents the relevant NTB-preference correlation coefficients for agricultural and industrial goods, respectively. Statistically significant positive values (at the 95 percent confidence level) appear for none of the preference-granting areas. Significant negative values of r appear for none of the agricultural products and for Austria, Ireland, the Nordic countries, and Switzerland in the industrial sector. We conclude, therefore, that there is virtually no evidence that the product-distribution of NTBs and preference offers systematically coincide to such a degree as to pose a serious threat to the effectiveness of the preference scheme. The two variables appear to be either unrelated or inversely related, indicating for the above-named countries significant differences in the product-distribution of NTBs and preference offers.

If, on the basis of available data, we can reject the notion of a general danger to the generalized preferences from the aggregate product-distribution of nontariff obstacles among the industrial countries, this nevertheless does not preclude the possibility that such a danger may indeed exist for individual product groups. While analysis is difficult due to the limited available degrees of freedom ($N = 10$), some general conclusions seem possible.

Table 5-11 presents simple correlations between the frequency of NTB applications and preference coverage in the case of product groups for which $r > 0.30$. Since the critical value of r rejecting the null hypothesis at the 95 percent confidence level is 0.55, a significant positive relation exists only for processed vegetables, meat and fish preparations, beverages, and discontinuous man-made fibers. For these product groups, liberal (restrictive) preference offers seem to be associated with a high (low) NTB-incidence, and the beneficial effects of the liberal preference offers may be partly neutralized. Statistically significant negative correlations exist for glues and albuminoidal substances, manufactured wood products, and footwear. In the latter instance this is due to restrictive preference offers combined with very high rates of NTB-incidence. For these products, and for all others evidencing no significant correlation, there would appear to be little danger of NTB-induced compromise of the tariff preferences offered.

Table 5-10

Simple Correlation Across Product Groups between Frequency of NTB Applications and Preference Offers[a]

Preference-Offering Area	Computed Correlation Coefficient	
	Agricultural Products	Industrial Products
Austria	−0.05	−0.32
Canada	0.05	0.01
EEC	0.34	−0.02
Ireland	0.00	−0.45
Japan	0.39	0.07
New Zealand	0.17	−0.02
Nordic	−0.11	−0.21
Switzerland	0.11	−0.68
U.K.	−0.07	−0.08
U.S.	0.26	0.03
Mean	−0.06	−0.33

[a]For each preference-offering area, the value of r represents the simple coefficient of correlation between the product distribution of the preference offers and the product distribution of nontariff obstacles applied to imports of all manufactures and semimanufactures. The critical value of r to reject the null-hypothesis for agricultural products (N = 24) is 0.40 at the 95 percent level and for industrial products (N = 75) is 0.19 at the same level of confidence.

Data: Distribution of nontariff obstacles compiled from GATT sources and published in *Liberalization of Tariffs and Non-Tariff Barriers* (Geneva: UNCTAD Document TD/B/C.2/R.1, 1969). Trade data from United Nations Statistical Office, Statistical Papers, Series D, *Commodity Trade Statistics* (various issues), and OECD, Statistical Papers, Series C, *Trade by Commodities* (various issues).

Source: Ingo Walter and Joe W. Chung, "Non-Tariff Distributions and Trade Preferences for Developing Countries," *Kyklos*, February, 1971.

Nontariff Barriers and Effective Protection

In the preceding chapter the implications of NTBs for effective rates of protection were discussed, and yet the data presented here have been couched exclusively in nominal, market-access terms. The reason is the inordinate difficulty of converting nontariff barriers, including quantitative import restrictions, into their *tariff equivalents*—the ad-valorem rates of duty that would yield the same inside-outside price differential as that actually induced by the NTB. Few nontariff obstacles to market access can—by their very nature—be converted into tariff equivalents, and hence very few attempts have been made by economists to engage this problem empirically.

One notable exception is Robert E. Baldwin,[11] who has attempted to derive the degree to which domestic value-added is increased by tariffs, nontariff barriers, and the combinations of both for selected product groups. For the

Table 5-11
Correlation between Preference-Offering Countries for Selected Product Groups[a]

BTN	Products	Computed Value of r[b]
ex 07	Processed vegetables	0.74
ex 08	Processed fruits	0.42
ex 11	Malt, starches, gluten	−0.54
ex 16	Meat and fish preparations	0.55
ex 18	Cocoa preparations	0.33
22	Beverages	0.61
ex 24	Processed tobacco	−0.36
ex 27	Mineral fuels, oil	0.44
30	Pharmaceuticals	0.40
31	Manufactured fertilizers	0.33
35	Albuminoidal substances, glues	−0.92
ex 44	Wood products	−0.77
51	Man-made fibers (continuous)	0.35
56	Man-made fibers (discontinuous)	0.77
62	Other made-up textile articles	0.36
64	Footwear	−0.56
70	Glass and glassware	0.31
71	Pearls, stones, precious metals, jewelry	0.34
85	Electrical machinery	0.32
87	Road vehicles and parts	−0.41
93	Arms and ammunition	0.31

[a]High (+) values of r indicate that preference-offering areas apply *both* high (or low) preference and NTB incidence rates for the listed product-groups. High (−) values of r denote that when preference rates are high, the NTB incidence tends to be low, or vice versa.

[b]The null-hypothesis is rejected for N = 10 if the value of r exceeds 0.55.

Data: See Table 5-9.

Source: Walter and Chung, "Non-Tariff Distributions."

United States, only domestic measures leading to increased agricultural prices, quotas, the American Selling Price system of customs valuations, federal excise and transportation taxes, federal highway subsidies, and state and local retail taxes were considered, applied to 1964 and 1972 rates of duty.

For many product groups, nontariff barriers are not considered to add significantly to the effective rate of protection in the United States, and for many others their impact is to reduce effective protection—because of the increased costs incurred by import-competing suppliers. The most important instance of a positive impact of NTBs on effective protection is crude petroleum, natural gas and their products, while food products and textiles also show significant positive NTB effects. On the other hand, livestock and livestock products, tobacco manufactures, carpets and leather products, as well as chemicals show a substantial negative impact of NTBs on the effective rate of protection. Interestingly, the impact of NTBs on such major products as automobiles and trucks, machine shop products, stone and clay products, plastics, pharmaceuticals, paints, and furniture is also deemed to be negative.

Table 5-12 gives the aggregate results of the Baldwin study for 1964 and 1972, after the tariff reductions under the Kennedy Round had been fully implemented. Corresponding results for the United Kingdom (1972) indicate an 18 percent increase in the effective rate for primary products, 11 percent for intermediate and consumer goods, 17 percent for capital goods, and 13 percent overall. These results are of course only partially valid, but they do indicate the impact, both positive and negative, that NTBs may have the effective rate of protection.

Toward NTB Liberalization

To summarize the foregoing—the apparent structure of NTBs in the market-economy industrial countries—the application of nontariff measures seems to

Table 5-12
Nominal and Effective Rates of Protection in the United States, by Commodity Group, 1964 and 1972[a]

| | Nominal Rate, Tariffs Only[c] | | Effective Rate[d] | | | |
| | | | Tariff and Nontariff Measures | | Nontariff Measures Only | |
Commodity Group[b]	1964 (1)	1972 (2)	1964 (3)	1972 (4)	1964 (5)	1972 (6)
Primary products	.08 (.14)	.07 (.14)	.18	.17	.08	.08
Intermediate and consumer goods	.10 (.13)	.07 (.11)	.22	.18	.04	.07
Capital goods	.11	.06	.15	.07	−.01	−.01
Average	.10 (.13)	.06 (.10)	.20	.15	.03	.05

[a]Rates for 1972 include the effects of reductions agreed to in the Kennedy Round of GATT negotiations.

[b]Primary products include industries 1-10 (except 4) from the 1958 input-output table; intermediate and consumer goods cover industries 13-42; and capital goods cover industries 43-64.

[c]Figures in parentheses are nominal rates based on both tariff and nontariff measures; they are given only for groups that include industries where the effects of nontariff measures were estimated.

[d]Nontraded inputs are treated like traded inputs and excluded from value added.

Source: Robert E. Baldwin, *Non-Tariff Distortions of International Trade* (Washington, D.C.: The Brookings Institution, 1970), p. 165.

follow the pattern of national commercial policies in general. High cost, import-competing suppliers seem to be the prime beneficiaries of nontariff protection; these are most frequently agricultural or based on agricultural imports. Second in terms of frequency of NTB-shielding are the extractive industries and suppliers of crude materials. Nontariff protection of manufactures, on the other hand, is subject to far more irregularity in terms of its application to individual commodity groups and by individual countries—the only clear exceptions being in the textile and chemical-pharmaceutical areas.

If this analysis of the application of nontariff barriers is valid, and if the thesis concerning the deflection of protectionist effort from tariffs to nontariff restrictions is correct, then any successful new moves toward freer trade cannot be limited to tariffs alone. Rather, they will be applied on a broad front, to tariffs and nontariff barriers alike.

In part, the future of successful NTB liberalization depends upon whether agriculturally-based commodities are included; their exclusion would reduce the number of specific nontariff measures to be contended with quite materially. Yet it can be argued quite persuasively that many industrial countries—such as Canada, the United States, and Denmark—have a major stake in agricultural liberalization and will not tolerate the exclusion of that sector from future discussions. Moreover, there is no discrete "break" between agricultural and nonagricultural commodities, and it is difficult if not impossible to determine where one begins and the other leaves off. And precisely those nontariff measures most readily negotiated (Type I measures) are heavily concentrated in the agricultural commodity categories.

The next question quite obviously concerns the optimal way of approaching the reduction of nontariff barriers, under conditions of the multiplicity of legislative and administrative agencies involved in their implementation, and their close ties to a wide variety of domestic programs. Substantial progress has been made in liberalizing Type I restrictions, particularly quantitative barriers. Generally the results have been attained through bilateral negotiation inside and outside the GATT, with the aid of Articles XXII and XXIII of the General Agreement. The latter establish a procedure by which complaints by the contracting parties, whenever benefits that should be accruing to them under the GATT are being nullified by other countries, are transformed into mutual discussion or investigation by outside panels for conciliation.

Industrial countries filing successful complaints under the GATT have included Norway, the United Kingdom, Canada, France, Italy and the United States, while defendants have included Australia, Germany, France, Belgium, Sweden, and the United States. Particularly in the agricultural area, the GATT itself has taken the initiative in studying the entire problem of nontariff barriers and has consulted with the EEC on the impact of the Common Agricultural Program on trade in a variety of farm commodities. The GATT has also attempted to control the use of subsidies (Article XVI), and has recently opened the entire question of nontariff barriers for reconsideration by initiating a wide and comprehensive survey of the use of NTBs by the contracting parties and other countries.

Whether a great deal of progress can be made under the auspices of the GATT—given the multiplicity of factors governing nontariff restrictions—remains to be seen. This is particularly true in view of the case with which barriers that are "illegal" or not explicitly considered under the GATT provisions may be continued.

With respect to the strategy of NTB liberalization, several points stand out. If progress is to be made through traditional multinational trade negotiations, (a) prior authority to make concessions must be granted to the negotiators, and (b) estimates of restrictiveness must be developed for bargaining purposes. The first of these requirements will be difficult to meet, since NTBs are applied by a multitude of authorities: national legislatures, executive-branch agencies, and state-local governmental and quasi-governmental units. Moreover, as has been implied here, the development of points of bargaining will prove to be equally difficult. Both considerations will certainly serve to alter the character of the discussions from those prevailing in past multinational trade negotiations.

Another approach is the establishment of "codes of behavior" covering various types of nontariff measures and agreed to in advance by all participants. These codes could themselves be established by means of bargaining, according to restrictions of "special interest" to each country, and take effect over specified adjustment periods. Enforcement could then be left to the standard GATT adjudication procedure or to a special agency created for that purpose.

Yet a third alternative for the liberalization of NTBs would involve a procedural shift in the direction of sectoral free trade. Both tariffs and nontariff measures could be eliminated completely on selected commodity groups—chosen by means of intercountry bargaining—over transition periods tailored to market conditions prevailing in each industry. This approach, considering the total "package" of protective devices at once, would avoid the problem of compensatory increases of NTBs in response to reduced tariff rates. It would not, however, solve the question of delegation of authority, and postagreement ratification would probably be required.

Finally, NTB liberalization will certainly continue to be undertaken within the framework of existing or future regional economic integration schemes. Such projects involve agreements in which explicit provisions for the removal of nontariff measures are included. Moreover, the related problems of agricultural integration, harmonization of indirect taxes, subsidies, transport and competition regulation, and government procurement practices may themselves be attacked under regional integration programs, thereby getting at the root cause of many nontariff distortions to trade. Cohesive regional free-trade areas may also provide central institutions which can serve as sources of continuing initiatives for NTB liberalization and as agents in its implementation.

The experiences of the EEC and EFTA seems to indicate the rapid progress is more likely to occur under a more or less cohesive free-trade area than is possible under broad intergovernmental negotiation and consultation. This would appear to be especially so in the case of the more subtle kinds of NTBs and those whose economic impact is difficult to quantify or even identify. Whether or not a free-trade area is an appropriate device for the elimination of nontariff barriers depends upon the specific structure of nontariff protection existing within such a union, among the various participating countries. Indeed, if NTBs classified as Type II and Type III restrictions are important, the elimination of such barriers may well demand movement toward economic union well beyond the free-trade area stage, to include the coordination and harmonization of a variety of domestic policies and programs.

Notes

1. The short-circuiting of the national trade-policy decision process by means of nontariff barriers is more fully explained in Chapter 2.

2. Robert G. Hawkins, "The Economic Impact on the United States of a U.K.-Canada-U.S. Free Trade Association," in Thomas M. Franck and Edward Weisband, eds., *A Free Trade Association* (New York: New York University Press, 1968), p. 53.

3. SITC Revised, United Nations Secretariat, Statistical Office, *Statistical Papers*, series M, no. 34 (New York: United Nations, 1961).

4. The following sources were used, among others, in the compilation of the NTB inventory: (a) International Chamber of Commerce, *Non-Tariff Obstacles to Trade* (Paris: ICC, 1969), (b) A variety of GATT documentation released prior to 1968, (c) UNCTAD studies of quantitative import restrictions contained in the following documents: TD/B/C.2/26 and Corr. 1, TD/B/C.2/9, TD/B/82/Add. 2 and Corr. 1-4, TD/20 and Supplements, TD/B/AC.5/5, TD/B/C.2/R.1 Add. 1, and TD/B/C.2/83, as well as UNCTAD country-studies, (d) U.S. Office of the Special Representative for Trade Negotiations, "Preliminary Inventory of Non-Tariff Barriers," in Committee on Ways and Means, U.S. House of Representatives, *Foreign Trade and Tariff Proposals* (Washington, D.C.: GPO, 1968), and (e) Bureau of International Commerce, U.S. Department of Commerce, "Non-Tariff Inventory by Country" in ibid., part 9.

5. This section relies heavily on a paper by the author entitled "Non-Tariff Protection Among Industrial Countries: Some Preliminary Evidence," *Economia Internazionale*, 1972.

6. The following is based on a paper by the author and Jae W. Chung, entitled "The Pattern of Non-Tariff Barriers to International Market Access," *Weltwirtschaftliches Archiv* (Bd. 108), 1972.

7. For instance, see the debates in the fourth (1970) session of the

UNCTAD Committee on Manufactures, as noted in the proceedings (UNCTAD documents TD/295-TD/B/C.2/97).

8. The following relies on the author's paper "Non-Tariff Barriers and the Export Performance of Developing Countries," *American Economic Review*, Papers and Proceedings, May 1971.

9. The competitiveness factors are taken from a recent study by H.F. Lydall for UNCTAD, *The Performance of Developing Countries as Exporters of Manufactures to the Developed Market Economy Countries*, Document TD/B/C.2/91 (Geneva: UNCTAD, 22 December 1969). Because of high reliance on natural resource endowments, petroleum products and nonferrous metals are excluded in the competitiveness estimates, which are based on human capital-intensity, physical capital-intensity and the size of plant as determining variables. The NTB factors represent an enumeration of the specific NTBs bearing on individual product groups in the developed countries. See UNCTAD's *Liberalization of Tariffs and Non-Tariff Barriers*, annex II.

10. The following is based on Ingo Walter and Jae W. Chung, "Non-Tariff Distortions and Trade Preferences for Developing Countries," *Kyklos*, Fasc. 4, 1971.

11. Robert E. Baldwin, *Non-Tariff Distortions of International Trade* (Washington, D.C.: Brookings Institution, 1970).

6

Barriers to International Competition: Interfirm Competitive Behavior

Corwin D. Edwards

Tariffs and other measures that discriminate against imported goods not only impose governmental restrictions upon trade but also facilitate additional private restrictions. Domestic suppliers—protected by the additional costs and quantitative restrictions that their government imposes upon foreign goods at the frontier—are less exposed to foreign competition than they would be if the frontier were open. If they can agree among themselves to fix prices or otherwise to restrain trade, (a) they encounter less danger that sales of foreign goods in disregard of the restrictions—e.g., at lower prices—will undermine the agreement; and (b) where governmental barriers are sufficiently high to exclude imports, they can disregard foreign competitors entirely. Similarly, if domestic suppliers are few, their tendency to behave like monopolists or oligopolists will be less disturbed, or not disturbed at all, by the need to consider the impact of foreign competition. To the extent that the government closes its frontiers to imports, it enhances the opportunity for anticompetitive influences within domestic markets to attain strength and express their strength in domestic restraints of trade.

Students of restrictive business practices have long recognized that tariff and nontariff barriers to international trade are closely related to private restrictions. This connection has been expressed in such phrases as "The tariff is the mother of trusts"; in assertions that countries with low tariffs, such as England before the First World War, needed no antitrust laws; and in suggestions that when the American antitrust laws are violated an appropriate remedy would be reduction or abolition of the relevant tariff or other trade restrictions.[a] International free trade has been regarded both as a logical corollary of domestic policy that promotes competition and as a possible adequate safeguard for domestic competition.[b]

---

[a]Section 29 of the Canadian Act to Provide for the Investigation of Combines Monopolies, Trusts and Mergers authorizes the Governor in Council to reduce or eliminate a tariff if it appears to him, as a result of investigation or judicial decision, that customs duties are facilitating disadvantage to the public from agreement, arrangement, merger, or monopoly.

[b]Such a formulation is clearly inadequate in one situation—that in which the significant suppliers operate only in foreign countries and the competitive arrangements that they apply there have a restrictive impact upon the domestic market. The United States, for example, produces substantially no diamonds, neither gem stones nor industrial sorts. Restriction of the diamond supply and of the terms of sale thereof are consummated by foreign firms in foreign countries. Whether or not the United States chooses to apply a tariff to diamonds does not affect the degree of competition in supplying American buyers.

Where domestic supplies are substantial, the presumption is that—in the absence of governmental barriers—competition from imported goods will be possible and that domestic restrictions cannot exist if they are exposed to the possibility of such competition. Each of these assumptions, however, is only partly true.

Trade Potential in Services and Products

First, competition from imports is not always possible if barriers against imports are removed. For the entire field of consumer services, imports are irrelevant—for construction, retailing, dry cleaning, laundry, theatrical performances, barbering, and a host of other activities. Those who render the service might be of foreign origin, but their services cannot be. And the question whether or not foreign competitors may appear in the field depends, not upon trade barriers, but upon national policy toward the rights of foreigners to enter the country and to do business within it. A broad program such as that of the European Economic Community, including removal of barriers to migration, to international movements of capital, and to establishment and operation of business enterprises by foreigners, might introduce new competition into service industries; a program limited to reduction of obstacles to imports could affect products but not services.

For products, the possibility of importation is necessarily specific to the types of goods imported. Some are too perishable to be easily brought from a distance, and some are too heavy or bulky. For perishable goods, imports can be competitive only when they can be sold at prices high enough to justify such costs as protective packing, shipment under refrigeration, and perhaps air transport. For heavy or bulky goods significant import competition is likely to be possible only where transportation costs are not prohibitive, for example, in an area that can be easily reached by water. There is no general possibility that governmentally unrestricted importation can prevent restraints of domestic trade in such goods as bread or soft-skinned fruit or construction aggregates or cement.

The possibility of importation is further limited by convention, by law, and by nontariff barriers not of protective intent. Conventions of measurement and of design differ from one part of the world to another—use of metric systems of measurement or an alternative; use of electric current of different voltage; use of different types of electric plugs, and so forth. Foreign products that do not conform to the local convention are not easily usable. Similarly, regulatory requirements about the characteristics of goods differ in different nations, as noted in Chapter 4. Wholesome meat, properly labeled textiles, safe automobiles have meanings that are prescribed by applicable laws; and if the foreign product does not meet standards applicable to all products of its type it is unsalable even if explicit trade barriers exclude it.

In such cases casual importation is not feasible. The foreign product becomes available only if some part of the foreign supply is redesigned to meet the locally applicable conventions and regulations. This may take place if potential sales of the redesigned product are large and if conformity to local requirements is not too burdensome. Foreign automobiles, for example, are made salable in the United States by modifying foreign specifications to incorporate in the cars that are produced for sale here the safety and emissions characteristics required by American law. So long as there are differences in national conventions and regulations, these are likely to prevent the importation of a considerable number of products whose prospective sales are too small to justify such special adaptations.

For such instances, the competition-enhancing potential of government collaboration to remove barriers to international trade clearly depends upon the breadth of the effort. A program concerned only with tariffs and other explicit obstacles at the frontier leaves untouched the obstacles that are created by diversity of national conventions and regulations. A more ambitious program would include systematic effort to remove internal obstacles by harmonizing the national usages and regulations that create these obstacles. For automobiles, for example, it might include international agreement upon safety features that manufacturers must incorporate in new cars. The potential of such an effort in promoting competition from imports would be much greater than that of the less ambitious one; but this greater potential would be attainable only so far as the participating countries could agree upon norms of conduct and modify a large number of internal practices and rules to fit these norms. The efforts by the EEC to achieve such harmonization—e.g., in national regulations applicable to pharmaceuticals—demonstrate both that such agreements are not impossible and that they can be reached only slowly and arduously.

The possibilities of effective import competition as a barrier to anticompetitive business practices can be summarized as follows: Unless the program includes free movement of productive resources and freedom of establishment, import competition is not available as a curb upon private restraints of trade in service industries. Import competition can have an effect upon perishable goods only if these are expensive enough to justify special care, and its effect upon heavy and bulky commodities will be significantly limited by the costs of transporting them. Where products need to conform to national conventions of measurement, design or taste—or to national regulatory requirements—import competition can be a general curb upon restrictions only if the free-trade program includes ambitious and successful efforts to harmonize internal laws and usages;[c] otherwise, it can appear only in markets large enough to induce

---

[c]In an ambitious program of harmonization such as that of the EEC, efforts to create new competitive opportunities for foreign goods and foreign business enterprises are not likely to be successful unless they reach even further than has been indicated above. Where the enterprises of a country are handicapped in comparison with those of another by national legal requirements, they are likely to insist upon removal of the handicap as a necessary

foreign suppliers to adopt special specifications for the goods they export to particular countires.

Supplementary Private Restrictions

The presumption that where competition from imports is feasible it will in fact serve to reduce or prevent domestic business restrictions is likewise excessively optimistic. The fact that foreign goods can enter the market means that they can compete, not that they necessarily will. There are at least three other possibilities:

1. Domestic suppliers may be able to devise additional private restrictions that shut foreign goods out of the domestic market as effectively as a tariff or NTB.
2. Foreign suppliers who enter the domestic market may do so as participants in existing domestic restrictions.
3. Foreign suppliers may join with domestic ones in wider arrangements by which they undertake to stay out of the domestic market in return for similar abstention by domestic suppliers in foreign markets. In any of these ways new restrictions may extend, replace, or supplement the previous ones. So far as they do so, the competitive effects of a policy favoring freer trade will be nullified.

This kind of nullification is not likely to be complete. The restrictions by which the internationally available goods can be deprived of competitive effect are harder to apply than restrictions in closed markets. If they take the form of domestic restrictions, they must employ restrictive trade devices that were not previously needed. If they include the foreign suppliers, they must cover more firms and a broader geographic area transcending national political boundaries and must be substantively more complicated. Some anticompetitive arrangements cannot be so tightened as to close the national market, nor so enlarged as to become international cartels; and competition from imports is likely to weaken these or destroy them. Thus within the context of major efforts to promote freer trade, the possibility of importation will have procompetitive effects.

Without other policies designed to maintain competition, however, a substantial degree of private restriction is likely to remain both (a) in situations in which

---

corollary to removal of any protection that they have received from tariffs, NTBs, or regulation of the characteristics of commodities. The field for harmonization of laws may be thus extended to cover taxation, labor legislation, incorporation, patent rights, subsidies, and numerous other matters in which the applicable law affects the burdens and opportunities of business.

foreign goods cannot compete effectively and (b) in situations in which private arrangements preclude such competition.

The relation between tariff reduction and domestic laws governing competition differs in these two types of situation. Just as international trade in goods cannot significantly affect situations of the first type, so in such situations intercountry differences in the curbs that are applied to private business restrictions cannot significantly affect international trade. A country may use its domestic policy to attain whatever degree of internal competition it desires, without fear of the impact of different policies applied in other countries, nor fear of the impact of the diversity of national policies toward competition upon any policies of trade liberalization in which it may participate. In these situations, coordination of trade policy and competition policy is not necessary, and lack of coordination of national competition policies is not an obstacle to the effectiveness of trade liberalization.

In the second type of situation, competition policy and trade policy are closely related. Unless curbs are applied to the private restrictions that are capable of nullifying the effect of import competition, the competitive benefits from imports may be greatly diminished. Instead of appearing for all types of goods that are domestically restricted for which a substantial supply of imported goods would be practicable, these benefits will appear only where business efforts to tighten or extend restrictive arrangements are unsuccessful. Unless such a partial accomplishment is to be regarded as adequate, measures against private action that excludes foreign suppliers are indispensible corollaries of trade liberalization.

Types of Restraints Upon Competition

To differing degrees in different countries, restrictions to interfirm competition have been illegal or of doubtful legality. Here they will be discussed without reference to the legal curbs upon them. Subsequently, the adequacy of the curbs imposed by existing law, and the ways in which such curbs might be strengthened where they are inadequate, will be central topics.

Four general classes of restriction have been visible:

1. Restrictions imposed upon a country by enterprises that export to that country without encountering any significant supply from other sources, domestic or foreign.
2. Restrictions imposed within a country by enterprises that were not exposed to competition from imports, the latter having been excluded by governmental barriers to trade, private restrictive practices, or a combination of both.
3. Restrictions imposed within a country by the collaborative action of domestic and foreign firms, with the foreign firms participating in the domestic restrictions.

4. International restrictions, applicable in a number of countries and in-cluding participating suppliers in several.

Restrictions of each of these classes have existed in several forms; but some types of restriction have generally been impracticable in each class.

The first class of restrictions imposed from abroad upon a market that has no significant alternative source of supply is uncommon. Its existence depends not only on absence of substantial domestic production, but also upon the existence either of foreign monopoly or of effective restrictive agreements among all important foreign producers. Where the requisite conditions exist, as for nickel or diamonds, three forms of restriction are likely to be important—restriction or supply, price-fixing, and barriers to entry designed to foreclose opportunity to create new sources of supply. By limiting exports to a country, the foreign suppliers can impose scarcity by their own actions. By fixing prices they can determine the selling terms appropriate to that scarcity. Both of these practices have been unmistakable in the diamond industry. If there is a possibility that new sources of supply might be created in a domestic market, as has been true from time to time for chemicals when control by innovators was becoming precarious, foreclosure of opportunity for new firms can be undertaken in several ways—by agreements to withhold necessary technology or machinery, by localized temporary price wars intended to discourage or destroy new competi-tors, or by establishment of a local subsidiary, intended to remain small and yet to preempt enough of the local market to discourage ambitious newcomers.

The second class—domestic restrictions that involve exclusion of import competition—could not continue to exist under effective trade liberalization arrangements if it relied upon exclusion of imports by government action. It could continue to flourish, however, where private measures to exclude imports could be effectively used. The domestic restrictions themselves could, of course, be of any kind that might be domestically practicable and profitable. The exclusionary restrictions that would be necessary to support them, however, would be likely to take one or more of six forms: (a) closed pools of domestic patents might be employed to establish barriers which would expose imported goods to effective harrassment either by infringement suits or by denial of access to necessary technology; (b) collective reciprocal exclusive collaboration arrange-ments might be made with distributors, so that most important channels of distribution would be unavailable to imports; (c) a similar effect might be achieved by agreeing with distributors upon specifications about the characteris-tics of firms that should be regarded as eligible suppliers, shaping these specifications so that suppliers of imported goods were disqualified, and summarizing the results in "blacklists" or "whitelists"; (d) reciprocal trading arrangements might be made with important industrial users of the relevant product, so that sale by foreign firms to important customers would be foreclosed; (e) on various pretexts, recurrent harrassing boycotts might be fomented among distributors, transportation workers, or consumers; and (f) discriminatory prices and terms might be accorded by domestic suppliers to the customers or localities that were beginning to buy imported goods, so that sellers of imported goods must either lose sales or sell at unprofitable prices.

In the third class—restrictions with the collaboration of foreign participants—imported goods come into the national market, but suppliers of them collude in the restrictions that are imposed by the domestic suppliers. When this is the case, domestic restrictions can be of many kinds—price-fixing, allocation of markets or products, restriction of supply, restriction of distributive channels, or joint sale. However, they cannot include restrictions upon productive capacity or methods of production; and any restrictions that they imposed upon patents or use of unpatented technology must be limited to use within a single country, since the foreign operations of the suppliers of imported goods are not within the field of the agreement.

The fourth class—truly international competitive restrictions—differs in its potential according to its comprehensiveness. If there are important sources of supply outside of the international field that it covers, the ability of the participants to undertake restriction may be significantly limited. Such cases are roughly analogous to restrictions in a single country, with the area covered by the restriction treated as equivalent to that of the country and the rest of the world treated as "foreign." If, however, the field of restriction is comprehensively international, with no significant sources of supply left out, the field of possible restriction is significantly enlarged. In each country, domestic firms that wish to restrain trade in the domestic market may be able to induce foreign suppliers to agree to stay out of that market. For practical purposes, such a restriction involves reciprocal undertakings by domestic suppliers to abstain from some or all foreign markets. Thus, this type of restriction consists of arrangements to allocate national territories among participating suppliers.

The means of allocation, however, may vary. Perhaps the most common is agreement to allocate national patents, so that each firm, in its allocated territory, can use the patents of all participating firms as a barrier against intrusion, and by infringement suits could, if necessary, invoke the aid of the courts in policing this barrier. Other means of doing the same thing include allocations of rights in a trade mark, so that the intruder must either encounter legal obstacles or identify his product by an unknown name, and simple agreement to divide territories.

Though allocative agreements are likely to be the simplest, international agreements that include all significant suppliers may take many other forms. These include not only substantially everything open to restriction in a single country when foreign suppliers are participants, but also restrictions that are not feasible in the one-country case—restrictions of capacity and productive methods, and restrictions upon the rate of introduction of new technology.

The Size of the Problem

Although the nature of the problem of anticompetitive restriction of trade can be foreseen, its magnitude cannot. Since restrictive arrangements are normally clandestine, private estimates of their prevalence are obviously unreliable. In most countries what is reliably known about the prevalence of restrictions comes from records of public investigations and proceedings. But these tell little that is relevant about the prevalence of such practices. An official body can investigate only a few problems at a time. The scope and speed of action by different official bodies and the priority given by them to particular kinds of restriction vary widely; so does the legal vulnerability of a particular restriction under different existing laws. The restrictions covered by successive investigations may not have existed at any one time, and what was investigated may have been eliminated or significantly changed after the investigation. Much that is appropriate for investigation may not yet have been discovered or may still await official action. For such reasons, statistical summaries of official proceedings cannot tell us much about the relative number or total of types of restriction in the fields with which these proceedings are concerned.

In a few countries that maintain registers of restrictive agreements, official figures are available about the numbers of agreements containing particular kinds of restriction. Peculiarities of these figures make them difficult to use in estimating the numbers of restrictions that affect or might affect international trade.[1] Nevertheless, they provide, where they are available, a better basis than investigations and proceedings for such an estimate.

The number of private restrictions that have existed where governmental trade barriers have limited and distorted international market access is not, however, a good indication of the number that would exist if these governmental barriers were removed. It is reasonable to suppose that enterprises that lose protection by governmental barriers will have stronger incentives than before to try to use private restrictions as substitutes. It is also reasonable to suppose that where such efforts fail, private restrictions that existed previously may crumble under new competitive pressures from other countries.

With these limitations in mind, one can say only that available information about private restrictions in the recent past indicates persuasively that their number has been large enough to constitute a significant problem for the world trading community.

In 1963, the registrations that had been received by the European Economic Community included nearly 700 multipartite agreements, of which at least 135 involved participants in two states and at least 175 participants in more than two states.[2] Since the ground for registration was that the agreements restricted trade between states that were members of the community, the number of instances in which the trade of nonmember states was affected by these agreements does not appear in the foregoing figures. Many agreements probably covered only trade within the EEC. Nevertheless, it is reasonable to infer that a substantial number of the registered multipartite agreements had restrictive consequences outside the EEC as well as within it. In addition to these, multipartite agreements probably existed that were not subject to registration because they were applicable only to trade between one or more EEC countries and other parts of the world.[d] Moreover, the EEC had also registered about 480 bipartite agreements licensing patents or technical knowledge; and since such agreements often include restrictions upon export from the country in which the license is granted, some of these probably restricted trade with countries outside the EEC.

For nearly 500 of the EEC multipartite registrations, preliminary analyses of restrictions were available in 1963.[3] Though some of the categories were still too imprecise to have meaning, the analysis included 33 instances of allocation of territorial markets, 77 instances of maintenance of quotas of production, 173 instances of price-fixing, 60 instances of joint sale or purchase, and 57 instances of collective exclusive dealing. So far as the agreements that embodied these restrictions covered territory not subject to EEC's corrective action, the probability that they restricted trade outside EEC was high. In addition there were 156 instances of multilateral licensing and 43 instances of "technical cooperation"; and since such agreements often include provisions limiting competition among participants, these agreements, so far as they had impact beyond the EEC, may also be suspected of restriction not subject to corrective action.

In 1963, the requirements of single countries in which restrictive agreements were reported, though concerned primarily with restrictions in domestic markets, explicitly covered export agreements in some countries, and in other countries covered the export and international aspects of agreements that involved domestic restrictions also. Thus national registers included certain international agreements and certain national export agreements. About 100 registrations (in five countries) pertained to agreements that were apparently international in scope.[4] In these there were 38 agreements allocating territorial markets, 15 allocating the amount of export business, 12 allocating patent rights, copyrights, or trademarks, 27 establishing reciprocal exclusive or preferential dealing, 44 fixing prices or price relationships, 4 establishing joint sale, 10 establishing joint production, and 28 establishing joint use of trade marks, patents, or unpatented technology. Because the firms involved in some of the joint activities in production and sale may have been too small in the aggregate to have a substantial restrictive effect, some of these provisions may have involved merely attainment of an efficient scale of operation and may have resulted in no significant restriction. The other types of restriction, however, would not have been worth establishing had they produced no restrictive effect.

---

[d] If, for example, French and Belgian firms had agreed upon allocation of Latin American markets, this agreement would not have been subject to registration.

About 94 registrations (in four countries) pertained to agreements within a single country as to its exports.[5] Among them were 11 involving allocation of foreign markets, 4 involving allocation of goods to be exported, 1 involving allocation of foreign customers, 11 involving territorial allocation of patents, copyrights, or trademarks, 21 involving export quotas, 50 involving fixation of export prices or the level of bidding in foreign markets, 1 involving selection of the firm that would submit the lowest bid, 10 involving joint use of trademarks, and 2 involving joint exportation or joint sale in foreign markets. Only for the last type of provision was there any reasonable possibility that competition was not significantly restricted in export trade by the enterprises of the country.

Unilateral Control of Anticompetitive Practices

Control over restrictive business practices that is appropriate as a corollary to trade liberalization can be applied, of course, by a single country, even though the reduction of tariffs or other governmental trade barriers that have made it important were the result of concerted international action.

An example of such a policy is that of the United States since the inception of this country's trade agreements program. The United States has participated over the past several decades in international action to reduce tariffs, both through bilateral reciprocal agreements and through multilateral bargaining such as the Kennedy Round. Meanwhile, the American antitrust laws, unilaterally applied, have been an effective barrier to domestic private restraints of trade (including those designed to exclude foreign goods and those participated in by foreigners supplying such goods) and to international arrangements by which imports to or exports from the United States were privately restricted. Restraints have been condemned under these laws even if the acts or agreements through which American imports (or exports) were intentionally restrained were executed outside the United States and even if the participants therein were partly or wholly foreign business enterprises.[6]

These unilateral prohibitions of private restriction have terminated or drastically modified a series of important restrictive business activities. Allocation of world markets that included restrictions on foreign exports to the United States were condemned in the aluminum case, the titanium case, the tungsten carbide case, the alkali case, the incandescent lamp case, the antifriction bearing case, a chemical products case, and the prismatic glassware case.[7] Participation by foreign firms, acting partly outside the United States in restrictions applied in the United States, was condemned in the tungsten carbide case, the incandescent lamp case, and the Swiss watch case.[8]

But unilateral efforts to protect American trade from the restrictive effects of action outside the United States have been sometimes unsuccessful and usually beset by difficulties. Problems of jurisdiction, ignorance, inability to impose adequate remedies, and controversy with foreign governments have limited the effectiveness of American action.

Lack of jurisdiction has been a substantial obstacle. Where those who imposed restrictions were wholly beyond reach, the American authorities could not apply American law. Where some basis has appeared for legal proceedings, troublesome questions as to jurisdiction have arisen. In some cases the problem has been whether or not a foreign firm was sufficiently present in the United States to be subject to an American court's authority;[9] in other cases in which jurisdiction over the firm was clear, the question has been whether or not the firm's role in restrictive activity abroad was sufficiently direct to justify holding it responsible for resultant restrictive effects upon American trade.

Such problems have complicated almost every antitrust proceeding that involved activity by foreign firms or activity in foreign countries. In some instances they have resulted—e.g., the diamond case—in dismissal of proceedings against foreign defendants who were held to be insufficiently present to give the American court jurisdiction.[10] In other instances, lack of jurisdiction over some firms has necessitated that action be directed against only some of the firms that participated in the restriction with the hope—which has been justified to different degrees in different cases—that orders against these firms would make continuance of restriction by the others impossible.[e] In still other instances difficulties of proof have eliminated from the case parts of the total pattern of restriction for which the responsibility of the defendants could not be demonstrated to the court's satisfaction.[f]

---

[e]Examples are the prismatic glassware case, the aluminum case, and the incandescent lamp case. In prismatic glassware, a proceeding against an American firm, resulting in an order against it, was used to break up territorial allocations and preferential relationships between it and certain European firms. In aluminum, part of the case concerned the operations of an international cartel that restricted sales of aluminum in the United States by foreign companies. The court found that French, German, Swiss, British and Canadian companies were members of the cartel. Of these only the Canadian company was a defendant in the case. It was enjoined from participation in any similar cartel agreement covering American imports. In lamps, similar international cartelization played an important role both in restricting American export and import trade and in limiting the access of American independent firms to lamp making machinery. Though the cartel included the principal producers of Europe, the only European firm included in the case was Philips, over which American jurisdiction could be established. The part of the order that was designed to terminate the cartel directed the American firms not to participate in similar agreements with any manufacturer and directed Philips not to engage in any such agreement with any American manufacturer as to production in the United States or export to or from the United States. Relations between Philips and other European lamp makers remained untouched, even if they concerned American trade.

[f]The responsibility of an American firm for the conduct of its foreign subsidiaries is usually established by proof that it controls the subsidiaries. More ambiguous relationships, however, cause difficulty. In the aluminum case, the Aluminum Company of America was held not be party to the organization and operation of the international cartel, even though the Canadian company that had been active in the cartel had been spun off from this company, was controlled by the same few large stockholders, and had as president the younger brother of its chief executive. Direct evidence about the role of the chief executive of the American company was conflicting; and the structural connections between the two companies were not thought sufficient to justify holding the American company responsible for the Canadian company's actions.

Ignorance has also been a recurring handicap, hard to overcome by unilateral investigation. It is possible for American and foreign firms alike to hold meetings, make agreements, and keep many of their most candid records outside the United States, and for American firms to make arrangements affecting American trade through subsidiaries or affiliates not located in the United States. Where an arrangement is international, the documents in which its content and operation are described can be so dispersed that no single country contains a full documentary account of what is involved.[11] The American authorities may be unaware of restrictions that are imposed from abroad.[g] When they have grounds to suspect that such restrictions exist, they may seek to discover them by subpoena. If the desired documents are in the United States, subpoena of them causes no unusual difficulties even if what they contain is relevant to activities abroad. But if the documents are elsewhere, the subpoenas may involve such demands as that a firm doing business in the United States produce for the American authorities (a) documents that it possesses in other countries, or (b) documents possessed by its subsidiaries in other countries or by subsidiaries of such subsidiaries. Such demands are likely to be held valid by American courts except so far as their scope is thought to be unduly burdensome. Nevertheless, they are likely to involve resistance, litigation, and delay, so that the need to use them makes enforcement difficult.[12]

The difficulties in getting information have sometimes been enhanced by foreign governments. From time to time some governments have protested that American subpoenas of documents located in their territory were infringements of their sovereignty. In some countries corporation law is so interpreted that corporate officials may not transfer corporate documents abroad. In some countries what is demanded in an American proceeding may pertain to relations between a company and a government, or on some other ground may be regarded as secret under laws that impose secrecy upon particular kinds of activity. When an American grand jury called for documents about restrictions upon international trade in petroleum, for example, the governments of the United Kingdom, France, the Netherlands, and Belgium informed companies under their jurisdiction that disclosure of these documents would violate their laws. In Switzerland, where laws about secrecy are particularly strict, the penal code provides for fine and imprisonment for persons who make business secrets accessible to foreign official agencies. In Ontario, a law passed after an American subpoena had been sent to more than fifty Canadian pulp and paper companies forbids removal of business records relating to business in Ontario pursuant to subpoena by any authority outside Ontario.[13]

A third recurring handicap has been difficulty in devising effective remedies

---

[g]There is reason to believe, for example, that during the operation of the international radio cartel an American consular official wasted considerable time promoting sale of American radio sets in a country to which the cartel agreement had bound American producers not to sell.

for restrictions that involve conduct in other countries. This difficulty has appeared most clearly where markets have been allocated under an international agreement for exchange of patent rights, under which participants have obtained in their assigned territory the power possessed by all the patents held by the participating group. In terminating such a scheme, an American court can require participants who hold American patent rights to make these rights available to others who may wish to produce or sell in the United States. If it does no more, however, its remedy is both discriminatory and inadequate. The inadequacy consists in the fact that, though imports into the United States and production in the United States are freed from restriction, restrictions due to the scheme still prevent export from the United States to countries where there are counterpart patents. The discrimination consists in the fact that foreigners can now produce in the United States or export to it, whereas Americans who attempt the same thing in other countries would infringe the counterpart patents.

Termination of the scheme requires, therefore, that the court's orders cover the counterpart patents also. So far as American holders of foreign counterpart patents are concerned, this can be done; for such holders can be directed to grant immunity under their foreign patents to exports from the United States authorized under their American patents. If necessary they can also be directed to make their foreign patents available to producers in foreign countries. But similar treatment of the foreign patents of other firms is much more difficult. A foreign firm that is a defendant in a case probably could be subjected, as a matter of American law, to similar control of its foreign patent holdings. But if its business is primarily foreign, the severity of the restriction imposed upon it by such control would be disproportionately greater than that imposed by similar control over the foreign patents of American firms. Foreign firms that are not defendants cannot be subjected to corresponding orders, and therefore retain fully the power to exclude American suppliers that they obtained by the restrictive arrangement. The likelihood that the American court's remedy will be comprehensive enough to remove, without discrimination, all of the relevant restraints of American commerce is not very great.

Difficulties in applying such remedies have also sometimes been increased by foreign official action. The lamp and chemical cases provide clear illustrations. In the electrical case, the Netherlands government protested the decree that was proposed by the U.S. Attorney General on the ground that it involved extraterritorial jurisdiction over Philips. The objection applied particularly to the decree's proposed limitation of Philips' exercise of patent rights under patents granted by the Netherlands and by other foreign countries.[14] Whether or not as a result of this protest, the decree in the case exempted Philips from the broad prohibition of cartel agreements that was imposed upon the other defendants. Instead, Philips was enjoined only from agreements with United States manufacturers providing that such manufacturers refrain from exporting from the United

States or that Philips refrain from exporting to or producing in the United States. Moreover, Philips was explicitly exempted from requirements that it do or refrain from doing anything under the decree that was contrary to law in a country in which Philips was incorporated or did business.[15] Thereupon the Dutch government amended its Economic Competition Act so that Dutch firms, unless granted exemption, were forbidden "to comply deliberately with any measures or decisions taken by any other State which relate to any regulations of competition, dominant positions, or conduct restricting competition."[16]

While the chemical case was pending, the valuable British patents for nylon had been transferred from duPont to Imperial Chemical Industries (ICI), and had been exclusively licensed by ICI to British Nylon Spinners, a firm of which ICI owned a 50 percent equity share. The decree directed that the patents be returned to duPont and be subjected to the decree's general requirement that licenses be nonexclusive. British Nylon Spinners obtained from the British courts an interlocutory order preventing ICI from returning the patents, and this order was confirmed on appeal.[17]

In light of experience in enforcing the relatively severe antitrust laws of the United States, these laws, unilaterally applied, cannot be regarded as adequate corollaries for anticompetitive practices to broad-scale liberalization of governmental barriers to international access. They are sufficient to terminate private restrictions only where what can be discovered, reached, and corrected under American law is so much of the total pattern of restriction that the rest of it cannot continue. By this test they are adequate to remove a restriction that is applied to the domestic market by action that takes place largely in the United States. They are also adequate for a restriction applied to the American market from abroad if the participating firms whose action can be controlled by the United States—American suppliers or international firms domestically based—are indispensable participants in the restrictive agreement. But they are inadequate where, as in the case of diamonds, the possibility of supply from domestic sources is too slight to mitigate restriction applied from abroad.

They are only partly effective for international allocation of markets. Because of the incomplete knowledge that the American authorities have and the incomplete control that they can exercise over restrictive activities outside the United States by foreign firms, proceedings under the American law are likely to be, to an uncertain extent, ineffective and discriminatory. Sometimes they may even fail to terminate important restrictions on American imports; more often they may open American markets to foreign goods without correspondingly opening foreign markets to American goods.

Significant Recent Changes in Control

Since the Second World War, the legal status of private restrictions that affect international trade has changed significantly. Countries that had imposed weak controls on private restrictions have strengthened them, and countries that had imposed no controls have enacted them. At least twenty-five countries had such laws in 1964.[18] In addition, vigorous international arrangements for control of private restriction had been developed in the European Economic Community and in the European Coal and Steel Community, and rudimentary ones in the European Free Trade Association and the General Agreement on Tariffs and Trade.[19] This proliferation of legal controls changed in two ways the problem of private restrictions relevant to international trade.

First, it made such restrictions substantially harder to develop and to maintain. Before the Second World War, no major trading country except the United States and Canada attempted to prevent restrictive business agreements.[20] Indeed, several such countries gave such arrangements tacit or explicit approval.[21] In important trading centers, restrictive arrangements international in scope could operate with no fear that they would infringe the national law or incur hostile or suspicious national investigation. A country such as the United States, which used its own law to protect its own trade, could expect neither cooperation nor sympathetic understanding by governments that had jurisdiction over most of the trade of the world.

Today, national controls are applicable to restrictive business practices in a much larger part of the world's total trade. It is harder to establish the central office of a cartel in a country that is indifferent to the cartel's operations. And although they are uncoordinated, national investigatory powers are potentially available to examine a larger part of the total pattern of an international restrictive arrangement. The likelihood that the existence of such an arrangement will become known is also enhanced by the facts that eight countries require that most kinds of arrangements restricting domestic trade be reported to the government and that in seven of these countries some or all of what is reported is included in a public register.[h] There is an increased possibility that parts of an international restrictive arrangement will be discovered and will be held to be contrary to the law or policy of one or more governments that have effective jurisdiction over them.

Moreover, the United States is not now the only country that seeks to protect its own commerce against restrictive acts that take place beyond the national borders. German law covers "all restraints of competition which have effect in the area in which this act applies, even if they result from acts done outside such

---

[h]The full text of reported agreements is disclosed by Norway, Denmark, Sweden, Israel and the United Kingdom (though in the latter four countries a few agreements are kept confidential on grounds of public interest or undue harm to legitimate private interests). In the United Kingdom export agreements are reported confidentially and nothing about them is disclosed; but when an agreement restricts domestic trade, the whole of it, including any export restrictions, must be publicly registered. In Finland useful summaries of agreements are made public. In Austria, summaries are also published, but usually in unrevealing generalities. In the Netherlands, all reports are strictly confidential and only statistical summaries are published.

area."[22] Orders under the British Monopolies Act are applicable to acts or omissions to act outside the United Kingdom if the person engaging in such conduct is a British subject, a British corporation, or a person who carries on business in the United Kingdom.[23] Austrian law applies to "cartel agreements made abroad, insofar as they are to be implemented on the territory of the Austrian Federal Republic."[24] The laws of Denmark and Spain are applicable to restrictions that have effects in the domestic market, and thus may be capable of similar interpretation.[25]

The development of policies against private restrictive practices by the European Communities has enhanced the difficulties created for international restriction by the increased number of national laws. The treaty that established the European Coal and Steel Community forbids, in the field it covers, all types of restrictive agreements except those that provide for joint buying or selling or for specialization in producing, and provides that the excepted types must receive specific authorization.[26] It also requires prior authorization for mergers. The treaty that established the European Economic Community includes a broad prohibition of restrictive agreements likely to affect trade between member states, subject to possible exemption of agreements found to have broadly specified beneficial effects.[27] Implementing regulations under the treaty have made report of a restrictive agreement a prerequisite for a grant of exemption,[28] and have thus given both the community and the governments of member countries confidential information about a large number of restrictive arrangements. The treaty also forbids abuse of a dominant position so far as trade between member states may be affected thereby.[29] These prohibitions are applicable if the prohibited effect is found, whether or not the restrictive activity takes place in the countries between which trade is restricted and whether or not the firms engaging in the restriction do business in those countries.[30]

By virtue of the two treaties, the rules about restriction in the European Communities have been tightened in three ways: (a) the limits of national jurisdiction have been partly overcome, as indicated above; (b) certain prohibitions and controls that varied in character and strength from state to state are uniform in the treaties, with content that is generally stronger than that of the underlying national laws; and (c) since the EEC Treaty is municipal law in the member states, the duty to comply with it has filled gaps in the national legislation. Though Italy long considered but did not enact a domestic antitrust law, the provisions of the treaty are law in Italy; and though the domestic legislation of Belgium is applicable only to control of abuses of economic power, the treaty's prohibitions of cartels are law in Belgium.

But since the protective legislation of the European Communities pertains only to trade between the member states, even the international effect of their action to curb restrictive business practices is sharply limited. The rules of ECSC, for example, prevent comprehensive cartelization by steel companies within the community, but do not prevent these companies from collaborating in export trade. In 1963 eight national federations of steel makers, representing firms within and outside the community, were participants in an international agreement about export prices, the policies of which were apparently set by meetings held within the community. Nevertheless, under ECSC, relations among the community's steel firms had been sufficiently competitive that efforts to apply export quotas similar to those of the prewar international steel cartel had been unsuccessful.[31]

Diversity in Control

The proliferating legislation has also complicated the problems that grow out of diversity in laws. Before the Second World War, such problems arose between states that differed drastically in their basic policy—the few states that forbade or curbed restrictive business practices, the few states that made particular restrictions mandatory, and the large number of states that imposed no specific control over such matters. Though control of such practices is now the policy of all of the major industrial countries that accept private enterprise, such control is still absent in the great majority of national states. Thus problems of conflict of law and policy still exist where restrictions affect both the states that attempt to control restrictive business practices and those that do not. But alongside these problems, there are increasingly complicated problems of diversity of control in the states that apply control.

In the two dozen countries in which national control exists, the national laws differ in purpose, scope, substance, procedure, and safeguards, and no two laws are alike in all these respects.[32] Such uniformity as has been achieved is to be found in the operations of the European Communities; yet though each of the community treaties was negotiated by the same member countries, it is notable that the restrictive practice provisions that were applied by ECSC to coal and steel differed markedly in substance and procedure from those applied by the EEC to other industries.[i] Each national law and each of the community treaties has expressed the ideas and the play of forces from which it emerged. A wish to reduce the differences in the national controls has been demonstrated only by the establishment of uniform requirements and procedures in each of the community treaties for application of the treaty itself. But even among the member states of the Communities, the relevant national laws about restrictive business practices have not been made more uniform. Outside the Communities, controls have been wholly unmodified by desire to minimize their diversity.

---

[i]There are indications that the recent fusion of the executives of the two European Communities may be followed by deliberate effort to reconcile so far as possible the interpretations given to the two community treaties, and perhaps eventually to amend these treaties to make them more consistent. Time since the fusion has been too short, however, to permit assessment of the strength of this tendency or of the extent of its probable accomplishment.

The diversity of approach to a given problem may be illustrated by considering the way in which high gasoline prices were treated under the German law and the way the same problem might have been treated under the laws of the United States and several other countries.

The Arab-Israeli War of 1967 suddenly and drastically stopped the flow of petroleum products from Middle Eastern sources through the Suez Canal to Western Europe. Shortages of supply existed in European markets until the flow was reestablished by longer and slower shipments around the Cape of Good Hope. Prices of gasoline in Germany rose sharply at the time of the shortage, and after restoration of the flow these prices did not drop.

A proceeding was begun under the German Act Against Restraints of Competition. The relevant provisions of. this act define as "market-dominating" two or more firms between which "no substantial competition exists in fact" and which are not exposed to substantial competition from others and authorize the cartel authority to prohibit abuse by market-dominating enterprises.[33] The proceeding by the German Federal Cartel Office was based upon the belief that uniform increases in prices by the leading suppliers of gasoline and subsequent maintenance of these increases after restoration of supplies demonstrated both absence of substantial competition and abuse of the power thereby attained. Before decision was rendered in the case, the suppliers reduced their prices to approximately the levels considered appropriate by the office, and thereupon the proceeding was terminated.[34]

The behavior of German gasoline prices illustrates a common type of price behavior: rachet-like price adjustments in which price moves upward quickly but downward slowly if at all. This kind of pricing has been discussed as follows by a former president of the American Economic Association:

... the growing downward inflexibility of prices, which brings about a "rachet-action" and prevents differences in the rate of increase in productivity from being adjusted in a way consistent with a stable average price level. Such stability requires increases in some prices, roughly offset by decreases in others. The restoration of two-way price flexibility in response to changes in costs, where it threatens to disappear, is perhaps the most crucially needed single improvement in our imperfect market system.[35]

It is likely to be regarded by some observers as indicative of a price agreement and by others as a result of individual price decisions by firms that participate in an oligopoly position.

Let us examine its status under various antitrust laws by considering how the German gasoline problem would have been treated if it had arisen in countries other than Germany. For this purpose let us assume a hypothetical condition in which (a) perturbation in petroleum markets because of the interruption of supply was worldwide; (b) the firms that supplied most of the gasoline were international corporate combinations; (c) price movements for gasoline were elsewhere the same as in Germany; and (d) search for an antritrust remedy was undertaken by the antitrust authorities of the United States, the United Kingdom, France, the Netherlands, Denmark, and Norway. How would the problem have been formulated under the law of each country?

In the United States the relevant question would have been whether or not the firms involved had agreed upon prices. The facts treated in Germany as evidence of abuse of dominant power would have been considered as possible evidence of the existence of agreement. If an agreement had been found, its continuance or renewal could have been enjoined and the parties to it could have been punished. If the evidence had been insufficient to prove agreement, the American law could not have been applied.

In the United Kingdom two alternative procedures would have been available, one applicable if there appeared to be an agreement, the other if not. Under the first, registration of the price-fixing agreement would have been required.[36] Subsequently the agreement could have been terminated by judicial order unless the parties convinced a court that the agreement resulted in one or more of seven specified types of public benefit and that the benefits outweighed the detrimental effect of the restriction.[37] Under the second alternative, the conduct of the suppliers could have been referred to the Monopolies Commission for report as to whether at least one-third of the gasoline supplied in the United Kingdom or in a substantial part thereof had been furnished by two or more suppliers who, "whether voluntarily or not and whether by agreement or arrangement or not," had so conducted "their respective affairs as in any way to prevent or restrict competition."[38] If the commission had found that this condition existed and that it might be expected to operate against the public interest, the Board of Trade would have had the power to forbid observance of the arrangement or to fix or regulate the prices to be charged.[39]

In the Netherlands, too, alternative procedures would have been available. Under one, the appropriate minister could have decided provisionally and, after obtaining an advisory report from a part-time committee of private citizens, could have decided finally, whether or not the suppliers had a dominant position that had consequences conflicting with the public interest. If so, the minister would have had power to publish data about the matter and to impose upon the suppliers rules on prices or obligations to deliver to designated persons at customary prices.[40] Under the other procedure, if the minister thought that there was a price agreement, he could have invoked penalties for failure by the parties to register the fact;[41] and if he regarded the agreement as contrary to the public interest he could have suspended it or, after consulting the same committee, could have forbidden the parties to conform to part or all of it.[42]

In France a single procedure would have been available for agreement and for concentrated power. The issue would have been whether either of two conditions existed: (a) concerted action encouraging "artificial" price increase or hindering price reduction, or (b) activity characterized by manifest concentration of economic power that had the purpose or might have the effect of interfering with the normal operation of the market. Under either condition, the action in question could have been forbidden and subjected to possible prosecution unless it ensured "the furtherance of economic progress, particularly through increased productivity."[43] If a proceeding had been undertaken, decision whether or not the condition was thus justified and, if not, whether it should be prosecuted or informally terminated, would have been made by the Minister of Economic Affairs after an advisory report by a Commission on Combines and Dominant Positions containing a majority of nongovernment members.[44]

In Denmark the suppliers would have already been listed on a public register if a Monopoly Control Authority[45] had found that they were individually capable of exerting a substantial influence on prices or distribution or transport throughout the country, or in local market areas—or if there was any restrictive agreement among them capable of such an influence. Whether or not agreement was involved, registration would have subjected them to a requirement that they put no price increase into effect without approval by the authority.[46] Moreover, if the authority had decided that restriction by them (concerted or not) that impaired competition "must be deemed to result" in unreasonable prices, it would have negotiated to terminate these and, if negotiation failed, could have prescribed prices or price changes and could have issued orders terminating the relevant agreements, decisions, or practices.[47]

In Norway the prices charged by the suppliers, whether individually or concertedly set, would have been subject to a provision that broadly prohibits demand for, acceptance of, or fixation of prices "which are unreasonable." They would also have been subject to a broad grant of power to the King to issue rules about "maximum prices, minimum prices, price freezing, price calculation . . . maximum profit margins," and numerous other matters—and to amend or annul restrictive business agreements and other arrangements.[48] These provisions were supported by requirements that restrictive agreements and arrangements were forbidden until registered, and that enterprises must report their interconnections and restrictive provisions if they provided at least one-fourth of the national supply of a commodity or were subject to foreign control or, in the opinion of the Price Directorate, needed special supervision.[49] Officials could have enforced these provisions, or regulations under them, by criminal penalties and by forfeiture of excess prices, and persons who had paid excess prices could have demanded refund of the excess.[50]

With such diversity of national procedures and legal constructs, there would be little prospect of effective action to cope with our hypothetical gasoline problem if that problem were to appear on the international scale postulated. Some countries might indeed act, with substantial results within the country, as did the German government. Other governments might not act—perhaps because their laws provided insufficient basis for action, perhaps because the information available to them did not include information relevant to their action that was available to other governments, or perhaps because they could not mobilize the resources and political support needed to act effectively. If action were taken by all countries in which the relevant effects upon prices appeared, the time needed for the applicable procedures would differ greatly in different countries, and the remedies invoked where proceedings resulted in corrective action would differ in nature, immediate effectiveness, and promise of enduring effect. Moreover, the remedies that could have been applied might very well have been inconsistent with one another. The countries empowered to use corrective price orders might do so in a way that makes the resulting national levels of prices internationally discriminatory. In using the Sherman Act against an international price-fixing conspiracy, a United States court might order firms over which it had jurisdiction to terminate restrictive agreements applicable to shipments of oil from the Middle East, while the United Kingdom, under its Monopolies Act, might order British corporations and firms doing business in its territory to modify the agreements in prescribed ways but not to terminate them.

Yet the problem as stated is one in which the origins of challenged price behavior were international, the firms engaging therein were doing business internationally, the problems as to overcharges to consumers and acceleration of inflation were similar in all countries, and all countries considered corrective action necessary.

Even with this measure of agreement, and with awareness that concerted action by the affected governments would have been cheaper, better informed, and more effective than independent national procedures, concerted action would not have been possible in the present state of law and policy. Substantive differences in goals and in analyses of the proper way to attain them would have prevented agreement about how to act. These obstacles would have been buttressed by numerous procedural differences that have little importance but, nevertheless, make the action of each country idiosyncratic. The summary of measures that are now available to cope with problems such as the hypothetical gasoline case shows wide differences as to whether the significant problem is such a case is an unreasonable level of prices, lack of effective competition, or concerted action; whether or not a balancing of detrimental and favorable effects is appropriate; whether the appropriate remedy is punishment, a corrective order, precautionary control, or a negotiated settlement; and whether or not price control is a suitable remedy. Procedures are as diverse as substance: Registration may be required or not; proceedings may be conceived as law enforcement or as decisions of policy; and may be civil or criminal, wholly public or wholly private, conducted wholly by public officials or inclusive of private persons who give advice or participate in the decision process; and decisions may be by courts, commissions, or departmental officials.

Scope for International Cooperation

The foregoing discussion suggests two conclusions: First, that concerted international action is highly desirable in efforts to curb restrictive business practices that are international in scope; and second, that difficulties in establishing concerted action in this field are formidable, perhaps even more so than in establishing other institutions implementing trade liberalization on a regional or multilateral basis.

To what extent and by what means can these difficulties be overcome? Several past efforts and current experiments with joint action by governments against restrictive business practices have sought answers to this question along widely different lines.

The least ambitious answer consists of *seeking and seizing opportunities for mutual help and collaboration in particular cases*. Many different degrees and kinds of cooperation are conceivable. Officials responsible for action relating to restrictive business practices in different national political jurisdictions might, for example, furnish relevant information to one another, undertake investigations desired by other countries, consult one another about the scope of proceedings they contemplate undertaking and the effect of remedies they contemplate applying, use their own powers to help other countries obtain documents that have been sent abroad to evade examination, grant administrative and judicial comity to corrective action taken by other countries, and, by frequent exchange of views, increase mutual understanding and similarity in policies. So long as such cooperation takes place informally case by case, its accomplishments are likely to be slight because of two great difficulties.

The first difficulty is due to divergent interests. Any proceeding large enough to justify international cooperation is quite likely to affect the national interests of different countries differently. In the hypothetical gasoline case that was discussed above, for example, officials from Germany, Denmark, and Norway might have expressed an undiluted consumer interest. In the other four countries, to varying degrees, the attitudes of governments might have been affected by producer interests, governmental or private, that were strong enough to prevent full sympathy and support for repressive action by a foreign country against international oil companies. The effect of such cleavages of interest is likely to be greatest when the desirability of cooperation in each case is separately considered, without clear general policy.

The second difficulty is national legislation that limits discretion. In most countries, official action is subject to rules that limit the grounds upon which investigations can be undertaken, the right to use information officially obtained, and the grounds for and character of corrective action.[j] Informal

---

[j]In the United States, for example, those who enforce the antitrust laws may require that information be provided, but except as noted below, the requirement must be relevant to contemplated proceedings and the information obtained must be kept confidential except as

cooperation that seems desirable may be precluded by law in some countries and, being unavailable from these, may be rejected by other countries because it cannot be reciprocal.

If mutual aid by national authorities is to be significant, it must overcome these difficulties. It must be undertaken systematically by reciprocal agreement, so that each government's interest in refusing to cooperate in a particular case will be overcome by a duty to cooperate, supported by desire to be certain that other governments will continue to cooperate in cases where it has a vital interest. Legislative obstacles to cooperation must be replaced by laws that authorize cooperation in specified ways within specified limits. To establish cooperation along these lines would require, of course, a treaty determining the stituations in which there was a duty to cooperate, making explicit the kinds of assistance that one government could obtain from another in such situations, and thus requiring modifications of municipal law so far as necessary to make such assistance possible.

Such cooperation would be simpler than other kinds of collaborative action in two respects: First, it would avoid the necessity of establishing supranational bodies to conduct supranational proceedings. Second, it would minimize the need for participating governments to agree upon goals and substantive policies and procedures. Cooperation could be undertaken for types of problems in which the participating governments agreed that corrective action was needed and approved of the effects that corrective action by the other countries was likely to produce, whether or not the cooperating governments agreed with one another about the substantive and procedural concepts they used in moving from statement of problem to corrective result.

Thus far little has been done to ascertain the practicable limits of national cooperative action. An expert committee on restrictive business practices, that has been sponsored by the Organization for Economic Cooperation and Development (OECD) and its predecessor OEEC since the early 1950s, has brought together twice a year officials concerned with restrictive business practices in member countries and in the European Economic Communities. The committee has achieved some progress toward agreement about the nature of restrictive business practice problems by providing for exchange of information about recent proceedings, by developing agreed definitions of relevant terms, and by sponsoring studies of certain restrictive practices.

It has agreed upon such cooperation in proceedings as is consistent with the

---

it is disclosed in the course of such proceedings. A request by a foreign government would be insufficient basis for either an investigative demand or disclosure. Similarly, corrective orders under the American laws must be reasonably relevant to violations of those laws and could not be issued merely in support of action taken by another government. The Federal Trade Commission possesses further discretionary investigatory powers, not focused upon alleged violations of law, and may make public, at its discretion, almost anything that it may thus discover. Whether or not these powers could be used on request by a foreign government, without domestic reasons for their use, has not been tested.

laws of the participating governments and international organizations. However, since the experts in the committee operate at subordinate executive levels in the governments and international organizations from which they come, a resolution by them cannot be regarded as a binding obligation of the participating governments and does not purport to provide a basis for removal of any of the legal obstacles that might limit cooperation. Its significance lies not in what it has accomplished but in what it might foreshadow.

A slightly more ambitious program might provide for *consultation by governments in an effort to reach mutually satisfactory solutions for problems presented by restrictive business practices*. The nature, possibilities, and limitations of such a program can be ascertained by examining the two such programs that now exist, that of the General Agreement on Tariffs and Trade and the European Free Trade Association.

In 1960 the GATT adopted a recommendation that participating governments, upon request by one of their number, undertake bilateral or multilateral consultations with the applicant about restrictive practices, and that if a government agreed that the practice discussed involved effects upon international trade harmful to the objectives of the GATT it should "take such measures as it deems appropriate" to eliminate the effects. The program provided that the results of such consultations should be made available to the participating governments.[51]

In 1959, the treaty that established the EFTA included a declaration opposing concerted business practices that have as object or result "the prevention, restriction or distortion of competition" so far as these practices "frustrate the benefits" of the EFTA's action about tariffs and quantitative restrictions. Member states were authorized to complain to a council that represented them all, and the council was empowered, by majority vote, to examine the matter, to make recommendations to a member state, and, if the recommendation was not accepted, to authorize a member state to suspend observance of its obligations to the recalcitrant state under the treaty.[52] In 1965, this procedure was supplemented. A complaint sponsored by a member government was then informally discussed with that government by the government or governments within whose territories the parties to the practice are located, and if there is agreement that the practice exists and was incompatible with the Treaty, the governments having jurisdiction could take the action necessary for a remedy. Failure to reach agreement resulted either in informal discussions on a broader multilateral basis or in reference of the complaint to the Council. Matters informally settled were reported in general terms with care not to disclose "confidential facts." Formal recommendations or decisions by the Council were accompanied by a public report.

At the close of 1968, no action under the GATT resolution had been reported, nor was any action taken under the EFTA procedure before 1965. An announcement by the EFTA in December 1968 said that "a few" cases had been subsequently discussed, and reported that during or immediately after informal discussions three practices had been discontinued: payment of a loyalty premium to firms that agreed not to import, a collective bonus paid by a national manufacturer's association to retailers on a scale related to their purchases of domestically produced goods, and payments made by three companies to their jointly owned manufacturing subsidiary "in respect of equipment of the type made by the subsidiary but bought from foreign suppliers."[53]

Scant use of these consultative procedures was to be expected. The criteria for consultation under the GATT procedure are ill-conceived. Consultation takes place only on request by a presumably aggrieved government, and therefore must necessarily be limited to relatively few matters. If no government possesses information sufficient for a responsible complaint, there is no procedure for investigation and no obligation on other governments to investigate. Governments are left individually free to use their own concepts of harm and their own tests of whether a practice is harmful, and to take whatever action they please if they encounter a harmful practice. The obligation to consult is thus left bare of all elements of agreement or obligation that might make consultation meaningful.

In practice, the EFTA procedure partly avoids these defects. Informal consultations apparently begin "on the basis of some *prima facie* evidence," and, without formally announced obligation to do so, "the country approached will provide as much information as its own laws and practices allow."[54] Thus some pooling of information takes place, though limits to investigation and to disclosure of knowledge that were previously set by the national laws are not reduced by any international obligation to investigate or disclose what is relevant to the international problem. As in the GATT, use of procedures of *ad hoc* intergovernmental consultation in EFTA make it certain that the cases discussed will be few since, governments are left free to apply their individual views of what is harmful and how harmfulness is to be determined. In the absence of meaningful disclosure about the facts of cases that are informally settled, there is little room to develop from these cases general interpretative standards that international traders would understand and accept. In cases that cannot be informally settled, or settled on the basis of recommendations made by the council, the further procedures that are contemplated—imposition of discriminatory tariffs or quantitative governmental restrictions bearing upon exports from a recalcitrant country—are unlikely to correct private restrictive practices and are highly objectionable in themselves.

In the light of these examples, it seems clear that intergovernmental consultative procedures can be used, at most, for relatively few and relatively important problems; that they are unlikely to be effectively used unless they oblige participating governments to obtain and to pool relevant information and to modify domestic laws so far as necessary for this purpose; and that they are likely to be used only in cases where restrictions are both flagrant and simple unless the participating governments can reach meaningful agreements about such matters as what restrictions are appropriate for consultation and what kinds of results from restriction shall be deemed harmful. So far as such agreements on substance can be reached, a logical corollary would be for governments to agree that, where harm is found, they accept an obligation to take effective action to end it. The case for such obligation is strengthened by the ineffectiveness and undesirability of measures that authorize governments to protect themselves against private restrictions by imposing public restrictions, as provided in the EFTA treaty.

A consultative provision for effective future action in this respect would obligate participants to prevent and correct private restrictions that were likely to thwart the purposes of the treaty. It would also obligate them to assist other participants in fulfilling this obligation by making appropriate investigations of activities within their jurisdiction that were alleged to have harmful effects upon other participants, and to make relevant information available to other participants; and it would set forth, to the limit of possible substantive agreement, the types of restriction thereby subjected to investigation and corrective action and the tests of harmful effect that were applicable.

A consultative procedure thus amplified would differ from more ambitious forms of international collaboration in three important respects. First, it would depend upon use of national rather than international procedures for appraising complaints, conducting investigations, reaching conclusions, and applying remedies. Second, by virtue of these limitations, it would avoid requiring individual governments to use unpalatable means of investigation or remedial action. Third, it would also thus avoid requiring individual governments, contrary to their own conclusions, to accept decisions by others that particular practices were harmful under the agreed standards.

A still more ambitious program would *establish and use international means for action against restrictive business practices*. Examples of such programs are the restrictive business practice provisions of the European Community treaties and the activities under them. Proposals for international action were also developed but never put into effect in the draft Charter for an International Trade Organization,[55] the draft plan submitted by the *ad hoc* committee on restrictive practices to the United Nations Economic and Social Council,[56] and the draft Convention of the Council of Europe.[57] Though these programs differed in many particulars, they all contained the features that are essential to international action: definition of a goal to prevent specified types of restrictions; establishment of international procedures for identifying restrictive business practices, conducting investigations of them, reaching decisions about their harmfulness, and taking corrective action where appropriate; determination of the scope of international action and of the character of the international obligations assumed by the participating states.

A well-conceived program of this kind, such as that of the European Economic Community, can provide more comprehensive protection against restrictions than is possible under the less ambitious programs. It can cover cases of restriction that individually are too small to justify international consultation but that constitute in the aggregate serious obstacles to international trade. Because of this broader coverage, it can more easily develop precedents and standards for decision that become generally accepted, and can diminish the difficulties presented by conflicting national interests in particular cases. Its standards and precedents, uniformly applied, can go much further than a program of international consultation toward diminishing difficulties from diversity in national law such as have been discussed above. Because the deflecting influence of particular firms and business groups is likely to be weakened in a broader international program, its policies, like those of EEC, are likely to be less tainted by tolerance for restriction than the policies of the participating states.

Problems and Opportunities

But though the potential of a program of international action is great, the difficulties in setting up such a program are also great. States can more easily agree with one another to limit their own action, as in reducing tariffs, than they can to transfer to an international instrument powers of control over their own citizens. Doing the latter requires that they agree not only upon goals to be sought and business activities to be curbed, but also upon suitable ways of applying public authority to private conduct, and that they devise instruments of international action that can be used equitably in each state in spite of national differences in the way business operates and is organized. This is a formidable task even in countries that, like the members of the EEC, have common cultural, political, economic, or legal interests. It may indeed be impossible for states with fundamentally different views of the role of private business, the desirability of competition, the scope of personal rights, or the role of law. The fact that countries as numerous and diverse as those that participate in the GATT have accepted agreements that effectively limit their own freedom of action in international trade does not demonstrate that they could accept and apply a program for international action about private restrictions.

The nature of the difficulties that must be surmounted, even by states with similar history and similar economic, political, and legal institutions, is evident if one considers the problem of applying international control to business conduct in a field in which the degree of private freedom to do business differs from state to state. This problem appears in two important forms, each of which deserves discussion: (a) the existence of private competitive enterprise, regulated private enterprise, and public enterprise as ways in which the same activity is organized in different states; and (b) the existence of enterprises that are generally subject to substantial regulation in all states, but with major differences in the scope and methods of regulation.

The first difficulty can be illustrated by the example of the potash industry. In the United States potash is produced by private companies that are subject to the American antitrust laws. In Germany potash producers are private companies organized in a cartel that operates under an exemption granted by officials who apply the German cartel law. In Spain potash is produced both by private companies and by a government company. In France potash production is a government monopoly. In 1963 the French and German producers were making their foreign sales through a cartel that fixed resale prices, forbade buyers to buy from independent sources, and forbade reexport. These and other producers sold in England through a joint sales company.[58] An international program to prevent private restrictions could be applied to potash only if, first, the American insistence on competition and the German willingness to permit controlled cartelization could be somehow reconciled, and second, agreement could be reached upon the way in which the program was to affect the government enterprises of France and Spain. Unless government and private firms were subject to similar curbs upon restriction, the obvious discriminatory impact of the international program would be a major obstacle to acceptance of it by the disfavored countries.

The European Communities have sought to cope with this kind of problem by forbidding governments to undertake directly or indirectly the kinds of restriction that are forbidden to private firms. Article 90 of the EEC Treaty provides that member states "shall not in respect of public undertakings or undertakings to which they grant special or exclusive rights enact or maintain any measure contrary to the rules of this treaty," and makes particular reference to the articles that apply to private restrictions. The ECSC Treaty subjected cartel agreements to explicit approval. Moreover, Article 66(7) of this treaty empowered the High Authority to address to private or public enterprises that have a dominant position that protects them from effective competition "any recommendations required to prevent the use of such position for purposes contrary to those of this treaty," and provided that, if the recommendations were not carried out, prices and conditions of sale or programs of production and delivery to be applied by these enterprises could be fixed by the High Authority. Some similar means of making comparable controls applicable to private, quasi-public, and public commercial undertakings would be necessary in any international organization concerned with restrictive business practices.

The second difficulty—application of international control to industries that, in the participating countries, are normally subject to substantial regulation—is even greater. In modern states, regulation replaces competition as a provider of important safeguards for the public in a substantial segment of the economy. At the core of the regulated segment lie the industries that supply public transportation by rail and air, power from electricity or gas, communication services by telephone, telegraph, radio, and television, and banking and insurance services. What lies within the periphery varies considerably from state to state. It may include public transportation by water or road; production of oil, natural gas, and other minerals; supply of water; agricultural production and marketing; production and sale of drugs, milk, and other commodities related to health; and provision of various kinds of professional services.

Where what is regulated is of a kind that cannot enter into or directly affect international trade, there is, of course, little risk that private restriction will negate the benefits of tariff reduction. Diversity in regulations applicable to local public utilities is no obstacle to a free-trade area. Whether or not private restrictions upon professional services might thwart the removal of public restrictions would depend upon whether or not the latter program reached beyond tariff reduction to remove barriers to migration and to the practice of professions by foreigners.

But regulation covers goods (such as petroleum, drugs, and farm products) that can move in international trade; services of transportation and communication that can be rendered on an international scale; and domestic services (such as provision of credit and insurance) that can be rendered in support of export trade. In such fields the character of the applicable regulations may be directly relevant to international programs designed to control private restrictions.

In the relevant regulated fields, diversity in regulation is likely to cause two problems. The first appears wherever what one state entrusts to control by competition is subjected to public regulation in another state. This may be true for a whole industry, which is in one state competitive, in another state regulated. More pervasively, it may be true of specific aspects of industries in which states rely upon a mixture of regulation and competition. All states may intend that competition between regulated enterprises shall take place with respect to matters not explicitly regulated. Yet in one state regulations may be applied only to the right to engage in the business, in another only to the characteristics of what is sold, in a third only to the price that is charged, and in a fourth to all of these matters.

So far as—in regulated fields that are relevant to international trade—there exist such diversities in the scope of regulation, an international program to prevent private restrictions must cope with these diversities in one of three ways. One possibility is to remove diversity by international agreement to rely on competition in the respects in which there are differences, regulation being abandoned by states that have undertaken it. Another possibility is to remove diversity by general resort to regulation, competition being appropriately limited by states that had relied upon it. A third possibility is to retain the diversity but to modify the regulations in an effort to make their results, so far as possible, analogous to those expected from competition.

These are hard choices. It is certainly appropriate to expect that, in an international program that eliminates private business restrictions, particular states that have used public regulation to provide comparable restrictive benefits for private groups must abandon these regulations. But most public regulations have public rather than essentially private purposes. Since a state seldom, if ever, uses these except where it wants results that competition is not expected to produce, the difference between reliance upon competition and reliance upon regulation is likely to express, in such cases, choice between different values—present abundance or conservation, flexible prices or price stability—and to leave little hope that regulation can be used for results like those of competition. Moreover, a state's choice of regulation or of competition may express appropriate priorities in its own national problems, different from those of other states. Thus a state with a scant food supply may foster unlimited competitive fishing, while one well-fed from nonmarine sources may regulate fishing to conserve its dwindling numbers of fish.

Agreement in matters of this kind cannot be expected to be quick or easy. Yet if international control is to applied within the regulated segment of the economy, numerous choices of this kind are necessary, each likely to involve technical complexities and substantive problems peculiar to a specific aspect of a specific industry.

The second problem in the regulated area appears wherever that is regulated is subject, in different states, to regulations that differ significantly in substance or method of control. Though all states fix the price of a transportation service, each may apply different standards in setting the level of the price, may reappraise the price on different grounds and with different frequency, and may use bodies differently constituted to reach decisions by different procedures. As a result of these differences, producers or consumers in some states may incur discriminatory disadvantages, and treatment of the whole interstate area as a "common market" may be impossible.

The task of an international program in coping with such situations is even more difficult than in coping with the first problem. It involves not only the possibility of conflicting goals, as in the first case, but also needs to reconcile conflicting views about when regulatory authorities should act, how they should act, and what machinery should be used for the purpose. Though agreement upon economic purposes and methods is difficult, there is likely to be equal or greater difficulty in reconciling the political and legal institutions that are relevant to due process of law, supervision of the regulatory authority, and similar matters. So far as agreement is possible, two techniques are available for giving it effect. Either an international body can issue rules that require the participating states to harmonize their domestic regulations or the regulatory task can be taken over by the international body. The first of these alternatives is likely to be less thorough but more practicable.

In spite of the inherent problems involved, certain international controls applicable to regulated industries are apparently possible where problems are urgent. The EEC has developed such controls for both transportation and agriculture, and has moved more rapidly on the latter. In 1962, it broadly exempted from its treaty provisions about restricting those activities that constituted parts of national agricultural programs.[59] After long and severe disagreements, the member states developed the broad lines of an agricultural policy that necessitated a long series of decisions applicable to particular agricultural commodities and problems. Instead of setting up one or more specialized international bodies to exercise continuous regulatory control over agriculture, the EEC has specific mandatory rules to limit, channel, and harmonize the controls applied by the member states.[60]

In view of the great difficulties that confront the international economy in coping with diversity in regulated industries, the initial target of an international program in this field should be only that part of the problem that cannot be separated from the problem of private restriction. Power should be included in this program to identify state regulations that are designed to shelter private firms from competition in industries that, in other states, are subject to the rules against restriction. Where such regulations are identified, there should be power to require that they be terminated or appropriately modified.

The task of coping with regulations that express national idiosyncrasies of purpose or method is much less urgent. A program directed against private restrictions might be desirable and practicable without undertaking it. A program including it should go no further than to state a purpose to harmonize regulatory laws and to establish means by which whatever harmonization might prove practicable could be undertaken. But since such work must be slow, other things that are less difficult should not be deferred until its completion.

Notes

1. Registration requirements focus upon domestic affairs, omitting restrictions that take effect only in other countries and perhaps those that affect only export trade. Particular kinds of restriction are not registrable in all laws that provide for registration. In the statistics of restriction for some countries, the scope of the restrictions is not ascertainable—whether local, regional, or national—or the segments of the economy in which the restrictions appear are not given. The descriptive categories by which restrictions are classified are not wholly comparable. Moreover, to an unknown extent that probably differs under different registration systems, restrictions subject to registration have not been registered. For analysis of registration requirements, see Corwin D. Edwards, *Control of Cartels and Monopolies*, Dobbs Ferry, New York, 1967, Chapter 4. For analysis of registration statistics, see Corwin D. Edwards, *Cartelization in Western Europe*, U.S. Department of State, June 1964, pp. 3-27, 98.

2. That substantial numbers of agreements appropriate for registration had not been registered was generally believed. Estimates of the proportion of registrable agreements that had been registered ranged from 80 percent to as low as 5 percent. Of the total multipartite agreements registered, 493 had been processed when the published analysis was made. The figures about the number of countries in which there were participants pertain to these 493. See ibid., p. 25.

3. Ibid., p. 26. Since agreements often include more than one type of restriction, the total of restrictions listed for the 493 agreements was nearly 1200. Information is not available about the total number of agreements that included the types of restrictions selected for discussion below.

4. Ibid., pp. 21-24. Some of these registrations may have been for the same international agreements, registered in more than one country.

5. Ibid., pp. 18-21.

6. In the aluminum case (148 F.2d 416), Judge Learned Hand formulated the rule about liability as follows: "It is settled law—as 'Limited' itself agrees—that any state may impose liabilities, even upon persons not within its allegiance, for conduct outside its borders that has consequences within its borders which the state reprehends. . . . Two situations are possible. There may be agreements made beyond our borders not intended to affect imports, which do affect them, or which affect exports. Almost any limitation of the supply of goods in Europe, for example, or in South America, may have repercussions in the United States if there is trade between the two. Yet . . . it is safe to assume that Congress certainly did not intend the Act to cover them. Such agreements may on the other hand intend to include imports into the United States, and yet it may appear that they have had no effect upon them. . . . We shall assume that the Act does not cover agreements, even though intended to affect imports or exports, unless its performance is shown actually to have had some effect upon them. Where both conditions are satisfied, the situation certainly falls within such decisions. . . Both agreements . . . were unlawful, though made abroad, if they were intended to affect imports and did effect them."

7. U.S. v. Aluminum Co. of America, 148 F.2d.416 (1945); U.S. v. National Lead Company, 63 F. Supp. 513 (1945) and 332 U.S. 319 (1947); U.S. v. General Electric Co., 80 F. Supp. 989 (1948); U.S. v. United States Alkali Export Association, 86 F. Supp. 59 (1949); U.S. v. General Electric Co., 82 F. Supp. 753 (1949) and 115 F. Supp. 835 (1953); Timken Co. v. U.S., 83 F. Supp. 284 (1949) and 341 U.S. 593 (1951); U.S. v. Imperial Chemical Industries, Ltd., 100 F. Supp. 504 (1951); U.S. v. Holophane Co., 119 F. Supp. 114 (1954) and 352 U.S. 903 (1956).

8. U.S. v. Watchmakers of Switzerland Information Center, Southern District of New York, Opinion, December 20, 1962 (Commerce Clearing House, 1963 Trade Cases, #70,600); final judgment, January 22, 1964, modified January 7, 1965 (Commerce Clearing House, 1965 Trade Cases, #71,352).

9. The answer now appear to be "yes" if the foreign firm does business in the United States via an American subsidiary. See U.S. v. Scophony Corp. of America, 333 U.S. 795 (1948).

10. See U.S. v. De Beers Consolidated Mines, Ltd., Commerce Clearing House, 1948 Trade Cases, #62,248.

11. The so-called as-is agreement in the petroleum industry, for example, consisted of a master document to which effect was given by a whole series of national and regional agreements made by different corporations in different parts of the world. The whole program was available only to those who (a) knew the ties that linked numerous corporations incorporated in numerous states and (b) had access to the entire body of interrelated agreements. See Federal Trade Commission, Report on the International Petroleum Cartel, Staff Report Submitted to the Subcommittee on Monopoly of the Select Committee on Small Business, U.S. Senate August 22, 1952.

12. See the excellent discussions in Wilbur L. Fugate, *Foreign Commerce and the Antitrust Laws*, Boston, 1958, pp. 76-85, and Kingman Brewster, *Antitrust and American Business Abroad*, New York, 1958, pp. 474-488. A subpoena can direct the recipient to produce only documents over which he has control. At first glance, this limitation appears to preclude subpoenas that direct an American company to produce documents possessed by its foreign parent; but if the parent is doing business in the United States, through the subsidiary as agent or otherwise, the parent may itself be party to the case and subjected to subpoenas that pertain to documents elsewhere.

13. See Brewster, *Antitrust*, pp. 482-88.

14. Since the other European manufacturers were not defendants in the case, orders limiting Philips' use of its European patents would have subjected it to limitations not imposed upon the other European members of the lamp cartel. See Brewster, *Antitrust*, pp. 46-48.

15. U.S. v. General Electric Co., et. al., 115 F. Supp. 835, Decree, Sections VIII and XI.

16. Economic Competition Act., Section 39. See OECD, *Guide to Legislation on Restrictive Business Practices*, Netherlands, 1.0. Both the lamp decree and the petroleum grand jury subpoena were regarded as incentives for this amendment.

17. British Nylon Spinners v. Imperial Chemical Industries, Ltd., Court of Appeal, October 15-16, 1952; Chancery Division, June 23-24, July 9, 1954. See *International Aspects of Antitrust*, Part 2, pp. 1125-1136.

18. Edwards, *Control of Cartels and Monopolies*, pp. 25-26.

19. Ibid. For EEC see pp. 281-320; for ECSC, pp. 243-279; for EFTA, pp. 240-42; for the GATT, pp. 235-40. In 1964, EFTA's procedures about restrictive business practices had not been used. Since then EFTA has indicated, in general terms and without details, that a few cases of restriction have been informally discussed, with the result that restrictions were voluntarily terminated. See *EFTA Reporter*, December 13, 1968, p. 3.

20. In Europe in the interwar period, France occasionally applied the remnants of a Napoleonic law against agreements designed to get excessive profits by artificial means; Germany, Norway, and Denmark applied laws against "abuses" by cartels; Bulgaria and Yugoslavia authorized their authorities to invalidate restrictive provisions and dissolve cartels; Rumania provided for surveillance over cartels and control of their prices; and Sweden provided for investigation of cartels but not for corrective action. Some kind of legislation intended to limit private restrictions existed and was occasionally applied in South Africa and Mexico; and laws or constitutional provisions that had become dead letters existed in several other countries. See ibid. pp. 3-5, and Corwin D. Edwards, *Trade Regulation Overseas, The National Laws*, Dobbs Ferry, New York, 1966, pp. 3-12 (France); 155-59 (Germany); 281-86 (Norway); 225-28 (Denmark); 325-27 (Sweden); 546-50 (South Africa).

21. In the late 1930s mandatory cartelization was broadly possible under the laws of Japan, Germany, Italy, the Netherlands, Belgium, Latvia, and New Zealand, and import segments of industry had been cartelized by special laws or with governmental support in France and the United Kingdom. See Edwards, *Control of Cartels and Monopolies*, pp. 5-6 and his, *Trade Regulation Overseas*, pp. 9-10 (France), 77-82 (Netherlands), 134-36 (Belgium), 157-59 (Germany), 419 (United Kingdom), 592-97 (New Zealand), 650-54 (Japan).

22. *Act Against Restraints of Competition*, Section 98(2). See OECD *Guide to Legislation on Restrictive Business Practices*, Germany, 1.0.

23. The statutory provision—Section 10(4) of the *Monopolies and Restrictive Practices (Inquiry and Control) Act of 1948*—forbids application of orders under the act "to any person in relation to his conduct outside the United Kingdom unless he is a British subject, a body corporate incorporated under the law of the United Kingdom or some part thereof, or a person carrying on business in the United Kingdom." It provides, however, that "save as aforesaid, any such order may be so made as to extend to acts or omissions outside the United Kingdom." This statute still governs important kinds of restriction but is no longer applicable to agreements that are covered by the subsequent Restrictive Trade Agreements Act. The latter statute applies to agreements containing specified types of restriction if two or more of the parties do business in the United Kingdom and two or more parties accept restrictions. Thus it appears to be applicable to an agreement made abroad by which a foreign firm restricts the amounts or prices of what it exports to the United Kingdom, provided that (a) at least one other firm, whether doing business abroad or in the United Kingdom, accepts restrictions, and (b) the parties to the agreement include two or more firms, British or foreign, who do business in the United Kingdom.

24. *Cartel Act*, as amended, Section 2. See OECD *Guide to Legislation on Restrictive Business Practices*, Austria, 1.0.

25. Section 1(1) of the Spanish *Act Against Restraints of Competition* applies to practices "whose object or whose effect is to prevent, to distort, or to

limit competition in the national market or in a part thereof." Section 2(1) of the Danish *Monopolies and Restrictive Practices Control Act* applies "within trades in which competition, throughout the country or in local market areas, is restricted. . . ." In each statute applicability depends upon effect within the country and the language neither explicitly includes nor excludes situations in which such effects arise from action taken outside the country.

26. An agreement of the exempted type must be authorized if the High Authority finds (a) that it "will contribute to a substantial improvement in production or distribution (b) that it is essential and not unnecessarily restrictive for the purpose; and (c) that it cannot give the parties power to fix prices or limit supply nor protect them from effective competition. The authorization may be limited in time and may be subjected to specified conditions; and it may be revoked or modified. See Article 65 of the Treaty, OECD *Guide to Legislation on Restrictive Business Practices* ECSC, 1.0.

27. To be eligible for exemption, an agreement must contribute "towards improving production or distribution of goods or promoting technical or economic progress, must reserve to users 'a fair share in the profit which resulted,' and must not impose any restriction not essential for these objects nor give participants power 'to eliminate competition in respect of a substantial portion of the products in question'." See Article 85 of the Treaty, OECD *Guide to Legislation on Restrictive Business Practices*, EEC 1.0.

28. EEC Council Regulation No. 17, Articles 4-7, Ibid., EEC 1.1.

29. Article 86 of the OECD Treaty.

30. For example, a series of exclusive dealing agreements between Grundig, a German producer, and distributors in EEC countries bound Grundig to sell only to these distributors and prevented each of these distributors from exporting from the country assigned to him. The agreement that involved Consten, a French distributor, resulted in a decision by the European Court that the agreements were prohibited, since they prevented other enterprises than Consten from importing Grundig products into France and prohibited Consten from reexporting these products to other member countries. See the judgment of July 13, 1966, in cases No. 56-64 and 58-64 between S.A. Consten, Grundig Verkaufs GmbH, the governments of Italy and Germany, and the EEC Commission, ibid., EEC, 3.0 no. 2. and 3.1 no. 4.

31. Edwards, *Cartelization in Western Europe*, p. 27, and his *Control of Cartels and Monopolies*, p. 322. The price agreement was registered in the United Kingdom.

32. The laws of seventeen of these countries are compared in detail in Edwards, *Control of Cartels and Monopolies*. Monographs on the laws of thirteen of them are included in Edwards, *Trade Regulation Overseas*.

33. *Act Against Restraints of Competition*, Section 22. For this and the other foreign statutes cited, see OECD, *Guide to Legislation on Restrictive Business Practices*.

34. See Hans-Heinrich Barnikel, "Abuse of Power by Dominant Firms: Application of the German Law," *Antitrust Bulletin*, spring 1969.

35. J.M. Clark, *Competition as a Dynamic Process*, pp. 485-6.

36. Under Sections 14-18 of the Restrictive Trade Practices Act, a Registrar is empowered, when agreements have not been registered, to bring persons before the High Court for examination under oath as to the existence of an agreement, subject to penalties for false evidence, and can be authorized to make the registration the basis of information that he possesses.

37. Sections 20-21 of the same act. In practice the court habitually accepts undertakings by the parties to terminate their arrangements and refrains from issuing orders. Failure to do what has been undertaken can be punished as contempt of court.

38. *Monopolies and Restrictive Practices (Inquiry and Control) Act* of 1948, Section 3.

39. Ibid., Sections 6-7; Section 10 as modified and extended by Section 3 of the *Monopolies and Mergers Act* of 1965.

40. *Economic Competition Act*, as amended, Sections 24-28. As used in this law, the term *dominant positions* covers concertedly by agreement. There is no provision for hearings by the minister. Instead, the committee hears *in camera* those who apply to be heard, until it thinks itself sufficiently informed. (Section 25.)

41. *Economic Competition Act as Amended*, Sections 2 and 49.

42. Ibid., Sections 19-23. Rules about hearings are the same as in the case of dominant positions.

43. *Price Ordinance of 1945*, as amended, Articles 59 bis and 59 ter.

44. *Decree No. 54-97* of January 27, 1954, as amended. The commission reviews reports from government investigatory officials and written comments upon these reports by interested parties. It may hear *in camera* such interested persons as it wishes. It transmits to the minister with its own report the reports and comments that it receives. See Articles 3, 7-10, 12-13 of the decree.

45. This authority consists of a directorate whose head is appointed by the King and a board consisting of part-time persons appointed by the Minister of Commerce (a majority being independent of business affected by the act), under a chairman appointed by the King. See *Monopolies and Restrictive Practices Control Act*, as amended, Sections 3-5.

46. *Monopolies and Restrictive Practices Control Act*, as amended, Sections 6 and 24.

47. Ibid., Sections 11-12.

48. *Act on Control of Prices, Profits and Restraints of Competition*, Sections 18, 24, and 42.

49. Ibid., Sections 33, 34, and 36.

50. Ibid., Sections 52, 56, and 59.

51. GATT, "Decisions of the Seventeenth Session," L/1397, December 5, 1960, p. 17.

52. European Free Trade Association, "Text of Convention and Other Documents approved at Stockholm on 20th November, 1959," Articles 15, 31. (mimeo, 906, Her Majesty's Stationery Office, London).

53. *EFTA Reporter*, December 13, 1968, p. 3.

54. Ibid., p. 3.

55. U.S. Department of State, *Havana Charter for an International Trade Organization*, March 24, 1948, pp. 35-78.

56. *Report of the Ad Hoc Committee on Restrictive Business Practices to the Economic and Social Council*, E 2380, E/AC, 37.3, March 30, 1953.

57. Council of Europe, *Memorandum on the Recommendation of the Consultative Assembly for the Preparation of a European Convention for the Control of International Cartels and Draft Convention Prepared by the Secretariat General*, SG/R (51) 15, November 28, 1951, pp. 10-42.

58. Edwards, *Cartelization in Western Europe*, pp. 29-30. See also United Kingdom Monopolies Commission, *Report on the Supply of Chemical Fertilizers*, Her Majesty's Stationery Office, London, 1959, pp. 73-77, 87-92, 134-36, 180, 188-93, 209-210, 223-24, 227.

59. Council Regulations No. 26, April 4, 1962 and No. 49, June 29, 1962.

60. See for example, *EEC Bulletin*, September-October 1968, pp. 60-61.

7

The Multinational Corporation: A New Trade Policy Issue United States

Robert G. Hawkins

Introduction

An important new issue in the commercial policy debate in many countries concerns the multinational firm (MNC). MNCs have become the most important means of transferring capital and technology across national frontiers, as production by foreign affiliates has expanded more rapidly—via both acquisitions of existing facilities and expansion and creation of new facilities—than domestic output in most nations. While foreign direct investment has long been important in the extractive and primary industries, the most rapidly growing component in the postwar period has been in manufacturing—and more specifically in the overseas activities of U.S. manufacturing firms.

Accompanied by lower tariff barriers, declining transportation costs, and improved communications and travel services, the large multinational firm has become an important vehicle for rationalizing the international structure of production. Certainly not all activities of MNCs are enhancing to world economic welfare, as such factors as different national taxation systems and monopolistic advantages may enter into the decision to invest abroad, but still the ability of the MNC to marshall more information on foreign conditions, costs, and other terms of production, and to communicate and employ that information in its production and marketing decisions efficiently and rapidly is an important source of its presumed advantages over purely national firms.

Among the results of the successful growth of MNC operations relative to world output and of their dramatic flexibility in allocating production facilities internationally has been a growing concern that a need to control and regulate MNC activities was needed. The rationale for such regulation generally lies in actual or presumed advantages of the MNC relative to strictly national firms; such as ease in raising capital, in avoiding antitrust regulations, in minimizing environmental control costs, in securing control over raw materials, and the like. In almost every case, the actual or potential advantage accruing to the MNC rests with its ability to integrate decisions with respect to financing, production locations, and international trade within one decision-making unit.

This chapter draws heavily on the author's *U.S. Multinational Investment in Manufacturing and Domestic Economic Performance* and *Job Displacement and the Multinational Firm: A Methodological Review*, both published as Occasional Papers by the Center for Multinational Studies (Washington, D.C., 1972). The revisions were financially supported by the New York University Project on the Multinational Firm in the U.S. and World Economy. Research assistance by Elizabeth Webbink and helpful comments on earlier drafts by Timothy Stanley and Ingo Walter are gratefully acknowledged.

One of the major manifestations of this ability, especially in manufacturing industries, is to allocate (at the margin) or to reallocate (inframarginally) production schedules from one country to another. As production locations shift, trade patterns almost inevitably change, and thus MNC activities become a direct issue in the trade policy debate. But also, as production locations are changed from country to country, labor is displaced at one location, new employment is created in another, and a similar impact is felt on the suppliers of the industry. Thus the *trade* policy aspect of MNCs is intimately assocated with, and often gets translated into, the issue of their freedom of action. For example, a decision to begin production of a product abroad, which has been (or could be) produced domestically, and to import it back to the domestic market, might be thwarted with prohibitive barriers on the import goods or by controls over the initial foreign investment. The emergence of the MNC as an important force in the international economy, both as a transferer of capital and knowhow, and as an international trader, has added an additional dimension in the formation of trade policy positions.

This has, no doubt, been most dramatically true in the U.S. As indicated in Chapter 2, the growing importance of the MNC in manufacturing has further clouded the traditional lines between protectionist groups and liberal traders. In the past, it could usually be expected that both management and labor in a particular firm would unite on international trade matters. In import competing activities, management, labor, and supplier firms would tend to be protectionist, while firms and employees in export-oriented activities would tend toward a liberal trade position. With a multinational firm, however, it is not uncommon for the corporate management to be liberal traders and the production workers to be generally protectionist. There are, of course, important variations in patterns among the divisions of many firms. For example, a firm which manufactures components in a foreign affiliate—and retains some domestic production in similar lines—for import, assemblage, and sale in the U.S. may indeed be schizophrenic. The division managers and labor force capable of producing the components will likely favor both protection from imports and restrictions on new investments abroad. On the other hand, the managers and workers in the assembly and marketing operations for the final product will tend to be liberal-trade oriented. Each position is consistent with self-interest, as the former seek to preserve their jobs and parts of the company while the latter seek to ensure the competitive viability of their parts of the firm by keeping the cost of material inputs to a minimum.

As the capabilities for foreign production by American MNCs has expanded in the 1960s, especially in low-wage countries such as Taiwan, Singapore, and Mexico, the opposition of organized labor to foreign investment has strength-ened. It was evidenced first in the specific unions most directly affected by "foreign sourcing" by MNCs of components for assemblage in the U.S., for example the International Electrical Workers. But by 1971, the parent organizations of the union movement were swinging toward a protectionist position in general, with an anti-MNC rhetoric in particular. This culminated in 1972 in the AFL-CIO-supported Burke-Hartke bill, which would have not only authorized *general* import quotas, but also would have provided authority to restrict foreign investment by U.S. firms and the transfer of technology abroad.

Labor's concern over foreign investment is twofold. One is the more traditional protectionist concern about the displacement of American jobs by imports. To the extent that foreign direct investment adds to the capability for exporting back to the U.S. items which could be produced locally, it is contributing to the loss of U.S. jobs and should, for the worker's short-run interest, be prohibited. This could be done by restrictions on the imported products, or by restricting the initial foreign investment, or preferably by both.

The second concern is more recent and pervasive. It is that foreign production by MNCs sold in the local market or exported to third countries are substituting for American exports and thus also involve a loss of American jobs. In this case, however, the remedy cannot rest with U.S. commercial policy as traditionally defined, because tariffs or quotas will not protect the jobs. Rather, the remedy must lie in restricting the firm's activities in investing and producing abroad, and this can be done only through restriction of foreign investment, tax-disincentives for foreign production or foreign income, and other such measures not usually associated with trade policy.

While the distinction between the results of import competition in the local market and that due to substitution for exports by foreign production is useful analytically, the practical results are the same. Both involve an adjustment to a new international equilibrium in which, assuming exchange rates to be in equilibrium also, low productivity activities are phased out and resources are transferred to those in which there is a competitive advantage. This process occurs both within and without multinational firms, although there is a fair indication that MNCs may bring about the changes—giving rise to the need for adjustment—much more rapidly than other firms.

The debate has thus recently become focused on whether the foreign operations of multinational corporations (MNCs), on balance, displace American jobs or actually create jobs. Sometimes using the same data, different analysts have arrived at very different conclusions. This is, at least at the margin, an important question since worker dislocation and reabsorption represents the principal component of the cost of adjustment under any trade policy change. Assessing the costs of adjustment relative to the long-term benefits is the job of rational policy making.

This chapter attempts to assess the adjustment burden in the U.S. labor force from expanding operations of MNCs. It also seeks to identify the nature of the assumptions used to construct estimates of the domestic employment effects of multinational firms' foreign operations. It will examine the sensitivity of the estimates to the assumptions and present the net result of a set of "reasonable" but subjective and arbitrary assumptions.

The direct effects of foreign investment on U.S. employment, or jobs, can be classified this way:

1. The U.S. employment which would have occurred in the U.S. if the production of foreign affiliates could have been carried out in the United States. This, in turn, can be subclassified into employment associated with foreign affiliate production sold in foreign markets which otherwise could have been served by exports from the U.S., and employment associated with foreign affiliate output imported back into the American market and which could have been produced domestically.
2. U.S. employment created by the production of exports that would not have occurred in the absence of foreign subsidiaries. This also can be subclassified into employment associated with capital goods exports when a foreign operation is established, and employment created due to the marketing, service, and complementary product advantages that export sales from the United States receive as a result of the "local presence" of the foreign affiliate.
3. Nonproduction employment created in the American parent firm of a managerial, clerical, or service nature which arises solely because a part of the firms' operations are carried out abroad. This might be extended to cover U.S. management and other personnel who reside in the foreign countries, as they are "American" jobs even though performed abroad.
4. Employment created in the United States external to the MNC itself but involving performance of services for the MNC directly associated with the foreign nature of its operations—including legal and public relations services, management, engineering and financial consulting, and other supporting activities.

For simplicity, the employment effect described in the first category will be referred to as the "production displacement" effect, while the second type will be called the "export stimulus" effect. The third and fourth categories will be referred to, respectively, as the "home office" and "supporting firm" employment effects.

Implicit in the foregoing taxonomy is the fact that the study is confined to estimations of the *direct* effects of MNCs on U.S. employment. It does not consider the indirect effects of foreign investment on jobs, which might arise due to variation in the overall rate of economic growth, the substitution of capital for labor, and other such factors that may be indirectly affected by MNC operations. This omission would not seem to represent a major shortcoming, since most of the attributable "employment" effects would probably occur directly. Furthermore, the influence of government policies are likely to cloud the impact of MNCs on rates of growth and substitution of productive factors, especially since foreign direct investment is a small portion of total capital spending by American business.

The study is also limited to "manufacturing" industries. Foreign investment by firms in these industries are the most relevant cases involving the alleged "displacement" of American workers. Foreign investment in petroleum and other natural resource-based industries, and in the service industries, is fundamentally different in nature, often dictated by geographic and supply factors.

Finally, in calculating their effect on domestic employment, MNCs are treated here as identical with total U.S. foreign direct investment in manufacturing, regardless of the size or nature of the investing firm. This is required by the fact that aggregate data is used and no distinction can be made between truly "multinational" firms and "national" firms with limited direct foreign investment.

It should be expected that the occupational coverage of the different effects identified here will vary substantially. The production-displacement effect and the export-stimulus effects will fall predominantly on production workers, most heavily in the semiskilled and skilled occupational classes, although the impact will vary greatly by industry. On the other hand, the home-office and supporting-firm effects will involve jobs primarily in the managerial, clerical, and professional occupations. These differences in skill and occupation mix between the jobs displaced and those created as a result of MNC expansion do, of course, reflect the role of the multinational enterprise as a vehicle for structural change in U.S. production and employment. It dramatizes the nature of the adjustment process and the related costs of foreign investment to the national economy.

The following section approaches the issue by examining historical trends in foreign investment by United States firms and its relationship, or lack thereof, to corresponding historical trends in employment patterns, by manufacturing industry. The remainder of the chapter presents an assessment of the probable direction and magnitude of the employment effects outlined above.

Intensity of Foreign Investment and Disruption of the National Market

As an indication of whether domestic production displaced by MNCs is common or rare, various measures of growth for U.S. industries have been compared with the intensity of foreign direct investments in those industries. If new foreign production by U.S. firms has created a significant burden on the American economy, distinct from the adjustment and unemployment burdens imposed by other structural changes and cyclical factors, and from the deterioration of the overall U.S. competitive position before the adjustment of currency parities, the following should be found:

1. The deterioration in the trade balance for "high" foreign investment industries should be greater than for "low" foreign investment industries.

2. The growth in employment for "high" foreign investment industries should be lower than for "low" foreign investment industries.
3. The proportion of U.S. production exported should be low and falling in "high" foreign investment industries and the ratio of imports to domestic production should be high and rising.

Trade Balance and Foreign Investment

The export-import balance of the manufacturing sector deteriorated substantially in the 1960s, as did the trade balance in general. From an average surplus of $5.4 billion in 1963-64, it fell to a surplus of only $3.2 billion (excluding petroleum) in 1969-70. Individual industry balances are shown in Table 7-1. The industries have been rather arbitrarily divided between "high" and "low" foreign investment categories.

Industries which were higher than the average for all manufacturing, on the basis of the ratio, or change in the ratio, of production by U.S. foreign affiliates to domestic shipments, were called "high" foreign investment industries.[2] Based on the division into categories described above, it will be noted that the "high" foreign investment industries have had, in most cases, large surpluses. Paper and primary metals are the exceptions in this group, having shown consistent trade deficits.

Between the two periods (1963-64 and 1969-70), transport equipment experienced a dramatic decline in its trade balance of $2.5 billion. The U.S.-Canadian Automotive Agreement of 1965 accounted for a good part of this drop (about $1.3 billion between the years covered here), and the rest is explained by the rapid rise of Japanese and European car imports, neither of which reflected the influences of American foreign investment.[3] Less dramatic slippage among the "high" foreign investment industries occurred in electrical equipment and rubber products. Overall, the deterioration of the trade balance was $2.0 billion between 1963-64 and 1969-70, or $664 million when Canadian-U.S. trade in automotive products is removed. This is a modest downturn, most of which clearly resulted from forces other than foreign investment.

The "low" foreign investment industries have generally tended to record trade deficits. In half of these industries, the deficits rose in the period, while negligible changes occurred in two others. Significant improvements occurred in instruments, food products, and fabricated metals. Overall, then, the high foreign investment industries remain the net surplus industries, although those surpluses declined in the late 1960s. This falling off is mainly attributable to competitive and inflationary influences on U.S. trade, and to the special effect of U.S.-Canadian automotive trade.

Table 7-1

Trade-Balance Position—Exports Minus Imports, High vs. Low Foreign Investment Industries (Millions of Dollars)

| | Exports minus Imports | | |
High Foreign Investment Industries	Average 1963-64	Average 1969-70	Change
Chemicals	1,901	2,593	692
Machinery, Except Electrical	3,572	5,052	1,480
Electrical Equipment	891	414	−477
Transport Equipment	499	−2,021	−2,520
Paper and Paper Products	−660	−558	102
Primary Metal Products	−666	−1,567	−901
Rubber Products	89	−248	−337
Totals for High Foreign Investment Industries	5,626	3,665	−1,961
Totals Excluding Canadian-U.S. Automotive Trade	5,004	4,340	− 664
Low Foreign Investment Industries			
Instruments and Related Products	367	606	239
Food Products	99	959	860
Stone, Clay, and Glass Products	8	−103	−111
Fabricated Metal Products	398	604	206
Textile Mill Products	−433	−575	−142
Leather and Leather Products	−137	−587	−450
Furniture and Fixtures	−4	−185	−181
Printing and Publishing	124	171	47
Apparel and Related Products	−263	−971	−708
Lumber and Wood Products	−428	−425	3
Totals for Low Foreign Investment Industries	−269	−506	−237

Source: *U.S. Commodity Exports and Imports as Related to Output* (various issues), U.S. Department of Commerce.

Competitiveness and Foreign Investment

Two other sets of trade measures are shown in Table 7-2. These are the ratios of imports to domestic shipments and of exports to domestic shipments in 1963-64 and 1969-70, and the changes in those ratios between the two periods. Substantial change in these ratios over time would indicate major structural shifts in the domestic economy, or major shifts in the international competitive positions of certain industries. If foreign investment were a major adverse influence on the international competitive position, one would expect the high

Table 7-2

Various Employment and Trade Measures by Major Manufacturing Industry

SIC Industry	Absolute Change in Trade Balance 1963-64/1969-70 (Millions of Dollars) (1)	Imports/U.S. Shipments		
		% 1963-64 Ave. (2)	% 1969-70 Ave. (3)	Change (4)
Total Manufacturing	747	2.7	5.0	2.3
20 Food Products	−860	2.9	3.5	0.6
21 Tobacco Manufactures	38	0.1	0.3	0.2
22 Textile Mill Products	−142	4.6	4.3	−0.3
23 Apparel and Related Products	−708	2.5	5.1	2.6
24 Lumber and Wood Products	3	7.1	8.0	0.9
25 Furniture and Fixtures	−181	0.6	2.6	2.0
26 Paper and Allied Products	102	6.8	6.4	0.4
27 Printing and Publishing	47	0.4	0.6	0.2
28 Chemical and Allied Products	692	1.5	2.4	0.9
30 Rubber and Rubber Products	−337	1.5	3.3	1.8
31 Leather and Leather Prod.	−450	4.6	12.1	7.5
32 Stone, Clay, and Glass Prod.	−111	2.1	3.1	1.0
33 Primary Metal Products	−901	4.6	6.9	2.3
34 Fabricated Metal Products	206	0.9	1.9	1.0
35 Machinery, except Electrical	1480	2.0	4.0	2.0
36 Electrical Equipment	−477	1.8	5.0	3.2
37 Transport Equipment	−1522	1.5	7.8	6.3
38 Instruments and Related Prod.	239	3.9	5.4	1.5
39 Miscellaneous Manufactures	−413	6.7	11.5	4.8

Sources: Column 1–*U.S. Commodity Exports and Imports as Related to Output* (various issues), U.S. Department of Commerce; data for 1969-70 were obtained from prepublication worksheets, Department of Commerce.

investment intensity industries to have falling ratios of exports to domestic sales and rising ratios of imports to domestic sales.

Table 7-2 indicates that both the export-domestic sales and import-domestic sales ratios rose slightly between the two periods. For manufacturing as a whole, the former rose by 1.2 percent and the latter by 2.3 percent. There was, thus, a small increase in the "openness" of the U.S. economy, occurring on both the export and import sides.

More striking is the fact that the changes in the individual industry ratios were clustered in a fairly narrow range. The ratio of exports to domestic sales rose in fifteen of the nineteen industries, and three of the four which showed decreases were relatively low foreign investment industries. Also, the ratio of imports to domestic sales rose in all but one industry.

| | Exports/U.S. Shipments | | Annual % Growth in U.S. Shipments | Annual % Growth in Employment |
% 1963-64 Ave. (5)	% 1969-70 Ave. (6)	Change (7)	1963-64/1969-70 (8)	1963-64/1969-70 (9)
4.3	5.5	1.2	5.6	2.2
2.8	2.5	−0.3	5.1	−0.2
2.7	3.4	0.7	2.0	−1.3
2.0	1.9	−0.1	6.2	2.0
1.0	1.0	0.0	5.3	0.0
2.6	4.8	2.2	5.9	−0.3
0.6	0.6	0.0	6.8	2.4
3.3	4.1	0.8	6.5	1.8
1.2	1.3	0.1	7.4	2.7
7.3	7.7	0.4	6.7	2.8
2.5	1.9	−0.6	11.2	4.8
1.4	1.2	−0.2	3.8	−0.7
2.0	2.5	0.5	5.0	0.7
2.9	4.0	1.1	6.2	1.8
2.6	3.4	0.8	8.6	3.6
12.9	13.1	0.2	9.3	3.7
4.8	5.9	1.1	8.1	3.8
5.1	8.5	3.4	5.2	1.9
9.7	10.6	0.9	10.6	4.8
3.6	5.1	1.5	6.4	1.8

Columns 2-7—Trade data from same source as column 1; domestic shipments are from *Annual Census of Manufactures* (various issues), Department of Commerce.
Columns 8-9—*Annual Census of Manufactures* (various issues).

When the industries were divided, as above, into "high" and "low" foreign investment categories, there were only slight differences between the groups in the observed changes between the two periods. The ratios of both exports and imports to domestic sales rose for the high foreign investment industries, the former by 1.4 percent, and the latter by 2.8 percent. (When the influence of the Canadian-U.S. Automotive Agreement is removed from import sales, the change in the ratio is 2.4 percent.) For the low foreign investment industries, the export-domestic sales ratio rose by only 0.3 percent, while the import-domestic sales ratio rose by 1.0 percent. This suggests that the high investment industries are also the more dynamic trading industries. Such small differences in the relative size of these changes do not indicate major structural shifts resulting from the operations of foreign affiliates of MNCs. While changes in the competitive position of U.S. production were certainly apparent in this period, the evidence suggests that foreign production by U.S. firms was not one of the significant influences.

Domestic Employment and Foreign Investment

The ultimate test of whether foreign investment has had major disruptive effects domestically depends on the rate of change in domestic jobs and production. The final two columns of Table 7-2 contain the average annual growth rates of domestic shipments (at current prices) and numbers of employees, by industry, over the six-year period 1963-64 to 1969-70. This was an era of sustained high levels of new foreign investment following the surge of the early 1960s. On the other hand, the period was one of uninterrupted cyclical expansion of the economy, during which cyclically unstable industries would have been expected to expand employment and output at an above average rate. This does not appear to be a significant problem here, however, as some of the more cyclically-variable industries can be found in both the "high" and the "low" foreign investment categories.

Taking employment as the most relevant variable, the annual rate of expansion in all manufacturing over the period was 2.2 percent per year. Dividing the industries into the "high" and "low" foreign investment groups, the average growth rates were 4.7 percent per year for the "high" and 1.3 percent for the "low" foreign investment industries. At the broad industry level, then, there is no indication of dramatically heavy "adjustment" burdens from foreign investments at the aggregate level. The rate of expansion of manufacturing sales and employment in the United States has been rapid enough to absorb any potential or actual displacement due to rising levels of external production by MNCs. This evidence indicates that the heavy foreign investment industries are increasing in size *in the United States* faster than those industries which are less involved with foreign investment.

*Relationships between Foreign Investment
and Measures of Domestic Performance*

A slightly more rigorous means of examining the evidence in Table 7-2 is to compare the rankings of industries according to their intensities of foreign investment with their rankings according to the other variables under discussion. This serves as a check on the generalizations made above and alleviates the problem of arbitrarily dividing the industries into only two groups.

Correlation coefficients were calculated between the rank of an industry on the basis of the intensity of the foreign investment and its rank with respect to:

(a) the growth rate of domestic employment, (b) the growth rate of domestic sales, (c) the change in the trade balance, (d) the change in the import/sales ratio, and (e) the change in the export/sales ratio.

Two separate sets of rank correlation coefficients were calculated from the data in the table: one covers the entire nineteen manufacturing industries while the other excludes tobacco manufacturers and transport equipment. These exclusions were made on the basis that the foreign investment intensity rank for tobacco was misleading and that the U.S.-Canadian Automotive Agreement and surge of car imports from abroad made the transport equipment industry a special case which would tend to distort the results.

The coefficients are shown in Table 7-3. The Spearman rank correlation coefficient may vary from +1 to −1. A coefficient of +1 indicates that the ranks by industry on the two variables are identical, while a −1 indicates a complete reversal of ranks. A value of 0 would indicate complete absence of correlation among the ranks.

The results indicate that all of the measures are *positively* related to the intensity of foreign investment by industry. The coefficient for the growth in employment is statistically significant and positive, regardless of which industry coverage is used; this indicates that, on the average, industries with more intense foreign investment have experienced faster domestic employment growth and vice versa. The same is true of growth in domestic sales, although because of slow growth in tobacco sales in the late 1960s, the coefficient covering all industries is low and not statistically significant.

One might expect the high foreign investment industries to show a tendency for the trade balance to move adversely. Nevertheless, when the industries are treated individually as here, there is a fairly high and significant correlation between the intensity of foreign investment and positive (or smaller negative)

Table 7-3
Spearman Coefficients of Rank Correlation: "Intensity of Foreign Investment" and Domestic Performance Indicators

	All 19 Manufacturing Industries[a]	Omitting Tobacco Manufactures & Transport Equipment
Domestic Employment Growth Rate	.19	.47
Domestic Shipments Growth Rate	.09	.41
Absolute Change in Exports minus Imports	.28	.27
Change in the Imports/Sales Ratio	.11	.10
Change in the Exports/Sales Ratio	.23	.12

[a]Excluding petroleum manufactures and ordinance.
Data: Table 7-2.

changes in the trade balance. Thus the higher the foreign investment intensity, the more likely it will be accompanied by an improvement in the trade balance, and vice versa.

Aside from the export-sales ratio when all nineteen industries were included, the coefficients for changes in the ratios of trade to domestic sales show a positive but low correlation. Indeed, the coefficients are so close to zero that they reveal no statistical significance. There is no systematically observable relationship between intensity of foreign investment and changes in the ratio of imports or exports to sales, unless tobacco manufactures and transport equipment are retained.

Employment Growth at a Less Aggregate Level

One of the shortcomings of the above analysis is that it must be carried out at the high level of aggregation of the SIC two-digit industry. This limitation could conceal substantial dislocations within the industry groups. For example, a broad industry such as electrical equipment could grow rapidly, while large subindustries within it were declining as a result of growing foreign operations of MNCs.

To diminish this possibility, and to discover whether there are sizable intra-industry differences, growth rates of employment over the past decade were calculated at the three-digit-industry level for those industries deemed to be most intensive in foreign operations. The results are given in Table 7-4. While the period covered is relatively long and might conceal the fact that adjustment has actually been successfully completed within the period, any substantial dislocations which might arise as major segments of U.S. industries are transferred abroad should be visible. This trend would show up as a decline in employment in an industry and is the major adjustment burden which this study seeks to uncover.

But among these thirty-nine sub-industries which contain the heaviest foreign investment in manufacturing, only three had an absolute decline in U.S. employment in the past decade. And two of these appear to result more from technological change (gum and wood chemicals and reclaimed rubber) than from new foreign operations. Only one, building paper and board mills, may have lost jobs primarily because of foreign investment.

Only twelve of the thirty-nine industries failed to achieve an annual employment growth rate of at least 1.5 percent. Again, most of these twelve low-growth cases can be attributed to technological change, to shifts in local U.S.-market factors (aircraft), or to competition from foreign firms (blast furnaces and basic steel), rather than to American foreign investment. Some, such as industrial and agricultural chemicals and household appliances, were clearly the result of a combination of MNC operations and foreign competition.

To summarize, the conclusions which emerge are that (a) employment (and domestic sales) growth seems to be higher in industries with higher levels of foreign investment; (b) the changes in the trade balance in recent years, contrary to what might be expected, tend to be more favorable—or less unfavorable—in conjunction with higher foreign investment activity by industry; and (c) shifts in the ratios of exports or imports to domestic sales are mildly but positively related to the intensity of foreign investment. The rather small adjustment burden visible in this aggregative analysis is borne out by the pattern of employment growth at the more detailed level. The adjustment cost of foreign operations appears to have been small and isolated, while the domestic economic performance of the industries which claim the major share of American MNCs in manufacturing has been well above average. Specific plants and employees will sometimes be displaced, but most often, it appears, the rapid growth of foreign operations only causes the level of domestic operations to grow more slowly, but still at a higher rate than the average level for all U.S. manufacturing.

Measuring the Direct Effects of U.S. Investment Abroad on Domestic Employment

While the analysis above is indicative of the net result of foreign direct investment and domestic operations of these and other firms, the real question of the impact on employment can be answered only by a careful examination of what would have occurred had there been no direct investment abroad. The four direct effects on U.S. employment identified at the beginning of this chapter are as follows:

	Domestic Employment Impact
Local production displacement effect (DE)	negative
Export stimulation effect (XE)	positive
Home office employment effect (HE)	positive
Supporting firm employment effect (SE)	positive
Net employment effect (NE)	(?)

Using the above notation, we thus have the following relation:

$$NE = XE + HE + SE - DE \quad , \tag{7-1}$$

and each element must be estimated. This ignores the indirect, or "second order" effects which may result from altered levels of national income due to changing aggregate domestic investment (due to foreign investment).[4]

Table 7-4
Average Growth Rates in Total Employment: High Intensity, Foreign Direct Investment Industries, 3-Digit SIC Level, 1959-60 to 1969-70 (% per year)

SIC Industry		Growth Rate in Employment	SIC Industry		Growth Rate in Employment
	Paper and Paper Products			Chemicals and Allied Products	
261	Pulpmills	0.7	281	Industrial Chemicals	0.7
262	Papermills	0.4	282	Plastic Materials & synthetics	4.0
263	Paperboard mills	1.7	283	Drugs	2.1
264	Miscellaneous	2.2	284	Soaps, Cleaners & toilet goods	2.2
265	Paperboard containers & boxes	2.0	285	Paints & Allied	1.3
266	Building Paper & board mills	−6.5	286	Gum & Wood Chem.	−2.1
			287	Agricultural Chem.	0.2
			289	Miscellaneous	5.4
	Rubber and Plastic Products, n.e.c.			Primary Metal Industries	
301	Tires and tubes	0.8	331	Blast Furnace and Basic Steel	0.4
302	Footwear	3.4	332	Iron & Steel Found.	1.7
303	Reclaimed Rubber	−3.9	333	Primary Nonferrous metals	2.9
306	Fabricated Rubber Products	1.3	334	Secondary Nonferrous metals	1.5
307	Misc. Plastic Prod.	8.7	335	N.F. Rolling & Drawing	1.3

Machinery, Except Electrical

351	Engines & Turbines	2.4
352	Farm Machinery	2.1
353	Construction Mach.	2.7
354	Metal Working Mach.	3.0
355	Special Ind. Mach.	2.4
356	General Ind. Mach.	2.4
357	Office & Computing	5.7
358	Service Ind. Mach.	4.9
359	Miscellaneous	4.9

Transportation Equipment

371	Motor Vehc. & Equip.	2.0
372	Aircraft Parts	1.1
373	Shipbuilding	2.7
374	Railroad Equip.	2.7
375	Motorcycles, Bicycles & Parts	4.6
379	Miscellaneous	11.4

336	N.F. Foundaries	2.7
339	Miscellaneous	3.3

Electrical Equipment

361	Electric Test. & Distributing Equip.	2.0
362	Electric Ind. App.	2.3
363	Household Appl.	1.5
364	Electric Lighting & Wiring Equip.	2.3
365	Radio & TV Rec.	5.0
366	Communication Equip.	8.2
367	Elec. Comp. & Access.	4.9
369	Miscellaneous	3.0

Data: U.S. Department of Commerce, *Census of Manufactures*, various issues.

The Production-Displacement Effect (DE)

Two steps are required in estimating the impact on domestic employment of foreign direct investment that displaces U.S. output.[5] First, the volume of production displaced must be estimated. Second, the relationship between that volume of production and the number of workers required to produce it (labor input) must be estimated. The combination of the two factors provides a "job equivalent" estimate. That is,

$$DE = FQ\,(\,\alpha\,)\,(\,\ell\,)$$

where FQ is the volume of U.S. production abroad, α is the proportion of that output which could have been produced in the U.S. with retention of the market; and ℓ is the labor-output coefficient in the U.S. industries where labor is displaced.

This formulation presumes that the appropriate labor-output ratio is known. In applying such a ratio to the estimated foreign production displacive of U.S. output $(FQ\alpha)$, it is further assumed that the production techniques (at least labor productivity) in the foreign affiliate is similar to that in the U.S. parent firm. These assumptions are not really subject to verification with aggregate data, but it is hoped that the margin of error is sufficiently small to obtain rough orders of magnitude.

The estimation of the proportion of production by foreign affiliates which actually displaces U.S. output (α) is subject to even greater difficulties. Various alternatives are dealt with in a subsequent section.

The Export Stimulus Effect (XE)

This is the number of U.S. jobs generated in the production of U.S. exports which would not have occurred without the presence of foreign affiliates of U.S. firms and the foreign investment. These stimuli involve such things as: (a) capital goods exports to establish foreign production facilities; (b) raw materials and spare parts used in the production process and maintenance of such foreign affiliates; (c) exports of goods, produced in the U.S., complementary with goods produced and sold abroad by affiliates of U.S. firms; and (d) exports from the U.S. generated as a result of marketing and service personnel abroad whose presence is primarily connected with the foreign affiliate.

In attempting quantitative estimates of these magnitudes, the relationship may be formulated as follows:

$$XE = XF\,(\,\beta\,)\,(\,\ell'\,), \qquad\qquad (7\text{-}2)$$

where *XF* is total U.S. exports to (and through) affiliates and β is the proportion of such exports which result from the four factors described above. *XF* is a known quantity, but β must be estimated by assumption or by statistical methods. ℓ' is the relationship between exports and labor inputs. This is often estimated on the basis of the labor-output ratio in the relevant industries which, incidentally, may be different industries from those in which the displacement of U.S. production occurs (i.e., ℓ' may be significantly different from ℓ). These coefficients, as normally estimated, suffer from the same drawbacks described above for α and ℓ.

"Home Office" and "Supporting Firm" Employment Effects (HE and SE)

The general perception is that whatever jobs are dislocated by expansion of production in foreign affiliates are overwhelmingly "production" jobs. On the other hand, jobs created in the United States are a combination of production jobs due to the "export stimulus" effect and white-collar employment as a result of the two effects considered here. The very nature of foreign operations would appear to require more American jobs than a comparable amount of production in the U.S.[a] This follows from the fact that multiple sets of national laws, labor relations, accounting practices, community relations, and similar issues in the corporate environment are encountered in the case of an MNC, while this is not required of a firm with equal output but with U.S. operations only. This foreign-related, extra employment may be internal to the MNC (*HE*) or purchased from specialized support firms (*SE*) such as international law firms, management consultants, and the like.

Techniques for estimating these magnitudes are very rudimentary, but it is likely that the U.S. employment effects are positively related to the amount of foreign production. That is,

$$HE = f_1 (FQ); \quad \frac{\partial HE}{\partial FQ} > 0,$$

$$SE = f_2 (FQ); \quad \frac{\partial SE}{\partial FQ} > 0,$$

Clearly, however, the size of the coefficient relating them will vary from firm to firm, and industry to industry. Likewise, the distribution of such employment creation as between *HE* and *SE* will vary from firm to firm, depending on the

---

[a]One implication of this is that direct production costs abroad must be sufficiently lower than those in the United States to be able to offset the implied higher overhead (per unit of worldwide production) due to staff requirements associated with foreign production.

degree of "internalization" of such support functions. As yet, no systematic analysis has been attempted on these magnitudes. A very tentative methodology for *HE* is outlined in the next section.

Range of Estimates Under Differing Assumptions

The foregoing suggests that the estimates of job creation and job dislocation due to foreign investment depend heavily on the assumed value of various parameters, or coefficients. It also depends on the base, or coverage, of the foreign operations being analyzed. This analysis assumes that the "jobs" argument is relevant mainly in manufacturing production abroad by U.S. firms, and the total foreign production (sales) of foreign manufacturing affiliates will be used as the base. Since current sales are the result of past as well as current foreign investment (portions of which may have been financed from foreign sources), foreign production of U.S. affiliates represents a broader base for assessing the "job" displacement effect than the foreign investment by U.S. firms. Total foreign sales of U.S. foreign affiliates in 1968 were $59.7 billion. This represented an equivalent of about 10 percent of output (sales) in the U.S. in manufacturing, and had increased by an average of $5.1 billion per year since 1965.[6]

Production Displacement Effect (DE)

The two parameters (coefficients) needed to estimate the gross production displacement effect—when aggregate data are used—are the proportion of the foreign production which could have, on internationally competitive terms, been carried out in the U.S. (α) and the labor-output relationship (ℓ). The soundest method for estimating an overall production displacement effect would be to utilize individual ℓ's and α's for narrowly-defined industries, and sum up these individual industry estimates. This would be preferable because the extent of actual displacement by foreign-affiliate production and the labor intensity of output clearly varies significantly from industry to industry. But such detailed estimates are beyond the scope and capacity of this initial analysis, and aggregate parameters for all manufacturing will be employed in the hope that the bias generated by using such a broad average will not be great.

With respect to the labor-output relationship (ℓ), the most appropriate method by which to calculate the U.S. "job equivalent" of foreign affiliate production which could have been performed in the United States is to determine the American labor component in the value-added of U.S. manufacturing industries (direct-labor requirements) as well as the American labor component of material inputs from other industries (indirect-labor requirements). This combined figure could then be applied to the volume of sales by foreign affiliates which could have been produced in the United States (αFQ).

While the contribution of labor to value added is not readily available on an input-output industry basis with the industries weighted by foreign investment, there are calculations available of the labor requirements for U.S. exports and for import-competing production.[7] While these estimates of labor input requirements are weighted by exports or by import-competing production—and therefore will have different industry structures from that of the foreign production by U.S. affiliates—the latter should be more similar to export production than to import-competing production since few imports are from foreign affiliates. For this reason, the total employment-export production coefficient is shown in Table 7-5 as one alternative for the labor-output coefficient (ℓ). This value, taking into account merchandise exports only, is 63.7 workers per million dollars of output exported (or $15,700 in output per man).[b]

Another equally crude basis for establishing the labor-output relation is to use the ratio of total manufacturing employment to total product in manufacturing. This measure is also shown in Table 7-5, and the average for 1968-69 is 79.5 workers per million dollars of output in manufacturing (or $12,600 of output per worker). This measure does not take into account the indirect labor embodied in inputs from nonmanufacturing industries, nor does it reflect the structure of foreign affiliate production. It is implicitly weighted by the relative importance of industries in the United States, which may be very different from their relative importance in the production of foreign affiliates.

Thus neither of these measures are completely satisfactory as proxies for "ℓ,"

Table 7-5
Estimates of the Output-Employment Relation in Manufacturing

	Workers per Million of Output
(1) Total Labor Requirements in Manufacturing in U.S. Exports[a]	63.7
(2) Ratio of Employment to Gross Product in Manufacturing[b]	79.5

[a]Direct and Indirect Labor requirements in manufacturing output exported directly or indirectly through sales to other export industries. (C. Bowman, "Report on Employment Related to Exports," *Monthly Labor Review*, June 1969.)
[b]Calculated from "National Income and Product Accounts," in U.S. Department of Commerce, *Survey of Current Business*, June 1970 and *Census of Manufactures*, 1970.

---

[b]The main drawback to this coefficient is that the indirect labor component is actually the labor in manufacturing industries embodied in outputs which are transferred to other domestic industries which in turn undergo further processing and are eventually exported. The more appropriate indirect labor measure would be the U.S. labor embodied in material *inputs* into the manufacturing sector, the latter weighted by manufacturing exports.

but both are of a similar order of magnitude and will, as can be seen below, yield roughly comparable results. Being the readily available estimates, they are used as the basis for high and low assumptions concerning "ℓ."

The estimation of α—the proportion of foreign production which actually displaces potential output in the United States which could occur on a competitive basis—is even more problematical. Nor is there any direct evidence which allows one to infer a "reasonable" value for it.

Obviously, α may vary from 0 to 1, depending on the extent to which the foreign operations of U.S. affiliates could have been carried out in the United States on competitive terms. In Figure 7-1, the horizontal axis covers the range for α and on the vertical axis the resultant production-displacement effect (DE) is shown, based upon \$59.7 billion of total sales of foreign affiliates. Two

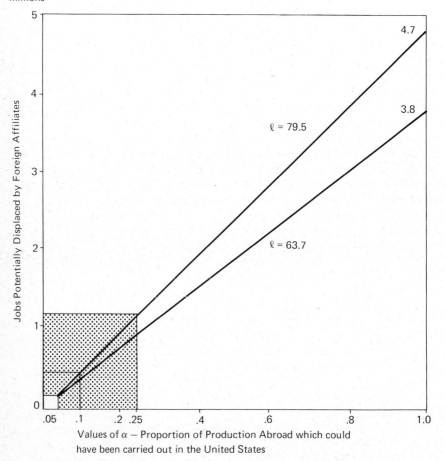

Figure 7-1. Sensitivity of Production Displacement Effect to the Value Assumed for α.

relations are plotted, each based on one of the values of ℓ (the labor-output relation) shown in Table 7-5.

The value with respect to α is more critical to the overall estimate of DE than is the value of ℓ. The maximum variation of the estimate of DE is from zero (if α is zero) to 4.7 million jobs if it is assumed that $\alpha = 1.0$ and $\ell = 79.5$. When the lower estimate for ℓ is used, the estimated production displacement effect is 3.8 million when α is 1.0.

The value which α actually takes between 0 and 1 cannot be determined precisely, but there is some evidence which suggests that it is at the lower end of the range. Case studies and questionnaire surveys of the reasons why firms invest abroad almost invariably indicate that defensive (or competitive) factors are paramount. That is, foreign operations seem to be most often established or expanded to retain market shares in the face of foreign competion.[8]

While this may be the frequent situation, some (no matter how few) decisions to invest abroad must have as the determining factor lower costs of production abroad—whether due to labor costs, material costs, taxes, or other—of an item which does not face competition from foreign firms. To the extent that this motive governs the investment, American labor is actually displaced by foreign production which could have occurred in the United States, and α must be greater than zero.

With these considerations, it seems possible to establish a realistic range within which the actual α may fall. At the lower extreme, surely 0.05 is sufficiently small to make it unlikely that the actual α is smaller. And given the evidence developed in the aforementioned studies, an outside upper limit of 0.25 would suffice. Assuming that the range of 0.05 to 0.25 is "reasonable" for α, the estimate of the "production displacement effect" on U.S. employment is from 190,000 at the low end to 1.2 million at the high end. This range is illustrated by the shaded area in Figure 7-1.

For illustrative purposes, the value of 0.1 is shown in the figure within the shaded range. But the size of the shaded area clearly indicates the extent to which employment effects depend upon the assumptions of the investigator, even when constrained by "realistic" limits suggested by other evidence.

Export Stimulus Effect (XE)

As noted in Equation 7-2 above, the jobs created due to additional export volume associated with the operations of foreign affiliates can be conveniently summarized in the relation

$$XE = XF\,(\,\beta\,)\,(\,\ell'\,).$$

The proportion of total U.S. exports to or through foreign affiliates (β) must be the product of an assumption at least as arbitrary as that associated with α above. The term ℓ' is the labor-output coefficient in those industries producing XF. Since at a highly aggregative level there is little reason to expect ℓ' (for industries producing for exports to affiliates) to be very different from ℓ (for domestic production displaced by production of foreign affiliates), the range for ℓ' is taken to be the same as that for ℓ. Thus, the high and low values used for ℓ' are those given in Table 7-5.

The limits for β again are, logically, 0 and 1. The higher the actual β, the more U.S. jobs owe their existence to the operations of foreign affiliates. The variation of jobs dependent on foreign affiliates (XE) with the possible levels of β are shown in Figure 7-2 for the two values of ℓ'.

The export base to which the range of βs is applied is \$8.7 billion. This represents about 33 percent of 1968 exports of U.S. manufactured goods. This proportion is based on data for 1966, the latest year for which sufficiently detailed data are available. United States exports which went to foreign manufacturing affiliates of U.S. firms amounted to \$7.1 billion, or 33 percent of the total exports of manufactures.[9] Most of this amount (\$6.1 billion) was exported by U.S. parents to their own affiliates, while an additional \$1.0 billion was exported by other U.S. firms. Assuming that these relationships were maintained into 1968, U.S. exports to foreign manufacturing affiliates would have been \$8.7 billion. The range of jobs dependent on the export stimulation effect is from zero, assuming that all exports would have occurred without foreign affiliates ($\beta = 0$), to 692,000 under the assumption that all exports to foreign affiliates were dependent on foreign operations ($\beta = 1$), and that the labor-output relation was 79.5.

The actual value for β within the range of 0 to 1 is difficult to estimate

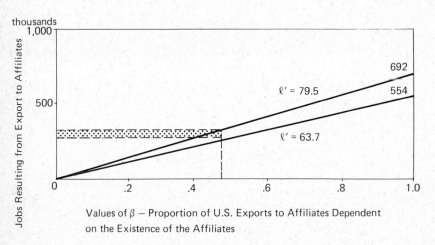

Figure 7-2. Sensitivity of Export Stimulation Effect to the Value Assumed for β.

empirically and thus must be made by arbitrary, and only partially defensible assumptions. One reason for the difficulty is the wide diversity of exports to the foreign affiliates. Some of these are clearly dependent on the affiliates' existence; others could conceivably be made directly to a foreign customer or to a foreign firm had the affiliate not been in operation. The question is ultimately one of how extensive is the competitive advantage given by the existence of foreign affiliates of U.S. firms to exports from the United States over those from foreign suppliers. Critics of multinational firms generally argue, implicitly, that the export stimulus effect is negligible (i.e., that β is close to zero).[10] Others have emphasized the interdependence of the parent's exports to affiliates and the foreign production, arguing that marketing, repair, and other services available in the foreign affiliate tend to increase sales of the parent.[11] This would imply that β is quite high.

While acknowledging that a very satisfactory method of estimating β is not feasible, a rough indication of the likely range can be attempted. This is based upon the presumption that exports to foreign manufacturing affiliates for different purposes will differ with respect to their dependence on the foreign affiliate, and in a broadly predictable manner. The categories of exports to affiliates were established in a survey of over 300 firms by the Department of Commerce in 1965.[12]

United States exports to foreign affiliates were divided into five categories: capital equipment; goods for further processing or assembly; goods for resale without further manufacture; other goods including operating supplies; and unallocated. In order to make a rough estimate of β, it is assumed that most of the exports to affiliates which were in the capital goods, other goods (operating supplies), and goods for further processing receive a distinct advantage from the existence of the foreign affiliate. Put differently, exports in these categories are presumed to be markedly higher because the affiliates were American-owned than they would have had the foreign affiliates been absent. On the other side, it is assumed that most exports of goods which were resold without further processing, and unallocated exports, could probably have been exported without the existence of the foreign affiliate. It is again acknowledged that some orders for parent company goods are probably stimulated by the affiliate, just as some capital goods exports would occur even if the subsidiary were not U.S.-owned.

For convenience, therefore, it is assumed that all exports to affiliates of the capital goods, other goods (operating supplies), and goods for further processing can be atrributed to the foreign affiliate. In the survey for 1965, exports in these categories amounted to 47 percent of total exports to the affiliates (by the parent and others). It is correspondingly assumed that all U.S. exports to affiliates in other categories would have been made even without the foreign affiliation. This amounted to 53 percent of the total U.S. exports to the surveyed affiliates.

Since there is no reason to suppose that the surveyed firms were atypical of all foreign affiliates (in manufacturing), nor that this percentage changes significantly over time, the 1965 percentage was used as a crude basis for approximating the "export stimulus" of foreign manufacturing affiliates in 1968. On this basis, the estimated β for Equation (7-2) is 0.47. The estimated flow of U.S. exports (XF) to foreign affiliates dependent on their existence is thus $4.1 billion. From Figure 7-2, it can be seen that the employment effect from the export stimulus (XE) is 325,000 for the high value of ℓ' and 260,000 for its low value.[c] The range between the two will be treated as a rough order of magnitude of the jobs dependent on the "extra" exports of the United States as a result of foreign subsidiaries in manufacturing.[13]

"Home Office" Employment Effect (HE)

The earlier estimate of the production displacement effect on employment (DE) supposes that all or a part of production by foreign affiliates could have been done in the United States, and translates that production into job-equivalents based on the United States employment-production relation. This employment concept includes both production and nonproduction workers. Yet the multinational firm does not transfer totally the management and other supportive functions to the foreign affiliate. Some of the management functions are retained in the parent, some are carried out in the host country by *Americans*, and some additional employees are needed simply because a part of the firms' operations are foreign.

Again, there is, at present, no acceptable methodology for estimating the magnitude of this "home office" effect. Raymond Vernon has suggested that 250,000 workers in American companies are dependent on the foreign operations of their firms, but his method of estimation is not outlined.[14] While the following method is highly arbitrary and must be carefully qualified, it does give an impression of the likely size of the effect.

It is assumed, first, that the ratio of non-production to production workers is the same for foreign affiliates as for U.S. production.[15] Assuming further that the ratio of non-production employment to sales is the same in the U.S. as in American affiliates abroad, the $59.7 billion of sales by foreign affiliates in 1968 would require approximately 418,000 non-production workers to support it.

Even if this figure is a realistic one, the central question in estimating HE is the share of these nonproduction jobs carried out by Americans and the share

---

[c]Calculated as follows:

$$XE = XF (\beta) (\ell')$$
$$XE = \$8.7 \text{ billion} \times 0.47 \times \ell'$$

where ℓ' is given the values of 79.5 and 63.7, respectively.

filled by local citizens or other foreigners in the host country.[d] Since no surveys exist upon which to base such a division, it is necessary to make an arbitrary but hopefully realistic assumption. For the estimates which follow, it is assumed that two-thirds of the additional nonproduction employment which results from foreign affiliate operations are manned by foreigners and one-third by Americans. That is, for each two management, clerical, or professional workers in the foreign affiliate, there is one such job in the U.S. parent. Casual observation suggests that this should not be far from the mark.

Based upon this pyramid of assumptions, the estimated "home office" employment effect (HE) is roughly 139,000 jobs.[16] It must be emphasized that this is only an indication of a probable order of magnitude of this effect.

Supporting-Firm Employment Effect (SE)

There is little question that firms and governmental agencies which supply services to multinational firms in support of their foreign operations employ a significant number of nonproduction workers, and some of these owe their jobs to foreign affiliates. The number can only be guessed, but it realistically should be much smaller than the home office effect. Robert Stobaugh has indicated that 100,000 jobs is perhaps a realistic figure.[17]

For purposes here, one-half of the home office effect, or approximately 70,000 will be used. The rationale is that, if the HE estimate is realistic, the impressionistic evidence as to the relative importance of purchased support to internalized services in a few MNCs suggests a 2 to 1 relationship. Little faith should be attached to such an estimate, however.

The Net Employment Effect and the Role of Assumptions

The estimates made above as to the magnitude of specific direct effects on U.S. jobs of foreign operations of American firms have depended, at each stage, on at least one critical assumption of a magnitude for which sufficient data for a statistical estimate is not available. Thus, although the assumptions actually made are deemed reasonable, there is no confirming evidence for most of them. This is a critical shortcoming of the illustrative set of estimates made here as well

---

[d]It is recognized that there is a slight bias in the estimate of 418,000 production workers due to the use of the ratio of nonproduction workers to domestic sales in the United States as the basis for the number of such workers connected with foreign affiliates. Some of the nonproduction workers in the United States are, in fact, those which are being estimated; i.e., owe their jobs to foreign affiliate sales rather than to production in the United States. Since U.S. production is ten times that of the foreign affiliates, this bias is negligible given the crudeness of the procedure.

as all of those studies which attempt to use aggregate data to arrive at aggregate estimates.

The estimates relating to the individual components of Equation (7-1) are brought together and summarized in Table 7-6, which also illustrates the critical role played by assumptions and combinations of assumptions in arriving at the net employment effect of American direct investments abroad. In those combinations shown in the table, the net effect may range from an addition of 240,000 U.S. jobs to a net loss of 666,000 U.S. jobs. This wide range is the result of (1) two different assumptions of the labor-output relation (ℓ and ℓ') and (2) two alternative assumptions for the proportion of foreign production which actually displaces U.S. output. The latter alternatives have already been

Table 7-6

Summary of Estimates of U.S. Employment Effects of Multinational Firms in Manufacturing under Alternative Assumptions, 1968

	DE (FQ = $59.7 billion)			XE (XF = $8.7)		HE	SE	NE
α	ℓ	Thousands of Jobs	β	ℓ'	Thousands of Jobs	Thousands of Jobs	Thousands of Jobs	Thousands of Jobs
.05	63.7	190	.47	63.7	260	139	70	+279
.05	79.5	238	.47	79.5	325	139	70	+102
.10	63.7	380	.47	63.7	260	139	70	+ 89
.10	79.5	475	.47	79.5	325	139	70	+ 59
.25	63.7	791	.47	63.7	260	139	70	−322
.25	79.5	1,200	.47	79.5	325	139	70	−666

Summary of estimating procedures and definitions:

$NE = -DE + XE + HE + SE$

$DE = FQ(\alpha)(\ell)$

$XE = XF(\beta)(\ell')$

NE = Net employment effect

DE = Production displacement effect

XE = Export stimulation effect

HE = Home office employment effect

SE = Supporting firm employment effect

FQ = Production (sales) of American foreign affiliates in manufacturing, 1968 ($59.7 billion)

XF = U.S. exports to foreign affiliates of U.S. firms, 1968 ($8.7 billion)

α = proportion of total production of foreign affiliates which could have been produced in the U.S. under world competitive conditions.

β = proportion of exports to affiliates which would not have occurred in the absence of the affiliates.

ℓ = Direct and indirect U.S. labor requirements per million of output in manufacturing carried out abroad.

ℓ' = Direct and indirect labor requirements per million of exports shipped to foreign affiliates.

constrained to a subjective "reasonable" range of 0.05 to 0.25 (for α). The extent of the range within which these "reasonable" estimates may fall is the important reason why sensible men may make contradictory statements about "employment effects"—and the preferred trade policy based on it—apparently using the same data to support them. The value within the range which lies closer to the truth cannot be known with existing information.

It is obvious from the table that the net employment effect is most sensitive to the assumption with respect to α. Thus, if one assumes that α is at or close to 0.05, the net effect ·(NE) will be positive. It would, in fact be positive, assuming the lower value for ℓ so long as α was less than 12.5. Above that level, the NE becomes negative. As noted earlier, case study and survey evidence suggest that α is very low while other lines of reasoning lead to higher values. If the actual value of α is in the 0.1 (shown in the table) to 0.15 range, as seems likely, and the estimates for the other effects are even approximately close to their true values, one may conclude that the net employment effect is quite small; that is, the jobs dependent on foreign operations approximately offset those dislocated by foreign operations. Given the nature of the estimating procedure, a low level of certainty must be attached, but within a range of 25,000 jobs net displaced or net created, the estimates fit comfortably with various combinations of assumptions. By the same token, different combinations (especially with a high value of α) will yield substantially higher net displacement estimates.

In short, unequivocal statements as to the impact of MNC operations on domestic employment must be rejected, as they are, perforce, built on concealed or open assumptions. This exercise can, at most, indicate (a) that the net result based on reasonable assumptions is not "large" relative to other labor-force magnitudes and adjustments, and that this result may be either positive or negative; and (b) that a not unlikely result is an approximate offset of job dependency against job displacement.

The Adjustment Problem and MNC Operations

While attempts to estimate the total jobs owing their existence to foreign operations and comparing them with employment displaced by foreign production may be useful in establishing rough orders of magnitude, they run the risk of focusing attention on inappropriate issues. The more important trade and investment policy issue involves the economic costs and benefits of such foreign operations to the U.S. economy. The "net job effect" is only one of a number of components in such a calculation.

Some foreign direct investment by MNCs displace particular workers in particular firms in specific industries,[18] but in most instances it is also true that such investment improves the allocation of the world's resources and represents a long-run benefit for the United States. That a flexible economy is able to concentrate its resources—capital, labor and managerial skills—in those pursuits which it can do relatively better inside the United States is an important component in the dynamic adjustment process. American real output and income tend to rise as a result of foreign investment, by permitting American labor to switch to higher paying and higher productivity occupations, by providing lower cost imports and by allowing higher returns on capital through repatriated earnings than would otherwise be the case. Quantitative estimates of these benefits from foreign direct investment have been conspicuously absent. Against these (uncalculated) benefits must be set the economic costs of reallocating labor and capital to other lines of endeavor, plus the output lost through their idleness due to a sluggish reallocation mechanism, which results from the transfer of MNC operations abroad. The short-run costs should be more than balanced by the long-run gains, and if not, a policy change should be made.

The central question is how burdensome are the real economic adjustments necessitated by changing MNC operations? On an annual basis, are they large compared to the benefits from the foreign investment which may accrue in the long run? Are they small compared to other adjustments constantly going on in the economy for other reasons? These are questions which cannot be answered unequivocally.

The above analysis and estimates of job displacement and creation do not represent a valid assessment of the current adjustments required as a result of foreign investment outflows; that is, of current foreign investment decisions. A worker can be "displaced" only once, for a given foreign investment, and to calculate—as above—the U.S. job equivalent of *all* current foreign production and then call it "displacement" is not valid. This output is the result of past foreign investments, and the point in time when the workers were initially displaced extends back over a number of years. The group of U.S. workers which might be displaced currently are those who would have been employed had the production of foreign affiliates not increased.

Assuming initially, that the entire increase in foreign affiliate production in a given year ($6.5 billion in 1968) gives rise to domestic economic adjustment, and that the same proportions applied earlier for average behavior also apply at the margin, an estimate of the annual new reallocation of labor can be made. This initial estimate excludes the adjustment which would have occurred anyway as a result of the loss of foreign sales by U.S. firms due to competitive forces operating in international markets. It seeks to estimate only the number of jobs displaced by new foreign production which could have been carried out competitively in the United States. Since alternatives for the value of α applied earlier to total foreign production of affiliates are not available to reflect the marginal relationship, nor the relationship between the changes in foreign production and changes in U.S. employment, the earlier average relationship will be applied here.

The appropriate concept for the maximum "reallocation affect" is the production displacement effect (*DE*) used earlier and not the net employment effect. Workers displaced must be retrained and reallocated regardless of whether foreign operations of the same firms create an equal or larger number of new jobs.

Using this method,[e] the new reallocation burden from the growth in foreign operations which could have, competitively, been retained in the United States, ranges from 20,000 workers to 121,000 workers. This is based on the increase in manufacturing production of foreign affiliates in 1968 ($6.5 billion), and a low combination of assumptions (α = 0.05 and ℓ = 63.7) and a high combination of assumptions (α = 0.25 and ℓ = 79.5). The more realistic mid-range (α = 0.1 to 0.15) yields approximately 40,000 to 60,000 for the high and low estimates of ℓ.

This estimate of the range within which the gross new dislocation of U.S. labor by the expansion of foreign affiliates is comparatively small (about 8 percent) in relation to the 1.5-2 million annual expansion in the U.S. labor force, or in relation to the recent unemployment level (5 million).

These labor displacement figures constitute an adjustment burden only if domestic U.S. demand fails to expand sufficiently to absorb a number of additional workers at least equal to the number nominally being released by the increased foreign output. The first part of this chapter presented considerable evidence that U.S. production has increased, on average, rapidly enough in the industries which are intensive in foreign affiliate operations to more than compensate for the workers nominally displaced by expansion of foreign production. Thus even the relatively small estimate of gross displacement may give a magnified impression of the actual adjustment burden. When absolute and identifiable displacement occurs it is of course concentrated in particular geographic areas and in particular unions associated with the production being displaced. The reallocation of these workers should be facilitated by improved adjustment assistance and advanced corporate and government manpower planning. The presumption that the reallocation burden should—or can—be avoided by restricting the foreign investment in the first place fails to take explicitly into account the long-term benefit to the economy of such investments.

Yet those who seek to make a trade and investment policy issue out of foreign production by U.S. firms implicitly ignore the potential benefits to other groups in the economy. This is characteristic of the strategy of interest groups involved in trade policy determination. The expansion of foreign production by MNCs has complicated the traditional alliances, and has, it appears, contributed to a back-lash against the trade liberalization of the earlier post-war period.

---

[e]In terms of the earlier equations: $\Delta DE = \Delta FQ\ (\alpha)\ (\ell)$. The calculations use earlier limits for α (0.1 and 0.25) and ℓ (63.7 and 79.5). ΔFQ is taken, for illustrative purposes, to be equal to the $6.5 billion in production of foreign affiliates in 1968.

Notes

1. Business International, *First Report on the Business International International Investment and Trade Study*. (New York: Business International, 1972); Emergency Committee for American Trade, *The Role of the Multinational Corporation in the United States and World Economies*, volumes 1 and 2. Washington, D.C.: ECAT, February 1972); National Association of Manufactures, *U.S. Stake in World Trade and Investment* (New York: National Association of Manufacturers, 1971); National Foreign Trade Council, *The Impact of U.S. Foreign Direct Investment on U.S. Employment and Trade* (New York: National Foreign Trade Council, Inc., November 1971); Stanley Ruttenberg, *Needed: A Constructive Foreign Trade Policy* (Washington, D.C.: AFL-CIO, October 1971); Robert Stobaugh and Associates, "U.S. Multinational Enterprises and the U.S. Economy." (Harvard Business School), 1971 (mimeo.); and U.S. Chamber of Commerce, *Multinational Enterprises Survey* (Washington, D.C.: U.S. Chamber of Commerce, February 1972). The wide range of these estimates stems from differences in the methods of calculation used by the researchers. They employ different assumptions, explicitly or implicitly, in making the calculations.

2. See Robert G. Hawkins, *U.S. Multinational Investment in Manufacturing and Domestic Economic Performance*, Center for Multinational Studies Occasional Paper No. 1 (Washington, D.C. 1972) Appendix Table 1.

3. Only 10 percent of U.S. auto imports in 1970 were from foreign affiliates of U.S. firms. See testimony of N.R. Danielian in U.S. Senate Committee on Finance, *Foreign Trade: Hearings Before the Subcomittee on International Trade*, May 17, 1971, p. 160.

4. In short, the matter of whether foreign investment actually lowers domestic investment, or leaves it unchanged, is bypassed. For an extended discussion of this problem in foreign investment, see G. Hufbauer and M. Adler, *Overseas Manufacturing Investment and the Balance of Payments* (U.S. Treasury Department, 1968), pp. 3-7.

5. For an evaluation of possible alternative estimating techniques, see Hawkins, *Job Displacement and the Multinational Firm: A Methodological Review*, Center for Multinational Studies Occasional Paper No. 3 (Washington D.C., 1972).

6. These data are from official Department of Commerce sources. For more detail on the growth and structure of foreign production of U.S. affiliates, see R. Hawkins, *U.S. Multinational Investment in Manufacturing and Domestic Economic Performance*.

7. See Charles Bowman, "Report on Employment Related to Exports," *Monthly Labor Review*, June 1969, pp. 16-20. See also, the testimony of Secretary Theodore Schultz in *Tariff and Trade Proposals*, Hearings before the House Ways and Means Committee (May 12-13, 1970), pp. 608-13.

8. See for example Stobaugh's "U.S. Multinational Enterprises," especially pp. 26-30; and *Business International, first report*.

9. Data are from the U.S. Commerce Department's 1966 Census, reported in Part 3: *U.S. Direct Investment Abroad, 1966: Manufacturing*.

10. For example, see Nat Goldfinger, "A Labor View of Foreign Investment and Trade Issues," in *United States International Economic Policy in an Independent World, Papers I* (President's Commission on International Trade and Investment), p. 924.

11. See Polk, et. al., *U.S. Production Abroad and the Balance of Payments*. (Conference Board, 1966) esp. pp. 112-114.

12. See *Survey of Current Business*, May 1969, pp. 34-49.

13. The low value (260,000) is surprisingly close to R.B. Stobaugh's estimate of 250,000 which was arrived at independently and evidently by a very different methodology. (See Stobaugh, "Multinational Enterprises," p. 31.)

14. Raymond Vernon, "A Skeptic Looks at the Balance of Payments," *Foreign Policy* (Winter 1971-72), pp. 63-64.

15. Calculations are based on data in the U.S. Department of Commerce, *Annual Survey of Manufacturers* (1969) and *Survey of Current Business*, October 1970, pp. 18-20.

16. This figure is substantially below the 250,000 estimated by Raymond Vernon, "Balance of Payments."

17. Stobaugh, "Multinational Enterprises," p. 31.

18. Some of the more important examples of plant closings are dramatically chronicled in the *Proceedings* of the AFL-CIO Conference on the Multinational Corporation, New York, 1970.

8

Potential Economic Benefits and Costs of Adjustment in Trade Liberalization

Robert G. Hawkins and
Rita M. Rodriguez

Various approaches are available with which to analyze the effects and desirability of arrangements for freer trade. This chapter employs the comparison of national industrial size, structure, and performance to address the question of what combinations of industrial countries have the most (or the least) to gain—from various perspectives—from bilateral or multilateral trade liberalization. This technique essentially bypasses the problem of price (and income) elasticities of demand and supply of exports and imports and deals with the national economic characteristics underlying the elasticities. We thus seek to discover for which groups of countries systematic trade liberalization makes economic sense.

The following chapter employs a complete, internally consistent econometric model of world trade involving three regions. This model, for which parameters were estimated on the basis of historical data, is used to simulate the results of the elimination of tariffs on the trade flows and balances of payments of the three regions.

Each of these methods of analysis, of course, has serious shortcomings. But they provide separate and hopefully complementary insights into the possible results of trade liberalization. Each appears to be suited to deal with the particular problem under analysis.

Irrespective of the method of analysis, the results of trade liberalization will depend primarily on: (a) the height of tariffs and restrictiveness of nontariff barriers to be reduced or eliminated; (b) the characteristics of production and cost structures of the trading partners engaged in the trade liberalization endeavor; and (c) the characteristics of demand in these countries. The levels and structure of national tariff rates have been considered in Chapter 3, and the configuration of nontariff barriers in Chapters 4 and 5. In this and the following chapter, the analysis focuses only on tariff reduction or elimination, and does not incorporate estimates of the impact of changes in nontariff barriers. The tariff reduction in trade liberalization determines the price change which consumers perceive, and the characteristics of their demand (nationally), that is,

The authors acknowledge with thanks the programming and computational assistance of Robert Haskell and N. Hill White, and the encouraging comments on an earlier draft by Sperry Lea.

193

price and income elasticity for particular products, will determine the change in the volume of consumption. Finally, the national production and cost structures will govern the changes in the international pattern of production. Each of these factors are dealt with, in differing ways, in these two chapters.

Trade Liberalization and National Economic Interests

National policy makers must face two sets of generally conflicting results from any effective move towards trade liberalization. On the one hand are the economic benefits from improved resource allocation. These will be manifest in lower prices for imports, higher prices for exports, economies of scale in export industries, and benefits from greater competition. On the other hand, these benefits can only be realized at certain economic costs. These costs take the form of short-run balance-of-payments problems, costs of reallocating resources domestically, and the costs of accelerating the demise of industries for which an international competitive advantage has long since been lost. No rational economic policy maker, from the national point of view, can ignore either set of considerations. Indeed, one of the fundamental jobs of national policy is to balance the benefits with the costs, at the margin, and to negotiate policy packages which give the greatest national benefits at least cost.

This chapter attempts to assign relative (not absolute) values to the benefits and costs of trade liberalization vis-à-vis particular pairs of countries. We will first discuss the theoretical foundations for the particular measures chosen as components of such benefits and costs, and then the formulation of available data into indexes for measurement of their relative intensity.

The Benefits

The economic benefits of trade liberalization have, in the literature on the theory of customs unions, been divided into two categories.[1] The first, the static benefits, arise as more efficient producers (nations) are substituted for less efficient producers (nations) at preliberalization levels of costs and productivities. From the individual nation's point of view, it is thus able to obtain greater amounts of a series of commodities at preliberalization costs, by importing from a lower-cost supplier instead of buying higher-cost local output. On the other hand, the output of local "relatively efficient" industries will expand, at the preexisting price level. Each unit of that exported output will, however, purchase a greater quantity of "import goods" than before. The result is the so-called static benefit of *trade creation*, in the terminology of customs union theory.

If trade liberalization is selective among the countries to which it is applied, and therefore discriminates in the treatment of imports from nonparticipants, there is the possibility that a nation may switch its imports from a lower cost nonmember to a higher cost member supplier, because the former still faces a tariff while the latter does not. This means that the efficiency of resource allocation is reduced, and the importing nation now pays more per unit of imports. This switching of foreign suppliers of imports is known as *trade diversion*, and constitutes a loss to the country concerned (and to the third country suppliers). Trade diversion, however, can arise only if trade restrictions are imposed or relaxed selectively among countries. Changes in trade restrictions by a country for all imports irrespective of national origin would involve only trade creation if barriers were lowered, or trade destruction if barriers were raised. In this analysis, an attempt is made to establish which pairs of countries may have potentially the most to gain (or to lose) by bilateral liberalization, and therefore trade diversion is implicitly dealt with as an undesirable result, to be minimized relative to trade creation.

Viner has argued that the benefits of a customs union (and, by extension, trade liberalization in general) will be greater the more rivalry, or competitiveness, there is between the economies of bilateral liberalizers and less the more complementary are their economies.[2] This argument stems from the supposition that if trade barriers are eliminated between two countries, and they have basically the same industry structure, then the lower-cost industry will survive and serve the two national markets (or the prices in the high-cost industry will be lowered to survive). Thus a large part of the output will be reallocated to a lower-cost supplier, thereby permitting a large saving of resources. Conversely, suppose the economies are complementary, country A produces X and country B produces Y. The potential for expansion of trade is small regardless of the removal of trade restrictions, since if B wanted X before, it had to get it from Y (or some other country) rather than internally, regardless of barriers.

Makower and Morton refined this prediction by showing that, while similarities in (competitiveness between) industrial structure were necessary for potential gains from trade creation; the actual gains will depend, positively, on the differences in costs of production between the two countries.[3] In short, if a foreign supplier is to be substituted for local producers, the national economic gain will be the larger the lower are his costs compared to ours.

While actual differences in national costs of production are almost impossible to measure satisfactorily, differences and similarities in industrial structure are measurable. This will be a major element in the comparison which follows. And since we cannot adequately observe differences in costs between countries, we assume implicitly that the structure of cost differences either adds to the effects of similarities in industrial structure, or are at least neutral.

It is also obvious, a priori, that the potential benefit of trade liberalization varies with the size of the liberalizing nations. The expected benefit from trade liberalization between a small and a large nation is limited by the supply capabilities of the small nation. The basic structure of a relatively small nation (e.g., Canada) would be substantially affected by its full integration with a large nation (the United States), while the impact on the latter—except in a few narrowly defined commodity groups—would be quite minor. Thus the relative benefit of trade liberalization will be greater (for both countries) the more comparable are their sizes, since each would then face similar constraints on their overall supply capabilities.

A third factor considered in this analysis of the potential benefit is "economic distance" between liberalizing countries. High costs of transport can prevent effective competition between suppliers in different countries even if tariffs and nontariff barriers are zero. The closer the countries (in terms of average economic costs of transporting commodities), the wider the range of products which would be effectively competitive in the absence of tariffs. And the smaller the group of commodities which would still have distinct separations between national markets because of the expense of transfer, the more beneficial (potentially) will be trade liberalization.

Proxy variables for each of these characteristics are developed for various nations, and an index is constructed for each as to its affinity for trade liberalization on a bilateral basis with each of the other nations. Using equal weights for all three characteristics, an overall index of "potential competitive overlap" is constructed between each pair of countries. To summarize, it is assumed that:

1. The more similar the industrial structure of output, the greater the likely benefit of trade liberalization between pairs of countries;
2. The more similar the economic size, the greater the likely benefit (relatively) from trade liberalization.
3. The closer, in terms of economic distance, are two countries, the greater is the likely benefit.

The Costs

The other set of considerations which a nation faces in deciding on a trade liberalization policy has to do with the cost of adjustment in the economy. These include the cost of reallocating resources as the industrial structure adjusts itself to the new trade pattern and the possibility of disturbances to the balance of payments. The analysis assumes that these costs of adjustment will be lower for the country whose exports expand relative to its imports.

This seems realistic for various reasons. The cost of reallocation will be smaller if new jobs and demand for output arise in export industries equal to or greater than the jobs and demand being displaced in import-competing industries, i.e., temporary unemployment of resources will be less if there is net upward pressure on aggregate demand. Also, regardless of the prevailing exchange-rate system, the country which suffers the deterioration in the trade balance due to trade liberalization will have a greater burden in adjusting than the country whose trade balance improves. Under fixed exchange rates, the deficit country must reduce costs and income relative to its competitors in order to regain the lost reserves while the surplus country need do little, if anything. If the deficit country's currency depreciates, its terms of trade decline, thus lowering real income.

If these assumptions are realistic, a nation would, *ceteris paribus*, prefer to liberalize trade with nations with which it would expect an improvement in its trade balance and avoid liberalization with nations where a deterioration would likely occur.[a] Put differently, a movement toward free trade would be more favorably received by a nation if it were to occur with a partner with which the expansion of exports would exceed the expansion of imports than if imports would likely expand more than exports.

While a large number of factors would govern the actual result of bilateral liberalization on costs of adjustment in any case, two are likely to have a systematic effect. These are the relative height of the tariffs (or nontariff barriers) being eliminated and the relative costs of production. The country with the higher overall level of tariffs (or, more precisely, effective rates of protection), assuming that there is not excess protection, would experience a larger increase in imports than exports if it eliminated, reciprocally, tariffs with a country with lower tariffs. Similarly, if a country has the lower preliberalization level of costs of production relative to its partner in liberalization, at the existing exchange rate, its exports are likely to expand relative to its imports, with the opposite holding true for the higher cost partner.

Both of these measures are essentially static, but costs and comparative advantage are constantly changing through time in a dynamic world. It is not feasible to isolate the various causal factors in international competitiveness and its change through time, but it is possible to employ a proxy variable which reflects the results of such change. This is the growth rate in industrial output of one country compared to another. High-growth countries generally experience more rapid growth in overall factor productivity than slow-growth countries and thus, with a fixed exchange rate and similar inflation rates, would find its goods becoming more competitive, through time, than its slow growth partner. Additional arguments could be made along these lines, but the essence is that comparative growth rates are used as a proxy for the various dynamic factors which affect the relative costs of adjustment to trade liberalization. Fast growing countries would bear lower costs of adjustment than more slowly growing countries.

---

[a]In actual practice, of course, trade negotiators attempt to vary their concessions and demands in an effort to "equalize" the trade-balance impact, and minimize the costs of adjustment. It is not feasible to vary the mix of the terms of liberalization in this analysis, however.

Empirical approximations, at the aggregate national level, are developed for each of these determinants of the cost of adjustment. The relative cost is then determined between each pair of potential trade liberalizers among the industrial countries with the intent of discovering with which group of nations any particular country would find a low cost involved with trade liberalization. Finally, again giving equal weights to each, an overall index of "cost of adjustment" is developed on a bilateral basis.

To summarize, the cost of adjustment facing a country in liberalizing trade reciprocally with a series of other countries will be as follows:

1. Costs will be higher the higher are its tariffs compared with those of each of the partners.
2. Costs will be higher the higher are its preliberalization cost levels compared with those of its partners.
3. Costs will be lower the more rapid the growth rate of real output in the recent past, compared to the growth rate of each of the potential partners in liberalization.

We turn now to the development of the empirical measures described above, and their use in the construction of the indexes of "potential competitive overlap" and of "potential costs of adjustment" for each pair of countries.

Competitive Overlap: Empirical Measures

The three components of this analysis are the similarity in industrial structure of nations, similarity of economic size, and economic distance between each pair. The characteristics of each of these measures will be examined, and the differences will then be used to construct indexes of similarity (or dissimilarity).

Industrial Structure

Consistent cross-country data of output by industry is woefully incomplete. Conceptually, the most appropriate data are those for value added by industry in each country. Such data has been collected and made fairly consistent by the United Nations for a number of countries for the year 1965.[4] Unfortunately, the data are available for manufacturing industries only and at the two-digit level of the Standard Industrial Classification. The complete industry breakdown is available for only nine advanced countries, none of which include any of the existing EEC members. For other analyses, the country coverage can be more extensive. The industrial structures, as illustrated by the percentage contribution by each industry to total value added in manufacturing, are shown in Table 8-1.

Table 8-1

Industrial Structure by Country: Percentage of Value Added in Total Manufacturing Accounted for by Each Industry, 1965

Industry	U.S.	Canada	Japan	Australia	Norway	New Zealand	United Kingdom	Sweden	Austria
Food	8.5	11.0	7.4	10.6	8.3	17.6	6.8	7.9	11.7
Beverages	1.8	3.3	1.9	1.8	3.1	2.3	3.1	1.1	3.7
Tobacco	0.7	1.0	0.0	0.9	2.9	0.7	1.0	0.3	3.3
Textiles	3.2	4.4	7.9	4.9	3.9	4.7	5.9	2.9	6.4
Clothing and Footwear	4.4	3.8	1.7	5.0	4.4	6.9	3.9	4.0	6.6
Wood and Cork Products	1.9	4.2	3.1	4.1	3.7	6.8	1.2	5.7	4.7
Furniture and Fixtures	1.5	1.7	1.5	1.3	3.4	2.3	1.5	1.4	2.7
Paper & Paper Products	3.7	8.4	3.6	3.3	6.8	5.3	2.8	7.9	3.6
Printing and Publishing	5.3	4.7	4.6	4.1	6.4	6.1	5.1	5.3	3.6
Leather Products	0.3	0.3	0.3	0.5	0.3	0.7	0.5	0.4	0.6
Rubber Products	2.5	1.6	1.5	1.5	1.0	2.0	1.6	1.3	1.6
Chemicals and Chemical Products	9.2	7.0	11.3	7.0	9.3	4.4	9.8	5.2	6.7
Petroleum and Coal Products	1.8	1.9	1.4	1.9	0.6	1.4	1.1	0.8	1.7
Nonmetallic Mineral Products	3.5	3.8	4.8	5.0	4.1	4.6	4.3	4.8	7.0
Basic Metals	8.3	8.6	8.9	10.7	9.6	0.7	8.1	8.0	7.4
Metal Products except Machinery	6.2	8.2	5.6	5.8	6.7	7.1	7.4	6.5	7.3
Machinery except electrical	10.0	5.0	9.2	8.8	4.6	6.9	10.8	15.9	6.2
Electrical Machinery	8.9	6.7	9.7	5.8	5.1	3.7	9.0	6.7	5.8
Transport Equipment	13.4	10.1	9.5	13.4	13.0	11.6	11.8	11.0	5.4
Other Manufacturing	4.0	3.3	5.2	2.4	1.9	3.2	3.6	2.0	3.6

Source: Calculated from data in appendix to Chapter 8.

In most cases, the contribution of a given industry does not vary greatly across country. Thus food, nonelectrical machinery, transport equipment and chemicals are important industries in all of the countries shown. On the other hand, industries which generally play a relatively small role (4 percent or less) in most countries are beverages, tobacco, furniture and fixtures, leather products, rubber products, and petroleum. This testifies to the predominantly industrial nature of the countries covered by the study. Austria and New Zealand are the countries that tend to be less industrialized on this basis. The closeness in relative contribution is particularly marked among the large countries like the United States and Canada.

Nevertheless, some substantial discrepancies between the relative importance of particular industries in various countries can be found. For example, paper and paper products in Canada and Sweden occupy a considerably larger role than in any of the other countries. Similarly, in Sweden, machinery (excluding electrical) accounts for 16 percent of total value added, a considerably higher proportion than in other countries.

As noted earlier, the intent is to develop a comprehensive bilateral comparison of similarities of industrial structure. We presume that if an industry occupies a similar relative position in two countries, it is at a similar stage of development in the two countries and therefore produces comparable, i.e., competitive, products. By aggregating the comparisons of individual industries, a measure of the degree of comparability of the industrial structures as a whole can be obtained for each pair of countries. If a large number of industries have similar relative importance in the two countries, chances are that each country is producing a similar array of commodities—their industrial structures are competitive.

Any comprehensive measure of the similarity in industrial structure across countries is subject to various limitations. One important limitation is that the actual degree of similarity in the industrial structures of the two countries may be obscured. This arises because of the degree of aggregation underlying industry definitions, a problem of substantial magnitude here. For example, the product mix in "textiles" may vary greatly among countries. Data availability make it impossible to correct this problem.

The measure used to evaluate industrial similarity takes the industrial structure of each country, as measured by the percentage of value added accounted for by each industry, and compares it with the same percentages for the other country. A comparison is carried out for each of the countries under study. Formally, the comparison involves:

$$\sum_{i=1}^{20} \left| \left(\frac{VA_i}{VA_a} \right)^a - \left(\frac{VA_i}{VA_b} \right)^b \right| ,$$

where the first term in parenthesis is the value added in industry i expressed as a proportion of total value added in manufacturing in country a, and the second term in parenthesis is the same proportion for country b. These differences are then summed for all twenty industries ($i = 1, \ldots, 20$), thereby implicitly giving each industry the same weight. For each country, identical calculations were carried out for each other country.

Because the sum of the absolute differences might well have a different "scale" from one pair of countries to another, and because the intent of the calculation is to provide a basis for comparison of industrial structure among pairs of countries, the absolute values of the expression above were "normalized" so that the range of variation was from 0 to 1.[b] The closer the normalized index is to 1.00, the more similar are the industrial structures of the countries compared and the closer to zero, the less similar. The results of these calculations are shown in Table 8-2.

According to the index, the U.S. industrial structure is most comparable to that for the United Kingdom. The relative comparability of the U.S. structure with the other countries are ranked in the following order, from the closest to the least close: Australia, Japan, Norway, Canada, Sweden, Austria, and New Zealand.

A comparable analysis for United Kingdom ranks the countries' places, in order of decreasing similarity, the U.S., Japan, Australia, Canada, Norway, Sweden, Austria, and New Zealand. The ranking for Japan is very similar to

Table 8-2
Index of Similarity in Industrial Structure, Selected Countries

	U.S.	Canada	Japan	Australia	Norway	New Zealand	United Kingdom	Sweden
Canada	.63							
Japan	.81	.52						
Australia	.86	.79	.64					
Norway	.69	.79	.41	.41				
N.Z.	.24	.40	.00	.45	.31			
U.K.	1.00	.64	.81	.72	.60	.19		
Sweden	.64	.67	.43	.62	.55	.29	.55	
Austria	.36	.69	.36	.64	.45	.41	.43	.24

Note: Indexes cover manufacturing only, for 1965 data. Indexes have been normalized to range from 0 to 1; the higher the index, the more similar the industrial structures.
Source: Calculated from data given in appendix to Chapter 8.

[b]The normalization procedure was to take the difference between the absolute value of any given index of similarity and the extreme value at the high (arithematic) end of the range, and divide that difference by the range. This normalization procedure was carried out for each of the indexes calculated in this chapter.

those of the United States and United Kingdom. For Canada, however, the order is altered considerably. In this case, the most similarity is found with Norway and Australia. Also, Canada finds its industrial structure more similar to Austria than to the United States, United Kingdom, and Japan.

To isolate a group of countries that, according to this measure, would expect to reap advantages from multilateral trade liberalization, we sought clusters of countries with high indexes of similarity among them. One such cluster, indicating a highly advantageous group for multilateral liberalization is the United States, Japan, Australia, United Kingdom, and possibly Canada. These five countries have industrial structures that, bilaterally, yield indexes of similarity above .79 (except for Japan and Canada, and Japan and Australia). Their industrial structures, as expressed by our measures, are thus rather similar.

The similarity indices for the remaining countries (Norway, New Zealand, Sweden, and Austria) show a mixed picture. Their indexes with the previous group are generally in the "moderate" range, with a few very close structures, and a few very dissimilar structures. Furthermore, the country pairs in the intermediate range do not always have industrial structures of similar levels when paired differently. Sweden, for example, has a moderately similar structure to the United States, United Kingdom, and Canada, but finds its industrial structure to be close to only two of the other countries in the intermediate group.

The most serious limitation of this analysis is the absence of data for the EEC countries, either individually or as a unit. The comparison among pairs of indexes of similarity would be much more valuable if such data were available, since surely Sweden, Austria and the United Kingdom comparisons with EEC countries have greater relevance than such comparisons with Japan or Canada. It was decided, however, that the available data did provide sufficient evidence of similarities and dissimilarities among non-EEC countries to be of some value in establishing the likely degree of competitiveness.

Size Comparability

Although similarity in industrial structure is one determinant of the economic benefits of freer trade, capacity or supply limitations imposed by differences in relative size are another important determinant. Even highly competitive economies may experience only mild expansion of trade if barriers are eliminated if they are of greatly different sizes. One country may have lower costs of production, but if it also has little capacity to expand production because of limited size, the increase in trade and welfare will be correspondingly limited.

Using the same data as above, the relative size of manufacturing industries, and of total manufacturing, in the advanced countries (excluding the EEC) were compared. As noted earlier, the data were for 1965 and thus ignores the relative size changes since then—for example, the more rapid growth of Japan. In addition, the conversion of each nation's production (value added) was done at the parity exchange rates existing in 1965, which assumes that those were equilibrium exchange rates. This clearly was not the case, and the comparisons must thus be taken only as rough orders of magnitude, but of some usefulness.

The size comparison is shown in Table 8-3. In the table, the size of the industry is expressed as a percentage of total value added by the nine countries combined.

For total manufacturing and for each industry, value added is strongly dominated by the United States, which accounts for 70 percent of the total value added in manufacturing and at least 60 percent in each industry. Japan and the United Kingdom account for approximately 10 percent each of total manufacturing. The fourth largest country is Canada with 4.5 percent of total manufacturing production. The remaining countries—Australia, Norway, New Zealand, Sweden, and Austria—each account for less than 2 percent of total manufacturing production.

In spite of the small percentages of the total production by countries other than the United States, there is considerable variation in the size of particular industries in the other eight countries. For example, Canada produces 7 percent of the beverages, 8 percent of wood and cork products, and 10 percent of paper and paper products for the group, but only 4.5 percent of all manufactures. Similarly, Japan produces 17.5 percent of textiles, but only 9.1 percent of all manufactures.

In order to compare the relative sizes of these countries, we calculated the absolute differences between each pair of countries in the percentage of combined value added for total manufacturing represented by each. More precisely, the "index of size comparability" is defined as:

$$\left(\frac{VA_m^a}{\sum_{j=1}^{9} VA_m^j} \right) - \left(\frac{VA_m^b}{\sum_{j=1}^{9} VA_m^j} \right) ,$$

where VA_m^a is value added in total manufactures, in country a, and $\sum VA_m^j$ is the sum of the value added in manufacturing for all nine countries. This difference was calculated between each pair of countries. These absolute differences were normalized so as to range from 0 to 1, the most similar in size being 1.[c] The results are shown in Table 8-4. The comparisons illustrate vividly the disproportionate size of the United States. Any comparison with the United States receives a low index. The most comparable other countries, compared to the United States in terms of size, are the United Kingdom and Japan. The low

---

[c]The same normalization procedure was used as earlier. See note b above.

Table 8-3
Relative Size of Countries, by Industry: Percentage of Combined Value Added Accounted for by Each Country, 1965

Industry	U.S.	Canada	Japan	Australia	Norway	New Zealand	United Kingdom	Sweden	Austria
Food	70.7	5.9	8.0	2.4	0.5	0.6	8.2	1.8	1.5
Beverages	62.3	7.4	8.5	1.7	0.8	0.3	15.5	1.0	1.9
Tobacco	69.4	5.8	0.0	2.2	2.2	0.3	14.3	0.9	4.6
Textiles	56.2	4.8	17.5	2.3	0.5	0.3	14.8	1.4	1.7
Clothing and Footwear	75.1	4.1	3.8	2.3	0.6	0.5	9.6	1.9	1.7
Wood and Cork Products	60.6	8.3	12.6	3.5	0.9	0.9	5.6	4.9	2.3
Furniture and Fixtures	69.6	4.8	8.7	1.6	1.2	0.4	9.7	1.8	1.8
Paper & Paper Products	66.1	9.6	8.5	1.6	1.0	0.4	7.4	4.0	1.0
Printing and Publishing	72.0	4.1	8.2	1.5	0.7	0.3	10.1	2.0	0.7
Leather Products	67.2	4.2	8.0	2.7	0.5	0.5	12.7	1.9	1.8
Rubber Products	78.8	3.3	6.2	1.3	0.2	0.2	7.6	1.1	0.7
Chemicals and Chemical Products	70.1	3.4	11.2	1.4	0.6	0.1	10.9	1.1	0.8
Petroleum and Coal Products	75.5	5.0	7.9	2.1	0.2	0.2	6.7	0.9	1.0
Nonmetallic Mineral Products	64.2	4.4	11.4	2.5	0.6	0.3	11.7	2.4	2.0
Basic Metals	69.5	4.6	9.7	2.4	0.6	0.0	10.0	1.8	0.9
Metal Products except Machinery	68.2	5.7	8.0	1.7	0.6	0.3	11.8	2.0	1.2
Machinery except electrical	71.5	2.3	8.6	1.7	0.2	0.2	11.3	3.2	0.6
Electrical Machinery	71.6	3.4	10.1	1.2	0.3	0.1	10.6	1.5	0.7
Transport Equipment	74.6	3.6	6.8	2.0	0.6	0.2	9.6	1.7	0.4
Other Manufacturing	70.8	3.8	12.1	1.2	0.2	0.2	9.3	1.0	0.9
Total Manufacturing	70.1	4.5	9.1	1.9	0.5	0.3	10.2	1.9	1.0

Source: Calculated from data in appendix to Chapter 8.

Table 8-4
Index of Size Comparability in Total Manufacturing of Nine Countries

	U.S.	Canada	Japan	Australia	Norway	New Zealand	United Kingdom	Sweden
Canada	.06							
Japan	.12	.93						
Australia	.02	.96	.90					
Norway	.00	.94	.88	.98				
N.Z.	.00	.94	.87	.98	.99			
U.K.	.14	.92	.98	.88	.86	.86		
Sweden	.02	.96	.90	1.00	.98	.98	.88	
Austria	.01	.95	.88	.99	.99	.99	.87	.99

Note: Values have been normalized to range from 0 to 1; the higher the value, the more similar the size.
Source: Calculated from data in appendix to Chapter 8.

values suggest that even when other countries have industrial profiles similar to that of the United States, the large difference in size of the countries involved will limit the capacity for trade expansion. If the cost structures after tariff reduction favored the products from the smaller country, U.S. demand could be rechanneled to this small country to a very limited extent because the latter's production capacity could supply only a limited amount of the larger American market. In particular instances, however, one country (e.g., Japan) could produce a very large proportion of American consumption in specific industries (like textiles). Also, this index provides only a bilateral comparison and is not a good indication of the benefits from multilateral trade liberalization.

Despite these limitations, and the additional one of omission of the EEC countries, the index does provide some useful indication of size comparability. The bilateral comparisons for those other than the United States all yield an index of over 0.80. Canada, Japan, and the United Kingdom all have manufacturing sectors of comparable size (indexes of size comparability of 0.92 or above). Similarly, Sweden, New Zealand, Norway, Austria, and Australia are quite comparable.

This suggests that, given the similarity of industrial structure, freer trade between these pairs of countries would not be disproportionately hampered by a size limitation. On the other hand, bilateral trade liberalization between countries of unequal size would have asymmetrical results. The smaller would be unhampered in securing the benefits of lower costs in the larger country, but the larger country would face supply limitations in the smaller country and thus would expect more limited benefits than if the trade liberalization were with a country of comparable or larger size. For the United States, then, bilateral freer trade would be more meaningful—at least from the point of view of size—with Japan, the United Kingdom, or Canada than with the other countries shown.

Economic Proximity

While the characteristics of economies with respect to industrial structure and size are important in determining the potential benefits of free trade, the costs of moving goods remains a hindrance. High costs limit the range of effective competitiveness between economies while low transport cost increase it.

The relevant measure of transport costs is one incorporating all of those elements which cause the price of a commodity to be higher in country of import than in the country of production. These include actual freight charges (both international and from point of production to point of debarcation), insurance, financing charges, higher risks of default and exchange rate variation, customs clearance charges, and the like. There are no satisfactory direct measures of such costs, and thus indirect or proxy measures must be used.

One possibility is physical distance between the principal ports in various countries. Unfortunately, this measure takes no account of the fact that transport costs may depend as much on the mode of transport and the type of route as on physical distance. In addition, it ignores the variation in costs of transport which result from differences in the commodity structure of trade between countries. As a percentage of value, transport costs range widely among commodity groups.

As a superior, but still highly imperfect proxy for relative transport costs between pairs of countries, the ratio of exports (f.o.b.), as reported by the exporting country, to imports (c.i.f.), as reported by the importing country, was calculated. Exports are ordinarily reported f.o.b., thus including price of the commodities (and inland transport) only, and excluding freight costs and other expenses incurred in transporting and landing the good in the importing nation. Imports, however, are normally reported c.i.f., thereby approximating their value landed in the importing country. (Notable exceptions are the United States and Canada, who report imports f.o.b.) Thus conceptually, the same trade flow is reported by the two countries on two bases. The difference between the value of the same trade flow as reported c.i.f. and its value f.o.b. should be the basis for a rough estimate of the cost of transport between two countries, based on the existing commodity structure of trade.

There are, of course, two trade flows between each pair of countries, and under this formulation, the economic distance between country A and country B will probably differ for A's exports to B and B's exports to A. This should be expected so long as the commodity structure of the trade flows are not identical.

This formulation was attempted for the nine countries for which the earlier indexes had been calculated. Conceptually, the formulation was as follows:

$$ED_{a,b} = \frac{\left[\dfrac{\text{Imports, c.i.f. } a \text{ from } b}{\text{Exports, f.o.b. } b \text{ to } a}\right] + \left[\dfrac{\text{Imports, c.i.f. } b \text{ from } a}{\text{Exports, f.o.b. } a \text{ to } b}\right]}{2}$$

where $ED_{a,b}$ is the economic distance between a and b, and the bracketed terms are the ratio of the two trade flows (of manufactured goods) expressed on a c.i.f. basis by the importing countries to the respective flows as measured f.o.b. by the exporting countries. These two values were averaged for the overall distance (or proximity) measure.

Several problems of data consistency and availability were encountered in these calculations. A major one, of course, is that the United States and Canada report imports f.o.b., and thus both elements in the brackets above could not be calculated. In each case, we were able to use only the export flow of these two countries as the basis for estimating ED. Also, while one nation's exports should be another's imports, this is not precisely the case in practice. Because of differences between countries in the timing of reporting, differences in data collection procedures, and other problems, it is not unusual for substantial differences in coverage to occur for what is ostensibly the same trade flow as measured by the two countries involved. One practical manifestation of this was a few instances in which the c.i.f. value for imports for a country, as reported by the importing country, was less than the f.o.b. export figure as reported by the exporting country. Such a situation, conceptually, is impossible, and when this occurred in our calculations, that flow was excluded and the measure relating to the opposite flow was used for ED.

While these are serious limitations, it seems unlikely that they are so serious as to make the estimates of the relative transports costs between pairs of countries seriously biased. As before, we normalized the calculations between each pair of countries so that the measure can vary from 0 to 1. The closer to 1 for any particular pair, the lower the relative costs of transport, that is, the closer the "economic proximity" and presumably the more meaningful a given reduction in trade barriers.

The results of the calculations for the nine countries are shown in Table 8-5. With the limitations described, these can at most be taken as rough approximations. Yet the values reflect the general a priori expectations, and are highly correlated to physical distance. The important exception, and surely a reflection of data aberrations, is the very high transport costs between the United States and the United Kingdom (the highest among all pairs of countries). This clearly makes no sense. The remaining bilateral comparisons between the United States or other countries do appear meaningful. As one would expect, the United States is most closely proximated by Canada, and European countries (except the United Kingdom) are all closer, economically, than Japan or Oceania. Japan, on the other hand, finds itself closest to Oceania, followed, surprisingly, by European countries and then the United States. These are, perhaps, distorted by the commodity structure of trade among these pairs of countries and by the distortions caused by existing barriers to such trade. It may well be that European countries limit Japanese imports more severely in high transport-cost

Table 8-5

Index of Economic Proximity between Pairs of Countries, 1968

	U.S.	Canada	Japan	Australia	Norway	New Zealand	United Kingdom	Sweden
Canada	.68							
Japan	.14	.07						
Australia	.00	.07	.60					
Norway	.28	.38	.23	.07				
N.Z.	.00	.07	.60	1.00	.07			
U.K.	.00	.28	.23	.14	.41	.14		
Sweden	.28	.38	.23	.07	.82	.07	.41	
Austria	.28	.38	.23	.07	.82	.07	.41	.82

Note: Based on the ratio of c.i.f. imports to f.o.b. exports of manufactured goods (SITC Divisions 5-9) for each pair of countries. The absolute values have been normalized so as to range from 0 to 1, the higher values indicating lower transport costs. Trade with and among EFTA members was treated as a unit (excluding the U.K.). Thus, Austria, Sweden, and Norway were assumed to be the same distance from each other, and each the same distance from the other countries, based on total EFTA trade with that country. Australia and New Zealand were treated as one unit relative to the other countries.

Source: Calculated from OECD, *Commodity Trade Statistics* (Series C), 1968.

items than in low transport-cost items, while the United States does not. To the extent that this type of explanation is valid, the use of existing trade patterns as a basis to estimate costs of transport may be misleading.

General Index of Potential Competitiveness

The preceding has developed three measures relating to the potential competitiveness among nine countries under freer trade. These measures may be combined, under various assumptions, into a single measure for each pair of countries. The basic comparisons in the form of normalized values for the three indexes of industrial-structure similarity, size comparability, and economic proximity are presented in Table 8-6.[d] Our a priori expectations are that, *ceteris paribus*, the closer the index values are to 1, the more potential economic benefit from freer trade between that pair of countries.

In deciding how to combine the indices into one common measure, the question of the relative importance (and reliability) of the measures must be faced. A simple but arbitrary solution was to assume that each was of equal importance and should therefore receive equal weight. This arithmetic mean attempts to wrap into one number an estimate of the relative potential competitiveness of the countries being considered. The arbitrary assignment of

[d]Normalized values provide a common scale for the three indexes.

equal weights leaves much to be desired, but with the limitations of the individual indexes outlined above, any refinement beyond this simple computation would probably involve false precision. It is obvious, however, that additional "overall indexes" can be calculated using whatever weights are considered more meaningful.

Table 8-6
Indexes of Competitive Overlap for Nine Countries

		U.S.	Canada	Japan	Australia	Norway	New Zealand	United Kingdom	Sweden
Canada	a)	.63							
	b)	.06							
	c)	.68							
	Ave.	.44							
Japan	a)	.81	.52						
	b)	.12	.93						
	c)	.14	.07						
	Ave.	.39	.52						
Australia	a)	.86	.79	.64					
	b)	.02	.96	.90					
	c)	.00	.07	.60					
	Ave.	.29	.61	.71					
Norway	a)	.69	.79	.41	.41				
	b)	.00	.94	.88	.98				
	c)	.28	.38	.23	.07				
	Ave.	.32	.72	.51	.49				
N.Z.	a)	.24	.40	.00	.45	.31			
	b)	.00	.94	.87	.98	.99			
	c)	.00	.07	.60	1.00	.07			
	Ave.	.08	.47	.49	.81	.46			
U.K.	a)	1.00	.64	.81	.72	.60	.19		
	b)	.14	.92	.98	.88	.86	.86		
	c)	.00	.28	.23	.14	.41	.14		
	Ave.	.38	.61	.67	.58	.62	.40		
Sweden	a)	.64	.67	.43	.62	.55	.29	.55	
	b)	.02	.96	.90	1.00	.98	.98	.88	
	c)	.28	.38	.23	.07	.82	.07	.41	
	Ave.	.31	.67	.52	.56	.78	.45	.61	
Austria	a)	.36	.69	.36	.64	.45	.41	.43	.24
	b)	.01	.95	.88	.99	.99	.99	.87	.99
	c)	.28	.38	.23	.07	.82	.07	.41	.82
	Ave.	.22	.67	.49	.57	.75	.49	.57	.68

a) Index of Similarity of Industrial Structure.

b) Index of Size Comparability.

c) Index of Economic Proximity

Data: See previous tables.

The overall indexes of competitive overlap range from 0.08 (between the United States and New Zealand) to 0.81 (for New Zealand and Australia). Most of the indexes fall between 0.40 and 0.70. For each country, potential partners in bilateral trade liberalization may be ranked according to the potential economic benefit and trade expansion. When this is done for the United States, for example, the countries which are most likely to yield meaningful benefits, in order of importance, are: Canada, the United Kingdom, Japan, Norway, Sweden, Australia, Austria, and New Zealand. Likewise, for Canada, the economic affinity, in decreasing strength, would be felt with Norway, Austria, Sweden, the United Kingdom, Australia, Japan, and the United States. For Japan, the United Kingdom and Australia seem most relevant for a potentially economically beneficial trade liberalization scheme, and the remaining countries less so. Japan and Canada are the United Kingdom's best prospective bilateral partners among the countries considered.

Thus, for purposes of overall policy-making, this analysis suggests that the United States would be most interested in bilateral or multilateral negotiations with the United Kingdom, Canada, and Japan. On the other hand, Canada would be interested in such negotiations with the United States but would also have stronger interests in negotiations with smaller countries (Australia, Sweden, Norway, and Austria), as would Japan and the United Kingdom, than would the United States. A reasonably strong economic case for liberalization appears to exist among one group of countries: the United States, United Kingdom, Japan, Canada, and Australia. Another case exists for links among the smaller countries—Austria, Norway, Sweden (each members of EFTA)—and also between these countries and particular members of the larger group—United Kingdom, Canada, and Australia.

It must be reiterated that this overall index should not be taken as a definitive measure of relative potential benefit, but only as a rough indicator of relative potential gains from freer trade. The shortcomings of it—including the poor data for the economic distance measure, the fact that the economic size index indicates the limits of potential benefit for the larger country but not for the smaller country, and the absence of data for the EEC countries—constrain its general validity and dramatize the need for care in its use.

Relative Costs of Trade Liberalization:
Empirical Measures

While the potential long-run benefits to an economy from freer trade may be a strong policy argument, governments must also consider the transitional costs in obtaining these gains. A country may fear a situation in which freer trade with one or more partners will see the other countries expand exports, capture markets, and prosper while its own industries' lack of competitiveness is exposed, factories close, and its balance of trade turns adversely. A country facing such a situation will be much more reluctant to negotiate trade liberalization—due to these expected higher costs of adjustment—while a country which is confident that its international competitiveness has been stifled by barriers abroad—that its expected costs of adjustment are low—will be eager to negotiate barriers downward.

In what follows, we assume that the transitional costs of trade liberalization would be high for the country which faces a deteriorating trade balance and retrenchment in its manufacturing industries, and low for a country whose industries expand. It is argued that three types of considerations will determine which, between a pair of countries, absorbs the major part of the adjustment burden. These are the comparative height of the tariff barriers to be eliminated, the relative costs of production prior to tariff reduction, and the "dynamic" behavior of the relevant industries in the two countries in the past. The lower tariff country, the lower production-cost country, and the most dynamic country will likely have the lesser adjustment problem and thus would welcome liberalization. Each pair of countries is compared on the basis of these three criteria below, and an overall index of relative adjustment ease is subsequently calculated.

Tariff Rate Differentials

Freer trade would tend to expand proportionately more, *ceteris paribus*, the exports of countries which previously had comparatively low tariffs and the imports of those which previously had relatively high tariffs. As a result, the balance of trade of countries with relatively low preexisting tariffs would tend to benefit more than those with relatively high tariffs.

The degree of overall protection of one country compared to another is very difficult to assess. But one indicator is differentials between "average" tariff rates. One calculation of such differentials is exhibited in Table 8-7 for the countries for which data are available. The data in Table 8-7 are the own-import weighted average tariffs of the country in the row minus the average tariff of the country in the column. For cases where the data are positive, the country in the row has a higher average tariff than the country in the column.

The data in the table reflect again the discussion in Chapter 3. Japan, the United Kingdom, and Canada have relatively high tariffs, while the United States was somewhat lower; but still higher than the external tariffs of Norway and Sweden.

The tariff differentials of Table 8-7 were normalized, as described above, so that the range of variation was from 0 to 1.00. High negative values in Table 8-7 are translated into numbers close to 1.00, indicating a presumed willingness of the country in question to liberalize trade with the other country, since the

Table 8-7

Tariff-Rate Differentials between Pairs of Countries, All Nonagricultural Commodities, Post-Kennedy Round Rates

(Average tariffs for all commodities in country in the *row heading* weighted by country's imports minus average tariffs for all commodities in country in the *column heading* weighted by this country's imports)

	U.S.	Canada	Japan	Australia	Norway	New Zealand	United Kingdom	Sweden	Austria
U.S.	–	−2.5	−3.6	n.a.	1.6	n.a.	−3.1	2.8	−5.4
Canada	2.5	–	−1.1	n.a.	4.1	n.a.	− .6	5.3	−2.9
Japan	3.6	1.1	–	n.a.	5.2	n.a.	.5	6.4	−1.8
Australia	n.a.	n.a.	n.a.	–	n.a.	n.a.	n.a.	n.a.	n.a.
Norway	−1.6	−4.1	−5.2	n.a.	–	n.a.	.0	.0	–
N.Z.	n.a.	n.a.	n.a.	n.a.	n.a.	–	n.a.	n.a.	n.a.
U.K.	3.1	.6	− .5	n.a.	.0	n.a.	–	.0	.0
Sweden	−2.8	−5.3	−6.4	n.a.	.0	n.a.	.0	–	.0
Austria	5.4	2.9	1.8	n.a.	.0	n.a.	.0	.0	–

Note: Tariffs are measured as the average tariff for all commodities in each country weighted by the imports of that country. This weighting system was preferred over a system using weights representing some average world or area trade flows. By weighting tariffs according to the country's own imports, we hope to obtain a better picture of what the relevant tariffs are to the specific country. This method however, has the disadvantage that the cases where the tariffs are high enough to deter most imports of a given commodity, the present weighting system biases downward the estimated tariff. No tariffs estimates are available for Australia and New Zealand. Tariffs on imports by one EFTA member from another are assumed to be effectively zero.

Source: Data in Chapter 3.

former's tariff is lower than the latter's. A value of one indicates the greatest advantage for the first country. On the other hand, a value of zero indicates the greatest disadvantage as between any pair of countries, that is, the first country's tariffs exceed the second's by an amount greater than for any other pair of countries. The results are presented in Table 8-8.

As expected, the countries in the row heading with the lowest numbers are Japan and Austria followed by Canada and the United Kingdom. This indicates an expected reluctance to negotiate reciprocal trade liberalization with the other countries. The countries with the highest general values are Norway and Sweden. In other words, Sweden and Norway have average tariffs which are below those of all the other countries which appear in the table. They thus would likely benefit from, say, an equal percentage tariff cut, depending on which other country was involved, from the point of adjustment problems.

Table 8-8
Index of Tariff-Rate Differentials between Pairs of Countries

	U.S.	Canada	Japan	Norway	United Kingdom	Sweden	Austria
U.S.	–	.70	.85	.37	.74	.28	.92
Canada	.30	–	.59	.18	.55	.09	.73
Japan	.22	.41	–	.10	.46	.00	.64
Norway	.61	.82	.89				
U.K.	.24	.45	.54				
Sweden	.64	.90	1.00		INTRA-EFTA		
Austria	.08	.27	.36				

Note: Values are normalized to range between 0 and 1. The closer the number is to 1 the lower the existing tariff rate of the country in the row headings, relative to the country in column headings.

Source: Calculated from Table 8-7.

These normalized values will be used below in the construction of a general index of relative "adjustment cost."

Comparative Costs

Countries with relatively lower-cost industries, at existing exchange rates and unit money costs of production, are likely to experience an expansion of exports compared to imports, while high-cost producers will find that their imports expand relative to exports, *ceteris paribus*. Defining and measuring an appropriate cost measure which can be used for comparisons across countries is a difficult task, and the measure developed here can only be taken as a crude proxy for a more comprehensive measure.

The measure employed is an approximation of output per unit of labor cost, or, more specifically, total value added as a ratio of total employee compensation in the industry. The higher the value added ratio, the lower are total production costs: (a) if production techniques (overall factor productivity) are identical across countries, (b) if factor input combinations are the same across countries, and (c) if markets are competitive (i.e., no monopoly elements exist). Each of these provisos are obviously violated in practice and as a result, the employee-compensation, value-added ratio is a highly imperfect measure of comparative costs.

Yet, the degree of bias is probably small enough to make this ratio useful for the purposes here. Employee compensation is a major proportion of total value added in almost all manufacturing industries in the countries under consideration and likely dominates the determination of that ratio. And separate evidence suggests that the capital-labor input proportions do not vary greatly from country to country.[e]

Despite these limitations, and the additional ones that the calculations are based on data for years prior to the currency realignments of 1971, the employee-compensation, value-added ratios are presented for the twenty manufacturing industries in the nine countries in Table 8-9.

For total manufacturing, Japan, with a ratio of value added to labor costs of 2.82, is by far the lowest-cost country and Sweden (1.78) the highest-cost one. The United States ranks among the lower-cost countries with a ratio of 2.15. This performance is followed by that of Canada and Norway with indexes close to 2.00. Further down is a group consisting of Australia, New Zealand and the United Kingdom, with indexes in the neighborhood of 1.90. The highest-cost country in the group is Sweden. The table shows that the ranking in productivity for total manufacturing is the result of a fairly consistent set of relationships among specific industries. When particular industries are analyzed separately, the ranking differs only slightly from the one obtained for the case of total manufacturing. The differences in ranking occur mostly among countries that have very close overall ratios for total manufacturing.

In order to compare the likely relative costs of each country under freer trade with each of the other countries, Table 8-10 has been prepared. Underlying this table is the sum of the (algebraic) differences in industrial productivity across all twenty industries, between each pair of countries. The importance of each industry in the total is weighted by its contribution in total manufacturing value-added in the country in question, i.e., the country in the row heading. More precisely,

$$DC_{a,b} = \sum_{i=1}^{20} \left[\left(\frac{VA_i}{EC_i}\right)_a - \left(\frac{VA_i}{EC_i}\right)_b \right] \left(\frac{VA_i}{\sum_{i=1}^{20} VA}\right)_a ,$$

where DC is the difference in comparative labor productivities between country a and b, VA_i/EC_i is the ratio of value added to employee compensation in industry i, and a and b are the country subscripts. The differences are weighted, according to the right term, by the relative importance of industry i in country a.

---

[e]While no direct data are available for capital inputs by industry or manufacturing across country, we attempted to appraise the degree to which factor intensities varied among countries. We used as a proxy measure for capital input "energy consumed," which was available for the twenty industries covered by this study, although some reported on one basis and others on another. We then calculated a ratio of energy consumed per employee, in total manufacturing for the eight countries for which data was available. While there was some variation across country, this was fairly limited and did *not* always correspond to one's intuitive expectation with respect to relative factor supplies.

Table 8-9
Ratio of Value Added to Total Employee Compensation, Manufacturing Industries in Nine Countries, 1965

Industry	U.S.	Canada	Japan	Australia	Norway	United Kingdom	Sweden	New Zealand	Austria
All Manufacturing	2.15	2.02	2.82	1.93	2.00	1.89	1.78	1.89	2.41
Food	2.53	2.15	3.18	2.30	1.62	2.26	2.39	1.54	3.09
Beverages	3.14	3.43	4.18	2.95	5.27	3.30	2.46	2.93	3.60
Tobacco	4.75	3.14	–	4.75	–	3.90	4.84	2.80	–
Textiles	1.90	1.79	2.42	1.83	1.95	1.77	1.65	1.37	2.08
Clothing and Footwear	1.80	1.54	2.32	1.71	1.83	1.65	1.61	1.30	2.30
Wood and Cork Products	1.78	1.68	2.36	1.79	1.96	1.61	1.77	1.52	2.43
Furniture and Fixtures	1.82	1.66	2.20	1.80	1.92	1.55	1.64	1.36	2.62
Paper & Paper Products	2.24	2.14	2.99	2.38	1.76	2.00	1.88	2.09	2.10
Printing and Publishing	1.96	1.77	2.41	1.80	2.04	1.81	1.75	1.47	2.17
Leather Products	1.50	1.61	2.60	1.70	1.96	1.79	1.57	1.47	2.44
Rubber Products	2.03	1.94	2.75	1.67	1.92	1.87	1.62	1.75	3.56
Chemicals and Chemical Products	3.74	2.69	4.73	3.32	2.66	2.84	2.35	2.27	2.84
Petroleum and Coal Products	4.27	2.65	7.14	6.29	2.65	2.58	4.16	5.53	5.34
Nonmetallic Mineral Products	2.24	2.25	2.80	2.11	2.16	1.83	1.90	1.63	2.45
Basic Metals	2.11	2.10	2.66	2.10	2.36	1.76	1.80	1.64	1.94
Metal Products except Machinery	1.93	1.87	2.35	1.69	1.78	1.73	1.75	1.53	2.07
Machinery except electrical	2.00	2.01	2.43	1.63	1.88	1.76	1.58	1.41	2.05
Electrical Machinery	1.96	1.81	2.88	1.71	1.91	1.77	1.65	1.51	1.92
Transport Equipment	1.87	1.93	2.85	1.48	1.56	1.63	1.55	1.36	1.97
Other Manufacturing	2.17	1.89	2.52	1.83	1.99	1.83	1.84	1.66	2.20

Note: Underlying values were in current prices and current wage rates.
Source: Calculated from Appendix to Chapter 8, and average employees by industry, United Nations, *Growth of World Industry, 1967*.

Table 8-10

Index of Comparative Efficiency between Pairs of Countries

	U.S.	Canada	Japan	Australia	Norway	United Kingdom	Sweden	New Zealand	Austria
U.S.	–	0.57	0.21	0.56	0.55	0.61	0.64	0.71	0.40
Canada	0.40	–	0.14	0.46	0.45	0.52	0.54	0.62	0.29
Japan	0.76	0.85	–	0.84	0.85	0.90	0.93	1.00	0.74
Australia	0.42	0.50	0.15	–	0.48	0.55	0.56	0.65	0.31
Norway	0.49	0.59	0.28	0.56	–	0.62	0.64	0.74	0.32
U.K.	0.36	0.44	0.10	0.44	0.40	–	0.52	0.60	0.27
Sweden	0.35	0.41	0.09	0.42	0.41	0.46	–	0.57	0.27
N.Z.	0.26	0.34	0.00	0.32	0.33	0.36	0.37	–	0.11
Austria	0.72	0.81	0.52	0.77	0.68	0.84	0.84	0.96	–

Note: Values are normalized to range from zero to one. High values indicate that the country in the row has lower costs (higher productivity) as compared to the country in the column.

Following the earlier practice, the absolute values of DC were normalized so as to range from 0 to 1. Values close to 1 in Table 8-10 thus indicate that a nation should prefer trade liberalization with the other country (in the column heading) because costs in the former are low compared to those of the latter, within the context of cost comparisons among all the countries. Conversely, values close to zero indicate a significant cost disadvantage compared with the other country, and one would thus expect a high burden of transitional adjustment from trade liberalization in that direction.

Weighting these implicit labor-productivity estimates by industry, Japan remains the lowest-cost country and New Zealand is the highest-cost country. Thus, when these two countries are compared, the index assumes the two extreme values of 0 and 1.00. As one would expect, when each of the other countries is compared with Japan, the index number is relatively high when Japan is in the row heading.

For specific countries, the potential partners in trade liberalization can be ranked according to this index—from those which are likely to cause little negative adjustment problems to those which may seriously disrupt local production. If this is done for the United States, for example, New Zealand, Sweden, and the United Kingdom would appear to make little adjustment trouble for U.S. industry, while Japan and Austria would evidently make the most. Canada, Australia, and Norway occupy an intermediate position.

While the underlying problems of this measure as an estimate of actual comparative costs are many, it does provide some insight into the fears of some nations in becoming associated with particular other countries in trade liberalization schemes. This certainly must be taken into account by national policy makers, and the index serves as a convenient starting point in that consideration.

Comparative Growth Rates

While cross-country comparisons of costs are important, they may give misleading indications of the actual structure of costs *after* the effects of trade liberalization are worked out, and do not necessarily reflect the dynamic forces altering cost structures through time. A comprehensive, but simple indicator of such forces does not exist, but one would expect, on a priori grounds, that the recent performance of one nation's industries compared to others' will provide a useful and simple approximation. As a proxy for recent performance, we chose growth rates in industrial production (not value-added), by industry, as the best available measure.

One may consider the growth experience in a given industry as a rough measure of its dynamism. While this growth may have been largely induced by developments on the demand side, supply considerations are also important, especially within the international context. That is, the industry's dynamism may have been the product of the industry's ability to adapt to new conditions, or the result of the industry's capability to create the conditions necessary for its expansion. The faster the growth of an industry in a country relative to the growth of that industry in its potential trade partners, the larger the possibilities for additional trade creation as a result of fewer barriers to exports. One important limitation occurs if the past growth has been due mainly to high tariff protection, but this seems unlikely except in a few special cases.

The average growth rate over the decade 1958 to 1968 for the twenty manufacturing industries for nine countries is shown in Table 8-11. The growth rates in total industrial production in most countries covered by the table vary between 5.25 and 6.20 percent. Out of these ranges are, on one side, Japan whose industrial output grew at a rate of 15.65 percent. On the other extreme, the United Kingdom and Austria had growth rates of 3.60 and 4.80 percent respectively. The well-known and extraordinary performance of Japan and the sluggish growth of the United Kingdom during this period were distributed widely among their manufacturing industries.

Certain industries have in general, grown more slowly than average in all countries while others have almost universally grown faster than average. Food, beverages, and tobacco industries have been slow-growing in most countries, as have textiles, clothing and footwear, except for their 8 percent growth in Japan. Wood and furniture industries have had moderately high growth rates only in Canada, Japan, Austria, and Norway. The chemical industry is the only industry for which all the countries studied experienced high growth rates. These high rates were in all cases, except Japan, above the rate for the respective country's

Table 8-11
Average Annual Growth Rates in Industrial Production for Selected Countries, Twenty Industries, 1958-68

Industry	U.S.	Canada	Japan	Australia	Norway	New Zealand	United Kingdom	Sweden	Austria
Total Manufacturing	5.90	5.85	15.65	5.25	5.45	6.20	3.60	5.95	4.80
Food	3.25	4.90	8.70	3.95	3.80	3.80	1.85	3.65	4.01
Beverages	3.25	4.90	4.30	3.95	4.75	4.60	4.55	2.87	4.30
Tobacco	2.90	4.90	6.75	3.95	1.00	6.10	n.a.	3.70	1.90
Textiles	4.80	7.90	9.80	5.35	.30	8.95	.49	5.30	4.35
Clothing and Footwear	4.25	3.15	8.30	4.25	3.10	2.10	2.27	2.80	5.90
Wood and Cork Products	1.45	5.30	6.70	4.20	7.10	2.40	3.80	5.05	8.10
Furniture and Fixtures	6.70	5.30	6.70	5.05	6.65	3.10	3.10	5.05	8.10
Paper & Paper Products	5.35	4.40	13.63	10.60	5.60	9.25	4.20	6.05	4.90
Printing and Publishing	4.55	4.55	5.25	6.30	5.60	7.40	4.20	3.75	3.15
Leather Products	1.95	2.10	10.40	1.20	n.a.	3.60	n.a.	1.26	.87
Rubber Products	6.70	3.75	13.77	6.45	6.05	5.95	5.15	5.30	8.95
Chemicals and Chemical Products	8.82	6.40	14.09	8.23	7.40	6.55	7.20	9.42	9.57
Petroleum and Coal Products	3.70	6.40	18.65	7.09	2.55	—	4.30	8.10	10.50
Nonmetallic Mineral Products	4.60	3.85	13.18	6.80	.49	5.51	5.15	35.50	6.30
Basic Metals	5.10	8.10	17.80	7.35	8.42	n.a.	2.24	8.35	2.86
Metal Products except Machinery	6.65	9.22	21.50	7.20	5.35	9.35	1.13	7.10	3.85
Machinery except electrical	7.40	9.22	21.50	7.20	5.49	9.35	4.70	7.10	4.01
Electrical Machinery	7.70	9.22	21.50	7.20	8.25	9.20	5.30	7.10	6.20
Transport Equipment	7.20	9.22	21.50	7.20	3.65	9.20	1.11	7.10	n.a.
Other Manufacturing	7.80	7.40	13.69	8.30	10.92	n.a.	5.90	12.45	n.a.

Source: United Nations, *Statistical Bulletin*, various issues.

total manufacturing production. Similarly, petroleum performed higher than average in most countries except the United States, the United Kingdom, and Norway. And, in general, the heavy manufacturing industries—metal products, machinery, both electrical and nonelectrical, and transport equipment—were above average performers except for the United Kingdom and Austria.

In order to obtain a bilateral comparison for each country with the other countries with respect to the relative dynamics of their respective industries, an index along the lines of those discussed earlier was constructed. This index was the sum of the algebraic differences between the two countries, in the growth rates of each of the manufacturing industries, weighted by the industry's relative importance in the first country. In symbols,

$$GD_{a,b} = \sum_{i=1}^{20} \left[(G_i^a - G_i^b) \left(\frac{VA_i}{\sum_{i=1}^{20} VA_i} \right)_a \right] ,$$

where GD is the overall growth difference between country a and country b, G_i^a is the growth rate in industry i in country a, and $VA_i / \sum_{i=1}^{20} VA_i$ is the relative contribution of industry i to total manufacturing in country a. These values were normalized (to range from 0 to 1) and are presented in Table 8-12. The country in the row is the subject country (country a) and the comparison is run for each country in the column. A value close to 1 indicates that the row country experienced a relatively high growth performance as compared with the other country. Zero indicates the widest difference in growth performance between that pair of countries, with the country in the row heading having the worst performance.

The pervasiveness of sizable growth differences noted above are obvious in the table. Japan on the high side and the United Kingdom and Austria on the low side emerge as the cases with widest divergences, regardless of which country's industrial structure is used as weights. Thus, Japan has exceedingly high values (suggesting little fear from reciprocal trade liberalization) while the United Kingdom and Austria have comparatively low values (implying fairly high potential adjustment problems). On this scheme, countries in general would find the United Kingdom and Austria desirable prospects for freer trade, from the perspective of adjustment costs, while the opposite is true for Japan.

On the basis of these comparisons, the United States (a mid-range country in average growth rates) would evidently find it least congenial to liberalize trade vis-à-vis Japan, and to a much lesser extent, Sweden, and most acceptable with the United Kingdom, Austria, Australia, and New Zealand. This, it will be recalled, is a similar configuration of countries to that yielded by comparisons in costs, as measured in the previous section.

Table 8-12

Index of Comparative Growth Performance in Industrial Production between Pairs of Countries (Normalized Values Ranging between 0 and 1)

	U.S.	Canada	Japan	Australia	Norway	New Zealand	United Kingdom	Sweden	Austria
U.S.		.47	.11	.48	.53	.50	.62	.44	.58
Canada	.55		.18	.51	.57	.54	.65	.48	.60
Japan	.90	.85		.87	.92	.89	1.00	.80	.96
Australia	.54	.49	.15		.57	.54	.65	.45	.60
Norway	.49	.45	.13	.45		.47	.59	.41	.54
N.Z.	.54	.50	.20	.50	.56		.63	.46	.57
U.K.	.40	.35	.00	.37	.43	.38		.32	.47
Sweden	.60	.54	.18	.55.	.61	.56	.69		.65
Austria	.48	.44	.14	.45	.50	.47	.57	.37	

Note: Values are normalized to range from zero to 1. Higher values indicate that the country in the row has had superior growth performance than the country in the column.

Overall Index of Costs of Adjustment to Trade Liberalization

In this section, three separate indexes have been developed which, it was argued, would be positively related to a country's willingness to enter into agreements to remove trade restrictions with a series of other countries. Fear of unfavorable turns in the balance of trade, or loss of competitiveness and domestic production, are costs which make policy makers reluctant to liberalize trade. The measures developed here are intended to identify the economic basis upon which such reluctance is based and to indicate its relative strength country by country.

The reservations about such indexes remain. Substantial data (and conceptual) problems are attached to each, and the overall usefulness is again limited by the absence of data for the EEC countries and by the failure to estimate indexes with alternative groups of countries instead of on a one by one basis.

Despite these deficiencies, and to reduce the possible danger of biases in any one, it is revealing to combine the three separate measures into one index to obtain a summary measure of likely concerns over adjustment problems of reciprocal trade liberalization among countries. Again, there is no precise way of determining which of the measures is more powerful or valid, whether one may substitute for (or complement) the others, and whether they are truly independent indicators. Thus, our arbitrary decision was to assign them equal weights by taking a simple average of the indexes for the differential tariffs, comparative efficiency, and comparative growth performance. These, together with the values for the individual indexes are shown in Table 8-13.[f]

The averages should indicate the relative interest that various countries in the row heading would have in eliminating tariffs vis-à-vis another country in the group of nine countries in the column heading. The column labeled "average" shows the simple average of the comparisons with the other eight countries for that country. The last column can thus be taken as a crude indicator of the direction of adjustment effects that might accrue if the country in the row were it to liberalize trade on a multilateral basis with all of the other countries. The higher the value (above 0.50) the smaller the likely adjustment difficulty; and the lower the value, the more likely that exports would expand less than imports (and thus cause more adjustment problems). A value around 0.5 would indicate that some countries would out-perform the country in question while others would not, with a net impact on the exports and imports of more or less equal proportion.

Using this as an approximate yardstick, the United States is in the mid-range, together with Australia and Sweden. Japan is the country for which the indexes definitely predict an expansion of exports relative to imports and hence has less fear of major adjustment costs. The United Kingdom, New Zealand, and to a lesser extent Austria and Canada are in the converse position, and might expect relatively high adjustment burdens as a result of multilateral trade liberalization.

For individual countries, the overall index provides a ranking of potential partners with respect to predicted adjustment burdens. For the United States, the countries to be most feared in bilateral reductions of barriers are Japan, Norway, and Sweden, while the United Kingdom, Canada, New Zealand, and Austria apparently offer little concern and might in fact provide new markets for export expansion.

For the United Kingdom, on the other hand, liberalization with New Zealand, Canada, and Australia would involve the least burden, followed by the United States, while Japan would likely impose substantial adjustment costs. Japan has most to fear from liberalization with Sweden and the United States.

While the overall index values would vary if different weights were assigned to the components, they do not appear to be overly sensitive to the weights assigned. Casual observation indicates that the overall conclusions would be little changed by altering the weights, and the values as shown are at least a reasonable first approximation of the probable ordering of relative adjustment costs.

---

[f]Since tariff averages are not available for Australia and New Zealand, the values in the average cells for these countries are the simple averages for the "comparative efficiency" and "comparative growth" indexes only.

Table 8-13
Overall Index of Costs of Adjustment to Trade Liberalization

		U.S.	Canada	Japan	Australia[a]	Norway	New Zealand[a]	United Kingdom	Sweden	Austria	Average with Other 8 Countries
U.S.	a)	—[b]	.70	.85	n.a.	.37	n.a.	.74	.28	.92	
	b)		.57	.21	.56	.55	.71	.61	.64	.40	
	c)		.47	.11	.48	.53	.50	.62	.44	.58	
	Average	—	.58	.39	.52	.48	.60	.66	.45	.63	.53
Canada	a)	.30	—	.59	n.a.	.18	n.a.	.55	.09	.73	
	b)	.40		.14	.46	.45	.62	.52	.54	.29	
	c)	.55		.18	.51	.57	.54	.65	.48	.60	
	Average	.42	—	.30	.48	.40	.58	.57	.37	.54	.43
Japan	a)	.22	.41	—	n.a.	.10	n.a.	.46	.00	.64	
	b)	.76	.85		.84	.85	1.00	.90	.93	.74	
	c)	.90	.85		.87	.92	.89	1.00	.80	.96	
	Average	.63	.70	—	.86	.62	.95	.79	.58	.78	.68
Australia[a]	a)	n.a.	n.a.	n.a.	—	n.a.	n.a.	n.a.	n.a.	n.a.	
	b)	.42	.50	.15		.48	.65	.55	.56	.31	
	c)	.54	.49	.15		.57	.54	.65	.45	.60	
	Average	.48	.50	.15	—	.52	.60	.60	.50	.46	.48
Norway	a)	.61	.82	.89	n.a.	—	n.a.	—	—	—	
	b)	.49	.59	.28	.56		.74	.62	.64	.32	
	c)	.49	.45	.13	.45		.47	.59	.41	.54	
	Average	.53	.62	.43	.50	—	.60	—	—	—	.53

N.Z.[a]	a)	n.a.	n.a.	n.a.	n.a.	n.a.	—	n.a.	n.a.	n.a.
	b)	.26	.34	.00	.32	.33	—	.36	.37	.11
	c)	.54	.42	.10	.41	.44	—	.50	.42	.34
	Average	.40	.42	.10	.41	.44		.50	.42	.34
										.39
U.K.	a)	.24	.45	.54	n.a.	—	n.a.	—	—	—
	b)	.36	.44	.10	.44	.40	.60	—	.52	.27
	c)	.40	.35	.00	.37	.43	.38	—	.32	.47
	Average	.33	.41	.21	.40	—	.49	—	—	—
										.32
Sweden	a)	.64	.90	1.00	n.a.	—	n.a.	—	—	—
	b)	.35	.41	.09	.42	.41	.57	.46	—	.27
	c)	.60	.54	.18	.55	.61	.56	.69	—	.65
	Average	.53	.62	.42	.48	—	.56	—	—	—
										.52
Austria	a)	.08	.27	.36	n.a.	—	n.a.	—	—	—
	b)	.72	.81	.52	.77	.68	.96	.84	.84	—
	c)	.48	.44	.14	.45	.50	.47	.57	.37	—
	Average	.43	.51	.34	.61	—	.72	—	—	—
										.43

[a]Tariff data is not available for Australia and New Zealand. Cells showing the "average" for these countries contain the mean of b and c only.
[b]–Indicates that the index is irrelevant for that combination of countries because each are already members of EFTA.

Source: Tables 8-8, 8-10, and 8-12.

a) Index of Tariff Rate Differentials
b) Index of Comparative Efficiency
c) Index of Comparative Growth Performance

Summary and Conclusions

This chapter has attempted to utilize economic data to address the questions of (a) which configurations of countries are most likely to produce significant improvements in world economic welfare if trade liberalization occurred and (b) what combinations of countries would result in relatively high (or low) economic costs of adjustment in the transition period following liberalization. A subsidiary question, but of paramount importance for any particular country, is how do potential partners in freer trade rank as to potential long-run benefits and short-term adjustment costs. The answers to these questions generally yielded different combinations or orderings of countries, as one would expect. Indeed, combinations of countries which are likely to produce the greatest long-run improvement in the allocation of resources are likely also to experience the greatest short-run costs of transition to the new world economic structure.

Relatively rough indicators of potential economic benefit and cost of adjustment were developed and combined into indexes involving bilateral comparisons, so as to facilitate comparisons between pairs of countries. The indicators employed in the "index of competitive overlap" were the industrial structure of the country, the economic size of the manufacturing sector, and the economic distance to each other country. Each pair of countries were compared with these measures, and while recognizing some conceptual and empirical inadequacy in the latter two, the three indexes were combined into the "index of competitive overlap."

The results indicated that substantial gains might be expected from trade liberalization—on a bilateral or multilateral basis—among the United States, the United Kingdom, Japan, Canada, and Australia. Also, benefits would arise from liberalization between or among, Austria, Norway, and Sweden, and in particular instances between one of this group and one or more members of the large country group, especially Canada and the United Kingdom. For the United States alone, liberalization with Canada, the United Kingdom, Japan, Norway, and Sweden would make most long-term economic sense, in decreasing order of expected benefit.

Three different measures were used as a basis for estimating the relative magnitudes of the economic costs of transition. These were predicated on probability that the burden of economic adjustment will be positively related to the adverse movements in the trade balance which might result from trade liberalization. Adverse trade balance movements are, in turn, likely to be greater if the partner country (a) has lower tariffs than the country in question; (b) has higher costs (as measured by the ratio of value added to labor compensation), and (c) has a less dynamic (slower growing) industrial base than its partner in liberalization. These characteristics were compared, on a bilateral basis, between each pair of countries for which the earlier calculations were carried out. They were then combined into a general index of "Cost of Adjustment."

The United Kingdom, New Zealand, Austria, and Canada are predicted to have relatively high adjustment costs as a result of trade liberalization with any of the remaining countries in the sample. Japan is expected to have adjustment problems with none of the other countries, while the United States, Australia, and Sweden occupy middle ground with expected problems vis-à-vis some countries, and no problems with others.

For any particular country, the two sets of indexes provide some of the information which policy makers must consider in planning trade policy. Each must face the play-off between potential long-term benefits and the short-run costs of adjustment. By considering the rankings of its potential liberalization partners according to the two sets of indexes, or considerations, individual countries may be able to decide which countries in combination with itself can provide the greatest potential long-term gain at the least likely short-term cost. For the United States, for example, liberalization with the United Kingdom and Canada would have substantial economic benefits and would likely present little if any adjustment burden. Liberalization with Japan, on the other hand, might be desirable from the long-term point of view, but disruptive in the short run. Similar configurations can be derived for other countries.

This analysis is weakened by its failure to include the EEC countries and by less than satisfactory refinement in some of the underlying indexes. It also proceeds from the presumption that total elimination of tariffs on a bilateral basis is the situation under consideration and derives its conclusions from that premise. This, of course, ignores the complexities of the actual negotiation process, in which partial removal of tariffs and nontariff barriers, and agreed upon safe-guards are part and parcel of the process of change in trade policy. Perhaps the most important contribution of the exercise is to indicate where and with which countries these safe-guards, partial and nonreciprocal concessions are not only desirable but essential.

Notes

1. The classic works on the theory of customs unions are James Meade, *The Theory of Customs Unions* (Amsterdam: North Holland, 1955); Tibor Scitovsky, *Economic Theory and Western European Integration* (Stanford: Stanford University Press, 1958) and Jacob Viner, *The Customs Union Issue* (New York: Carnegie Endowment, 1950). The dichotomy between "static" and "dynamic" effects employed here can be found in B. Belassa, *The Theory of Economic Integration* (Homewood, Ill.: Irwin, 1961), pts I and II.

2. Viner, *Customs Union Issue*, p. 51 ff.

3. H. Makower and G. Morton, "A Contribution Towards a Theory of Customs Unions," *Economic Journal* (March 1953), pp. 33-49.

4. United Nations, *Growth of World Industry, 1967* (New York, 1971).

Basic Data on Value Added by Manufacturing Industry for Selected Countries, 1965 (millions of dollars)

Industry	U.S.	Canada	Japan	Australia	New Zealand	United Kingdom	Norway	Sweden	Austria	Belgium	Germany	Italy	Netherlands
All Manufacturing	226,973	14,602	29,569	6,296	986	33,285	1,917	6,376	3,550	4,582	46,433	13,878	4,948
Food	19,403	1,619	2,208	670	175	2,269	159	507	418	646	680	1,601	606
Beverages	4,151	495	569	119	23	1,035	60	72	132	153	n.a.	n.a.	n.a.
Tobacco	1,766	148	—	58	8	364	57	24	118	37	n.a.	106	n.a.
Textiles	7,489	651	2,342	310	47	1,981	76	187	231	387	2,408	1,162	279
Clothing, Footwear	10,110	562	522	320	69	1,299	85	257	235	199	2,495	914	250
Wood & Cork Products	4,471	619	931	260	68	414	73	365	170	18	4,558	n.a.	n.a.
Furniture & Fixtures	3,612	252	453	86	23	503	66	95	96	187	n.a.	n.a.	n.a.
Paper & Paper Prod.	8,430	1,234	1,089	213	53	954	131	510	129	98	n.a.	291	171
Printing & Publishing	12,099	692	1,378	262	61	1,710	123	341	129	148	n.a.	466	298
Leather & Leather products	900	56	108	37	7	170	8	26	25	12	n.a.	112	72
Rubber Products	5,681	241	450	100	20	554	20	85	57	28	5,833	230	n.a.
Chemicals	20,956	1,036	3,361	446	44	3,276	180	336	240	288	n.a.	n.a.	n.a.
Petroleum & Coal products	4,168	278	436	120	15	374	13	51	60	72	n.a.	n.a.	n.a.
Nonmetallic Mineral products	7,996	560	1,425	320	46	1,460	79	308	252	267	2,708	848	221
Basic Metals	18,924	1,264	2,650	677	8	2,729	184	511	263	446	4,805	875	209
Metal Products Excluding Machinery	14,164	1,199	1,667	368	70	2,466	129	416	260	n.a.	n.a.	n.a.	n.a.
Machinery excluding Electrical	22,762	742	2,736	559	68	3,617	89	1,019	220	267	n.a.	n.a.	n.a.
Electrical Machinery	20,256	981	2,878	367	37	3,005	99	430	209	n.a.	n.a.	n.a.	608
Transport Equipment	30,541	1,486	2,814	814	115	3,947	250	707	192	n.a.	n.a.	997	375
Other Manufactures	9,094	489	1,561	156	32	1,201	38	130	128	139	n.a.	250	155

Source: Calculated from data provided by the United Nations, *Growth of World Industry, 1967*. National currency values were converted to dollars at the parity exchange rates existing in 1965.

227

9

The Effects of Tariff Liberalization on International Trade Flows and the U.S. Payments Balance: An Estimate from a World-Trade Model

Rita M. Rodriguez and
Robert G. Hawkins

One of the impediments to trade liberalization is an imprecise and inadequate understanding of the results and benefits of freer trade. As noted in the previous chapter, national policy makers are faced with a series of alternative situations, each of which involves potential benefits (from better allocation of resources) and costs (as a result of transitional adjustment in the national economies), which carry a high degree of uncertainty. While analyses such as that in Chapter 8 may assist in ordering the likely benefits and costs, no estimate as to the magnitude of likely effects from an altered trade policy was provided.

This chapter attempts to provide such an estimate for one (among many) possible scenarios of trade liberalization. It utilizes a fairly standard world-trade model to derive quantitative estimates of relationships between relevant economic variables,[1] and then it introduces a changed set of variables which would likely result if trade policy were changed in a particular way. The intent is to obtain an estimate of the impact of that change in trade policy on the volume (and value) of international trade, so that a benchmark—a rough order of magnitude of the expected effect—can be obtained for at least one such scenario. Other alternative trade policies, with which we do not deal, will then at least have a frame of reference from which their effects can be examined.

A formal econometric model has certain advantages over other methods for predicting the results of policy changes. While the immediate effect of trade liberalization, for example, will be on prices in international trade and in turn on trade flows, tariff changes and the concomitant changes in trade constitute only the first steps in a chain of actions and reactions which work their way through the economies of the trading partners. For example, national incomes will change, induced price changes will occur, and international capital movements will likely be affected. Almost every economic variable which is determined by aggregate demand and supply will be influenced by these changes, and these will feed back through the determinants of exports and imports to become again reflected in the balance of payments of individual countries.

Special thanks go to Dr. Rudolf Rhomberg of the IMF, who made the model available to us, and to Mr. Grant Taplin of the IMF staff whose advice and collaboration were invaluable in adapting the model to our needs. The International Monetary Fund contributed computer time required to reestimate the equations and to obtain the simulated solutions of the model.

229

To estimate a combined impact of these first, second, and higher-order effects of changes in trade policy, it is necessary to have a framework within which some or all of these interactions are taken into account in a quantitative fashion. This can only be provided by a formal econometric model.

Description of the Model

The model employed is a slightly simplified and modified version of the IMF world-trade model.[a] The world is divided into three areas and the model estimates trade and payments flows among those areas. The main modification of the original model was to transfer two countries—Canada and Japan—from the "Rest of the World" area to the Western Europe area. This was done in an attempt to group all of the "developed" countries except the United States together, under the presumption that major trade liberalization initiatives will involve all of the developed countries on a more or less equal basis while a very different policy is more likely as between the advanced and the developing countries. In this version of the model, the three regions (excluding Communist countries) include: (a) the United States, (b) Western Europe, Canada, and Japan (other developed countries—ODC), and (c) the rest of the world (ROW).

The Variables in the Model

For each region, relationships are established for merchandise and various service imports from the other two regions. A region's exports are the combined imports of the other regions from it. The functional relations are briefly as follows:

1. Merchandise imports (by either the United States or ODC) from either of the remaining regions depend positively on (a) the level of national income (in real terms) and (b) the relationship between domestic prices and import prices.
2. Merchandise imports of ROW are determined by its total foreign exchange receipts (payments by the United States and ODC) and its payments for service imports.
3. Payments for transportation services by any region to another region depends on the volume of trade and on an upward trend term.
4. Payments for tourist expenditures depend on national income and on an upward trend term.
5. Payments of income on foreign investment depend on the stock of total foreign assets in one region owned by another region.

---

[a]The full set of equations and precise definitions of the variables are presented in the appendix to this chapter.

6. Payments for "other" services by one region to another is determined by income, or by time trend, or by certain "special events."
7. The export price index is determined by domestic prices (GNP deflator), the volume of exports, and a time trend.
8. The proportion of ROW imports which come from the U.S. or ODC regions is dependent on the ratio of the export prices of U.S. and ODC.[b]

It was decided to employ a variation of the model in which national incomes and domestic prices are treated as exogenous variables, i.e., as determined outside the model. Also treated exogenously was the unemployment rate, the exchange rate between currencies, and the foreign investment position of one region in each of the others. Similarly, the current account balance of the rest of the world was taken as given rather than determined in the model. A final omission, due to poor statistical results, is the relationship determining trade in services between ROW and ODC.

Implicitly, the model makes the quantity demanded of imports (exports) dependent on the national income at home (abroad) and on relative prices. Supply factors enter the equations through the price variables. Export prices, in turn, depend on movements in domestic prices and on the quantity of exports.

Interactions of the Variables

The primary purpose of the model is to provide mutually-consistent relationships within which to estimate the impact of a change in trade policy. The first step, however, is to estimate the relationships between the variables. The estimated equations are presented in the appendix. The parameters were estimated by ordinary least-square regression methods, on annual data for the period 1953-67.

The parameters of the model provide indications of the responsiveness of the dependent variables to changes in the determining variables in the system. Due to the objective of the analysis, the focus is on the effects which changes in prices—in response to elimination of tariffs—and in income, as an assumed consequence of freer trade, all have on the trade flows of the regions involved. Thus primary concern is with the structural sensitivity of trade to changes in prices and incomes as manifested in the model. How much will merchandise imports change if import prices or national income vary by 1 percent? As with

[b]In the actual regression analysis, export prices of the rest of the world were included as explanatory variables for imports of the U.S. (ODC) from the ODC (U.S.). The additional variable was not statistically significant or with the a priori correct sign. The inability to include the export price of the alternative source of imports unfortunately rendered it impossible to measure potential "trade diversion" effects of tariff elimination among the advanced countries only. That is, the imports rechanneled from the rest of the world into the other developed area in response to the elimination of tariffs on goods imported from the latter cannot be estimated.

all econometric models, an answer to the question for the future uses the relationships which existed in the past, and thus tacitly assumes that the relationship is unchanging through time. But the estimated elasticities over past data are superior to no information at all, and Table 9-1 presents the income and price elasticities estimated from the model.

Comparison of the price elasticities of demand for imports of the two industrialized areas (the United States and ODC) shows two important characteristics. First, as economic theory and previous empirical studies lead one to expect, imports of the developed countries are more sensitive to changes in prices of imports from the other industrialized area than to changes in the prices of imports from the rest of the world. Second, U.S. imports are in general more sensitive to changes in prices than are those of ODC. The first characteristic can be explained in terms of the commodity composition of imports from each area. Imports from industrialized countries generally comprise goods with a higher degree of processing than imports from the less developed areas, which include a large percentage of raw materials. In developed economies, imports of manufactured goods find greater competition from domestically-produced goods—and thus larger price sensitivity—than imports of raw materials which are more dependent on limitations in domestic supply—and thus less price sensitive.

The second characteristic might suggest stronger competition between imports and domestic goods in the United States than in the other industrialized countries. Yet given the period over which the equation was estimated (1953-67), one expects that the commodity structure of U.S. exports as compared with ODC exports may be the answer. The United States may have tended to export goods which did not have local competition in the ODC while

Table 9-1
Estimated Income and Price Elasticities of Demand for Merchandise Imports[a]

	Price Elasticity	Income Elasticity
U.S. Imports from:		
Other Developed Countries	−1.85	1.65
Rest of the World	−0.62	0.52
Other Developed Countries imports from:		
United States	−1.03	0.62
Rest of the World	−0.30	1.07
Elasticity of substitution between U.S. and other Developed Countries Exports to Rest of the World	−2.69	—

[a]The elasticities are the coefficients of linear equations which were estimated on the logs of the variables. The elasticities are all statistically significant at the 99 percent confidence level.

Source: Appendix to Chapter 9.

the latter were breaking into the U.S. market with commodities which were already being produced there. While these underlying forces are beyond the scope of our study, their consideration may shed light on whether the elasticities in the future will be as high as or higher than during the period covered.

The relatively low-price elasticities of demand for imports from the rest of the world imply that a reduction in export prices in the developing countries will produce a decrease in their export earnings. A price increase, on the other hand, will produce a considerable increase in export earnings. Again, this reflects the commodity composition of trade of the ROW.

It is interesting to note that the elasticity of substitution between the two industrialized areas for exports to less developed countries (ROW) is a relatively high 2.7. This could be explained by the high degree of substitutability which exists between manufactured goods of the United States and of other developed countries.

The sensitivity of a region's imports to changes in its income is measured by the income elasticities in Table 9-1. United States imports from other developed countries are highly responsive to changes in U.S. income. However, changes in imports from the United States are less than proportional to changes in incomes in ODC. Thus, if economic growth in both the United States and ODC were at the same rate, the model predicts that the United States would develop a merchandise trade deficit vis-à-vis the other industrialized countries. Again, this may reflect a certain sensitivity of the parameters to the period over which the estimate is made—a period during which the U.S. trade balance was deteriorating and those of other developed countries were, on average, improving. At the same time, the United States was growing relatively slower than the average for ODCs. This configuration of circumstances has a number of sources, some of which had trade policy origins (the formation of the EEC and EFTA), and others had supply origins (the penetration of the U.S. market by foreign cars, steel, textiles, etc. from countries whose capacity to produce—and export—had been restored in the 1950s and 1960s). In any event, the relative size of the income elasticities of demand for imports from each other of the United States and ODC could not persist in the very long run without major strains on the international monetary system. We assume, however, that they would persist in the relatively short run, or to 1975 as is analyzed below.

Imports from the less-developed countries, however, will increase faster to the ODC than to the United States (elasticities with respect to income of 1.07 for ODC and 0,63 for the United States).

Estimating the Impact of Tariff Elimination: Assumptions

The equations estimated, encompassing behavioral relationships among economic variables, will be used to estimate the impact of elimination of tariffs by the developed regions. The objective is to assess the economic changes that a reciprocal elimination of tariffs would produce, rather than make a precise forecast of the levels that trade and income would achieve under the new conditions. That is, the concern is not with the precise magnitudes, but with the question: Given a certain world economic structure, if trade barriers were eliminated among the advanced countries—and some economic variables are thereby predictably affected—by how much will other economic variables change? A forecast requires an accurate prediction of every variable which is determined outside the system—for example, exchange rates, domestic prices, national incomes, and so on—while our intent is only to predict the likely changes in the exogenous variables most likely to be affected by trade liberalization. In what follows, the estimates of the model assuming no trade-policy changes are compared with the estimates of the model when trade liberalization is assumed to affect the export prices and the income variables, that is, with the simulated trade flows with free trade among the advanced countries.

While the values of the independent (determining) variables are changed to reflect the impact of tariff elimination, the same structural equations are employed (the same relationships between variables) to estimate the results of that change. Thus we ignore any potential feedback which freer trade might have on the relationships between the relevant variables which might alter them from the average 1953-67 values found in the regressions. We thus implicitly assume that the responsiveness of trade flows to prices, incomes, and so on, will be the same within a freer-trade environment as it was, on average, for the last fifteen years.

This is necessitated by a lack of information about the magnitude of structural changes which tariff removal would produce. Though it is reasonable to assume that improved communication will be triggered and will make consumers more aware of products in partner countries, and thus change the relations between trade flows and their determinants, we know very little about the nature of such changes. Instead of speculating about such changes, we prefer to consider our estimates of trade flows with tariff elimination to be biased downwards.

To isolate the economic impact of trade liberalization within the context of the model, the number of variables whose values are modified are limited so as to consider only the direct effects of the policy change. The values of these variables were changed on the basis of estimated tariff rates and judgment. The price change measures the results of the elimination of tariffs among the participating developed countries. The changes in the national income of the respective regions, which are made on the basis of assumption, are intended to reflect the alterations in economic growth induced by the increased specialization and gain from international trade. The level of national income may be altered by tariff elimination due to change in imports and exports which affect national income through the multiplier, and indirect effects of more efficient resource allocation in response to the new trade patterns.

Finally, changes in the investment position are assumed, so as to incorporate a priori considerations about capital flows in the context of tariff elimination. These, however, are completely subjective and do not affect, nor are they affected by, the estimates of the model.

Assumption 1: United States import prices from other developed countries (ODCs export prices to the United States) are reduced by 7 percent and the prices of imports of other developed countries (United States export prices) are reduced by 5.7 percent. These percentages are the implicit tariff rates on imports of one region from the other. It is assumed that neither the United States nor the ODCs reduce tariffs on imports from ROW. The levels of national income and foreign investment flows are unaffected.

The assumed tariff reductions are derived from the overall average of nominal tariffs weighted by the trade of the EEC, EFTA, Japan and Canada, imposed by the two groups on each other's products. The average includes not only manufactured goods (with slightly higher average tariffs) but also crude materials and semimanufactures. Agricultural commodities are excluded from the average. Trade policy relating to agriculture is so intractable and problematic that general tariff elimination would probably not be able to include agricultural commodities (see Chapter 11).

Our rationale for excluding the ROW from the tariff elimination is that trade between the two advanced regions and ROW is relatively price insensitive. Also, even if the ROW were to enter into a general scheme of tariff elimination, special safe-guards would undoubtably be applied by the advanced countries to limit the increase in imports of sensitive items for which developing countries have a substantial supply potential. It is equally unlikely that the countries in the ROW region would be in a position to grant meaningful tariff concessions to the advanced countries, given the use of import restrictions in the overall economic planning procedure, and import substitution and export stimulation policies in particular. In short, it seemed less of a violation of realism to exclude the ROW region from the assumed tariff elimination than to include them as full participants.[c]

Assumption 2: Import prices (tariffs) are reduced as under assumption 1. In addition, U.S. real national income increases by 1 percent and that of other developed countries increases by 2 percent. Foreign investment positions remain unchanged.

This admittedly arbitrary set of assumptions is intended to reflect the increment to national incomes which the direct and indirect effects of trade

---

[c]Another practical consideration is that a reliable tariff estimate for that region is not available.

liberalization would likely produce. These would arise because of an increase in the efficiency of the international allocation of resources, possible economies of scale, and the benefits of increased competition. While it is not feasible to estimate precisely this impact on the two regions, it is reasonable to expect that it would be substantially larger in the other developed countries than in the United States, because of the relatively "closed" nature of the U.S. economy, and the large size of the already integrated U.S. market. The scope for potential benefit is less, relative to total output, in the United States than in the other advanced countries, despite the limited integration already achieved in Europe.

One alternative to assuming what appear to be reasonable orders of magnitude for the "income effect" of trade liberalization would have been to use a version of the econometric model which made the regions' national incomes endogenous, that is, jointly determined with the trade variables by relationships in the model. This option was rejected because of the greater complications in estimating the relationships, which would have reduced their reliability. Also, the model is capable of treating only Keynesian "multiplier" effects on income from additional trade flows, while the more important effects being considered resulted from structural and allocational change and not from the straight-forward mutliplier process.

Assumption 3: Import prices (tariffs) are reduced and real national income is increased as under assumption 2. The international investment positions (stock of total foreign assets) of each developed area in the other developed area are increased by 10 percent as a result of tariff elimination.

Although the pure theory of international trade predicts that tariffs stimulate foreign investment and, by inference, that tariff reduction would allow trade to substitute for investment,[2] there is considerable evidence to suggest that the geographical structure of trade is highly correlated with the geographical structure of foreign investment. In breaking down international market imperfections, trade and investment often seem to be complements rather than substitutes. For this reason, and because the atmosphere within which major trade liberalization would occur is likely also to be conducive to international investment, we have assumed an increase in such investment under assumption 3. The magnitude of the increase is debatable, but we chose 10 percent, again arbitrarily, as being a conservative rough order of magnitude. Since the stock of international investment is a determinant of certain of the service items, this assumption affects the overall impact of the trade liberalization.

The impact of these three alternative situations on merchandise trade accounts of all three regions, and on the service accounts for the United States, were estimated for 1967 and 1975. In each case, the estimated payments and receipts among the regions with the current tariff rates are compared with the estimated values under each of the three sets of assumptions for liberalization. The last year for which complete data were available at the time of estimation was 1967, and thus it serves as the year on which to base one set of effects.

It was also considered appropriate to obtain an estimate for a future year after the induced effects on income and investment would have had time to work themselves out. The exogenous variables, therefore, are their actual values in 1967 and the projected values for 1975. The projections are based on the extrapolation of a linear trend for the period 1953-67. These assumptions would be totally inappropriate if our objective were to "forecast" the actual values of the items in the balance of payments in 1975. But the intent of the analysis is only to obtain a comparison of the situations which would prevail with and without elimination of tariffs, *ceteris paribus*. A percentage estimate is thus of the most value, and is not highly sensitive to the assumptions used in obtaining the trend value for 1975.

Simulated Results of Tariff Elimination

Estimated Effect on Merchandise Trade

The largest impact of tariff removal will, of course, be on merchandise trade flows. The estimated changes in trade flows among the three regions under assumption 1 and assumption 2 for 1975 are presented in Table 9-2. If allowance is made only for the elimination of tariffs (assumption 1), the volume of world trade would increase by an estimated $4.7 billions. If in addition, allowance is made for increase in the national incomes of the United States and other developed countries, as stated in assumption 2, the volume of world trade would increase by $7.8 billions. These increases represent increments of approximately 4 percent and 6 percent respectively to the expected level of world trade without tariff changes.

The absolute increase in U.S. exports are smaller than those of the ODC region. Under assumption 1, exports of United States to ODC increase by $1.8 billions, while the exports of the ODC to the United States increase by an estimated $2.8 billions. This represents an increase in ODC exports to the United States of 11.46 percent but only a 7.75 percent increase for U.S. exports to ODC. When income growth is taken into account under assumption 2, U.S. exports to ODC increase by $2.1 billions (9.08 percent) while the exports of the other developed countries to the United States increase by $3.2 billions (13.32 percent).

The imbalance in export expansion for the two industrialized regions are a result of the elasticities estimated by the model for the past relationships, mainly differences in the price elasticities of demand for imports from the other region.

Table 9-2
Estimated Changes in Merchandise Trade Flows in 1975 Among Three Regions Due to Elimination of Tariffs by U.S. and ODC (billions of U.S. dollars)

Exports From / To	U.S.	ODC	ROW	Total Imports
		Assumption 1		
U.S.	–	+2.801	0	+2.801
ODC	+1.792	–	0	+1.792
ROW	–0.081	+0.185	–	+0.104
Total Exports	+1.711	+2.986	0	+4.697
		Assumption 2		
U.S.	–	+3.253	+0.100	+3.353
ODC	+2.099	–	+1.146	+3.245
ROW	+0.160	+1.044	–	+1.204
Total Exports	+2.259	+4.297	+1.246	+7.802

The United States not only has shown a higher responsiveness to changes in import prices than the ODC, as noted earlier, but also U.S. import prices are assumed to be reduced by a slightly larger percentage than the import prices of the ODC, that is, the average U.S. tariff rate is marginally higher than that for the ODC.

When the assumed derivative increases in income are taken into account, the exports of each of the two developed areas increase by more nearly equal percentages than when only the tariff elimination is considered under assumption 1. The assumed percentage increase in income is 1 percent for the United States and 2 percent for the ODC. This by itself will tend to make U.S. exports grow faster than those of the ODC; however, the combination of a lower income elasticity of demand for imports by the ODC and the high income elasticity of demand for imports by the United States from the ODC partially offsets the tendencies resulting from the the differences in growth rates.

The estimates also predict that the ODC would be able to expand exports more than the United States as a result of the increase in imports by the ROW.[d] A partial explanation of this difference is the way in which the estimating equations were specified. The export price variable for the United States was determined by U.S. domestic prices (GNP deflator) and the volume of U.S. exports. In the case of the ODC, export prices proved to be a function of

---

[d]The small changes in imports of the ROW under assumption 1 when only export prices of industrial countries are altered are due to some changes in the foreign exchange receipts of the ROW that are originated on service items which are a function of trade volume of the two areas combined.

domestic prices only; export volume was not a statistically significant determinant. While this may involve some misspecification, it may also be a fairly accurate reflection of export price behavior in the two regions. In the United States, export prices have been more volatile than abroad, perhaps reflecting the fact that U.S. exporters consider export sales more of a residual than their foreign competitors. If so, export levels as an index of pressure of domestic demand and domestic supply limitation would be a significant determinant. In ODC countries, however, exporters may give the export market first priority so that expansion of export sales at constant prices occurs regardless of local supply limitations or demand pressures. In that case, the export volume would not be a determinant of export prices.

Given the structure of the two relationships, the elimination of tariffs leads to an increase in exports by the United States and ODC, but the export prices of the United States also rise, as volume expands, while the export prices of the ODC are not affected by the expansion of their exports. The ratio of U.S. to ODC export prices is thus altered, inducing the ROW to switch some imports from the U.S. to the ODC. This suggests, then, that trade liberalization among the advanced countries would result in a lower share for U.S. exports in the markets of the developing countries.

Under assumption 2, the exports of the ROW expand more due to the growth in ODC than from the increase in demand assumed for the United States. The income elasticity of demand for imports from the rest of the world region is higher for the ODC region than for the United States. In addition, the larger percentage increase in income in the ODC than in the United States has been assumed.

Summary of the Estimated Impacts on
Merchandise Trade Balances

The estimates of changes in exports and imports for the regions are shown in Table 9-2. For the United States, it is obvious that the total increase in imports is estimated to be larger than the total increase in exports, under either assumption. The opposite is true for the ODC. Thus, changes in trade flows induced by tariff elimination seem likely to deteriorate the merchandise trade balance for the United States and improve it for the ODC. The ROW trade balance would deteriorate slightly under assumption 1 and improve considerably under assumption 2, perhaps the more realistic one.

Keeping in mind the significant reservations concerning the use of the model, it is useful to examine the impact on the balances of trade for each area of trade liberalization under the alternative assumed conditions. These figures represent, at best, only general indications of the trends that these balances would be likely to exhibit. Table 9-3 presents balance of trade figures for each area for 1967 and

Table 9-3
Merchandise Trade Balances and the Effects of Tariff Removal (Current U.S. Billion Dollars)

	U.S.		ODC		ROW	
	Balance	Effect of Tariff Removal	Balance	Effect of Tariff Removal	Balance	Effect of Tariff Removal
1967						
Without Tariff Removal						
Actual	3.477		−6.198		2.721	
Model solution	2.826		−5.441		2.616	
With Tariff Removal						
Assumption 1	2.156	−0.679	−4.694	+0.747	2.538	−0.078
1975						
Without Tariff Removal						
Model solution	0.385		−1.837		1.451	
With Tariff Removal						
Assumption 1	−0.705	−1.090	−0.642	+1.195	1.347	−0.104
Assumption 2	−0.709	−1.094	−0.784	+1.053	1.493	+0.042

1975 for assumptions 1 and 2. These are also compared with the actual trade balances for 1967 and with those estimated by the model without trade policy change.

Assuming tariffs remained as they are, the tendencies from 1967 to 1975 would be for a substantial decrease in the trade surplus of the United States and for a similar improvement in the trade balance of the ODC—of $3.1 and $4.4 billion respectively from the actual balances for 1967. The predicted impact of tariff removal by the United States and ODC will accentuate these trends in their balances of trade. In the estimates for both 1967 and 1975, tariff removal would turn the U.S. trade surplus into a trade deficit, of $700 million in 1975. This would represent a deterioration of $1.1 billion due to tariff removal. For the ODC, however, their combined trade deficits would be reduced considerably, by a similar magnitude. The ROW merchandise trade balance would be little affected. Considering the tariff removal affect only, it would be harmed by $100 million. If the indirect effects on income assumed here are achieved, a slight improvement might be expected.

Estimated Effects on Service Items
and the U.S. Current Account

When service items in the balance of payments are considered together with the trade balance, the predicted effects of tariff removal for the United States is more optimistic from the balance of payments perspective. Since our concern is mainly with the impact on the United States, estimates of the effects on the service items in the ODC and ROW regions are not shown. The results for the United States, under all three assumptions are shown in Table 9-4. The effects of growth as projected to 1975 are shown, both assuming constant tariffs and removal of tariffs, under each of the assumptions.

For the service account of the United States vis-à-vis the ODC region, tariff removal is estimated to increase U.S. receipts from ODC by more than the increased payments of the United States to this area, for each assumption. The predictions are thus that the U.S. surplus on service accounts with the ODC countries would increase with tariff removal, ranging from $40 million to $350 million, depending on assumption. The most important item in this estimated improvement is the growth in U.S. receipts of dividends and interest from investments abroad under assumption 3. Under assumptions 1 and 2, which assume that foreign investment is unaffected by tariff removal, the change in the service accounts between the United States and ODC would be negligible (1-2 percent). Under assumption 3, however, an equal percentage increase (10 percent) in investment in foreign assets in the two industrialized areas increases the receipts on income from foreign investment by the United States to a much greater extent than the increase in such income for ODC. The result is that U.S. service receipts from ODC increase over 8 percent while the U.S. payments to ODC increases by less than 5 percent. This improvement on U.S. service account should be taken as an outside upper limit.

In the U.S. service account with the ROW, receipts substantially exceed payments, both currently and as projected to 1975 without changes in trade policy. This relationship is maintained under the assumptions concerning the results of tariff removal between the United States and ODC. While under assumption 1 the U.S. balance on services with the rest of the world region would decline slightly, under the more realistic assumption 2, and also under assumption 3, the U.S. service balance would be improved—again slightly. In every case, the estimated percentage changes in U.S. payments to or receipts from ROW are small (less than 3 percent) and the corresponding changes in the net balance are also small.

As one would expect, the general impact of tariff removal on the service accounts is quite small relative to the (absolute or proportional) change in merchandise trade flows. For the United States, reciprocal tariff removal with the ODC region would have a very small (1-3 percent) effect on the service accounts, and the net effect would range from a slight ($68 million) adverse impact under assumption 1, to the more realistic positive impacts of $134 million and $391 million under assumptions 2 and 3 respectively.

That these magnitudes are minor when compared with the impact on trade account discussed above can be seen from the lower row in Table 9-4. There are presented the overall estimates for the current account (combining the trade and service estimates). The estimated impact of tariff removal on the United States

Table 9-4
U.S. Current Account and the Effects in 1975 of Tariff Removal

	Projected 1975 Value Without Tariff Removal	Projected Values with Tariff Removal							
		Assumption 1			Assumption 2			Assumption 3	
		Value	Change	% Change	Value	Change	% Change	Value	Change	% Change
		(Current U.S. billion $)			(Current U.S. billion $)			(Current U.S. billion $)		
Export of goods and services										
Merchandise exports										
To ODC	$23.116	$24.908	+1.792	+ 7.75%	$25.215	+2.099	+ 8.08%	$25.215	+2.099	+ 9.08%
To ROW	10.904	10.823	−0.081	− 0.74	11.064	+0.160	+ 1.47	11.064	+0.160	+ 1.47
	34.020	35.731	+1.711	+ 5.03	36.279	+2.259	+ 6.64	36.279	+2.259	+ 6.64
Service receipts										
From ODC	9.526	9.631	+0.105	+ 1.10	9.712	+0.186	+ 1.95	10.294	+0.768	+ 8.06
From ROW	7.418	7.400	−0.018	− 0.24	7.566	+0.148	+ 2.00	7.566	+0.148	+ 2.00
	16.944	17.031	+0.087		17.279	+0.334		17.860	+0.916	
Total receipts	50.964	52.762			53.558			54.139		
Imports of goods and services										
Merchandise imports										
From ODC	24.430	27.231	+2.801	+11.46	27.683	+3.253	+13.32	27.683	+3.253	+13.32
From ROW	9.205	9.205	—	—	9.305	+0.100	+ 1.09	9.305	+0.100	+ 1.09
	33.635	36.437	+2.802	+ 8.33	36.988	+3.353	+ 9.97	36.988	+3.353	+ 9.97
Service payments										
To ODC	8.843	8.912	+0.069	+ 0.78	8.937	+0.094	+ 1.06	9.262	+0.419	+ 4.74
To ROW	3.636	3.722	+0.086	+ 2.36	3.742	+0.106	+ 2.92	3.742	+0.106	+ 2.92
	12.479	12.634	+0.155		12.679	+0.200		13.004	0.525	
Total payments	46.114	49.071			49.667			49.992		
Current account balance	4.851	3.692	−1.159	−23.89	3.890	−0.961	−19.81	4.146	−0.705	−14.53

ranges from an adverse movement in the current account of $1.2 billion under assumption 1 (a reduction in the projected current account surplus in 1975 with existing tariffs of 24 percent) to an adverse impact of $700 million (14.5 percent of the projected 1975 surplus) under assumption 3. The range of variation of the final estimate on the current account among the assumptions is relatively narrow, despite the diverse ingredients of assumptions. It should be noted, however, that these estimates deal only with the current account impact, and ignores the implicit adverse impact of assumption 3 on the U.S. capital account. Equal 10 percent increases in the foreign investment position of the United States in the ODC and vice versa would result in a substantially larger outflow from the United States rather than inflow.

Conclusions

This chapter has attempted to quantify, albeit in a crude way, the probable impact of general trade liberalization on international trade flows and current account balances. It has utilized a comprehensive and internally consistent world-trade model encompassing three regions to derive its estimates. It has limited its commercial policy alternatives to reciprocal removal of all tariffs (excluding those on agriculture products) by the United States and other developed countries, and has ignored the complications of nontariff barriers to trade and the tariff policy of the developing countries, which are the main elements in the rest-of-the-world region. Finally, the variation of the model employed makes the national incomes and domestic prices of the region exogenous variables, which introduces various shortcomings of consistency and interdependence, but permits a tractable focus on the specific relationships under discussion.

Thus the model, as applied, has a number of shortcomings, and only a limited range of effects of tariff removal have been explored. Because of the form of the model used, certain of the effects of tariff removal (on changes in national income and in foreign investment) have been determined by assumption.

Despite these limitations, and considering the resulting tentative nature of the findings, the estimated effects on the trade of the three regions and on the current account of the United States appear not only plausible, but clustered in a narrow range—less dependent on the assumptions than on the value of the empirical estimates of the functional relationships. The model predicts that the exports of each area would increase, and that the volume of world trade would increase roughly 5 percent as a result of reciprocal tariff removal by the advanced countries.

The technique used here of naïve projection for the variables to 1975 based on their trend values from 1953 to 1967 yielded an estimated substantial deterioration in the U.S. trade (and current account) balance, and a roughly equal increase in the trade balance of the other advanced countries. While such a projection was largely mechanical, its general predictions were already borne out by 1971, and its implications for stress on the world monetary system were manifest in the alterations in exchange rates and currency crises in 1971 and 1972. An important implication of this naïve projection of the model is that the pre-1971 structure of national economies, and their relationships with external payments and receipts, would almost certainly lead to increasing international monetary disequilibrium. As a result, nations demonstrated both a greater proclivity to use trade policy for balance of payments purposes and a lessened desire to engage in broad negotiations to reduce or eliminate reciprocally trade barriers.

More importantly, the model predicts two developments which are intimately related to trade negotiations. First, the reciprocal elimination of tariffs only among the developed countries would significantly harm the U.S. trade balance and yield an improvement in the trade balance of the other developed countries—as a group. While this assumption of a particular policy change is not intended as a prediction of what is likely to occur at the next trade negotiations, these estimated results are sufficient to explain why it is an unlikely trade policy posture. While the benefits of freer trade may be substantial (in real economic terms), the costs of adjusting to tariff changes must also be considered. And a significant deterioration in the current account balance of a principle negotiating partner indicates a high adjustment cost, and that negotiating partner is likely not to agree to mutual reduction or elimination of trade barriers which would result in it.

The estimates here—showing an expected sizable reduction in the U.S. merchandise trade balance combined with a very small net improvement in the service accounts—would indicate that the United States, in order to equalize more generally the adjustment burden, would offer less than complete elimination of its own tariffs in return for elimination by other advanced countries, or other possible *quid pro quos* such as unilateral removal of foreign NTBs to U.S. exports, safeguards for U.S. domestic producers, and other such devices. Put differently, the model indicates why simple, across the board tariff elimination will not work, and why tedious and complex negotiations are the more likely result.

Finally, the model predicts that full tariff elimination among themselves by advanced countries would have little impact on the current accounts of the developing (ROW) countries. Considering the impact of the tariff removal alone, as one would expect, the trade diversion effect on the exports of the LDCs is negative, but surprisingly small. On the other hand, assuming any sizable indirect effect on the national incomes of the advanced countries will stimulate LDC exports sufficiently to offset the adverse direct effect. This suggests that, in the short run, LDCs have a credible case for the extension of unilateral tariff concessions by the advanced countries if the latter liberalize trade among themselves. Such preferences, or their absence, should not however be expected to initiate a major change in the trade positions of the LDCs.

Notes

1. Rudolf R. Rhomberg and Lorette Boissonneault, "Effects of Income and Price Changes on the U.S. Balance of Payments," *IMF Staff Papers*, March 1964.

2. See R.A. Mundell, "International Trade and Factor Mobility," *American Economic Review*, June 1957, pp. 321-35.

3. Rhomberg and Boissoneault, "Income and Price Changes."

4. Ibid., pp. 116-22.

Appendix to Chapter 9

This appendix describes the econometric model used to estimate the impact of eliminating tariffs reciprocally among the noncommunist, developed countries on the trade flows of the United States and the group of other developed countries.

Additional details of the model can be found in an article by Rhomberg and Boissoneault in which the model, without our alterations, is presented.[3] The major change for this analysis was to move Japan and Canada from the "Rest of the World" region and into the European countries region, which we call other developed countries (ODC). This then gave a three-sector world as follows: (1) a sector including the OECD advanced countries other than the U.S. (ODC); (2) the United States; and (3) the rest of the world, including developing countries and the Communist countries. New equations were estimated on data from this configuration of countries. We then simulated the introduction of the elimination of tariffs between the ODCs and the United States. The results of that simulation were described in the text.

The basic structure of the model is straightforward. The values for each of the current account items—payments and receipts—of each region is determined by a series of exogenous variables, except that the export price index of the United States and ODC is determined endogenously. National income, domestic (internal) prices, and the level of foreign investment by one region in another are the principle exogenous variables. These, and the explicit relationships estimated, are shown below.

In the following sections are: (1) the precise definitions of variables in the model and their symbols, (2) the estimated equations and their measures of significance, and (3) the sources of the data.

List of Variables

Exogenous variables

Y_i = GNP in current prices and 1958 exchange rates, in billions of U.S. dollars ($i = 1,2$).

U_i = Number of unemployed as a percent of civilian labor force ($i = 1$).

I_{ij} = Investment position of region j in region i, at year end, i.e., total foreign assets including short-term and nonprivate, in billions of U.S. dollars.

P_i = Implicit price deflator (1958 = 1; $i = 1,2$).

V_2 = Implicit exchange rate of European OECD countries plus Canada and Japan vis-à-vis U.S. dollar (1958 = 1), i.e., these countries' GNP in current U.S. dollars and 1958 exchange rates divided by GNP in current U.S. dollars and current exchange rates.

$WTBK$ = Foreign workers admitted for temporary employment in U.S. agriculture, in thousands.

H_2 = Change in inventories of European OECD countries plus Canada and Japan in current prices and 1958 exchange rates.

B_3 = Autonomous current account balance of the rest of the world, i.e., net exports of goods and services from national income accounts less balance of endogenous current account items.

t = Calendar year minus 1952.

Jointly dependent variables

M_{21}^{as} = "Extraordinary" imports of automobiles and steel from Western Europe into the United States, in billions of U.S. dollars in 1954 prices. This variable is used as an adjustment to M_{12} (U.S. imports from Western Europe) and represents (1) the excess (for 1956-60) of automobile imports for 1955 and for 1961, and (2) an independent estimate for extraordinary steel imports at the end of 1959 and beginning on 1960 as a result of the steel strike in the United States.

M_{ij} = Value of merchandise imports into region j from region i, in billions of U.S. dollars.

F_{ij} = Payments for transportation services by region j to region i, in billions of U.S. dollars.

V_{ij} = Payments for tourist travel service by region j to region i, in billions of U.S. dollars.

D_{ij} = Payments of interest and dividend by region j to region i, in billions of U.S. dollars.

O_{ij} = Payments for other private services by region j to region i, in billions of U.S. dollars.

P_{xi} = Export unit value index in U.S. dollars (1958 = 1).

Equations

Region 1: United States

	$\overline{R}^2$	DW	$SE/\overline{X}$

1. In logs $\quad \dfrac{M_{21}}{P_{x2}} - M_{21}^{as} = -3.416 + 1.653\ \dfrac{Y_1}{P_1} - .205\,U + 1.850\ \dfrac{P_1}{P_{x2}}$

$\qquad\qquad\qquad\qquad (4.62) \quad (6.51) \qquad\quad (2.27) \qquad (3.15)$

     .993   1.556   1.35

2. In logs $\quad \dfrac{M_{31}}{P_{x3}} - .497 + .521\ \dfrac{Y_1}{P_1} - .120\,U + .617\ \dfrac{P_1}{P_{x3}}$

$\qquad\qquad\qquad\quad (1.36) \quad (4.13) \qquad\quad (2.70) \qquad (3.45)$

     .978   1.067   1.04

3. $\quad F_{21} = .179 + .026\ \left(\dfrac{M_{21}}{P_{x2}} + \dfrac{M_{31}}{P_{x3}} \right) + .080\,t$

$\qquad\qquad\quad (2.42) \quad (2.86) \qquad\qquad\qquad (8.26)$

     .988   1.032   3.77

4. $\quad F_{31} = .197 + .0320\ \left(\dfrac{M_{21}}{P_{x2}} + \dfrac{M_{31}}{P_{x3}} \right)$

$\qquad\qquad\quad (3.62) \quad (9.76)$

     .871   .616   7.86

5. In logs $\quad V_{21} = -3.690 + 1.358\,Y_1$

$\qquad\qquad\qquad (23.40) \quad (23.53)$

     .975   1.557   0.00

6. $\quad V_{31} = .0139 + .000771\,Y_1 + .003\,t$

$\qquad\qquad\quad (.35) \quad (5.82) \qquad (8.36)$

     .997   1.758   1.85

7. In logs $\quad D_{21} = -2.086 + 1.332\,I_{12}$

$\qquad\qquad\qquad (15.69) \quad (14.99)$

     .941   1.386   0.00

	$\overline{R}^2$	DW	$SE/\overline{X}$

8.
$$D_{31} = -1.78 + .0306\,I_{13} + .0146\,t$$
$$(6.74) \quad (5.38) \qquad (4.75)$$

	$\overline{R}^2$	DW	$SE/\overline{X}$
8.	.962	1.360	12.91

9. In logs
$$O_{21} = 3.793 - 1.856\,Y_1 + .0769\,t$$
$$(2.13) \quad (2.63) \qquad (4.51)$$

9. In logs	.952	1.792	0.00

10.
$$O_{31} = .0388 + .000274\,WTBK + .00653\,t$$
$$(1.53) \qquad (5.73) \qquad\quad (3.84)$$

10.	.690	1.495	10.27

11.
$$P_{x1} = .278 + 1.294\,P_1 + .00711\left(\frac{M_{12} + M_{13}}{P_{x1}}\right) - .0214\,t$$
$$(1.25) \quad (5.19) \qquad (3.59) \qquad\qquad\qquad (3.78)$$

11.	.964	1.859	.83

Region 2: Western Europe plus Canada and Japan

12. In logs
$$\frac{M_{12}}{P_{x1}} = -.716 + .615\,\frac{Y_2 - H_2}{P_2} + .214\,\frac{H_2}{P_2} + 1.03\,\frac{P_2}{P_{x1}R_2}$$
$$(1.40) \quad (3.09) \qquad\qquad (5.28) \qquad\quad (2.12)$$

12. In logs	.973	1.219	1.60

13. In logs
$$\frac{M_{32}}{P_{x3}} = 1.492 + 1.073\,\frac{Y_2 - H_2}{P_2} + .0585\,\frac{H_2}{P_2} + .295\,\frac{P_2}{P_{x3}r_2}$$
$$(4.48) \quad (8.33) \qquad\qquad (3.12) \qquad\quad (1.72)$$

13. In logs	.995	.750	0.59

14.
$$F_{12} = .210 + .0585\,M_{12} + .0183\,t$$
$$(5.02) \quad (8.26) \qquad (2.96)$$

14.	.991	1.924	2.51

	$\overline{R}^2$	DW	$SE/\overline{X}$
15.	.853	.675	9.45
16.	.988	2.134	0.00
18.	.928	1.515	0.00
20.	.822	1.538	0.00
21.	.928	1.976	5.25

15. $\quad V_{12} = .200 + .000779\ Y_2$
$$\qquad\quad (4.78)\qquad (9.08)$$

16. In logs $\quad D_{12} = -1.891 + 1.292\,I_{21}$
$$\qquad\qquad\quad (31.33)\quad (34.27)$$

17. $\quad O_{12} = -.256 + .00227\,P_2$
$$\qquad\quad (14.94)\quad (13.49)$$

18. In logs $\quad P_{x2r2} = .00341 + .299\,P_2$
$$\qquad\qquad\qquad\qquad (13.49)$$

Region 3: Rest of the World

19. $\quad B_3 = M_{13} + M_{23} + F_{13} + V_{13} + D_{13} + O_{13} - M_{31} - M_{32} - F_{31} -$
$$\qquad\quad V_{31} - D_{31} - O_{31}$$

20. In logs $\quad \dfrac{M_{13}/P_{x1}}{M_{23}/P_{x2}} = -.398 - 2.694\,\dfrac{P_{x1}}{P_{x2}}$
$$\qquad\qquad\qquad\qquad\quad (79.48)\quad (8.11)$$

21. $\quad F_{13} = -.158 + .126\,\dfrac{M_{13}}{P_{x1}}$
$$\qquad\quad (2.14)\quad (13.51)$$

	$\bar{R}^2$	DW	SE/$\bar{X}$
22. $V_{13} = -.528 + .0381 \left(\dfrac{M_{31} + M_{32}}{P_{x3}}\right) - .0245\, t$ (6.91) (8.20) (2.98)	.985	1.759	5.15
23. In logs $D_{13} = -1.363 + .372\, I_{31} + .802\, (M_{31} + M_{32})$ (6.74) (2.60) (3.01)	.976	1.320	6.41
24. $O_{13} = -.0495 + .0165\, (M_{31} + M_{32}) + .0207\, t$ (1.02) (6.12) (4.63)	.990	2.249	3.10
25. $P_{x3} = .766 + .0181 \left(\dfrac{M_{31} + M_{32}}{P_{x3}}\right) + .0379\, t$ (14.41) (5.60) (6.62)	.831	1.536	1.50

The numbers in parentheses below coefficient estimates represent the t statistic.

$\bar{R}^2$ = coefficient of determination adjusted for degrees of freedom.

SE/$\bar{X}$ = Standard error of estimate as a percent of the sample mean of the dependent variable.

DW = Durbin-Watson test statistic.

Data and Sources

The data and sources used in the model are well described in the above mentioned article[4] and not included in this section. The new data employed for these estimates were for Canada and Japan, the two countries that had to be excluded from the rest of the world area and included with the Western European area. Below we list the variables and sources used to obtain the relevant data for these two countries.

$M_{12}, M_{13}, M_{21}, M_{31}$ Department of Commerce, *Survey of Current Business*

P_{x2}, P_{x3} Price indices—International Monetary Fund, *International Financial Statistics*

                     Weights—Exports reported by Canada, Japan and OECD Europe, for 1962-64. OECD, *Overall Trade by Countries*, 1966.

$F_{ij}, V_{ij}, O_{ij}, D_{ij}$ *1960-67* Department of Commerce, *Survey of Current Business*, June 1968.

                     1953-59 Canada—Department of Commerce, *Balance of Payments Supplement*, 1963 edition.

                     Japan—Extrapolation of time trend for 1960-67.

I_{ij} Canada—Department of Commerce, *Survey of Current Business*, June 1968.

                     Japan—Derived from data on flows of capital and sparse information on some types of security stocks and interest rates.

M_{23}, M_{32} 1960-67 OECD, Series A
                     1953-59 OECD, Series I

Y_2, H_2 International Monetary Fund, *International Financial Statistics*, various issues.

10 Trade Liberalization and Economies of Large-Scale Production

Morris Goldstein

One of the principal arguments in support of freer trade in industrial products is that it offers potential economies of scale to most, if not all, of the participating nations. The basic argument is that the elimination of tariff and nontariff barriers will lead to decreases in the average cost of production in the plants, industries, and national economies of the member nations. These average cost decreases are expected to accrue primarily from two sources: (a) increases in both the size of plants and in the volume of production of the surviving suppliers due to the increased access to foreign markets, i.e., rightward movements along a declining long-run average cost curve, and (b) the forced adoption of more efficient production techniques and other positive changes in the character of competition, resulting from the increased intrusion of foreign firms into domestic markets, i.e., downward shifts of the long-run average cost curve.

While there is no denying the alluring intuitive appeal of the economies-of-scale case for freer trade, national policy makers might well express legitimate doubts about its practical importance for a variety of reasons.

First, if such potential economies of scale exist, we are at this time unsure about their probable size for any particular nation. Detailed cost studies for different sizes of plant—for a large number of industries and for a large group of countries—are available on only a very limited basis. And yet such cost studies are a *sine qua non* of estimating economies of scale in the traditional sense. Alternative methods of estimating economies of scale, such as engineering cost estimates, the survivor technique, and production function estimates, have been applied to few countries other than the United States, Canada, and the United Kingdom; and even where applied, the results have been less than reliably conclusive. Given this impressionistic character of the empirical evidence on the size of potential economies of scale, the benefits associated with these economies are open to question.

Second, the lack of empirical evidence on potential economies of scale among nations is in no small part traceable to the as yet unresolved problem of how to

The author wishes to acknowledge his indebtedness to Solomon Fabricant, Robert Hawkins, Ingo Walter, Daniel Saks, H.G. Georgiadis, Edward Denison, Lawrence Krause, Walter Salant, and John Tilton for their helpful comments and suggestions on earlier drafts of this chapter. The author remains of course solely responsible for the present text, and the views expressed therein are the author's alone and not necessarily those of the International Monetary Fund.

255

isolate and measure economies of scale independently from other causes of variation in costs among firms. Isolating the influence of economies of scale on the average cost of production when other factors, such as differences in technology, changes in factor prices, changes in plant or industry location, and differences in the quality of the factors of production also influence the average cost of production, has plagued the existing methods of measuring economies of scale. Until economies of scale can be independently identified in the production function, we cannot be certain that our presumed measures of scale economies actually do measure economies of scale instead of a host of related factors.

Third, the cost savings associated with economies of scale are, by definition, long run in nature (when all adaptations to a particular size of plant, industry, or economy have taken place), and therefore no account is taken of the short-run costs of adjustment incurred in moving, both backward and forward, along the long-run average cost curve. In fact, however, it is the very fear of short-run adjustment costs, especially as regards possible large-scale employment losses in import-competing industries, which has prompted some policy makers to favor a gradual reduction of tariff and nontariff barriers rather than more ambitious trade liberalization endeavors.

Finally, and most important, economies of scale represent but one argument among many for freer trade, and it assumes importance only in so far as it contributes toward the implicit primary goal of raising real national income per capita in each of the participating countries.

This chapter takes a closer and more cautious look into the economies of scale case for freer trade and draws attention to some oft-neglected sources and interpretations of economies of scale which are of particular interest to proposals for trade liberalization.

What are Economies of Scale?

Economies of scale have been defined almost exclusively in economic theory with reference to the simplest and most restrictive productive unit, the single-plant firm which produces a single standard product. For such a firm, "Economies of scale are the potential reductions in average unit costs which are associated with higher levels of productive capacity, with capacity measured in terms of the number of units of the standard product which can be produced per unit of time."[1] Economies of scale, so defined, are then expressed by the shape of the firm's long-run average cost (LAC) curve which shows "the lowest possible cost of producing at any scale of output when all possible adaption to that scale of plant has taken place."[2] Economies of scale are said to exist if the firm's LAC curve is downward sloping, and the optimum scale of plant is indicated by its lowest point. Where the firm's LAC curve is L-shaped, the levelling-off point on the curve indicates the minimum optimum scale (MOS) of plant.

The sources of economies of scale for the single-plant, single-product firm are both numerous and varied and have been treated at length in the literature.[3] They can be briefly classified as follows: (a) indivisibilities in capital equipment, (b) economies of massed reserves in inventory holdings, (c) economies in certain types of capital equipment, such as tanks, pipelines, and compressors, where the increase in cost of such equipment is less than proportionate with the increase in capacity (sometimes known as the "0.06 rule"),[4] (d) more efficient production techniques associated with higher output, (e) increased specialization of both labor force and capital equipment, (f) increases in efficiency of workers resulting from the increased experience associated with higher cumulative levels of output (learning by doing), and (g) savings in bulk transactions (large scale handling and shipping).

It should be noted in passing that, although these definitions of sources of economies of scale are rather straightforward for the single-plant, single-product firm, the measurement of such economies involves serious difficulties.[5] If accounting cost data are employed to determine differences in unit costs among different sizes of plants, it is virtually impossible to hold other things equal, and therefore it is extremely difficult to determine whether observed differences in average unit costs are attributable to different plant sizes or to differences in other factors—for example, plant location, age of equipment, the level of technology employed, factor prices, management ability, accounting methods, and so forth. However, even if we could solve all of the problems associated with making unit cost comparisons for different sizes of plant, the results would be of little value in appraising potential economies of scale attributable to freer trade if we are comparing single-plant, single-product firms. This is because such firms are the exception rather than the norm in the real world, and because scale takes on a more comprehensive, more multidimensional meaning when applied to multiplant multiproduct firms.

Economies in Multiplant and Multiproduct Firms

In the real world, firms usually operate more than one plant and produce more than one product, and there must be economic reasons for doing so, that is, the list of sources of economies of scale must be extended to include these economies.

Firms may grow horizontally over time. They produce a wider range of products either to guard against insufficiency of demand for the original product or products, or because several products can be produced jointly for technical reasons, for example, coal gas and coal. Economists have investigated the problem of incorporating the multiproduct case into economies of scale, and some comments in this regard bear repeating: "For multi-product plants and firms, scale is a multi-dimensional concept. The scale of production may be changed not only by altering the overall capacity to produce more of all products, or more of some products only, but also in other ways, such as by altering the length of production runs or the extent of standardization."[6] By decreasing the range of products it produces, as well as lengthening production runs, the firm may be able to decrease average unit cost, due to (a) the spreading out of setting-up costs, and (b) the increased efficiency of workers as their tasks become more standardized. This assumes, however, that the firm is able to maintain its previous sales volume with the more limited product variety.

With the protection afforded by trade barriers removed, firms in small countries may conclude that their quickest route to economies of scale resides in limiting their exports to those products in which they have the greatest international competitive advantage, and in so doing, lengthening production runs for these products. One economist has suggested that productivity differentials between the United States and Europe are better explained by differences in the length of production runs than by differences in plant sizes.[7] Much of the productivity differential between U.S. and Canadian firms is also no doubt linked with the relatively large product variety and short production runs of Canadian firms, induced in turn by the limited size of the Canadian market as compared with their American counterparts.[8]

Firms also may be able to reduce average unit costs by operating several optimal-scale plants due to economies of large-scale management, economies of large-scale distribution, and pecuniary economies of large-scale buying from suppliers. Often these multiplant economies will be accompanied by another source of cost savings—the extension of the firm via the integration of preceding or succeeding processes, i.e., vertical integration. The economies associated with the vertical integration of firms have been investigated, and it has been argued that vertical integration will give rise to economies in production if the integrated firm can perform a series of successive production processes more efficiently than they could be performed by a number of single plants or firms, each of which performed only one function. Indeed, vertical integration appears most likely to occur where technologically complementary productive processes can be brought together in a single plant or firm.[9]

Unfortunately, the empirical evidence on multiplant economies is so limited as to prohibit a meaningful prediction about their future importance in trade policy considerations. A study of U.S. firms illustrates that, where multiplant economies exist, they are usually quite modest in size—i.e., the unit cost of production and distribution of firms with several plants of MOS being typically about 1 to 2 percent below those of a firm with one plant of MOS.[10] Nevertheless, there is little justification for concluding that significant multiplant economies do not exist in other industrial countries.

It is well to take note of the fact that the United States operates the world's largest plants and industries (see below). In addition, the available evidence also suggests that the United States operates the largest firms. Of the 500 largest individual firms in the Western world, 306 are American.[11] Even in the EEC, the typical large firm is less than one-half the size of its counterpart in the United States.[12] Faced with increased competition from much larger U.S. firms in the international economy, smaller firms in other countries may discover that the only way they can successfully compete with large U.S. firms is to merge with other small firms, and thereby gain access to multiplant and multifirm economies. It is reported that the merger between Agfa of West Germany and Gevaert of Belgium enabled these firms to reap considerable cost savings by concentration of the two companies' worldwide sales network.[13]

It has also been suggested that the recent rapid increase in the price of technical equipment necessary to carry on basic research and development may force smaller firms in fast-growing industries to pool their research efforts, if not merge, in order to attain the critical mass necessary for profitably developing cost-saving innovations.[14] Further, if antitrust policies in some of the industrial countries are modified in the future to recognize possible economies-of-scale benefits in the evaluation of mergers, then the future size-distribution of firms in these countries will be much influenced by the availability of multiplant and multifirm economies.[15]

Until the theory of the firm adequately accounts for multiplant, multifirm, multiproduct scale-economic phenomena, and until we have better empirical information on the cost savings associated with it, it will not be possible to evaluate definitively the importance of such economies under freer trade, but it is already clear that these factors cannot be ignored in any meaningful interpretation of economies of scale.

Economies of Scale in Marketing and Distribution Costs

It is useful, when considering economies of scale for individual components of total unit cost, to think of the firm as "engaging in a series of distinct operations; purchasing and storing materials; transforming materials into some finished products, and some semi-finished products into finished products, storing and selling the outputs; extending credit to buyers, etc."[16] Each one of the functions which the firm performs can be thought of as having its own average-cost curve, and there is no a priori reason why the shape of the average cost curve for one function should be the same as the average cost curve for other functions. The traditional definition of economies of scale is expressed in terms of potential decreases in average (total) unit costs, and so provides no information on which of the components of total cost are especially sensitive to economies of scale. The empirical information that exists on economies of scale for components of total cost employs engineering cost estimates and pertains almost exclusively to production cost. This situation often results in the exclusion of potential economies of scale in distribution costs. It is clear that costs associated with marketing and transportation are nevertheless real costs for operating firms, and there is also no reason to conclude that these types of costs are any less responsive to scale economies than are production costs.

Potential economies of scale in distribution costs become an important factor under trade liberalization for a number of reasons. In order for firms to reap economies of scale under freer trade, they must successfully penetrate foreign markets. If these firms are selling a perfectly homogeneous product, they must possess a free-trade cost advantage for this product vis-à-vis the domestic producers of this product (unless the foreign firms are willing to quote prices below costs, and thereby incur short-term losses). Transportation costs, therefore, assume importance since firms that wish to export to a foreign market are likely to incur higher transport costs than domestic firms within that market for at least two reasons: (a) foreign firms are likely to be producing farther from the market destination than domestic firms and therefore will have to transport their goods farther; and (b) there is evidence of significant discrimination in transportation rates for international, as compared to national, transportation.[17]

The importance of transport costs for a particular export commodity will depend on the supply and demand elasticities for the product in question and on the ratio of the freight rate to the delivered piece of the product (the freight factor).[18] Where both the price elasticity of demand and the freight factor are high for an export product, high transport costs can limit the volume of trade and, therefore, the ability of firms to reap economies of scale from freer trade. From a global point of view, transport costs, *ceteris paribus*, diminish the volume of world trade by partially obscuring relative differences in production costs. To the extent that transport costs diminish the volume of trade, they likewise diminish the welfare gains associated with greater allocative efficiency. The greater the potential economies of scale in transportation costs, and the lower the future level of these costs, the less restrictive will such costs be to the volume of trade generated by liberalization measures.

In addition to economies in transport costs, economies of scale in marketing (advertising) costs assume significance once it is recognized that most of the relevant firms are likely to be exporting differentiated products for which selling costs may be a *sine qua non* for successful entry into the foreign market. A recent study of consumer goods industries in the United States shows that advertising, via its effect on product differentiation, acts to raise the height of entry barriers in these industries. It argues that new entrants in these industries may be forced to choose between selling at a price below the established brands or incurring heavy selling costs. The process by which advertising acts to raise entry barriers is described as follows: "First, high prevailing levels of advertising create additional costs for new entrants which exist at all levels of output. Because of buyer inertia and loyalty, more advertising messages per prospective customer must be supplied to induce brand switching as compared with repeat buying. . . . Moreover, the costs of penetration are likely to increase as output expands and customers more inert or loyal need be reached. . . . In addition, the effect of advertising on firm revenues is subject to economies of scale which result from the increasing effectiveness of advertising messages per unit of output as well as from decreasing costs for each advertising message purchased."[19]

The larger are the potential economies of scale in advertising costs, the less of a barrier will such costs be to firms hoping to expand the size of their market by increasing their export sales. It should be recognized, however, that even if new entrants into a market are willing to incur substantial selling costs to penetrate a foreign market, existing firms within the market may partially frustrate this attempt by proportionally increasing their own selling costs—up to the point at which all available economies in these costs are exhausted.

Since marketing costs are the revenue-inducing elements that make economies of scale in production cost possible, and transportation costs act to limit the competitive effectiveness of already realized economies of scale in production, the role of large-scale economies in distribution costs should not be overlooked in the assessment of total potential economies of scale deriving from trade liberalization.

Information, X-Efficiency, and the Level of Technology

One of the most repeated and forcefully argued claims for freer trade on the part of nations which operate relatively small sizes of plant is that the induced expansion of the market will permit them to exploit the superior levels of technology associated with relatively larger sizes of plant. Whether or not this is a valid claim can only be decided by reference to empirical evidence on differences in technology and differences in unit costs between smaller and larger sizes of plant (such evidence is reviewed below). The very preoccupation, however, with the *shape* of the long-run average cost curve—i.e., differences in unit-costs between small and larger sizes of plants—may well obscure an equally important potential source of cost savings which is independent of the size of plants, and which involves downward shifts of the entire LAC curve. These are cost savings which can be exploited by inducing plants of all sizes to move closer to their respective optimum techniques of production.[a]

One economist has suggested just such an approach to cost savings, which he calls "X-efficiency." X-efficiency centers on the motivation of managers and workers to bestir themselves to produce closer to the optimum. The primary attraction of potential increases in X-efficiency is that such cost reductions do

---

[a]It should be noted that the traditional long-run average cost curve assumes that each size of plant is employing the optimum technique of production available to it. As we shall show, however, there are reasons for suspecting that this assumption is a poor one in the real world.

not involve additional capital or increases in depreciation of existing capital; rather, "the methods usually involve some simple reorganization of the production process—e.g., plant-layout, reorganization, materials handling, waste controls, work methods, and payment by results."[20]

It is well to recall that most studies on the benefits of reducing or eliminating restrictions to trade have shown that computed benefits attributable to reallocation of resources—i.e., allocative efficiency—turn out to be very small, usually less than one month's growth of GNP annually. The effect of trade liberalization on X-efficiency, however, may turn out to be very significant for firms operating both small and large plants. The conclusion that freer trade will lead to positive changes in X-efficiency is suggested by two factors: (a) by fostering greater contact among nations via an increased volume of trade, more and better information should become available to nations as to the optimum techniques of production for different sizes of plant; and (b) by increasing competition among nations via the increased intrusion of foreign firms into domestic markets, freer trade provides the stick with which firms are forced to move closer to their optimum techniques of production.

Although the empirical evidence on X-efficiency is as yet too sketchy to evaluate, there are signs that certain industrial and developing countries are large potential gainers because of their seemingly low present level of X-efficiency. A recent study of the industrial organization and performance of Great Britain rejects the small-plant size explanation of low British productivity in favor of an essentially X-efficiency interpretation of British management: "the wide variation of simple efficiency among British firms suggests, in turn, . . . that British management resources are of lower quality than those of other industrial nations."[21] It can be reasonably argued that other countries, which like Great Britain display low levels of "residual productivity,"[22] should consider the effects of freer trade on efficiency levels in existing sizes of plant, as well as its effect on efficiency from building plants closer to minimum optimum scale.

The Size of the Market: Technological vs. Competitive

The traditional definition of economics of scale also leaves unanswered another question which is of critical importance in any trade liberalization scheme, namely the question of whether there will be sufficient demand to absorb the greater output associated with the building of larger size plants. In fact, it is just such a lack of demand that presently prevents the exploitation of economies of scale in most countries.

Although it can be stated unequivocally that economies of scale are limited by the size of the market, the related question of what is the minimum size of the market, which permits plants, firms, and industries in the economy to capture all potential economies of scale, is a much more difficult one to answer. In this regard, it is useful to employ the distinction between the minimum size of a market in a *technological* sense and the minimum size of a market in an economic or *competitive* sense. A market can be considered too small technologically if it is too small to provide an adequate outlet for the full-capacity output of the most efficient productive plant in a given industry. A market can be said to be too small in an economic sense if it fails to provide the competitive conditions necessary to spur the utmost efficiency and to lead to the establishment of the most technically efficient plants.[23] It can be expected that the technological optimum size of market is reached very much sooner than the economic optimum.

The traditional economies-of-scale definition emphasizes the technological cost savings arising from the building of larger size plants—made possible, in turn, by an expansion in the size of the market. These cost savings are represented by rightward movements along a declining LAC curve. Technological cost savings are classified as economies internal to the plant, firm, or industry. Technological cost savings are, therefore, confined to those countries which previously operated less than optimal-size plants. Many observers have concluded that all such technological cost savings can be captured in a country with a population of fifty million people or an output of fifty billion dollars.[24] It should be recognized, however, that the largest developed country, the United States, is likely to have a powerful voice in trade negotiations, and the resultant liberalization must therefore offer some prospective benefits to the United States. However, it has been shown that most industries the United States already operate multiple plants of MOS or greater, suggesting that farther technological economies are not likely to be very significant.[25] In contrast, by making possible an increase in the number of firms which operate MOS plants in each industry, trade liberalization is likely to offer significant increases in competition and efficiency to a country even as large as the United States. Such economic or competitive cost savings can be represented by a downward shift of the LAC curves of all plants, firms, and industries in the economy, and are more appropriately classified as economies external to the plant, firm, or industry.

The smaller countries can likewise expect to gain appreciably from the competitive cost savings initiated by freer trade. In fact, it has been indicated that in these countries most industries are more highly concentrated than their counterparts in the United States. Bain has computed the percentage of workers employed by the twenty largest plants for thirty-four industries in eight countries. The findings reveal a central tendency for the seven countries other than the United States to have from moderately (Japan 17.8, Italy 20.4, France 23.3) to substantially higher (Canada 37.7, United Kingdom 37.2, Sweden 44.4, and India 80.1) degrees of plant concentration than the United States (17.8).[26] Since higher levels of concentration *ceteris paribus*, usually reflect lower levels of competition, the potential cost savings from increases in trade-generated competition for these countries is likely to be greater than that for the United States.

It is evident, then, that in appraising potential economies of scale deriving from freer trade, competitive cost savings external to the plant cannot be ignored. If expansion in the size of plants is unaccompanied by an appropriate competitive atmosphere, there is nothing to ensure that the cost reductions brought about by economies of scale are passed on to the consumer in the form of lower prices; instead, these cost reductions would less desirably be reflected in an increase in monopoly returns.

Cost Savings for New Firms

Economies of scale, traditionally interpreted, envisage the cost savings made possible by an expansion of the market as being distributed among the existing firms in the economy. As such, this interpretation ignores the effects of an expanded market on the birth of new firms, which could not have previously entered the market due to the insufficiency of demand for their specialized product or service, i.e., the vertical disintegration which a larger market permits.[27] This process is merely a logical extension of Adam Smith's famous axiom that division of labor is limited by the extent of the market.

Consider a firm engaging in a series of distinct operations. Each function which the firm performs can be viewed as having its own average cost curve. If the size of the national market is small, it will not be possible for the firm to abandon those functions subject to increasing returns to another firm or industry which will specialize in this function in order to take full advantage of the increasing returns.[28] However, once the national market expands, such a contracting-out procedure will be possible, since there will then be sufficient demand to allow the new firm to sell its output. If the cost savings associated with increased specialization in the economy outweigh those cost savings attributable to increased vertical integration of firms (the opposite of the contracting-out procedure), then, this tendency toward greater specialization will continue as the economy matures and grows. As new firms which perform increasingly specialized functions establish themselves in the market, other new firms desirous of entering the market are able to draw on their specialized services and set up new operations more efficiently. The business directory of any metropolitan phone book offers persuasive evidence of the extent to which the large U.S. market offers subcontracting and specialization opportunities.[b]

Once again, countries with relatively small national markets are especially susceptible to cost savings from increased specialization following an expansion in the size of the market. Whereas Canadian and British firms often produce most of the component parts necessary for their final product, their American

---

[b]The author wishes to thank Solomon Fabricant for very helpful discussions on this point.

expected that the import-competing industries in these countries will suffer some decreases in sales. These sales decreases can, in turn, be expected to lead to employment losses as well as to negative economies of scale in these industries. It is therefore necessary that we discuss some of the factors which will determine the extent of the effects of freer trade on import-competing industries, and also how these effects should be evaluated.

First, in assessing the expected impact of freer trade on the import-competing industries in member countries, a distinction should be made between standardized products and differentiated products. In the case of standardized products, trade liberalization is likely to lead to greater specialization across industries, as those firms with a competitive advantage expand their output and those with a competitive disadvantage contract their output. Under these conditions, it may not be too misleading to expect that each dollar of increased imports displaces one dollar of output in the less efficient import-competing industry. For standardized products, therefore, the impact of freer trade on the import-competing industries will be a function of the resultant increase in imports.

The increase in imports of a particular product in a particular market resulting from a reduction of the tariff on that product can be calculated as a product of: (a) the price elasticity of demand for that product; (b) the percentage reduction in the tariff or equivalent NTB; and (c) the previous volume of imports of that product in that market.[31] Given the expected increase in imports resulting from freer trade, the expected decrease in output in the import-competing industries can be estimated. This expected decrease in output could then be applied to the industry's elasticity of employment with respect to output and to its LAC curve to determine both the employment losses and the average cost increases (negative economies of scale), resulting from liberalization.

In the case of differentiated products, freer trade may lead rather to greater specialization within industries,[32] and this, in turn, may lead to substantially less disruption in import-competing industries than would be the case with standardized products. If freer trade leads to greater specialization within industries, then industries may be able to produce at near their earlier scale, but in a more limited variety of products; here, scale is appropriately defined to include multiproduct economies. The adjustment effects of freer trade in these industries would then depend on the production changes necessary to alter the product mix. The experiences of the EEC and EFTA, where there have been relatively few bankruptcies and no disappearances of entire industries, suggests that specialization within industries is a very likely possibility under broad-scale trade liberalization.

In addition to the moderating effect of intraindustry specialization on the expected disruption of import-competing industries, there are other factors which may ease the impact of freer trade. If tariffs are eliminated once and for all, the sudden increase in export production may lead to a rise in member country export prices if the elasticity of export supply is low in the short run. The greater the increase in export prices, *ceteris paribus*, the lower will be the resulting increase in imports. It has been estimated that close to one-half of U.S. tariff reductions (in 1954-56 and 1955-59) have been offset by increases in supplier export prices.[33] The hypothesis that significant increases in exports will lead to rises in export prices would appear to apply with particular relevance to many of the Western European countries which are already employing labor at levels near capacity. A second factor which could moderate the expected contraction in the import-competing industries would be a substantial increase in real income, which would permit both domestic output and the increase in imports to be absorbed.

If we accept the fact that freer trade will impose some real costs, in the form of employment losses and negative economies of scale, on import-competing industries in member countries, the next question that must be addressed is how these costs should be evaluated. They should certainly not be passed over as insignificant adjustment costs. Although recent studies have concluded that the aggregate amount of employment losses following trade liberalization are not likely to be large (as a percentage of the labor force) for a country like the United States, there are nevertheless likely to be differences in impact among industries, and for some industries the employment losses may be significant.[34] For example, it has been estimated that three United States industries, textile mill products, apparel, and miscellaneous manufactured products, would account for over one-third of the total U.S. job loss resulting from free trade in industrial products.[35]

If the particularly hard-hit industries are also relatively large employers of low-skilled, minority group workers, then trade liberalization may, at least in the short run, be in conflict with the goal of a more equitable distribution of income. If the laid-off workers can be retrained at government expense and rapidly reemployed in the expanding export industries or elsewhere in the economy, then the costs of adjustment become less serious, although they are hardly likely to disappear.

If, then, it can be expected that free trade will impose not insignificant adjustment costs on the import-competing industries, should such costs be avoided? In fact, they should not, since an attempt to avoid employment losses and negative economies of scale in the import-competing industries would sacrifice the consumption benefits from freer trade. The consumption benefits from freer trade accrue in the form of lower prices for consumers as high cost domestic producers are displaced by lower cost foreign producers.[c] Those

---

[c]It should be noted that consumption benefits are not in conflict with economies of scale in the export industries for an individual country. What is of concern to the individual country regarding economies of scale in the export industries is the effect of these economies on export prices and on the country's terms of trade, which in turn affect the country's real income.

negative economies of scale that do occur in the import-competing industries add to the adjustment problems in these industries by raising the average unit cost on the contracting output, but where the industry's LAC curve is not steeply sloped, the average unit cost increase may not be great. In addition, the average cost increases incurred by the import-competing firm, when combined with the increased competitive pressure of foreign firms entering the market, may motivate the inefficient import-competing industries to become more efficient and thereby arrest their own contraction. In any case, the consumption benefits accruing to the whole economy should not be sacrificed in order to prevent cost increases from occurring among inefficient domestic producers.

International Comparisons of Economies of Scale: Some Caveats

The importance of economies of scale under freer trade must depend to a large extent upon their probable size. As indicated earlier, it is not yet possible to objectively determine the size of potential economies of scale caused by freer trade for even a single country, much less for a large group of countries. Neither the accounting-cost approach, the engineering cost-estimate approach, the survivor technique, nor the production-function approach yields an estimate of economies of scale consistent with its multidimensional nature in the real world.[d] The existing empirical estimates of economies of scale must, therefore, be considered only partial information. Yet, by piecing together some of these pieces, we may be able to obtain an impression of the size of at least some of the more important components of potential economies of scale resulting from freer trade.

Empirical measurement of economies of scale has been directed almost exclusively at estimating technological economies internal to the plant or to the industry, i.e., those economies represented by movements along the LAC curve. In our attempt to appraise the magnitude of these potential internal economies of scale, we shall be focusing primarily on two questions: (a) Are the existing sizes of plants different among the industrial countries, and if so, is there a positive relationship between plant size and plant efficiency; and (b) Are the

---

[d]The principal difficulty with both the accounting-cost approach and the production-function approach is their inability to separate the influence of economies of scale on the average cost of production from other factors which also influence the average cost of production. In contrast, the engineering-cost approach is able to hold other things constant and therefore is most consistent with the assumptions underlying the LAC curve. The engineering estimates, however, suffer from the defects that engineers often forecast costs incorrectly and that their cost estimates refer to hypothetical rather than actual plants. The survivor technique suffers from the drawback that a particular size class of plant may grow relatively in importance over time for reasons other than relatively higher efficiency, e.g., nature of antitrust policy, change in technology, a desire for prestige associated with bigness, and so forth.

existing sizes of industries different in participating countries, and if so, is there a positive relationship between industry size and industry efficiency? Since internal economies of scale represent only part of total economies of scale, we shall also note some efforts to obtain an impression of economies of scale more closely associated with the growth of the entire economy (both internal and external economies) by examining the role of economies of scale as a source of past economic growth in a number of industrial countries.

Before moving to the empirical evidence on technological economies of scale among nations, we should keep a number of caveats in mind. First, such studies almost invariably involve comparing output and output per worker (or unit-labor cost) in plants or industries in one or more countries with comparable measures for the larger plants and industries in the United States. Since per capita real income is higher in the United States than elsewhere, this is understandable. Nevertheless, to conclude that the economic efficiency of the United States will be replicated for other countries, once these countries achieve plant sizes, industry sizes, or a national market size equal to that of the United States is unwarranted. To do so would ignore differences among countries in the quantity and quality of other sources of economic growth. Fabricant has examined the relationship between the size and efficiency of the American economy and concluded that we must look to factors such as the very large stock of tangible and intangible capital, the huge U.S. investment in research and development, and the exceptional natural resources in the United States, as well as to the vast size of the American economy, in attempting to explain its high efficiency.[36]

Second, the very interpretation of economies of scale as the relationship between output and output per worker is suspect for a number of reasons. First, in cases where there is a positive relationship between plant or industry size and capital intensity, the relationship between output and output per worker in the larger plants and industries will reflect an upward bias. Productivity comparisons based on output per unit of total factor-input would produce more meaningful results; unfortunately such data is at present unavailable on a multi-country basis. Second, since output is included in both the size and efficiency measures, if an error is made in the measurement of output, then a similar error will be made in the measurement of output per worker, thereby producing a misleadingly high correlation.[37] And third, economies of scale postulate a relationship between output and average unit cost, rather than a relationship between output and output per worker. To the extent that other components of average unit cost, such as cost of materials and administrative costs, differ between plants and industries across countries, then comparisons of output and output per worker will yield a misleading picture of potential total economies of scale among countries.

The direction of causation between output and output per worker is also by no means entirely clear. Does higher output, via economies of scale, cause higher productivity, or does higher productivity, by shifting the industry's supply curve downward, cause an increase in output which is sold?[38] In some industries high output may lead to high productivity, while in other industries it may be high productivity which leads to high output. In short, for all of the reasons indicated above, high correlations between output and output per worker should not be taken as conclusive evidence of the existence of potential economies of scale in many national economies.

The Plant Size–Productivity Question

The first question which must be confronted in making international comparisons of plant sizes is what measure of plant size is most appropriate for size comparisons? Should we compare plants on the basis of number of workers employed, assets, actual output, or capacity output? Since we are interested in the size of plants chiefly for the purpose of testing for economies of scale, actual output is the preferred measure since economies of scale describes a relationship between output and average unit cost. Most available studies of plant size among nations are, however, based on an employment measure of size. A ranking of countries by plant size, based on employment, will be identical to ranking of plant size based on output only if labor productivity is equal among all countries. To the extent that labor productivity is higher in plants with the most workers, then, plant-size rankings by employment understate the relative size of the largest plants. Since labor productivity is higher in the United States then elsewhere, U.S. plant size is understated in the employment-based studies which will be presented below.

Bain has collected data on comparative plant sizes for eight countries—the United States, Canada, the United Kingdom, Sweden, France, Italy, India, and Japan.[39] By estimating the average number of employees in the twenty largest plants in the national industry for thirty-four industries, Bain is able to rank the eight countries by their median size of plant, as well as to estimate the range of plant sizes around that median. The results are reproduced in Table 10-1. The dominant conclusion is that the United States has by far the largest plant sizes, with only the United Kingdom relatively close. A secondary point of note is the particularly wide dispersion of plant-size relatives in Japan and Canada.

Bain's findings are supported in a recent study of plant sizes for the United States and four of the common-market countries by Swann and McLachlan.[40] Their results, reproduced in Table 10-2, indicate that the United States has a smaller proportion of its employees (in manufacturing) working in smaller plants and a strikingly larger proportion working in its largest plants. The country closest to the United States in plant size by this account is West Germany.

The available evidence on plant size therefore indicates that France, Japan, Italy, Canada, India, Belgium, and Sweden operate plants which are substantially smaller than those in the United States. In addition, the size of plants in the

Table 10-1

Summary of Findings Concerning Average Sizes of the Twenty Largest Plants in Thirty-Four Industries, Expressed as Relatives to U.S. Plants

Country	Number of Industries Covered	Median Plant Size Covered	% of Industries with Plant Size Relatives of 70 or Above	Range of Relative (excluding smallest and largest)
U.S.	34	100	100	100-100
U.K.	32	78	53	24-131
France	31	39	19	11-89
Japan	31	34	26	12-155
Italy	32	29	6	8-70
Canada	14	28	14	5-117
India	22	26	5	2-64
Sweden	27	13	0	6-43

Data: Joe Bain, *International Differences in Industrial Structure*, Table 3-3, p. 39.

United Kingdom and W. Germany is also smaller than in the United States, but to a lesser degree. The conclusion that many industrial nations operate plants smaller than the United States is, however, by itself not a compelling reason for building larger size plants in these countries, unless it can be demonstrated that smaller plants have higher average unit costs than larger plants. It is to this question that we now turn.

The conclusion that there is a positive relationship between plant size and plant efficiency emerges from Joe Bain's valuable study, *International Differences in Industrial Structure*. Bain employs engineering cost estimates, developed in an earlier study of U.S. manufacturing industries,[41] to estimate relative plant efficiency in twenty-four industries, for the United States, the United

Table 10-2

Distribution of Plant Sizes in Manufacturing in the United States and the EEC (% of Total Employment by Establishment Size Class)

		Number of Employees per Establishment				
		1-49	50-99	100-499	500-999	1000 +
(1958)	W. Germany	15.0	9.6	30.3	12.8	32.3
(1954)	France	19.0	11.9	34.0	12.9	22.3
(1955)	Italy	21.0	11.7	30.0	12.9	24.4
(1956)	Belgium	28.0	10.4	27.2	11.4	23.0
(1958)	U.S.	14.6	8.7	28.0	12.4	36.3

Data: D. Swann and D.L. McLachlan, *Concentration or Competition: A European Dilemma?*, Table 1, p. 9.

Kingdom, Sweden, Canada, France, Japan, Italy, and India. By adopting a number of heroic assumptions, for example, that in each particular industry, minimum optimal scale of plant is the same in all countries, Bain is able to estimate the percentage of workers employed in plants of reasonably efficient scale in each of the twenty-four industries, for each of the eight countries. By assumption, this percentage is 70 for the United States. A summary of the results is reproduced in Table 10-3.

The third column in Table 10-3 provides a measure of substandard efficiency in plant scale. The lower the number in column (3), the higher is the relative efficiency of the country's plants. Column (4) gives an arithmetic mean for the substandard industries of the percentage of workers employed in plants of reasonably efficient scale. Therefore the higher the number in column (4), the greater is the relative efficiency in the inefficient industries. The findings suggest that there is a high incidence of inefficiently run small plants in all of the seven countries, except the United Kingdom. In these countries, a dominant proportion of industries had a larger proportion (about 80 percent greater) of workers employed in inefficient small plants than did the United States.

Another study, by Gates and Linden, reinforces the conclusion about a positive relationship between plant size and plant efficiency.[42] The study compares output and unit costs in domestic and foreign plants of U.S. firms. Where output of the foreign plant was less than 5 percent of that of the U.S. plant, unit costs in the foreign plant were 31 percent *higher*. When the foreign to domestic output ratio rises to 5-10 percent, the foreign to domestic cost ratio falls to 99 percent. Further increases in the foreign to domestic output ratio to 10-25 percent, 25-50 percent, and over 50 percent, bring down the foreign to

Table 10-3

Summary of Findings Concerning Comparative Incidence of Inefficiently Small Plants in 24 Industries in 7 Countries

(1) Country	(2) Number of Industries Covered	(3) % of Industries in Which $<70\%$ of Employees Work in Reasonably Efficient Plants	(4) Mean % of Employees Working in Reasonably Efficient Plants for Industries in which (3) is <70 percent
U.K.	22	32	54
Sweden	22	82	48
Canada	8	75	46
France	20	75	48
Japan	23	75	46
Italy	23	91	42
India	16	56	33

Data: Joe Bain, *International Differences in Industrial Structure*, Table 3-10, p. 64.

domestic unit cost ratios to 96 percent, 86 percent, and 74 percent, respectively.

The empirical evidence, therefore, suggests that although the relationship between plant size and plant productivity is imperfect, there may be substantial potential technological economies of scale on the plant level available to most industrial nations. If these nations can expand the size of their markets and increase both the size of plants and the proportion of output produced in plants of reasonably efficient scale, then savings in average unit costs should be forthcoming.

The Industry Size-Productivity Question

Analogous to the plant size-productivity question is the question of whether industries are of different sizes in different countries, and if so, if there is a positive relationship between industry size and industry efficiency? Analysis of economies of scale on the industry level also takes account of multiplant, multifirm economies, both of which are excluded in the plant size studies.

Most of the existing empirical studies of the industry size-industry efficiency question have compared manufacturing industries in only two or three countries, most usually in the United States, the United Kingdom, and Canada. An early study examined output and output per worker in forty-four American and British industries.[43] The simple correlation between these two variables was 0.79, suggesting that a high labor productivity was most prevalent in the larger industries. A study of output and output per worker in twenty-two industries in the United States and Canada came to the same conclusion.[44] After excluding those industries which serve local and regional markets, and which therefore do not directly benefit from a larger national market, the rank correlation coefficient between output and output per worker was 0.76.

It was also discovered that the larger was the American output level relative to Canada in an industry, the greater was the U.S. productivity advantage over Canada for that industry. These findings lead to the conclusion that market size was probably the factor most responsible for productivity differentials between the two countries.

The relatively small size of the Canadian market has also been advanced as a factor contributing to Canada's weak international position: "Among the problems of Canadian manufacturing industries, one of the most important is the difficulty of attaining a sufficient volume of output to reduce unit cost to levels which are competitive internationally...."[45] The available empirical evidence therefore suggests that both the United Kingdom and Canada could reap economies of scale if freer trade permitted them to expand their market size and to increase the size of their industries.

Trade liberalization ought to offer potential economies of scale to more than two or three already large countries, and it would be helpful to have information on industry size and industry efficiency for a larger group of countries. Heretofore, such information did not appear to be available. We are however able to present data on industry size and industry efficiency for eleven industrial countries. The data are for twenty SITC manufacturing industries in 1965. Industry size is defined as the ratio of value added for industry i in country j to total value for industry i for a total of fifteen countries. Industry efficiency is defined as direct labor cost per unit of value added in industry i for country j. The industry efficiency data are available for eleven of the fifteen countries for which industry-size data exist. It should be understood that the estimates of industry size and industry efficiency presented below suffer from the same limitations and are therefore subject to the same caveats as the studies reviewed earlier in the paper. Their only advantage over earlier studies is that they cover a wider range of countries.

The data on relative industry size for fifteen countries appear in Table 10-4. The most striking conclusion from the relative industry-size comparisons is the overwhelming size dominancy of the U.S. industries. United States manufacturing value added accounts for approximately 57 percent of total manufacturing value added for the fifteen countries. In only four of the twenty industries, namely, textiles, wood and cork products, leather products, and petroleum and coal products, is the U.S. share less than 50 percent of total value added. In contrast, in no other individual country except for West Germany is there even one national industry which accounts for 15 percent of total value added. Although the data for West Germany are very incomplete (data for only eleven of twenty industries are presented), it appears to be the country second to the United States in industry size. Following West Germany in industry size are the United Kingdom, Japan, Canada, and Italy. The remaining nine countries account for less than 5 percent of total value added.

In Table 10-5 eleven of the same fifteen countries are compared on the basis of direct labor cost per unit of value added for each of the same twenty industries.[e] On the basis of this *very imperfect* measure of industrial efficiency, the eleven countries rank as follows (from the most efficient to least efficient for all manufacturing)—Japan, Austria, United States, Canada, Norway, Australia, the United Kingdom, Netherlands, Sweden, Belgium, and New Zealand. Comparing the country labor-cost rankings with the country industry-size rankings discloses that those countries which possess the relatively largest industries do not, in every case, also operate the most efficient industries. Japan, Austria, and Norway each have industrial labor-cost efficiency rankings above those suggested by their relative industry size. On the other hand, the United States, the United Kingdom, and Belgium display labor-cost efficiency rankings below their industry size rankings.

---

[e]Direct labor cost refers to labor costs originating in that industry and excludes labor cost incurred in that industry's principal supplying industries in the process of supplying inputs to the subject industry.

Table 10-4

Share of National Industries in International Total of Value Added, by Industry, 1965, 15 Countries (Percentage of Total Value Added by 15 Countries)

Industry	U.S.	Canada	Japan	Australia	Italy	Netherlands	Norway
All Manufacturing	57.2	3.7	7.4				
1. Food	61.9	05.1	07.0	02.1	05.1	01.9	00.5
2. Beverages	59.5	07.0	08.1	01.7	–	01.1	00.8
3. Tobacco	62.7	05.2	00.0	02.0	03.7	02.7	02.0
4. Textiles	41.8	03.6	13.0	01.7	06.4	01.5	00.4
5. Clothing & Footwear	58.0	03.2	02.9	01.8	05.2	01.4	00.4
6. Wood & Cork Products	35.7	04.9	07.4	02.0	02.7	00.6	00.5
7. Furniture	61.2	04.2	07.6	01.4	05.8	01.4	01.2
8. Paper & Paper Products	62.6	09.1	08.0	01.5	02.1	01.2	00.9
9. Printing & Publishing	58.0	03.8	07.7	01.4	02.6	01.6	00.6
10. Leather Products	42.2	03.6	06.9	02.3	07.2	04.6	00.4
11. Rubber Products	63.7	01.7	03.3	00.7	01.7	–	00.1
12. Chemicals & Chemical products	74.6	03.1	10.2	01.3	05.4	02.0	00.5
13. Petroleum & Coal Prod.	48.2	04.9	07.8	02.1	–	–	00.2
14. Nonmetallic Mineral Products	56.0	03.3	08.5	01.9	05.1	01.3	00.4
15. Basic Metals	52.6	03.7	07.8	02.0	02.5	00.6	00.5
16. Metal Products	59.9	04.4	06.1	01.3	04.3	01.2	00.4
17. Nonelect. Machinery	59.9	01.9	07.2	01.4	03.0	00.8	00.2
18. Electrical Machinery	58.3	02.8	08.2	01.0	03.3	01.7	00.2
19. Transport Equipt.	64.9	03.1	05.9	01.7	02.1	00.7	00.5
20. Other Manufactures	67.3	03.6	11.5	01.1	01.8	01.1	00.2

–Denotes missing observation for that industry

Data: United Nations, *Growth of World Industry, 1967.*

It must be emphasized again that unit labor cost is only one component of total unit cost. Differences in observed unit labor costs between countries does not permit a rational conclusion to be drawn about their relative industrial efficiencies, unless one also knows the behavior of other components of total unit cost, such as average materials costs, average selling and distribution costs, and so forth. For example, if we relied only on the intercountry estimates of industry size and industry efficiency presented above, we might conclude that the United States operates the largest industries, but not the most efficient ones. However, a study by Gates and Linden of 147 companies which operate both in the United States and abroad, indicates that the United States has a comparative disadvantage in unit labor costs, unit plant overhead costs, and in unit selling and distribution costs, but it has an offsetting comparative advantage in materials

Portugal	New Zealand	Belgium	U.K.	Sweden	Denmark	Austria	West Germany
00.4	00.5	02.0	07.2	01.6	00.6	01.3	02.1
–	00.3	02.1	14.8	01.0	01.1	01.8	–
–	00.2	01.3	12.9	00.8	01.6	04.1	–
01.4	00.2	02.1	11.0	01.0	00.5	01.2	13.4
–	00.3	01.1	07.4	01.4	00.6	01.3	14.3
00.3	00.5	00.1	03.3	02.9	00.5	01.3	36.4
00.7	00.3	03.1	08.5	01.6	00.8	01.6	–
00.4	00.3	00.7	07.0	03.7	00.5	00.9	–
–	00.3	00.8	09.6	01.9	00.3	00.7	–
–	00.4	00.7	10.9	01.6	00.9	01.5	–
00.8	00.1	00.2	04.1	00.6	–	00.4	43.3
–	00.1	00.8	09.9	01.0	00.7	00.7	–
–	00.2	01.2	06.6	00.9	–	01.0	–
00.4	00.2	01.6	08.8	01.8	–	01.5	16.3
00.1	–	01.3	08.0	01.5	–	00.7	14.2
00.2	00.2	01.3	09.1	01.5	–	00.9	15.6
00.1	00.1	00.9	09.5	02.6	–	00.5	11.0
00.2	00.1	01.0	08.6	01.2	–	00.6	12.1
00.1	00.2	00.7	08.3	01.5	–	00.4	08.9
00.4	00.2	01.0	08.8	00.9	00.5	00.9	–

costs.[46] If the industrial efficiency data were amended to include information on other components of total unit costs, such as unit materials costs, the United States might then appear to have the most efficient industries, as well as the largest industries.

Given the data limitations of the existing empirical studies on industry size and industry efficiency, it is difficult to come to any meaningful conclusion about the potential size of economies of scale on the industry level for any of the industrial countries. Like the evidence on plant level economies, however, the evidence does suggest that the sign of the relationship between industry size and industry efficiency is positive, implying that most prospective industrial countries, especially the smaller ones, can expect to gain at least some technological economies of scale on both the plant and industry levels.

Table 10-5
Direct Labor Costs Per Unit of Value Added, by Industry, 1965, 11 Countries

Industry	U.S.	Canada	Japan	Australia	Netherlands	Norway	New Zealand	Belgium	U.K.	Sweden	Austria
All Manufacturing	.465	.495	.354	.517	.532	.500	.641	.625	.529	.562	.415
1. Food	.395	.464	.314	.435	.515	.615	.650	.322	.442	.417	.323
2. Beverages	.318	.291	.239	.339	.448	.189	.341	.451	.303	.406	.278
3. Tobacco	.210	.318	–	.210	.448	.082	.357	.667	.256	.206	.060
4. Textiles	.525	.559	.412	.546	.661	.512	.727	.727	.565	.605	.479
5. Clothing & Footwear	.555	.648	.430	.584	.615	.545	.770	.707	.606	.622	.435
6. Wood & Cork Prodts.	.562	.596	.423	.560	.591	.510	.658	.582	.620	.565	.402
7. Furniture	.550	.602	.453	.554	.591	.519	.737	.672	.644	.608	.381
8. Paper & Paper Prdts.	.446	.467	–	.420	.505	.566	.478	.704	.499	.531	.476
9. Printing & Publishing	.511	.564	–	.555	.545	.490	.680	.581	.553	.571	.459
10. Leather Prdts.	.666	.622	.384	.588	.575	.509	.679	.735	.558	.635	.410
11. Rubber Prdts.	.494	.575	.364	.600	–	.522	.571	.868	.534	.618	.280
12. Chemicals & Chemical Products	.267	.371	.211	.301	.392	.375	.440	.634	.352	.425	.352
13. Petroleum & Coal Prdts.	.234	.376	.140	.159	–	.377	.180	.465	.387	.240	.187
14. Nonmetallic Mineral Products	.447	.444	.356	.474	.498	.462	.612	.692	.545	.526	.407
15. Basic Metals	.473	.476	.375	.475	.443	.423	.611	.719	.569	.556	.514
16. Metal Products	.518	.533	.425	.590	.592	.561	.651	.789	.579	.571	.484
17. Nonelectrical Mach.	.500	.597	.411	.612	.592	.531	.708	.703	.569	.631	.488
18. Electrical Machinery	.510	.551	.347	.584	.446	.522	.661	.989	.564	.604	.521
19. Transport Equip.	.536	.516	.351	.673	.689	.641	.735	.496	.614	.643	.506
20. Other Manufactures	.460	.529	.396	.547	.639	.501	.600	.494	.547	.542	.455

–Denotes missing observation for that industry.

Data: United Nations, *Growth of World Industry, 1967.*

Economies of Scale for the Entire Economy

Since national policy makers are more likely to be concerned about the effects of freer trade on economies of scale for the entire economy rather than for a particular plant or industry, we should like reliable estimates of potential economies of scale for the entire economy of each country. Unfortunately, very little empirical work has been done in regard to estimating economy-wide economies of scale for a large number of countries. In attempting to estimate economies of scale for an entire economy, the accounting-cost approach and the engineering cost-estimate approaches must be discarded in favor of the production-function approach. The only existing study of this type is Denison's attempt to estimate the contribution of various sources of economic growth, economies of scale among them, to the past growth of nine Western countries: the United States, the United Kingdom, Belgium, Denmark, France, Germany, the Netherlands, Norway, and Italy.[47]

This study develops an independent estimate of the contribution of economies of scale to economic growth in each of the nine countries by disaggregating the residual, output per unit of input, into several components, one of which is economies of scale. Examining U.S. economic growth in the 1950-62 period, it attributes 33 percent of this growth to increases in labor input (adjusted for quality change), 25 percent to increases in capital input, and 42 percent to increases in output per unit of input (the residual). Within the 42 percent contribution of the residual, economies of scale are estimated to have contributed 11 percent to the total real growth rate of 3.32 percent per year. Taking Northwest Europe as a whole, this study applies nearly the same procedure, and estimates the contribution of economies of scale to the real growth rate of 4.78 percent to be 20 percent.[48]

Although gains from economies of scale appear to have been an important source of productivity gain in the countries studied, there is no precise objective way to measure such gains. The national economies-of-scale estimates must, therefore, be considered as educated guesses. The contribution of economies of scale is the sum of three components: (a) economies of scale, both internal and external, arising from the growth of each country's domestic market, independent of changes in the size of local markets or in barriers to international trade; (b) economies of scale arising, in all countries other than the United States, from a "disproportionate allocation of increased purchasing power to products where, once the markets became available, existing techniques for large scale output could be adopted (from the U.S.) with an above average reduction in unit costs.";[49] and (c) economies of scale arising from the independent growth of local markets, via population shifts and increased automobile ownership.

In estimating the component of economies of scale that arise from the growth of each country's domestic market, Denison assumes that the percentage gains from economies of scale diminish as the size of the national market increases (assuming technological and managerial knowledge remains constant). By qualitatively weighing the views of other economists, the author arrives at a figure of 10 percent for the contribution of economies of scale in the United States. He therefore concludes that if 10 percent is used as an estimate of U.S. gains from economies of scale, then a percentage above, but not greatly above, 10 percent should be used for gains from economies of scale in European countries, since their national markets are considerably smaller than the U.S. market—their economies are less subject to diminishing returns to economies of scale.

When the gains from increases in the size of the domestic market are added to the gains (in the European countries only) resulting from the application of known technology and to the gains arising from the independent growth of local markets, a final figure for the contribution of economies of scale to the 1950-62 growth rate in each of the nine countries is obtained. The results of Denison's calculations are shown in Table 10-6 below.

The contribution of economies of scale to the growth rates in Germany, Italy, and France was especially significant. The reason for the relatively large contribution of economies of scale in these three countries lies not in an exceptionally rapid growth in their domestic markets, but rather with large shifts in their consumption patterns in response to income elasticities, which in turn permitted the application of existing U.S. technology in producing these products. Thus Denison's second component of economies of scale explains most of the variance in country gains from economies of scale in this period. Denison's findings can be interpreted as encouraging to supporters of trade liberalization since they indicate that economies of scale is an important source of increase in real national income per capita. On the other hand, the aggregate estimates also suggest that the percentage gains from economies of scale are

Table 10-6
Contribution of Economies of Scale to the Growth Rate, 1950-62

Country	% Contribution of Economies of Scale
Germany	28
Italy	26
France	26
Denmark	23
Norway	20
Netherlands	20
Belgium	19
U.K.	19
U.S.	12

Data: Edward F. Denison, *Why Growth Rates Differ*, Brookings Institution, 1967, p. 255.

likely to be smaller in the future than in the past, especially in the larger countries, as the size of domestic markets reach and surpass minimum optimum scale, and as shifts in consumption patterns (via income elasticities) toward products which can readily be produced under significant economies of scale become less likely.

Concluding Observations

This chapter has attempted to identify and assess various factors concerning potential economies of scale which might occur with freer trade. Many considerations which were shown to have policy significance have been left unanswered in the traditional treatment of economies of scale or empirical estimates of their magnitude.

Reliance on the traditional definition of economies of scale overlooks many of their aspects most relevant to trade liberalization. More specifically, (a) economies of sale relating to multiproduct, multiplant firms are often ignored; (b) by concentrating on unit-cost decreases, economies of scale in marketing and distribution costs are given too little attention; (c) by focusing on the differences in the techniques of production between small and larger sizes of plant, the effects of freer trade on motivating firms of all sizes to move closer to their individual optimum techniques of production are passed over; (d) by interpreting the size of the market necessary to permit economies of scale in a technological sense (internal economies), the market size necessary to reap economies of scale in a competitive sense is often disregarded; and (e) by ascribing potential economies of scale to existing firms within a market, the effects of freer trade on new firms desirous of entering the market are disregarded.

Two additional questions specifically associated with the uncertain nature of expanded production under freer trade were considered. One relates to the importance of the stability of demand for economies of scale. To the extent that demand uncertainties associated with production for export and production for the home market are significantly different, economies of scale induced by the former may be less than those induced by the latter. If this difference in fact exists, then estimates of past economies of scale in the domestic market may be a poor indicator of potential economies of scale resulting from increased export production under freer trade. A second question concerns the uncertain fate of the import competing industries under freer trade. Are negative economies of scale in the import-competing industries to be evaluated by the same criteria as positive economies of scale in the export industries? It was argued that they should not, since the negative economies in the import-competing industries are most appropriately viewed as long-run adjustment costs. And the fate of the import-competing industries under freer trade will be strongly influenced by whether this leads to greater comparative advantage across industries (interindustry specialization) or to greater comparative advantage within industries (intra-industry specialization).

The more recent empirical studies on economies of scale on the plant, industry, and economy levels were reviewed, and new data on the relative size and relative efficiency of twenty SITC manufacturing industries for eleven countries were introduced. It was concluded that potential scale economies at all three levels have been identified, but their magnitude under any particular posture of trade liberalization has yet to be estimated.

If potential economies of scale under freer trade are to be evaluated in a better informed and more rational manner than in the past, they will have to be interpreted in a more multidimensional context and each of these dimensions will have to be investigated more closely on both the theoretical and empirical levels.

Notes

1. C. Pratten and R.M. Dean, *The Economies of Large-Scale Production in British Industry*, (Cambridge: Cambridge University Press, 1965), p. 12.

2. Ibid.

3. For a good discussion of the sources of economies of scale internal to the plant, see Bela Balassa, *The Theory of Economic Integration* (Homewood, Ill.: Richard D. Irwin, 1961), Chapter 6.

4. The 0.6 rule was discovered by engineers as a shorthand method of measuring increases in capital costs as capacity expands; the rule suggests the increase in cost will equal the increase in capacity to the .6 power. For an empirical test of the .6 rule and of economies of scale, see Frederick T. Moore, "Economies of Scale: Some Statistical Evidence," *Quarterly Journal of Economics*, May 1959.

5. See C.A. Smith, "Survey of the Empirical Evidence on Economies of Scale," *Business Concentration and Price Policy* (Princeton: Princeton University Press, 1955), pp. 213-30.

6. Pratten and Dean, *Large-Scale Production*, p. 11.

7. Statement by P.J. Verdoorn in E.A.G. Robinson, eds., *The Economic Consequences of the Size of Nations* (London: Macmillin, 1960), p. 346.

8. For a thorough treatment of the effects of a limited market on Canadian industry, see Ronald I. and Paul Wonnacott, *Free Trade between the United States and Canada* (Cambridge: Harvard University Press, 1967).

9. Joe Bain, *Industrial Organization* (New York: John Wiley and Sons, 1966).

10. Ibid.

11. *Fortune Magazine*, July and August, 1964.

12. D. Swann and D.L. McLachlan, *Concentration or Competition: A European Dilemma?* (London: Chatham House, 1967), p. 12.

13. Ibid., p. 15.

14. Bela Balassa, *Trade Liberalization Among Industrial Countries* (New York: McGraw-Hill Book Company, 1967), p. 121.

15. Swann and McLachlan, *Concentration or Competition?* pp. 43-53.

16. George Stigler, "The Division of Labor is Limited by the Extent of the Market," *Journal of Political Economy*, June 1951, p. 187.

17. See John M. Munro, *Trade Liberalization and Transportation in International Trade* (Toronto: University of Toronto Press, 1969), Chapter 1.

18. Ibid., p. 195.

19. William S. Commanor and Thomas A. Wilson, "Advertising, Market Structure, and Performance," *Review of Economics and Statistics*, November 1967, pp. 425-6.

20. Harvey Leibenstein, "Allocative Efficiency and X-Efficiency," *American Economic Review*, June 1966, p. 396.

21. Richard Caves, "Market Organization, Performance, and Public Policy," in R. Caves, ed., *Britain's Economic Prospects* (Washington, D.C.: Brookings Institution, 1968), p. 295.

22. By low residual productivity, I am referring to a relatively low figure for the contribution of output per unit of input to a country's real growth rate; see Edward F. Denison, *Why Growth Rates Differ*, (Washington, D.C.: Brookings Institution, 1967), Chapter 21.

23. Tibor Scitovsky, "International Trade and Economic Integration as a means of Overcoming the Disadvantages of a Small Nation," in E.A.G. Robinson, ed., the *Economic Consequences of the Size of Nations* (London: Macmillan, 1960), p. 283.

24. See Robinson, *Size of Nations*, p. xix, and Richard N. Cooper, *The Economics of Interdependence* (New York: McGraw-Hill Book Company, 1968), p. 79.

25. Joe Bain, *Barriers to New Competition* (Cambridge: Harvard University Press, 1956), Chapter 3.

26. Joe Bain, *International Differences in Industrial Structure* (New Haven: Yale University Press, 1966), p. 43.

27. Unfortunately, the empirical question of whether increases in national markets over time have been associated with decreases in vertical integration remains an unanswered one for most countries. However, a recent study for the United States suggests that there has not been any discernible increase in the degree of vertical integration in the U.S. corporate sector for the period 1948-65. If anything, there may have been a decline. See Arthur B. Laffer, "Vertical Integration by Corporations, 1929-65," *Review of Economics and Statistics*, February 1969.

28. George Stigler, "Division of Labor," p. 187.

29. For two classic applications of the permanent-transitory dichotomy to problems of consumption and investment, respectively, see Milton Friedman, *A Theory of the Consumption Function* (Princeton: Princeton University Press, 1957), and Robert Eisner, "A Permanent Income Theory for Investment," *American Economic Review*, June 1967.

30. Tibor Scitovsky, *International Trade*, p. 284.

31. For application of this formula to large scale tariff liberalization, see Balassa, *Trade Liberalization*, p. 75.

32. The introduction of the terms *interindustry specialization* and *intraindustry specialization* and their application to large-scale tariff liberalization, owes to Bela Balassa; see his *Trade Liberalization Among Industrial Countries*, pp. 86-92 and his "Tariff Reductions and Trade in Manufactures Among the Industrial Countries," *American Economic Review*, June 1966.

33. M.E. Kreinin, "Effects of Tariff Changes on the Prices and Volume of Imports," *American Economic Review*, June 1961, p. 317.

34. See Walter S. Salant and Beatrice N. Vaccara, *Import Liberalization and Employment* (Washington, D.C.: Brookings Institution, 1961), pp. 193-210.

35. M.E. Kreinin, "Trade Arrangements Among Industrial Countries: Effects on the United States," in Bela Balassa, ed., *Studies in Trade Liberalization*, (Baltimore: Johns Hopkins Press, 1967), p. 39.

36. Solomon Fabricant, "Study of the Size and Efficiency of the American Economy," in E.A.G. Robinson, ed., *The Economic Consequences of the Size of Nations*, p. 35.

37. Ibid., p. 48.

38. For a good discussion of this direction of causation question, see Richard Caves, "Market Organization," p. 297.

39. Bain, *International Differences*, p. 39.

40. Swann and McLachlan, *Concentration or Competition?*, p. 9.

41. Bain, *New Competition*.

42. Theodore Gates and Fabian Linden, *Costs and Competition* (New York: National Industrial Conference Board, 1961), p. 129.

43. D. Paige and C. Bombach, *A Comparison of National Output and Productivity of the United Kingdom and the United States* (Paris: Organization for Common Economic Cooperation, 1959), p. 64.

44. John H. Young, "Some Aspects of Canadian Economic Development" (unpublished doctoral dissertation submitted to Cambridge University, 1955), p. 86.

45. H. Edward English, *Industrial Structure in Canada's International Competitive Position* (Ottawa: The Canadian Trade Committee, 1964).

46. Gates and Linden, *Costs and Competition*, Chapter 3.

47. Edward F. Denison, *Why Growth Rates Differ* (Washington, D.C.: Brookings Institution, 1967).

48. Ibid., pp. 299-301.

49. Ibid., p. 237.

11 Trade Liberalization and the Agricultural Impasse

Ernest H. Preeg

Analyses based on the theory of comparative costs reveal the agricultural sector as a shining example of the actual or potential gains from international trade and specialization. Wide differences among nations in available arable land, climate, and population density should all reflect substantial cost differences from one country to another and point to a trading pattern wherein the "bread-baskets" of the world would export basic foodstuffs to the populous areas less fortunately endowed by nature or geography.

The case is illustrated by the differences in value-added per farm worker in 1967, a rough proxy for differences in costs of production. These were as follows: the United States $6,350, Canada $4,450, the United Kingdom $3,180, France (1966) $2,000, West Germany $1,830, Italy $1,600, Japan $930.[1] Table 11-1 provides further supporting data on national differences in support prices for wheat, arable land, and population.

The classic example of an enlightened trade policy for agricultural products was the repeal of the British Corn Laws in 1846, which permitted the import of low-cost food from abroad in exchange for exports of British manufactures. However, the experience of recent decades has been—overall—a gradual reversal of the free-trade concept embodied in the Corn Laws. Indeed, the United Kingdom entry into the European Common Market in 1973 will involve the adoption by the British of the variable import levy system of the European Community, which is highly protectionist in concept and the antithesis of the 1846 initiative.

The limited progress achieved in liberalizing agricultural trade since World War II, which has probably been more than offset by increased trade restrictions in certain key product categories, has been particularly disappointing when compared with the very substantial progress made by the non-Communist industrialized countries in lowering barriers on trade in industrial products. With each succeeding multilateral trade negotiation under the GATT, the dichotomy between progressively lower trade barriers on industrial products and continued import restrictions on agricultural products has widened, and we are now at the point where the two categories of trade can hardly be viewed as parts of a single world trading system.

The views expressed are personal and do not necessarily reflect those of the U.S. Government.

Table 11-1

International Comparison of Support Prices for Wheat, Arable Land, and Population

	(1) Support Price for Wheat (Dollars per Ton, 1971-72)	(2) Arable Land (Millions of Hectares, 1964-69)	(3) Population (Total) per Hectare of Arable Land (1969)	(4) Percentage of Population in Agriculture (1965)
Argentina	1.21	23.9	1.0	18
U.S.	1.25	174.5	1.2	6
Canada	1.35	43.4	0.5	11
Australia	1.65[a]	44.4	0.3	10
U.K.	2.10	7.3	7.6	4
United Arab Republic	2.61	2.7	12.0	55
Sweden	2.74	3.1	2.6	13
India	2.76	159.7	3.4	70
Brazil	2.83	29.8	3.0	48
France	2.98	17.6	2.9	18
Germany	2.98	7.6	7.7	11
Italy	2.98	12.2	4.4	24
Japan	4.76	5.0	20.5	24
Switzerland	4.86	0.4	15.5	10

[a]1970-71.

Sources: *Review of the World Wheat Situation, 1970/71*, (International Wheat Council, London), Appendix Table VI, p. 78; *Production Yearbook 1970*, (FAO, Rome, 1971) vol. 24, Tables 1, 4 and 5.

This peculiar situation not only runs contrary to the objective of seeking maximum gains from trade, but in a broader policy sense has become increasingly difficult to justify for major exporters of agricultural commodities. Such countries rely heavily on increased access to foreign markets for farm products in order to achieve overall balance in their international accounts. In essence, it would appear that post-World War II trade liberalization has been biased against countries that happen to have an international competitive advantage in agricultural products, including the United States, Canada, Australia, New Zealand, and certain developing nations.

This basic problem—or impasse—in agricultural trade liberalization is frequently explained in terms of agricultural production representing a unique social/political problem in all countries, wherein one cannot expect an open trading system similar to that which governs industrial products. According to this thesis, each country has some form of domestic support program for agriculture which is related to deeply held convictions such as the need for national self-sufficiency in food, income parity for those employed in the farm sector, and the role of the small farmer as a mainstay of a democratic political system. Free trade in agriculture would undermine these national policies, and thus cannot be permitted.

In fact, however, the problem of agricultural trade is far more complex than indicated by this traditional rationale, which in any event is of diminishing relevance as the number of farmers continues to decline and small farms are merged into large, corporate "agribusiness" entities. There also appears to be more hope than implied in the standard rationale for agricultural protection, and that the seemingly intractable impasse in agricultural trade policy of the past quarter-century is amenable to a more rational trading system during the course of the 1970s and 1980s. An understanding of these prospects rests on at least four unique characteristics of trade in agricultural products that have hindered the kind of steady progress in liberalizing trade that has taken place for industrial products.

World Supply/Demand Relationship

First, efforts toward a more efficient world-trading system incorporating the agricultural sector have been hampered by an uncertain longer-term outlook with respect to the global supply of and demand for food. The degree of self-sufficiency in food production has risen quite substantially during the past decade in Western Europe, the traditional commercial market for agricultural commodities, while Japan has steadily grown into a major importer of food.

Perhaps of greater importance in the longer term, however, is the net agricultural trading position of the developing countries. A number of developing countries have made substantial recent progress in increasing food production, but the outlook remains highly uncertain. Aside from the ultimate Malthusian spectre, there is in any event widespread malnutrition in many parts of the developing world, which could well absorb existing or potential surpluses of food production in the more affluent countries, if the appropriate financing and marketing arrangements could be made.

The changing geographic picture of food surplus and deficit areas is illustrated by net export levels in grains over the past several decades, including a U.S. Department of Agriculture projection for 1980 based on a continuation of present policies.[2] Asia, including Japan, has shifted from the role of a small net exporter of grains in the late 1930s to a major net importer of 30 million tons in the mid 1960s, and is projected further to be a net importer of 60 million tons in 1980. Western Europe, on the other hand, is expected to be a net importer of only some 15 million tons by 1980 compared with about 25 million tons in the mid 1960s. As an indication of the uncertainty of developing-country demand, the Department of Agriculture made alternate assumptions about productivity trends and price levels, and projected net grain imports for all developing countries for 1980 ranging from 10.5 million tons to 52.1 million tons, with 35.8 million tons the estimate based on continuation of present policies.

Rapid Structural Change

Secondly, efforts to improve the international trading system with respect to agricultural commodities are further complicated by the continual and at times rapid shifts from relative labor-intensive to capital-intensive farming. This structural change took place in the United States over the past three or four decades and has been unfolding in Europe and Japan at a much faster rate in more recent years. Table 11-2 shows the relative and absolute decline in the agricultural labor force which has occurred in North America, Western Europe, and Japan since 1957.

During these periods of rapid structural change, which include not only a substantial exodus of farmers to urban areas but also a consolidation of small family farms into larger, capital-intensive units, governments tend to be particularly solicitous of the demands of the marginal producers—often the small farmers—and to resist steps toward trade liberalization which would aggravate their position by accelerating the rate of change. Moreover, this structural change at the same time brings about rapid productivity gains which, if in combination with support policies based on the higher cost structure of the marginal farmer not yet modernized, can become an important stimulus to increased production in the highest cost, least efficient producing countries.

Table 11-2
Agricultural Employment in Selected Countries

	Percentage of Civilian Employment in Agriculture				Annual Rates of Change in Employment in Agriculture	
	1957	1960	1965	1970	1960-65	1965-69
Canada	15.2	13.3	10.1	7.7	−2.7	−2.2
United States	9.3	8.3	6.1	4.4	−4.5	−4.9
Japan	34.3	30.2	23.5	17.4	−3.8	−3.7
United Kingdom	4.4	4.1	3.3	2.9	−3.8	−3.6
EEC:	23.2	21.0	16.4	12.8	−	−
of which						
France	24.6	22.4	17.7	14.0	−3.6	−3.6
Germany	16.3	14.0	11.1	9.0	−3.9	−3.8
Italy	35.6	32.8	26.1	19.6	−5.5	−5.1

Sources: O.E.C.D., *Labour Force Statistics 1959-1970*, p. 40; and *Structural Reform Measures in Agriculture*, (Paris, 1972), p. 21.

Incompatible National Domestic Policies

Third, each major nation, or in the case of the European Community a group of nations, has an internal policy to support and stabilize agricultural incomes in a way which moderates market forces and usually affects trade. But these internal policies vary greatly from country to country.

The United States, for a number of important commodities, has a combination of price-support and acreage-limitation programs, which attempt to insure that remunerative price levels to farmers do not result in excessive production. In conjunction with this internal support policy, quotas are applied to imports, as appropriate, to prevent them from undermining the domestic policy by driving down internal prices. The United Kingdom, on the other hand, has a "deficiency payment" system (in the process of being phased out), whereby world market prices determine the level of consumer prices, while farmers are paid a supplementary or "deficiency" payment to make up the difference between the market price and what is determined by the government in its annual review as an equitable return to the farmer.

The European Community's Common Agricultural Policy, as applied to grains and other basic commodities, is based on an internal price level jointly determined by the member governments which remains constant throughout the community during a given time period. In order that lower-price imports do not undercut the internal support price, a variable import levy is applied which is calculated to make up the difference between the world market price and the internal price plus a small margin in favor of domestic producers.[a] In effect, domestic producers can market as much as they are able at the internal support price, while imports are only permitted to supply the residual internal demand. Moreover, products not sold on the internal market are eligible for an export subsidy sufficient to market the product abroad.

In view of these differing national approaches to internal support, it is particularly difficult to develop a single, mutually compatible, international trading system. Almost all domestic policies are trade restrictive in one form or another, making world market prices ineffective as arbiter between supply and demand. As a result, there is no clear conceptual answer to some basic questions of agricultural trade: Which countries end up with the surplus production when there is global overproduction? Which countries receive the windfall gains or losses from international prices which, as the result of varying internal policies, are artificially low or high? To the extent that the poorer countries, on equity grounds, receive highly concessionary or grant food aid, who pays the bill?

---

[a]More specifically, the variable levy system is a complex one which imposes variable import charges on a number of basic agricultural commodities and also on processed food products and meats on the basis of the proportion of basic commodities contained in them—for example, the variable levy on beef is based on the existing internal-external price difference for various feed grains, weighted by the amount of each used per unit of beef.

Timing of European Integration

Finally, a more liberal trading system for agricultural products, either among the industrialized "market-oriented" trading countries, or on a broader basis to include the developing countries and the socialist countries of Eastern Europe and Asia, has been stymied over the past fifteen years by the process of European economic integration. As described further in the next section, internal farm policy formulation and implementation by the members of the European Community has been a long and drawn out internal political struggle, which for the Europeans has generally taken priority over the need to deal with the interests of trading partners abroad. This inward-looking attitude of the Europeans in the field of agricultural trade has been a disappointment to the community's trading partners, particularly agricultural exporting countries such as the United States, Canada and Australia. At times this impasse over agricultural trade has come close to disrupting trade policy on a much broader basis. A possible consolation to this situation is that the Europeans now appear to be entering a new and more comprehensive stage of economic integration which should permit a more outward-looking position in matters of agricultural trade.

The Postwar Record

The circumstances outlined above have, together, constituted a formidable impediment to trade liberalization in the agricultural sector. Still another factor, in this case institutional, has been the inadequacy of the international trading system and its institutional machinery, primarily as embodied in the GATT, for dealing with the issues of agricultural trade. A central concept of the GATT is that protection, to the extent necessary, should be in the form of tariffs, and that other restrictions, including quotas, should be terminated except under certain specified circumstances. Despite some exceptions, most notably in the textile sector, this principle has generally prevailed with success in the field of industrial trade.

For agricultural trade, the GATT provides for exemption from the "tariffs-only" approach under narrowly defined conditions where "necessary to the enforcement of governmental measures" (Article XI). Presumably, however, the bulk of farm trade should, under the terms of the GATT, come within the tariff-only oriented system. Nevertheless, nontariff barriers remain widespread in the agricultural field, mostly in apparent or flagrant violation of the GATT provisions. A 1962 GATT study of thirty-four countries, for example, reported that nontariff restrictions covered 87 percent of wheat production, 84 percent of butter, 59 percent of cheese, and 52 percent of sugar.[3]

The credibility of the GATT as an effective instrument for dealing with agricultural trade was dealt a particularly hard blow in 1955 when the United States, the foremost proponent of liberalized trade for farm products, sought and obtained a broad waiver from its GATT obligations in order to implement Section 22 of the Agricultural Adjustment Act. Import quotas were subsequently imposed on a number of products including cotton, wheat, peanuts, and certain dairy products.

Still another major if not mortal undermining of the adequacy of the existing GATT provisions with regard to agriculture was the adoption of the aforementioned variable levy import system by the European Community. These levies might, from a legal point of view, be considered a form of "tariff," consistent with the GATT, but in practice—as described in the previous section—the variable levy system can be the ultimate protectionist device, changing from day to day, with no upper limit, and eliminating effective competition between domestic and imported products at any price.

The major trading nations have, of course, been aware of these problems, including the inadequacies of the GATT provisions for dealing with agricultural trade. In 1958, in anticipation of the trade impact of the European Community, a committee of independent experts under the chairmanship of Gottfried Haberler was commissioned by the GATT to examine a number of questions in the field of trade policy, including agriculture.[4] The committee report emphasized the high levels of protection, the accumulation of surpluses by low-cost producers, and the inability of existing GATT rules and procedures to cope with the problem. A number of recommendations were made, primarily directed to the industrialized countries, to liberalize trade in primary products. The subsequent review of the report by governments, although characterized by one observer as picking out "with single-minded cynicism those points of the report which fitted their own case best without endorsing the policy of the report as a whole,"[5] did result in proposals for a new round of multilateral negotiations that would deal in a more comprehensive way with barriers to international trade in farm products.

The subsequent "Dillon Round" of GATT negotiations in 1960-62, however, was unable to act on these proposals because the European Community had not yet agreed on the specifics of its Common Agricultural Policy. Few significant concessions were made in the agricultural sector in the Dillon Round and, with respect to the community farm policy, some countries, including the United States, reserved their GATT rights for future negotiations for a time when the precise effects of this policy became known.

The Kennedy Round of GATT negotiations in 1963-67 became in many respects a captive of the impasse in agricultural trade, even though the final results were modest in the agricultural field compared with the very substantial reductions accomplished in barriers to industrial trade.[6] The negotiating objective for agriculture was, at the outset, defined only in vague terms: "In view of the importance of agriculture in world trade, the trade negotiations shall provide for acceptable conditions of access to world markets for agricultural products ... in furtherance of a significant development and expansion of world trade."[7]

Subsequently the United States, in particular, insisted that progress in the industrial sector be linked to parallel movement toward this objective for agriculture. The European Community, on the other hand, was unable to make specific offers until its internal policy was determined, a lengthy and tortuous process not completed until the summer of 1966. Even at this point, however, there was still basic disagreement on what would constitute acceptable conditions of access to world markets, and the final negotiating period in the spring of 1967 centered largely on what would be the minimum acceptable agricultural concessions for an overall agreement.

The results of the Kennedy Round can best be described in terms of two categories of products: grains, meat, and dairy products—for which comprehensive commodity arrangements were attempted—and all other products. In the latter category, total 1964 imports by the major industrialized countries were $11.1 billion, of which $3.6 billion was already duty-free before the Kennedy Round.[8] Of the remaining $7.5 billion of dutiable imports, $3.9 billion, or 52 percent, received tariff reductions as a result of the negotiations. In many cases, however, barriers other than tariffs were also in effect, making a qualitative appraisal of the trade-creating effects of these reductions virtually impossible.

Broad commodity arrangements were attempted for grains, meat, and dairy products in recognition of the interplay of domestic support policies for these products on world trade, and hence the need to deal with more than direct border restrictions if, in fact, a "significant development and expansion of world trade" were to be realized. These three sectors were also the core of the emerging variable levy system of the European Community which, among other things, required a renegotiation of previous GATT commitments by Community member states.

Commodity arrangements have had a lengthy and somewhat ambivalent history over the postwar period. Provision for such agreements was contained in the International Trade Organization (ITO) Charter of 1948, which was never ratified, but these sections were not carried over to the GATT. It was widely recognized that comprehensive agreements might be the only sensible approach for commodities where national policies had overriding effects on market conditions. But agricultural exporters, such as the United States and Commonwealth countries, were generally highly suspicious of and negative toward such arrangements, seeing them as a form of cover for more protectionist policies by the importing countries.

A particularly significant initiative by the French in 1961, the so-called Baumgartner-Pisani proposals, called for "market organization" for trade in basic agricultural commodities, starting with grains. The proposed policy would raise world prices to a "normal" level, never clearly defined, and in turn utilize the additional revenues gained thereby to finance shipments of surpluses to under-nourished nations unable to afford imports.

The experience of the Kennedy Round in the commodity field was largely an elaboration of such European concepts to organize markets confronted by the agricultural exporters' demands for guaranteed access for their products to the European and other commercial markets. The initial European offer was to bind, under certain conditions, internal support levels. The exporters rejected this approach because the anticipated internal support levels would almost certainly lead to increased production in the high cost-importing areas, particularly the European Community, while no provision was offered to give imports acceptable access to these markets.

Toward the end of the Kennedy Round, a more complete conceptual framework for a grains arrangement was put forward by the Europeans, including a proposed commitment not to exceed a specified self-sufficiency ratio—in other words reserving a given share of the market for imports. However, agreement on specific levels of self-sufficiency and other elements of such a comprehensive approach was not reached, and in the end a more modest arrangement was agreed upon, consisting of a joint food aid commitment of 4.5 million tons of grain per year for three years, and price ranges for wheat trade subject to the Prices Review Committee. For meat and dairy products nothing was accomplished in the quest for comprehensive commodity arrangements.

Since the conclusion of the Kennedy Round on June 30, 1967 there have been no serious attempts to negotiate an improved trading system for agriculture, although a number of subsequent developments have, if anything, increased the urgency for taking constructive joint actions.

First, the International Grains Arrangement has not worked out satisfactorily. The food aid commitments were implemented but the price ranges to be maintained on world markets, without operative provisions for joint actions in circumstances of global surplus or deficit, were not upheld. When increased production reached world markets in 1968, the Prices Review Committee was unable to agree on concerted action and, as provided in the agreement, prices were then permitted to drop below minimum levels. This dispelled any illusion about the adequacy of the International Wheat Arrangement.

Second, the European Community's variable levy system continues to take its toll on imports from nonmember countries. As shown in Table 11-3, the degree of community self-sufficiency in grains rose from 85 percent in 1958 to 94 percent in 1968/69. Moreover, the increase in European support prices relative to world market prices has made the farm policy an increasing burden to European economies: in 1969 for example, the Community support price for wheat was 214 percent of the world wheat price, 195 percent for soft wheat, and 197 percent for barley.

Perhaps the most striking development, indicative at least in part of the distortions in trade from the existing variable levy system, has been the marked

Table 11-3

European Community Self-Sufficiency in Agricultural Products and Relative Prices, 1958 and 1968-69 (%)

Product	EEC Self-Sufficiency, 1958	EEC Self-Sufficiency, 1968-69	EEC Producer Prices as a Percentage of World Market Prices, 1958-59	EEC Producer Prices as a Percentage of World Market Prices, 1968-69
Hard wheat	n.a.	60 ⎫	149	214 ⎰
Soft wheat	93	120 ⎭		195 ⎱
Barley	n.a.	107	134	197
Feedgrains	78	n.a.	–	–
All grains	85	94	–	–
Sugar	99	103	131	456
Beef	89 ⎱	89	147	169
Veal	102 ⎰			
Pigmeat	100	99	118	153
Poultry	93	98	n.a.	n.a.
Eggs	n.a.	n.a.	130	141
Butter	n.a.	113	n.a.	504
Cheese	n.a.	102	n.a.	n.a.

Source: Francis Knox, *The Common Market and World Agriculture: Trade Patterns in Temperate-Zone Foodstuffs* (New York: Frederick A. Praeger, 1972), Tables 7 and 16.

differences in the observed trends in Community imports of grains and oilseeds, particularly soybeans. These two categories of products are to a certain degree substitutes as animal feed, but whereas grains come under the variable levy import system, soybeans enter the Community duty-free as a result of GATT commitments undertaken by the Europeans before soybeans were of major commercial significance in trade. As a result, between 1960-61 and 1971 U.S. exports of oilseeds and products increased from slightly less than $200 million per year to $839 million, while over the same period U.S. exports of grains were up only modestly from an average annual level of $317 million in the early period to $423 million in 1971 (see Table 11-4).

Third, enlargement of the European Community to include the United Kingdom and other countries poses a new threat to nonmember exporters, particularly with regard to the British market which will now be subject to the Community farm policy. On the other hand, the anticipated high cost of the Common Agricultural Policy to the United Kingdom has been a major concern for the British, which together with growing disenchantment from various quarters within the European Community itself about the existing farm policy and its cost, indicates a growing constituency within Europe for modification of the present system.

These recent developments will influence the prospects for major new

Table 11-4

U.S. Agricultural Exports to the European Community ($ Millions)

	1960	1961	1970	1971
Products subject to the variable levy	299	443	454	448
Of which:				
Feed grains	197	186	324	345
Wheat	46	173	77	59
Rice	7	15	21	18
Rye	4	6	–	1
Total Grains	254	380	422	423
Poultry and eggs	29	46	13	10
Products not subject to the variable levy	800	715	1,105	1,353
Of which:				
Cotton	313	233	19	53
Fruits and preparations	46	57	67	61
Vegetables and preparations	12	13	22	19
Oilseeds and products	198	179	665	839
(Soybeans)	(15)	(15)	(220)	(262)
Tallow	38	31	33	33
Tobacco	88	97	124	151
Total	1,099	1,157	1,559	1,800

Source: *Foreign Agricultural Trade of the United States*, March 1972 (USDA), pp. 28-29.

multilateral trade negotiations scheduled to begin as early as 1973. The preliminary preparations for such negotiations have been under way during 1972 in the GATT as well as in the OECD, where a special group of experts has been preparing a report on an action program for trade policy in the 1970s. There is little question that agriculture will play a central role in the course of any future trade negotiations.

A Program for the 1970s

A successful action program for the 1970s in the field of agricultural trade will likely have to consist of two distinct parts: agreement in principle on broad objectives, in view of the confused conceptual framework of the past decade; and adoption of shorter-term specific objectives that will result in substantial movement toward the longer term goals.

Regarding broad objectives, the basic question is whether a consensus now exists, particularly among the major industrialized countries, that the present pattern of production and trade in basic farm products involves a highly inefficient use of resources and that therefore steps should be taken in the direction of a more rational system with greater market opportunity for low-cost producers and corresponding disincentives to increased high-cost production. This need not entail a reduction in farm incomes for individual farmers, since a system of incentives could be devised that would maintain incomes while at the same time working toward more efficient patterns of production and trade.

The corollary to this basic objective, in view of the importance of domestic programs, is that trade agreements in basic commodities would have to include some form of commitment on domestic policy. Commitments might include limits on total support to farmers, adjustment assistance or other incentives to ease the transition of marginal farmers to more productive employment and to divert low-yield acreage to alternate use, or more fundamental structural reform of the agricultural sector. As an example of the last category, Europe probably should give greater relative emphasis to high-value products, such as meat and dairy products, while the structure of support prices in recent years has tended overall to shift production toward low-value grain production. An internal Community policy, for both internal and external objectives, could be devised to reverse this trend through changes in relative support prices or other means.

Finally, to the extent that there is a consensus to stimulate the transfer of abundant food production in rich countries to the undernourished parts of the developing world, there would likely be a need for a coordinated approach for exports to these "noncommercial" markets.

The short-term specific negotiating objectives for the next several years are, of course, much more difficult to define at this point, and their elaboration must be left to unfold during the anticipated negotiations of the mid-1970s. However, in the context of those negotiations, although multilateral in concept, an important point of departure will be the dominant roles of a few key participants. The United States, Canada, Australia and New Zealand, although with some differences in product emphasis, will likely constitute an exporter group jointly pressing for greater access to the principal commercial markets in Europe and Japan. To a large extent, there will probably be a central element of bilateral United States-European Community negotiations, pitting the largest exporter against the main unresolved issues of European agricultural policy after EEC enlargement.

This basic negotiating context for new trade negotiations leads to two final observations. First, the agricultural negotiations will inevitably be linked to areas of negotiation in industrial trade, where the multilateral balance of interests will be quite different in character. In one sense, this provides an opportunity for a balanced overall agreement which might not be possible in the agricultural sector alone. On the other hand it may, as in the past, put agriculture into a central position as a critical factor in determining whether the overall trade initiatives in future years can be successfully concluded. Since the agricultural impasse will likely be one of the most difficult, if not *the* most difficult set of issues in the trade-policy field, this could result in agriculture assuming far greater importance to overall commercial relations than is indicated by its share of total world trade.

Second, and related to the previous point, the international economy today is more than ever a system of "political economy." With important and often growing roles of government affecting trade, particularly in the agricultural field, a stable and mutually beneficial trading system can only be maintained on the basis of political understandings that economic objectives will be pursued jointly, and that each participant is willing to gear its domestic economic policies to achieve a reasonable balance between internal and external interests. If, on the other hand, domestic policies consistently serve domestic interests at the expense of foreign interests, today's highly interdependent world economy will quickly regress. The domestic economic costs of international constraints, under conditions of imperfect competition and rather inflexible national economies, is belatedly receiving its deserved scrutiny.

For agricultural trade, however, with appropriate safeguards to avoid disruptive effects on individual farmers, the opportunities for multilateral gains from trade should still, under the circumstances of the 1970s, be clearly worth the mutual effort.

Notes

1. V.L. Sorenson and D.E. Hathaway, "The Competitive Position of U.S. Agriculture," *United States International Economic Policy in an Interdependent World* (Papers submitted to the President's Commission on International Trade and Investment, Washington, D.C., 1971), p. 817.

2. *World Demand Prospects for Grain in 1980*, Foreign Agricultural Report No. 75, (U.S. Department of Agriculture, December 1971), p. 78.

3. GATT Programme for Expansion of International Trade, *Food in Agricultural Products*, Second and Third Reports of Committee II, (Geneva, 1962), p. 18.

4. See Gerard Curzon, *Multilateral Commercial Diplomacy*, (Michael Joseph Ltd., 1965), pp. 179-85.

5. Ibid., p. 182.

6. See Ernest H. Preeg, *Traders and Diplomats*, (The Brookings Institution, 1970), esp. Chapters 9 and 15.

7. Ministerial Resolution adopted May 21, 1963. See GATT press release 793, May 29, 1963.

8. See GATT press release 992, June 30, 1967.

12 Trade Relations with the Third World: Preferential Aspects of Protective Structures

Harry H. Bell

Contemporary journalism was only too ready to characterize as a "failure" the second session of the United Nations Conference on Trade and Development (UNCTAD) held at New Delhi in early 1968. It was easy to ridicule the interminable caucusing of disparate groupings of African, Asian, and Latin American delegations trying to maintain the semblance of coalition. And indeed most of the resolutions that came out of UNCTAD II were limited to platitudes or procedural matters. Yet at least one of the resolutions was destined to have not only symbolic but also practical importance in improving the political atmosphere of future relations between poor and rich countries. The concept of a system of nonreciprocal and nondiscriminatory trade preferences (GSP) by industrial countries for exports of developing countries was barely six years old at the time. It appeared to challenge not only the first article of the GATT, but also the accepted trade-negotiating technique—multilateral application of trade concessions via the unconditional most-favored-nation (MFN) clause based on a more or less finely-calculated bilateral balance of reciprocity. Whereas the GSP idea had been bitterly opposed at the first UNCTAD (1964) by the United States, Japan, Sweden, and the Scandinavian countries, the requisites of U.S. popularity in Latin America prompted President Johnson to announce a rather startling change of position on this issue at the Punta del Este meeting of American presidents in 1967.

It was still more remarkable that, in the face of apparently insoluble complexities, the negotiations of the next two and a half years culminated in a further consensus, in late 1970, whereby the major industrial nations committed themselves to proceed with actual implementation of their respective unilateral tariff reductions in favor of developing countries under GSP. Again, this was only made possible by a major shift on the part of the United States, which dropped its insistence that safeguard mechanisms and other main features of the industrial countries' GSP offers be identical. In return, the countries of the European Economic Community (EEC) agreed to the establishment of machinery advocated by the United States to ensure reasonable burden-sharing among the preference "donors."

And yet it is ironic that by the time of UNCTAD III in Santiago two years later (April-May 1972), the United States was the sole major country in default on its commitment to implement GSP. The EEC was the first to put its scheme in operation in July 1971, closely followed by Japan and Norway (August and October, respectively), with the offers of the United Kingdom and most other donor countries taking effect at the beginning of or during 1972. Canada promised early legislative action. The American delegation stood alone, and could only reaffirm its support for GSP in principle and commend the implementing countries. They could offer no definite prospects of U.S. action.

It was enough for the U.S. spokesmen to refer to the dramatic events affecting the U.S. international economic and monetary position during 1971 to show that it would have been extremely dangerous to introduce preference legislation into a Congress that was already in a preelectoral mood and spawning such protectionist legislative proposals as the Hartke-Burke bill. What the U.S. representatives neglected to mention, however, was that there had been no preparatory effort at an earlier stage to educate the Congress—let alone public opinion—on what the GSP was all about, not just in the context of the strategy of economic development, but especially with respect to the role that the GSP might play in attenuating the disruptive effects of proliferating regional and bilateral preference arrangements on the whole international trading system.

In this and the following chapter, we shall explore the question of preferences as an aspect of general discrimination in international trade. What are they? What are the historical precedents? How can they benefit developing countries, and to what extent have they succeeded in the past? What is the outlook for the GSP, and for the formation of North-South trading blocs? The answers are of singular importance for assessing the efficacy of commercial policy as an agent of economic development.

Introduction

According to the 1968 UNCTAD II resolution, the objectives of the GSP were to increase the export earnings of developing countries, to promote their industrialization, and to accelerate their rates of growth. Yet it would be naïve to believe that it was entirely such developmental concerns—or the desire to appease the developing nations politically—that finally persuaded the industrial countries to reach their positive consensus on trade preferences. Indeed, there are good grounds for doubting that the preference-giving countries will *in fact* substantially liberalize access of labor-intensive goods from low-wage developing countries to their domestic markets, since strict safeguards are being imposed with respect to quantities and prices to preclude "market disruption." And liberal critics point out that by being unilateral, in the sense of an act of grace, the scheme renders developing countries helpless to resist increased use of quantitative restrictions in the guise of safeguards.[1] Since exports of manufactures from developing to developed countries have in any case been accelerating during recent years even without benefit of the GSP, the critics claim that it would have been better to concentrate on eliminating nontariff barriers, not on obtaining tariff preferences.[2]

One important consideration in favor of GSP, that has received insufficient attention thus far from the standpoint of the major industrial countries, is that it offers interesting possibilities for de-escalating the commercial rivalries associated historically with colonial and postcolonial preferential trading systems, especially with respect to the "reverse" preferences given by developing countries to their metropolitan powers in reciprocity for access to their markets. From the outset, the United Kingdom has seen in GSP a means of diverting to other countries some of the impact of its heavy concentration of imports of consumer goods from Asian countries of the Commonwealth Preference Area. The British are also relying on the GSP to contribute to a solution of their problems of divestment of Commonwealth responsibilities in connection with entry into the Common Market. The latter point is equally important to the charter members of EEC, which in addition find that the GSP offers a convenient way of disarming Latin American and other foreign critics of EEC trading policies and of avoiding the indefinite extension of new special relationships toward more and more countries. Moreover, to the extent that the GSP can be made to decrease the incentive for developing countries to give reverse preferences to the enlarged Common Market, it has an important role to play in the economic strategy of the United States, Japan, and other outsiders. Lastly, the GSP can be viewed as an alternative to the frequently-proposed special U.S. preferential relationship with Latin America—a relationship that offers little real advantage to either side but which, if consummated, might well be tantamount to a declaration of commercial warfare against Europe and precipitate division of the world into hemispheric spheres of economic and political influence.

Each of the foregoing considerations illustrates the point that the policy alternative posed by GSP is *not* a simple choice between preferences for developing countries on the one hand and nondiscrimination in international trade on the other. Consequently, efforts to compare the admittedly modest foreseeable benefits of the GSP—either in terms of increased exports or in terms of the maximum possible transfer of tariff revenue—with the costs of an alleged abandonment of GATT principles miss the relevant issue.[3] We already live in a world that is discrimination-ridden as well as tariff-ridden. There are preferences and there are preferences. Some are more orderly than others and may even be reasonably compatible with maintenance of a world economy based on multilateralism. Some have great potential for mischief and can lead toward disintegration of the world economy. The task is to ensure that the GSP, which is already an accomplished fact, is kept in the first category and to reduce discriminatory practices of the latter category.

This chapter takes as a point of departure a definition of discrimination (or preferences) as the geographical dimension of differentiated protective structures, in the belief that this approach—as distinguished from the usual legalistic approach—gives useful insights into the relationships between the product (or industry) differentiation of tariffs and geographic discrimination, the problems of measuring margins of preference, as well as some of the implications of the theory of effective protection as applied in the domain of preferential trading. The point is emphasized that the usual analytical assumption of infinite foreign supply elasticity is highly unrealistic in most preference situations, particularly where developing countries are concerned. A corollary is that there is an essential asymmetry in the trade and price responses in preferential relationships between developed and developing countries, and this is an important reason why the reciprocity involved in so-called reverse preferences is not comparable to that involved in economic-integration groupings among industrial countries. Finally, a parallel is also drawn between the economic inefficiencies resulting from extreme product differentiation of tariff structures and those resulting from "pathological" patterns of discrimination, exemplified by the bilateralism that prevailed in Europe just before and after World War II.

The second part of this chapter as well as Chapter 13 are devoted to an historical-institutional survey of the principal special-preference systems inherited from the British and French colonial regimes. The danger of formation of North-South trading blocs is implicit in the dynamics of the EEC's "association" policies. These tendencies are related to the recurrent proposals for a Western Hemisphere preferential area linking the United States and Latin America. There follows a background analysis of the main features of the GSP, as agreed upon in the OECD and UNCTAD, as well as the differences among the versions applied by various participants, including a detailed scrutiny of the EEC version.

Differentiation of Protection

Nominal Tariffs

In the broadest sense, policy related to trade preferences is almost synonymous with commercial policy in general. A trade preference is really nothing more or less than another form of discrimination in international commerce, and it is the essence of protective measures that they always "discriminate"[a] among goods that cross national customs frontiers—with respect to product-origin, product-class, or both. Protective measures are mainly thought of as *import* barriers (tariffs, quotas, exchange restrictions, and the like), but in the modern theory of protection they also include discriminatory measures affecting exports: duties and controls to restrain exports and various kinds of subsidies to promote them.

[a]The term "discrimination" is used in a broad sense here. In a narrower sense, it is frequently limited to denoting treatment more restrictive than most-favored nation (MFN).

And, although their intentional use is rather rare, measures that subsidize particular imports likewise fall within the same conceptual schema.

Protective measures affect the relative prices of goods. It has therefore been found convenient to define and measure levels of protection by the price differentials thus determined. In recent theoretical literature, the notion of "nominal" tariffs has been used to describe the level of protection, where the international price disparities for particular products are expressed in ad valorem percentages of a particular world-market price. The nominal tariff rate is normally rate of duty shown in the national tariff schedule, when the latter is expressed in or convertible into ad valorem terms and provided that it is not redundant, i.e., not so high as to make the import of duty-paid goods prohibitive. If one introduces an important further analytical condition—the "small country" assumption that the price elasticities of foreign supply and demand are infinite or very high (i.e., that the importing country's own commercial policy will not affect its terms of trade)—then the nominal tariff rate also measures the proportion by which the domestic price can be higher than it would have been under free trade.

Effective Tariffs

The notion of nominal tariffs is distinguished from that of the "effective" tariff rate. As noted in Chapter 3, this is also expressed in ad valorem terms, but applies not to the prices of products as such, but to the value added in processing the products when firms are not vertically integrated and therefore have to purchase their material inputs. Taking account of the fact that the intermediate inputs are usually subject to customs treatment different from that of the final product, it expresses the *net* effect of the protective regime on the productive process. Again taking recourse to various assumptions, the effective rate of protection expresses the degree to which the protective structure raises or lowers the value added in particular industries or productive processes as compared with that under free trade.[4] Effective rates are very hard to measure empirically, at best, and there are many unresolved theoretical issues.[5] It is nevertheless agreed by most authors that the pattern of differentiation of effective rates of protection gives some indication of how protective measures pull resources from one sector of a country's economy to another, thereby affecting welfare and (static) efficiency and frequently tending to frustrate comparative advantage. Relatively high effective rates may even lead to creation and maintenance of whole branches of production entailing a net loss of resources to the national economy. In any case, viewing tariff structures in terms of effective protection improves insight into the practical behavior of governments and industrial pressure groups in tariff negotiations and explains the characteristic tendency of nominal-rate tariff structures to "escalate" from low or zero duties on raw materials to progressively higher duties at more advanced stages of processing.

Geographical Discrimination

Tariff theory has, however, limited its analysis of the differentiation of nominal and effective tariff rates to the product-by-product and industry-by-industry dimensions. For simplicity of exposition it invariably abstracts from the fact that levels of protection are also likely to be differentiated along a geographical dimension. But just as, by definition, protection must involve discrimination between at least two categories of products,[b] so it must also discriminate between a domestic market and at least one foreign market. Such geographical discrimination ceases to be trivial and definitional as soon as a third area is singled out for special treatment. We then move into the domain of the theory of customs unions or, more generally, the theory of preferential or discriminatory trade.[6] Here it is mainly the spatial differentiation of tariff rates that is analyzed, to the neglect of the profile of protection by products and industries. Understandably, there are very few theoretical works that have attempted to cope rigorously with the multidimensional differentiation of protective structures and then only at a level of abstraction that bears little resemblance to the real world of economic institutions as it has evolved from historical political processes.[7] Moreover, formal customs-union theory has thus far been almost exclusively concerned with the static concepts of world welfare and efficiency as analyzed in terms of "trade creation" and "trade diversion." It often assumes away precisely those aspects (dynamic growth effects, external and internal economies of scale, etc.) that are the major nonpolitical considerations motivating preferential-trading arrangements.

The Temporal Dimension

In addition to being differentiated productwise, industrywise, and areawise, levels of protection also differ in the time dimension—in some countries quite widely. One must consider not only the process of adjustment called forth by autonomous changes in the product and area coverage or the magnitude of a preference, but also the complex interaction of autonomous movements of domestic prices with those of the international prices that filter through the protective regimes. An elementary example is the fact that ad valorem equivalents of specific and mixed duties may change significantly, even in the absence of legislative changes, thereby leading to significant changes in the measure of

---

[b]A uniform tariff on all importables, accompanied by a uniform export subsidy on all exportables, would be indistinguishable from a change in the exchange rate.

protection provided. Unfortunately, no comprehensive time series of tariff index numbers exist to facilitate temporal analysis of protective structures.

Complications of Defining and Evaluating Preferences

Margins of Preference, Relative
Prices, and Supply Elasticity

Other complications plague the study of preferential trading relationships when one comes to measure the degree of preferential (discriminatory) treatment. Margins of preference are normally expressed, for convenience, as the percentage-point difference between the MFN tariff rate and the preferential tariff rate. They reflect only approximately, at best, the price advantage enjoyed by the preferred supplier relative to MFN sources. For example, there is a minor anomaly of proportionality inherent in the usual arithmetic of calculating the preference margins.[c]

A more consequential problem, and one that goes to the crux of the preferences issue, is that the standard small-country assumption—i.e., that the country being considered faces infinite or very high elasticities of foreign supply and demand—is only likely to be fairly realistic vis-à-vis the world market as a whole, not with respect to all the particular preferential compartments that may be carved out of it. In the case of a broad economic grouping of industrialized countries like the European Common Market, especially when enlarged by new members and by free-trade arrangements with other countries, it may be reasonable to assume very high elasticities for most industrial products traded within the group—in which case the "world-market" prices facing any given member country may well be those determined by intracommunity competition. (One test for this condition is the existence of a strong export surplus in the products in question on the part of the other members of the community towards the outside world.)

On the other hand, developing countries are likely to show relatively low supply and demand elasticities. The short-term supply curve of an individual developing country for most industrial goods typically rises steeply and then becomes vertical. In this case, a preference to the developing country will *not* affect prices or total imports into the preference-giving area, and any stimulus to

---

[c]If the preference and MFN rates are 25 and 50 percent ad valorem, respectively, the margin of 25 percentage points implies a price differential of only

$$\frac{1.50 - 1.25}{1.50} = 16\ 2/3\%\ \text{or}\ \frac{1.50 - 1.25}{1.25} = 20\%$$

depending on which rate one puts in the denominator. This discrepancy can be neglected in dealing with "industrial countries" tariff systems where MFN rates are of the order of 10 percent or less and preferential rates are zero.

the exports and levels of production in the preference-beneficiary country will be very limited. Such incremental exports from the latter as do occur will constitute trade diversion (from nonpreferred third-country suppliers) and not trade creation (in competition with the domestic industry of the preference-giving country). The amount of the preferential remission of duty would normally accrue as a windfall term-of-trade effect to the preferred country and could be viewed as equivalent to a transfer of foreign aid.[8] Some or all of the windfall could be taxed, thereby assuring its effective repatriation, but this would counter incentives to invest in the longer-term development of the new export opportunities. In some circumstances, notably when the scope for preferential trade is limited by tariff quotas that leave no room for expansion of the existing flow, the windfall may even be captured by the importing middlemen in the preference-giving country. Various outcomes are possible, depending on market structure and on the procedures established by the governments concerned.

To be sure, given the possibility of international investment and transfers of technology, even small developing countries like Hong Kong, Singapore, and Taiwan may have a relatively high supply elasticity for many labor-intensive manufactured products over the medium term. This may also be true of developing countries already having a large production of the goods in question that could be diverted from the domestic market—at substantial real cost—if the trade preference is supplemented by special export incentives. With such relatively elastic supply in the preferred countries, there will be more possibility of a substantial downward impact on domestic prices in the preference-giving country and trade creation can occur.[d] Although this is a "good thing" from a free-trade economist's point of view, since it increases welfare via consumer surplus, it will be political anathema, and steps will probably be taken to minimize or eliminate the possibility of trade-creating effects.[9]

Finally, in the case of "reverse" preferences given by developing countries to developed countries under reciprocal preference arrangements—and especially where these are given to a group of developed countries such as the EEC—the foreign supply elasticity may well be very high, comparable to that of the world market as a whole. While the price in the preferred developed countries will determine the price in the preference-giving developing countries, in this case there will be no trade-creating effects since there is unlikely to have been any prior domestic production in the latter. There will be a pure and simple diversion of any trade that would otherwise have come from outsiders. As a general proposition, however, areawise discrimination requires abandonment of the a priori "small-country assumption" that underlies most of the analysis of the relative price implications associated with the nominal-tariff concept.

---

[d]The exclusions and sensitive lists laid down by preference-giving countries under UNCTAD Generalized System of Preferences provide a good check list of which products are expected to be in elastic supply in developing countries.

*Applicability to Preferences of
the Effective-Tariff Approach*

Partly for this reason, the concept of effective tariffs has not been formally integrated into the theory of customs unions and preferential trading. Geographical differentiation of levels of protection appears to be incommensurate with tariff differentiation in the industry as well as the product dimension. The fact that some imports are coming in from MFN sources and some from preferential sources complicates the analysis of a country's tariff profile, and *ad hoc* judgments have to be made as to which tariffs determine the levels of nominal and effective·protection.[10] Fortunately, most analysis of preferential trade-diversion effects on trade flows can be handled in terms of margins of preference as customarily calculated, but the effective-tariff concept is logically necessary for elucidating the response by import competing producers facing preference-induced trade creation effects.

Harry Johnson has raised the point that the new theory qualifies somewhat the previously accepted generalization that trade creation necessarily implies a more efficient use of resources and trade diversion, just the contrary.[11] Data are wholly lacking for empirical exploration of this aspect, and any tentative policy conclusions that might be reached on the basis of static analysis of the effects on world-welfare and efficiency would be subject to revision in the light of the dynamic and political considerations that are the main justifications adduced for particular preference schemes.

The effective-protection approach also throws light on an important issue that has arisen in connection with the controversy over the need for generalized preferences in behalf of developing countries. Some critics claimed that,[12] even before the Kennedy Round, the MFN tariff rates of industrial countries were already so low on the average that even zero duties would not stimulate developing countries' exports significantly. But as noted in Chapter 3 low *average* tariffs conceal the continued existence after the Kennedy Round of a number of "high" tariff peaks, especially for textiles and other labor-intensive exports of special interest to developing countries. More important, however, the prevailing pattern of escalation of nominal tariff rates from lower toward higher productive stages makes the total protective effect much higher than that indicated by the nominal tariffs on the more processed products, since the domestic processors benefit from relative subsidization of the cost of their material inputs.[13]

Discriminatory Quotas

Many protective measures that discriminate areawise do not involve formal tariffs, but rather such nontariff barriers as outright quantitative restrictions, discriminatory use of exchange controls, barterlike arrangements, and (of increasing importance) bilateral understandings whereby certain trade partners are persuaded to bear the onus of limiting their own exports. With some difficulty, the theory of protection has demonstrated the tariff-equivalence of quotas in terms of either their relative-price effects or their trade-flow effects, but here again much of the analysis depends on the small-country assumption of high or infinite foreign supply elasticity, an assumption that is usually unrealistic where industrialized countries are facing developing-country suppliers. To be sure, the brunt of discriminatory quotas or voluntary restraints is borne by the most competitive (supply-elastic) sources, so that these countries are confronted with the whole nominal tariff implicit in the quantitative import restriction plus the tariff. The excess over the tariff would then measure the approximate margin of discrimination (adverse margin of preference) as compared with third countries effectively enjoying access restricted only by the formal tariff. Whether this could be quantified empirically would depend on availability of internationally comparable price data. On the other hand, it is difficult to see how such implicit margins of relative preference and discrimination could be derived with respect to source countries of intermediate competitiveness that are subject to quotas which, while somewhat restrictive, are relatively less stringent. Therefore the notion of a quantifiable margin of preference is practically useless where NTBs are concerned.

Product Discrimination

Reverting to ordinary tariffs, several other problems arise in the evaluation of margins of preference or discrimination. The extremely detailed differentiation of tariff nomenclatures reflects in part the bargaining process that has characterized years of international negotiations based on reciprocity between principal suppliers. Concessions theoretically extended on an MFN basis are often so narrowly defined that they discriminate between close substitutes produced in different countries. The Tariff Schedules of the United States (TSUSA) are replete with such "product preferences." Some are almost as thinly disguised as the most famous example: the special rate accorded by Germany in its trade treaty of 1904 with Switzerland with respect to "large dappled mountain cattle or brown cattle, reared at a spot at least 300 meters above sea level and having at least one month's grazing each year at least 800 meters above sea level."[14]

Where goods are close substitutes, and serve the same needs and require similar degrees of fabrication, this practice can be used to accord effective preferences to a particular supplier in every respect but juridically. To the extent that this has resulted from the principal-supplier negotiating rule, has likely been biased in the past against products from developing countries. Since about 1967, however, deliberate efforts have been made to reverse the bias. With the technical help of the Customs Cooperation Council in Brussels, UNCTAD is attempting to persuade industrial countries to give especially favorable customs treatment to handmade and handicraft products as distinguished from those that are machine-made.[15] It is hoped that such products that are not considered to compete strongly with the home production of industrial countries could at least be separated out from preference exception and "sensitive" lists.[e]

It is not easy to distinguish the type of "product preferences" described above from the more general phenomenon that any tariff differentiated by products will "discriminate" in some manner as among countries with different export-mixes, reflecting their different resource endowments, relative-cost structures, and so forth. Such differences in the levels of average tariffs facing particular countries cannot be called margins of preference and—since the geographic effect is likely to be unintentional, incidental, and inevitable as long as there is product-differentiation of protection—the word "discrimination" is surely too strong. However, protective structures in most industrial countries do appear to discriminate against labor-intensive products at higher stages of production,[16] as well as against temperate agricultural products at all stages. Since the comparative advantage of a number of developing countries is believed to lie in the exchange of these products for more technologically-intensive goods, such countries may understandably perceive the situation as an inequity justifying compensatory discrimination in the other direction. It has been pointed out that the Kennedy Round reduced the MFN tariffs applied by the United States, the United Kingdom, and the EEC on manufactured goods of export interest to the developed countries themselves by substantially more than the reductions on other manufactures.[17]

Assuming comparable price and income elasticities, this might be expected, *ceteris paribus*, to lead to a relatively more rapid mutual expansion of trade among industrial countries and thereby to reduce the already small share of developing-country exports in world trade in manufactures. Other things are not equal, however. The developing countries' share in total imports of manufactures into developed market-economy countries has actually increased slightly during the sixties, from 5.1 percent in 1962 to 5.5 percent in 1969.[18]

Such arguments can be double-edged, moreover. Similar invidious comparisons—which in any case depend on the range of product classifications considered and how they are weighted in calculating averages—can and have been used to show that the GSP, to the extent it is effective, will "discriminate" in favor of a few Asian and Latin American countries already having a substantial industrial base. And the GSP will discriminate against the "least developed among the developing countries," whose potential exports are either raw materials already facing little or no tariffs or food products on which the protection will not be significantly affected by GSP.

---

[e]The EEC has introduced a special system of duty-free quotas for handicraft products outside the framework of its GSP scheme. Characteristically, it did this as discriminatorily as possible, by special bilateral arrangements with a limited group of beneficiary countries.

Content Preferences

All preference schemes, and especially those (such as free-trade areas) where the participants apply different tariffs towards outsider countries, must have "rules of origin" providing, *inter alia*, for limits on the amount of inputs from nonpreferential sources which can be embodied in goods eligible for preferential treatment, and ensuring that these have been substantially transformed. Otherwise trade channels will be distorted by the direct or indirect reexport of goods originating from outside the preference area. In determining what constitutes "substantial" transformation, European countries apply a criterion based on specified processing operations and/or a change in heading under the Brussels Tariff Nomenclature. The United States and Canada require that a certain minimum percentage of the final value be added in the beneficiary country.

Differences in the definition or operation of the origin rules can themselves substantially affect degrees of preference or create new preferences, although this could hardly be expressed as a margin of preference in terms of the nominal tariff concept. The United States permits a maximum foreign content of only 20 percent by value in goods imported preferentially from the Philippines. On the other hand, free entry is accorded to goods from the Virgin Islands, Guam, and American Samoa that have up to 50 percent foreign content. These insular possessions are juridically outside the U.S. customs territory, and, for historical and other reasons, their own imports from third countries occur at relatively very low duties (Virgin Islands) or duty-free (Guam, Samoa).

Several years ago it became highly profitable for U.S.-owned watch companies to import semifabricated components from Hong Kong for finishing, final assembly, and packaging in these dependencies for reexport to the mainland for sale within the shelter of the U.S. protective tariff. The 50 percent of value added locally created badly-needed industrial jobs in the territories, and the arrangement meets all infant-industry criteria. If unrestricted, however, it would constitute a "super-preference," in that the plants on the islands have a customs advantage, not only over third countries in the American market, but also over the U.S. domestic producers themselves by virtue of getting semifabricated inputs at or near the lowest world-market prices.

Theoretically this would seem to suggest an ingenious solution of the problem of what to do about the "least developed among the developing countries" under the GSP: to give them in effect "subsidized" access through operation of the effective-tariff principle. Indeed, the UNCTAD Secretary-General has called for application of very liberal origin rules to imports from the least-developed countries, including the principle of "cumulative treatment" whereby the permitted transformation could occur in more than one developing country.[19] That this demand is not likely to be accepted is indicated by the U.S. experience. Watches finished in the Virgin Islands captured such a large share of the American market that the United States felt obliged to impose a quota limitation, equal to one-ninth of domestic consumption, against imports from its own island possessions—even though they might well be considered among the "least-developed."

Another type of "content preference" has resulted from the practice of exempting from duty that part of the total value of a product processed abroad that represents the value of inputs produced in and previously exported by the importing country. Under Article 806.3 of U.S. tariff legislation, this applies to items made from U.S.-produced metals, provided some further processing occurs in the United States. Under Article 807, it applies to U.S.-produced components assembled abroad without further substantial processing. A complementary Program of Border Industrialization was established by Mexico in 1965 and provided for duty-free temporary import in bond of machinery, equipment, parts, and raw materials. The combined result, known as the "twin-plants complex," has promoted a rapid increase in Mexican-American trade, mainly carried out by subsidiaries of international corporations, to the intense displeasure of the U.S. labor movement.

A number of other countries have comparable special regimes for what is known as "active" and "passive" transit trade. Territorial contiguity with the United States has given Mexico a particular advantage in exploiting the possibilities of such content preferences, and low transportation costs plus very low wage levels have also made it possible for even the least-developed country in the Western Hemisphere—Haiti—along with Barbados and other Caribbean countries to participate in the worldwide "sourcing" activities of multinational firms.[20] Hitherto this had tended to be concentrated in a few very-low-wage Asian countries: Hong Kong, Taiwan, South Korea, Singapore.

It is characteristic of this trade that only *part* of the production process—usually the most labor-intensive—is transferred abroad, not whole industries or plants. This is in harmony with the principle of international specialization in terms of relative factor abundance, but by the same token increases the vulnerability of the system to the protectionist backlash exemplified in the Burke-Hartke Bill of 1971. The developing countries concerned find themselves in a more dependent position vis-à-vis the international firms sponsoring the arrangements than would be the case if there were free entry for the entire product, as under GSP. Political repercussions of a withdrawal of the special customs facilities could also be serious. In any case, in the present world business environment, international firms have shown great ingenuity in searching out and exploiting new ways of obtaining competitive cost advantages, even where these appear to involve only a few percentage points of nominal tariff. A U.S. Tariff Commission official has commented that the experience with "content preferences points toward the probability that a broad grant of tariff preferences to developing countries would accelerate the present trend toward locating some labor-intensive operations in such countries, whether by local initiative or by subsidiaries of international corporations."[21]

Pathological Profiles of Protection

The Uniform-Tariff Ideal

Theoretical considerations recommend strongly against the dispersion of rates of protection by product and by industry. "In the absence of monopoly power in trade, an undifferentiated tariff structure is the most efficient way of achieving a given amount of restriction. . . . Also, given a differentiated structure, a lessening of the differentiation may be a movement toward greater efficiency."[22] The uniform-tariff ideal must be qualified, to be sure, in the light of "second-best" policy considerations in a world that is already tariff-ridden and where considerations of industrialization, revenue, the balance of payments, and the terms of trade override those of static efficiency and welfare.[23] Moreover, even from the static-analysis point of view, uniformity of effective rates takes precedence over uniformity of nominal rates and—except in the case where the latter are completely uniform across the board—itself requires some escalation of nominal rates. But even where the infant-industry and similar arguments for protection are strongest, as in developing countries, OECD and World Bank studies have held that reasonably justifiable levels of effective protection do not exceed 10 to 20 percent.[24]

Perverse Effects of Tariff Structures
in Developing Countries

The OECD and IBRD studies cited above, among others, document the extremely high and erratically differentiated rates of nominal protection that have been applied in a number of developing countries in the name of import-substitution policies. They have pointed out that this has necessarily resulted in patterns of incentives that are ill-chosen even with respect to the objectives sought. In particular, the price-raising effect of the protective system, in conjunction with exchange-rate overvaluation, discourages exports, especially nontraditional exports of manufactures. Indeed, after allowing for currency overvaluation, the rates of effective protection for potential export industries are likely to be negative unless special measures are taken to reduce the protection-inflated costs of inputs into exporting industries.

The strong association between the height and variability of levels of protection in many developing countries and their lack of success in promoting exports of diversified manufactures has been exemplified by the major countries of Latin America, with the partial exception of Mexico, throughout most of the postwar period.[25] Tariff averages are notoriously unreliable and depend very much on the method of weighting. However, one comparison showed the following average heights of tariffs (including exchange premia and certain other charges, where applicable) about 1962: Brazil 170 percent; Argentina 137 percent; Chile 134 percent; Colombia 106 percent; and Mexico 62 percent.[26] The dispersion of the rates was almost unbelievably high, especially in Chile and Colombia with standard deviations of 227 percent and 176 percent, respectively.

During the next six years, however, all of these countries except Chile accomplished more or less far-reaching reforms of their tariff and exchange-rate systems, resulting in sharp reductions of both the average height and the dispersion of rates of protection. The Brazilian reforms of February-March 1967 appear to have reduced the average tariff of that country to about 42 percent. To be sure, since there was continued exchange-rate overvaluation, the Brazilian protective system was still biased against exporting even after the reforms, but the subsequent policies of minidevaluations, liberal recourse to customs draw-backs, and strong fiscal and credit incentives for exporting now appear to have changed the picture substantially. Brazil's exports of manufactured goods have finally begun to show really spectacular growth, albeit from a small base. The share of industrial products in total exports rose from 12.4 percent to 16.6 percent between 1969 and 1970.

High and erratically-dispersed rates of protection also characterize India and Pakistan, but in both countries this has resulted more from use of quantitative restrictions and complicated administrative controls than from tariffs. Pakistan obtained fairly rapid growth of manufactured exports in the latter sixties by using a "bonus voucher scheme" to create a special export rate of exchange to offset the cost disability inherent in that country's protective regime. In India the protection-supported prices on the domestic market for exportable manufactures other than textiles are 50 percent to 300 percent higher than the f.o.b. export realization. Export incentives ("import-entitlement" and, later, "import replenishment" supplemented by "cash assistance") are administratively cumbersome and inadequate to offset the bias against exporting. (The premature abolition of the entitlement scheme offset most of the temporary advantage of the 1966 devaluation.) Supplies of steel and other inputs needed for export processing are frequently unobtainable.

Indian exports of diversified manufacturers have therefore continued to lose ground. Meanwhile, Hong Kong, with virtually no protection at all, has been exporting more manufactured goods to the industrialized countries than the entire South Asian subcontinent plus all of South America put together.[27]

It has been pointed out that those developing countries that were the leaders in the campaign for GSP were precisely the ones whose manufactured exports appear to have been hindered more by their own commercial policies than by the much lower barriers in the industrialized countries. Critics of the scheme suggested that, since these countries were priced out of the market anyway, new preference margins would not significantly expand their exports; they would do better to "put their own house in order." While this argument had considerable justification, it neglected to take account of the fact that there was already in process a doctrinal evolution away from crude import-substituting protectionism with export pessimism in several of these countries.

Brazil is now demonstrating that a combination of tariff reform, more current exchange-rate adjustments and less rapid inflation, more sophisticated use of drawbacks and duty-free temporary imports to reduce costs of inputs, plus some recourse to discriminatory techniques, may have dramatically rapid effects in lowering the threshold of the relative-price barrier and increasing the elasticity of export supply. Meanwhile, the worldwide sourcing activity of multinational firms is radically expanding the role of international intraindustry specialization.

These recent developments suggest that the principal contribution of GSP may well turn out to be the incentive given to the most protection-ridden developing countries of South America and South Asia to indeed "put their houses in order." This is not without risk. To the extent that it does occur, and India, for example, were to rationalize its own protective system to the extent necessary for comparative advantage to operate, it might soon be considered more "disruptive" to industrial country markets than Hong Kong. Should that occur, regardless of apparent tariff preferences, the imposition of tighter nontariff restrictions by Europe and the United States might well substitute of the trade-inhibiting role hitherto exercised by hyper-protection and relative-price distortions on the Indian side. "The essential task of international economic cooperation will be, therefore, to make sure that countries which want free trade can have some opportunity to practice it."[28]

Pathological Patterns of Discrimination

The Ideal of Most-Favored-Nation Treatment

With universal free trade being out of the question in practice, the next-best international trading system, from a static-allocational point of view, is simple discrimination between two areas: the domestic market and the rest of the world. The unconditional MFN single-column tariff with no exceptions corresponds, in the geographical dimension, to the uniform-tariff concept in the product dimension. However, the limits of the domestic market are politically defined and subject to change. National states or parts of states may be absorbed by territorial expansion; overseas colonies may secede but retain links to the mother country; several states may form a customs union or free-trade area to broaden their markets or as a way-station to closer political union; outlying border zones in neighboring countries may need attachment to a natural hinterland. Derogations from the unconditional MFN principle to cover these situations are easily justified within the scope of Articles I and XXIV of the GATT, or by waivers from the Articles. Other derogations have been rationalized on historic, strategic, or simply *ad hoc* grounds.

The MFN clause itself is a juridical, not an economic concept. In its unconditional form, it is supposed to operate as an ingenious "golden rule," observance of which keeps the confrontation of national commercial policies from degenerating into bilateral economic warfare, even though considerable scope is left for bilateral bargaining between principal suppliers.[29] As institutionalized—first by legal precedent in innumerable commercial treaties and later in the GATT—the term "most-favored nation" has long been a misleading one. New Zealand, for example, has a five-column tariff,[f] the *second highest* set of rates constituting the so-called MFN tariff. Nevertheless New Zealand represents a relatively moderate array of geographical discrimination with preferences compared to some others, such as the EEC. Even the United States, despite its doctrinal commitment to nondiscrimination, applies penalty rates to various Communist countries and gives tariff preferences to Canada (under the Automotive Products Act of 1965), the Philippines (expiring in 1974), the Virgin Islands, Guam, and American Samoa, the Pacific Trust Territory, Puerto Rico, and Cuba (still on the books but a present in abeyance). Additional preferences, of a nontariff nature, are created by the Sugar Act quotas given to a number of countries (partly as a function of their lobbying effectiveness), and by the petroleum quotas, which favor Canada and Venezuela over other producers. Various degrees of nontariff areawise discrimination also arise through the operation of the U.S.-instigated "voluntary" bilateral quotas for meat, steel, textiles, and so forth.

Despite the prevalence of such derogations from MFN, about half the total imports of manufactures into the industrialized countries still take place under MFN tariffs. Most of the remainder (trade within the EEC and EFTA blocs) take the form of quasi-domestic trade. This latter portion will of course greatly increase after the expansion of the EEC and the new bilateral arrangements between EEC and nonmember European countries. Although it will surely not be to the liking of the United States, Japan, and other outsiders, the situation among the non-Communist industrial countries (at least with respect to non-agricultural products) will remain a fairly orderly system as long as the deviations from uniform treatment follow general criteria, are the result of multilateral arrangements, and do not fluctuate too erratically over time. Moreover, the amplitude of preferential margins is limited by the MFN tariffs, now at historically low levels and which may be reduced further in another round of multilateral negotiations.

Bilateralism

One can contrast such a system, imperfect though it may be, with what we can call "pathological" discrimination in import policy: extremely differentiated

---

[f]General, MFN, British Preferential, Canadian, and Australian rates.

across both country and product; changing rapidly from year to year or even month to month; characterized by extreme amplitude of implicit margins of discrimination and preference; and in which the arsenal of discriminatory measures includes not only tariffs and quotas but also broken cross-rates of exchange. Such pathological discrimination was prevalent in Europe during the immediate pre-and-post World War II periods and reflected the widespread use of bilateral payment and trade-quota arrangements and barterlike compensation deals that implicitly involved broken cross rates. It is recalled that the chaos of bilaterally discriminatory arrangements was gradually eliminated in Western Europe during the 1950s, in two stages. First, following establishment of the European Payments Union, (EPU) an intra-European liberalization program created a regional zone of mutual preferences. Transitional discrimination against the dollar area was sanctioned by the Organization of European Economic Corporation (OEEC) in more or less overt conflict with the GATT. Only after dissolution of EPU and establishment of convertibility under IMF rules was the emphasis shifted toward elimination of discriminatory quantitative controls vis-à-vis the dollar area and Japan.

Pathological bilateral discrimination still dominates the trade relations of the Socialist countries in their relationships with each other and with developing countries. Less important remnants of the bilateral system also exist among a number of developing countries, especially in the Middle East and Africa.

Proliferation of Overlapping Preferences
among Developing Countries

Perhaps more serious at the present time are the possibilities of a pathological degeneration of the highly complex networks of preferential trading relationships now proliferating among groups of developing countries. These have been justified in terms of "self-help" and the laudable objectives of regional and subregional integration, interregional trade expansion among developing countries, and solidarity of the more advanced toward the less-developed and landlocked countries. In general the industrial countries have been sympathetic to these schemes, and the normal GATT criteria for customs unions and free-trade areas have been explicitly or tacitly waived. Cynics might ascribe this spirit of toleration to a hope that the developing countries will get so involved in the complexities of negotiating new trade arrangements with each other that they will somehow be diverted from pushing their competitive labor-intensive exports into the industrial countries' markets.

To illustrate these complexities let us take the example of Chile. Chile gives several types of preferences within the Latin American Free Trade Area: LAFTA-wide concessions for hundreds of minutely-defined "national-list" items; particular concessions to four less-developed countries in the grouping (including Uruguay, despite its relatively high GNP); and separately negotiated sectoral concessions under the "complementation" agreements to which Chile has chosen to adhere. At the same time it participates, at the subregional level, in the Andean Group's automatic linear trade liberalization program, which is coupled with adoption of a minimum common external tariff intended to lead to a minimum margin of preference within the subregion. Also, there are additional special concessions to the two less-developed countries of the Andean Group. At the intercontinental level, Chile is a member of the group of sixteen geographically-dispersed developing countries which, by a protocol sanctioned by the contracting parties of GATT in February 1972, will exchange reciprocal preferential tariff margins for some 500 items. Finally, it may be noted that the Chilean trade regime even applies the principle of geographic preferences within its own territory, in the form of special free-entry or reduced-duty privileges for the Department of Africa and certain other provinces and departments in outlying parts of the country.

The real trade coverage of all these various concessions is still very limited. The LAFTA national-list procedure permitted each participant to "pick and choose" the items for which it was easiest to meet the requirements of an 8 percent annual reduction in the weighted average of tariffs on intra-LAFTA trade. Individual concessions were revocable and substitutable. A four-year interruption of the whole process had to be declared in 1969, after most participating countries reached the point beyond which there was a threat of real trade-creating competition with domestic industries. Another LAFTA procedure, which had required a four-stage selection of items to be accorded free entry at the end of the scheduled twelve-year transition, never got beyond the first stage of negotiation. No substantive agreements at all have been reached in such major sectors as agriculture, petroleum, automobiles, and iron and steel. Those few industrial complementation agreements that have been worked out cover minute subsectors that are of interest mainly to international firms, and in any case the preferential commitments involved are limited to the specific signatory countries. They thus involve additional discrimination within the LAFTA family.

The bogging-down of LAFTA over the problems of balancing national gains and losses has been matched by similar or more dramatic crises in most of the other integration groupings among developing countries, notably the Central American Common Market (CACM), the Central African Customs and Economic Union (UDEAC), the East African Community (EAC), and the Maghreb.[30] Essentially, no country is willing to accept significant inroads (trade creation) into its own market or to risk any process of regional allocation of industries that would limit its own future ability to claim a national share of each industry.

A special problem from the international point of view arises where, as in LAFTA, the external tariffs are extremely high. Such preferential intra-area cuts as are made can be highly trade-diverting. Those countries within the area that manage to benefit from the wide margins of preference acquire a vested interest in their partners' high external protection. The whole system tends to inhibit the tariff reforms that would be necessary to reduce the cost disabilities and distortions that indirectly frustrate exporting. Thus the pathological levels and dispersion of the profiles of external tariffs have an adverse influence on the preferential regimes, making them more fragmented and disorderly and compounding the difficulties of successfully attaining real integration. It was suggested several years ago that GATT approval of preferential arrangements among developing countries should be conditional on establishment of maximum ceilings on the rates of external protection (ideally in terms of effective rates).[31] Such a condition would be politically impossible today, however.

As a final consideration, the potential availability of deep margins of preference in the tariff structures of many developing countries constitutes a standing invitation to industrial countries to seek reciprocal arrangements involving an extension of the system of postcolonial "reverse preferences." This issue is discussed below.

Special Preferences for Developing Countries: The Colonial Background

If the issue of preferential treatment of developing countries' trade appears to arouse more emotion and controversy in the United States and elsewhere than, say, the U.S.-Canadian Automotive Products Agreement or even the formation of full customs unions among industrialized countries, this may reflect connotations inherited from textbook interpretations of the colonial rivalries among the Great Powers during the period between the end of the nineteenth century and the outbreak of the First World War. Americans brought up on John Hay's enunciation of the Open-Door Policy in China might be surprised to read, in a U.S. Tariff Commission report published half a century ago, that "the United States pursues the policy of preferential trade relations with its colonies"[32] and still more surprised to learn that this is still at least partially true.

In any case, it is important to trace the historical background of the colonial preferences, out of which have evolved what are now called "special" or "reciprocal" or "North-South" preferential systems. Following the Tariff Commission report already cited,[33] one can distinguish three historical periods. From the voyages of discovery in the fifteenth century through the Napoleonic Wars, mercantilistic attitudes and chartered-monopoly practices dominated the colonial rivalries. The second period, which lasted until about 1875, was based on relatively free trade, as far as most colonial powers were concerned, although the liberal orientation only reached France with Louis Napoleon—and then only for a brief interval. Thereafter the trend was toward a revival of domestic protectionism accompanied by a new nationalism in colonial commercial policy.

There were, to be sure, important exceptions and lags. The Netherlands continued to adhere to the open-door policies of the previous period. In Great Britain the imperialistic policies of Joseph Chamberlain were rejected at the turn of the century. However, the white dominions were already beginning unilaterally to grant preferences to British goods, and these began to be reciprocated by the mother country during and just after the First World War. It was not until the Ottawa Conference of 1932 that the free-trade principle was renounced and a full set of two-way preferential tariffs was systematized among the United Kingdom, the dominions, and many of the colonial possessions. Of particular diplomatic importance was the inclusion of India in the preferential system, since this broke with the network of open-door treaties that had been carefully built up with respect to all East Indian and Asian countries (except the Philippines).

Because colonies, protectorates, and spheres of influence were acquired at different periods and in the face of international pressures of different intensities, a variety of regimes existed within the imperial system, as is shown by a survey as of the early 1920s.[34] The highest degree of mutual preference was generally that resulting from the assimilation policy, as applied by the United States to Puerto Rico; by Japan to Formosa and Korea; and by France not only to the overseas departments, but also to Indo-China, Tunisia, Madagascar, New Caledonia, Guiana, and Gabon. Reciprocal differentiated tariff regimes falling short of full assimilation to the metropolitan customs area characterized the relationship of Great Britain with its dominions, its Western Hemisphere colonies, Cyprus, and Fiji; of Italy with Eritrea, Somalia, and Libya; of Portugal with all its overseas dependencies except Macao and Portuguese Congo; and of the United States with the Philippines.

The nondiscriminatory open-door policy was traditional in most British Crown Colonies outside the Western Hemisphere and in the Dutch East and West Indies. In other areas—Morocco, the Conventional Basin of the Congo, the German colonies, and various parts of Oceania—it resulted from the treaties whereby major international confrontations had been settled just short of war. The open-door pledge referred to only to nondiscrimination in the dependent territory and did not imply free trade. In several cases, such as Morocco and the Congo, there were treaty obligations limiting the height of the colonial tariffs. Free trade in the literal sense existed in Central Africa until 1890 and in India until 1894. Thereafter, it was retained only in certain transit ports: Hong Kong, Aden, the Straits Settlements, Djibouti, and so forth.

The main aspects of colonial commercial policy dealt with (1) the import-duty regime, (2) the export-duty regime in the colonies, and (3) the import-duty regime in the metropole toward products from the colonies. More incidental features related to intercolonial trade, shipping restrictions, and rights of establishment. What are now called "reverse" preferences—those encouraging sale of the metropole's manufactures in the colonies—were clearly the uppermost consideration. Colonial export duties were generally low and imposed primarily for revenue purposes, but where there were preferential exemptions or differential rates on unprocessed foodstuffs and raw materials this again benefited only the industry of the mother country.

Preferences on imports from the colonies were irrelevant for most products, since little or no protective duties applied to raw materials anyway, and few colonies (in contrast to the relatively developed British dominions) had any exportable production of manufactures susceptible of sharing in the protection of the mother country's home market. On the other hand, these "preferences in favor of developing countries" (enjoyed, to be sure, mainly by European plantation owners) were more important for those tropical colonial products that were subject to high revenue duties—tea, coffee, cocoa, vanilla, and spices—and for those that competed with the protected agricultural production of the mother country—especially sugar, tobacco, and rice.

Whether the colonial producers or the metropolitan consumers benefited from the preferential margins depended, of course, on supply elasticities, i.e., on whether the colonies or outsiders were the marginal suppliers. For such homogeneous goods, relatively small margins of preference were sufficient to concentrate the colonial trade in the metropolitan market. The narrowness of the British preference margins established on most colonial products in 1919 reflected this consideration. On the other hand, colonial products from their assimilated colonies entered France, Japan, and the United States on a completely duty-free basis and thus enjoyed relatively wide preferences.

The eighteenth-century notion of the *pacte colonial* justified colonial commercial policy as an implicit contract between equal parties. On the one hand, the colonial market was to be a market "preserve" for the manufactures of the metropole; colonial products should only be exported to the metropole; and transportation in both directions was to be monopolized by metropolitan shipping. As a *quid pro quo*, the colonial products would receive preferential treatment in the metropolitan market.

The rationale of today's special-preference systems is essentially no different. But now the stress is laid on the preferential access of the developing countries to the patron countries' market, and it is the "reverse" preferences that provide the *quid pro quo* required to maintain the semblance of reciprocity.

Post-Colonial Preferences:
The Commonwealth/Sterling-Area Complex

Evolution of the System

The two-way system of British Imperial Preference reached its greatest scope and highest preference margins about 1937. By that time, according to an authoritative study,[35] about 60 percent of imports from British preferential countries were accorded preference in the U.K. market, while "reverse" preferences for U.K. goods imported into the dominions and colonies covered a comparable proportion of trade (55-57 percent). The average preferential margin on all trade in each direction was about 10 to 12 percent ad valorem; since this incorporates a substantial weighting of nonpreferential trade, the average margins on preferred goods were of the order of 19-20 percent, with many individual margins much higher.

During the decade that included World War II, the scope of preferences was somewhat reduced and the average margins on all trade between the United Kingdom and its preference area declined to about 7 percent in each direction as of 1948. This reflected in part the effects of inflation on the incidence of specific and mixed duties, but also the effects of several rounds of MFN tariff negotiations between the United States and the United Kingdom, Canada, and India just before World War II and of the first GATT round in 1947.

Thus at the time major colonial possessions were becoming independent and the constitutional structure of the Empire was being transformed, it might have appeared that the British preferential system was in the process of being eroded. This would have been a considerable victory for U.S. diplomacy, which had used strong political means to force on reluctant British negotiators far-reaching commitments regarding nondiscrimination in the context of such documents as the Atlantic Charter (1941), the Mutual Aid Agreement of 1942 ("Article Seven"), and the draft Charter of the International Trade Organization (ITO).[36] In the summer of 1947, however, the abortive British return to convertibility collapsed in the ruins of the Anglo-American Financial Agreement. As a result, the wartime sterling-area-dollar-pool arrangements were reinforced.

For the next ten years commercial discrimination would take the forms of both Commonwealth Preference and the rationing of dollar-exchange allocations for imports, even in those countries of the sterling area that were not themselves suffering from dollar shortage. This dual discriminatory system was further complicated by the fact that the memberships of the two clubs overlapped only partially. Canada, which gave and received Commonwealth preferences, was itself discriminated against by the dollar-pool system. On the other hand, a number of open-door Commonwealth sterling countries received preferences from the United Kingdom and discriminated against dollar trade, but did not give substantial "reverse" preferences to British goods. A further blow was dealt the U.S. antidiscrimination campaign in 1948, when efforts to achieve dismantlement of tariff preferences through the ITO also collapsed.

Although successive rounds of GATT negotiations brought about some further erosion of preferential margins on a number of products, the quantitative importance of preferential trade into the United Kingdom began to increase; the weighted average margin of preference on all U.K. imports from the Commonwealth (which had fallen to about 5.5 percentage points as of 1957) widened again to above 7 percent by 1962.[37] This reflected a greater relative importance of manufactured goods (which enjoy a higher preference), a development which in turn was presumably associated with the trade-promoting effect of the availability of the preferences. Meanwhile, the average margin of reverse preference received by British exports to Commonwealth countries rested at about 6.5 to 7 percentage points for all exports to the area, which meant that the range of margins for particular goods in particular areas was still very wide.[38]

After the Kennedy Round

Very substantial narrowing of Commonwealth Preference margins has occurred as a result of Kennedy Round reductions of MFN tariff rates (only partly offset by reductions in nonzero preferential rates). The cuts were implemented over a five-year period, the final stages taking effect as from January 1, 1972. Moreover, in January 1972, the United Kingdom decided to levy tariffs on cotton goods from developing Commonwealth countries which, although subject to quotas, had previously been admitted with duty-free preference. The original intention had been to substitute tariffs for the quotas, but when the time came it was decided to retain quota controls and in addition impose tariffs!

In addition to these major erosions of the margins, the value of Commonwealth Preference to developing countries was further diluted when—again in January 1972—the United Kingdom introduced its version of the GSP. As in the case of the other countries granting generalized preferences, the U.K. scheme affected the industrial products falling within Chapters 25 through 99 of the Brussels Tariff Nomenclature (BTN), excluding mainly various textiles and products subject to revenue duties.[39] Beneficiaries of the U.K. GSP scheme correspond mainly to the membership of the so-called Group of 77 (actually ninety-six developing countries), with minor additions and deletions, plus the dependent territories of the United Kingdom and of the other donor countries.[40] Thus all developing countries of the Commonwealth Preference Area (CPA) are beneficiaries of GSP, which will affect them in several ways.[g]

In order to give a summary quantitative expression, in terms of margins of preference, to these recent developments affecting the preferential status of the

[g]"First, for those products which are covered by the scheme (27 percent of United Kingdom dutiable imports from the Commonwealth beneficiaries) they will share their Commonwealth preferences with the other beneficiaries under the scheme. On the other hand, there are products for which GSP treatment is duty-free while Commonwealth preferences are limited to a reduction of most-favored-nation rates. For such products, exports from Commonwealth beneficiaries will receive preferential treatment relative to those from industrial Commonwealth countries which are not beneficiaries under the scheme. It should also be recognized that developing countries enjoying Commonwealth preferences stand to benefit from preferential tariff treatment in markets of the other preference-giving countries." UNCTAD Document TD/124/Add.1, 9 March 1972.

developing countries in the CPA (Kennedy Round, tariffs on cotton goods, and U.K. implementation of the GSP), tariff averages for various categories of industrial goods were calculated on the basis of a stratified randomized sample consisting of 325 specific products of interest to developing countries.[41] These are presented in Table 12-1. Overall averages have also been calculated for two aggregate groupings of products (BTN 1-24 and SITC 5-8), using two alternative methods of weighting the product categories—i.e., according to the composition of U.K. imports and OECD imports from all developing countries. For present purposes the more useful aggregative product grouping is that covering manufactures and semimanufactures (SITC 5-8) and the more useful weighting is that based on U.K. imports from all developing countries.

Subject to caveats with respect to spurious precision, and assuming *inter alia* that a generally comparable mix of products is available from Commonwealth and non-Commonwealth beneficiaries of the GSP, reference to Table 12-1 permits us to summarize the main conclusions (for manufactures and semimanufactures) as follows:

1. The Kennedy Round, as modified by imposition of tariffs on cotton textiles and nonimplementation of the "ASP Package," resulted in a reduction of the average margin of preference given by the United Kingdom for products from the developing Commonwealth by about 40 percent (from about 10.2 percentage points to about 6.1 percentage points).
2. The average margin of preference obtained by GSP beneficiaries not belonging to the CPA is about 5.1 percentage points.
3. GSP beneficiaries belonging to the CPA will obtain whichever regime is the more beneficial for particular product categories. Although this will only slightly improve their average margin of preference in the U.K. market, through obtaining free entry for some products previously subject to nonzero preferential duties, they will still have a significant relative advantage vis-à-vis non-Commonwealth GSP beneficiaries (6.2 vs. 5.1 percentage points).

In any event, the U.K. GSP scheme is only a transitional arrangement, bridging the period until January 1, 1974, when it will have to be aligned with the EEC scheme then in effect. This points up what may be one of the most important justifications of the whole GSP exercise, to which we shall revert later. This is its potential function in facilitating the merger of the Commonwealth and EEC preferential systems without undue hardship for any developing countries and without triggering a trade war with the United States. It will be argued that this will depend on whether nonreciprocal generalized preferences can be made more atractive to developing countries than the postcolonial systems based on reverse preferences.

Table 12-1

Estimates Average Margins of Preference Given by U.K. to Commonwealth Developing Countries (Pre- and Post-Kennedy Round) Compared with U.K. GSP Offer

	U.K. Imports from D.C. 1968[a]	OECD Imports from D.C. 1969[a]	Average MFN Tariffs		Margins of Preference		
			Pre-Kennedy (1967)	Post-Kennedy (1972)	Commonwealth Pre K.	Commonwealth Post K.	GSP Offer
BTN 1-24 (Agricultural Prods.)	25%	27%	(Not Calculated)				
Industrial Raw Materials	14%	18%	2.7	1.3	2.3	1.3	0.9
Fuels	34%	33%	0.2[b]	0.1[b]	0.2	0.1	0.1
Chemicals	1%	1%	13.4	9.3[c]	13.4	9.3	9.3
Textiles	3%	2%	20.8	16.9[d]	10.0	6.5	4.2
Iron & Steel	–	1	13.0	10.5	13.0	10.5	10.5
Nonferrous Metals	11	8	4.5	3.2	4.5	3.2	3.2
Other Semimanufactures	6	3	11.8	6.8	11.3	6.5	6.8
Machinery & Transport Equipment	1	2	16.6	10.1	14.3	8.7	10.1
Clothing	3	3	29.7	23.0[d]	19.1	7.9	0
Other Finished Mfgrs.	2	2	20.9	14.2	20.9	14.2	14.2
Total	100% (4814 Mn)	100% (40601 Mn)					

Averages Weighted by U.K. Imports from Developing Countries (col. 1)

BTN 25-99 (Industrial Products)	75%	5.2	3.5	4.2	2.5	2.0
SITC 5-8 (Manufactured Products)	27%	12.7	9.0	10.2	6.1	5.1
Commonwealth Preference + GSP:					6.2	

Averages Weighted by OECD Imports from Developing Countries (col. 2)

BTN 25-99 (Industrial Products)	73%	4.9	3.3	4.0	2.4	1.9
SITC 5-8 (Manufactured Products)	22%	13.9	9.9	11.1	6.7	5.6

aData: OECD, *Commodity Trade Statistics, Series B.*

bExcludes revenue duties.

cTakes account of nonimplementation of Kennedy Round "ASP" Package.

dTakes account of reimposition of duties on cotton textiles from Commonwealth sources, effective January 1, 1972.

Before ending our comparison of Commonwealth Preference with GSP, we must recall that we have thus far ignored nonindustrial products, particularly certain foodstuffs that pose serious problems for which GSP has no answer. Among these are sugar and bananas, for both of which the West Indian Commonwealth countries enjoy a preferential market in the United Kingdom sheltered by a combination of tariff and nontariff measures.

Trade Effects of Commonwealth Preferences

Projections of the effects of customs unions and other preferential trade arrangements are frequently based on a more or less mechanical application of import-demand or substitution elasticities that have simply been assumed a priori or have been empirically derived from time-series data unrelated to a customs-union or preference situation. Historical experience with Commonwealth Preferences has been largely ignored, although it offers a number of analogies with the competitive situation expected to prevail under the UNCTAD Generalized System of Preferences.

A recent study, using cross-section linear-regression techniques, has indicated that (with certain obvious exceptions such as pulp, paper, and wood, which are Canadian export products) Great Britain and other Commonwealth countries as a group have benefited significantly from Commonwealth Preference in the Canadian market.[42] Indeed, it was estimated that in the absence of preferences, United Kingdom exports to Canada of goods now subject to them would have been 30 percent less in 1966 than they actually were. This reflected price elasticities of Canadian demand for British goods ranging from −3.1 for the metals category to −7.1 for earthenware. Thus "reverse" preferences given to developed countries having fairly elastic supply capability are clearly important determinants of trade flows.[43] On the other hand, the study was unable to find meaningful relationships between the share of developing countries in total Canadian imports, on the one hand, and preference margins, on the other hand, even at the 10-percent level of significance.

The difficulties of demonstrating statistical relationships between trade flows from developing countries and preference margins have also been brought out in a study which attempted to test the Latin American claim that Commonwealth Preference has in effect limited the flow of imports into the United Kingdom from Latin America and biased the composition of such trade against manufactures.[44] In general, it found insufficient data at the proper level of disaggregation either to corroborate or to reject the hypothesis that, for particular and comparable products, there will be a tendency to import more of competitive goods from preferentially tariff-free sources than from sources subject to the full tariff. There was no apparent relationship between the margins of preference and the difference in amounts imported from preferential and nonpreferential sources. Also, such relative-price information as was obtainable from trade unit-values seemed totally unaffected by tariff differentials.

We have already alluded to the characteristic inelasticity of export supply in developing countries and to the resulting problem for identification of trade responses to price or other influences operating from the demand side. This suggests that another approach may be more fruitful than the above-mentioned tests with such ambiguous or inconclusive results. Instead of comparing the export performance of different countries—subject to different protective regimes—in a given market, one might compare the relative performance of the same country—with a given amount of exports effectively available—in different markets in the same period of time, and then determine whether this appears to be systematically influenced by the existence of a margin of preference in one of the markets.

For such an exercise we choose as the dependent variable the ratio between the given developing area's share in 1967 U.K. imports and its share in the total imports of the same product classification in twenty-four developed market-economy countries (including the U.K.) in the same year.[45] The Relative Penetration Ratios (RPRs)[h] thus normalized exclude, in effect, supply influences as well as size-of-market and income effects. We hypothesize that the developing areas' shares in U.K. imports would be expected to be approximately the same as their shares in the ensemble of the industrial countries, i.e., that the RPRs would be about unity except to the extent that special factors existed.

Our model disregards the distance variable, since, with respect to most products and most Commonwealth supplier countries, the United Kingdom is probably located near the "center of gravity" of the total market of the industrialized countries.[i] Systematic upward deviations of the observed RPRs from unity are attributed mainly to (1) the different commercial policies of the industrial countries, and (2) a variety of historical, commercial, and even cultural factors that are lumped together as "special trade ties" between the United Kingdom and its former dependencies. While the commercial-policy influences affecting the denominator of the RPR could be very complex—reflecting *inter alia* the different heights of tariffs, quantitative restrictions, and other measures applied by the United States, EEC, Japan, and other developed market-economy countries—it seems reasonable to attribute much greater importance to the discriminatory effects of U.K. commercial policy on the numerator of the ratio. Such discrimination is quantified (approximately) in the margin of Commonwealth Preference, which we take as our independent variable.[46]

Table 13-2 presents the results of linear regressions run in accordance with the above model. Two different levels of product aggregation of the trade and

[h]A 2 percent minimum cutoff is used for the developing Commonwealth countries as a whole and 1 percent for the individual regions.

[i]Admittedly, freight cannot be disregarded as a factor in Japanese imports from Southeast Asia and U.S. imports from Caribbean Commonwealth countries.

Table 12-2
Regression of "Relative Penetration Ratios" of Commonwealth Countries in U.K. Market against Margins of Preference in United Kingdom—1967

Regression	Area	Range of Products	Level of Aggregation	No. of Product Groups n	Intercept (s.e. in paren) a	Regression Coefficient (s.e. in paren) b	R^2	F	Mean "RPR" $\bar{Y}$	Mean Pref. $\bar{X}$	Implicit Price Elasticity e
A.1	Developing Commonwealth	SITC 2-8	2-digit (P of I sample)	31	1.12	0.1106 (0.0307)[c]	.31	12.98	2.21	9.83	5.5
A.2	India	SITC 2-8	2-digit (reg. sample)	18	0.58	0.1367 (0.0511)[b]	.31	7.17	2.35	12.93	6.6
B.1	Developing Commonwealth	BTN 24-99	4- or 5-digit	103	1.21 (0.245)	0.1106 (0.0178)[c]	.28	38.53	2.52	10.93	4.9
B.1a.	Developing Commonwealth	SITC 2-3	4- or 5-digit	32	1.33 (0.148)[a]	0.1445 (0.0336)[c]	.38	18.51	1.64	2.19	9.0
B.1b.	Developing Commonwealth	SITC 5-8	4- or 5-digit	71	1.18 (0.506)	.1169 (0.0310)[c]	.17	14.25	2.92	14.87	4.6
B.2	South Asia	BTN 25-99	4- or 5-digit	46	1.25 (0.292)	0.1331 (0.0230)[c]	.43	33.37	2.49	9.33	5.8
B.2a.	South Asia	SITC 2-3	4- or 5-digit	21	1.44 (0.210)[a]	0.1094 (0.0470)[b]	.22	5.40	1.68	2.24	6.7

B.2b.	South Asia	SITC 5-8	4- or 5-digit	25	0.54 (0.822)	0.1719 (0.0492)c	.35	12.21	3.17	15.28	6.3
B.3	Hong Kong Singapore, Malaysia	BTN 25-99	4- or 5-digit	70	0.94 (0.542)	0.1291 (0.0325)c	.19	15.75	2.89	15.17	5.1
B.3a.	Hong Kong Singapore, Malaysia	SITC 2-3	4- or 5-digit	6					1.68	0.50	
B.3b.	Hong Kong Singapore, Malaysia	SITC 5-8	4- or 5-digit	64	0.29 (0.757)	0.1643 (0.0435)c	.19	14.29	3.01	16.55	6.4
B.4	Africa	BTN 25-99	4- or 5-digit	25					4.33	4.44	
B.5	Western Hemisphere and Other	BTN 25-99	4- or 5-digit	9					1.57	3.00	

Dependent Variable (Y): "Relative Penetration Ratio" = $\dfrac{\text{Area's Percentage Share of Total U.K. Imports}}{\text{Area's Percentage Share of 24 Dev'd Countries Imports}}$

Independent Variable (X): MFN Tariff Rate *minus* Commonwealth Preference Tariff Rate

"Implicit Price Elasticity": $\dfrac{b}{Y}(100 + X)$

aSignificantly different from 1.0 at 5 percent level.
bSignificantly different from zero at 5 percent level.
cSignificantly different from zero at 1 percent level.

tariff data were used, in view of the likelihood of large errors of observation in matching average tariff margins to aggregative product classifications.[47] Considering the obvious shortcomings of the model and of the data, it is rather surprising to obtain R^2's which indicate that the regressions explain a third or so of the total observed variance of the RPRs.[j]

Moreover, the regression coefficients (b's) are all significant, tending to confirm that a relationship does indeed exist between the size of the margins of preference—even where calculated from nominal tariffs—and the concentration of exports in the market of the preference-giving country as compared to other countries. In terms of implicit price elasticities, calculated at the means, this effect seems rather powerful. Other things being equal, a 1-percent price advantage resulting from the preference might be expected to increase the relative market share of the Commonwealth developing area in the U.K. market by about 4.5 to 6.5 percent for diversified manufactures. An even higher elasticity of about 9 percent is indicated for crude materials, which are likely to be more homogeneous. Capital equipment items, for which price influences are expected to be relatively unimportant compared to other competitive factors, were not exported by Commonwealth developing countries in 1967 in sufficient quantities to appear in the samples.

Although the estimated constant terms of the regressions have large standard errors, it is nevertheless in accord with expectations that those intercepts that are significant are greater than unity. This might be interpreted as representing the effect of "trade ties," which tend to concentrate Commonwealth trade in the U.K. market even without preferences. On the other hand, Hong Kong's special arrangements with U.S. and Japanese firms are such that it is not surprising that the intercepts for Southeast Asia are below the normalized level of 1.0.

One should not read too much into this exercise, given the data limitations and the fact that most of the variation of relative trade shares is clearly not attributable to the tariff-preference effect. However, analysis of the "residuals" is useful as a rough indication of the relative "preference-sensitivity" of different kinds of products. In regression A.1, for example, SITC subgroups 42 (vegetable oils) showed more than twice as much concentration of imports from the developing Commonwealth in the U.K. market than would have been estimated from the regression. This is, of course, the sort of low-value-added commodity where the protective effects of a relatively low nominal tariff on output are greatly magnified in terms of effective protection. In regressions B.1b. and B.3b., Hong Kong footwear and cutlery also appear much more than proportionately preference-sensitive. On the other hand, Indian iron and steel is far below the regression line in B.2., and other information confirms that the pattern of Indian

---

[j]Regressions A.1 and A.2 were also run in log-linear transformation, which raised the R_2's from 0.31 to 0.35 and 0.36, respectively. However, the linear regressions are easier to analyze.

steel exports has reflected temporary supply and demand situations to which tariff preferences are irrelevant.

Notes

1. See Richard N. Cooper, "Third World Tariff Tangle," *Foreign Policy* (May 1971), pp. 35-50; Benjamin I. Cohen, "Tariff Preferences for the Third World," *Intereconomics* (no. 9, 1970), pp. 285-88.

2. This argument would be more convincing if use of quantitative restrictions against developing countries had not already been increasing rapidly, *before* introduction of GSP, or if some progress had been made in obtaining their elimination through GATT. See Chapters 4 and 5.

3. Most estimates of increased exports are in the range of $0.5-$1.5 billion and of the maximum revenue gain of the order of $0.5-$0.6 billion, depending on assumptions as to safeguard measures, elasticities, and projected trade growth in the absence of preferences. See, for example, Christopher K. Clague, "The Trade Effect of Tariff Preferences," *Southern Economic Journal*, 38, no. 3 (January 1972), p. 379-89; "Tariff Tangle," p. 39.

4. See W.M. Corden, *The Theory of Protection* (Oxford: Clarendon Press, 1971), Chapters 2 and 3, Bela Balassa and Associates, *The Structure of Protection in Developing Countries* (Baltimore: Johns Hopkins Press, 1971), Chapter 1. See Corden's Appendices I and III for a brief history and selected bibliography on effective protection.

5. See articles by Herbert G. Grubel and William P. Travis, in H.G. Grubel and H.G. Johnson, eds., *Effective Tariff Protection* (Geneva: GATT, 1972).

6. See Jaroslav Vanek, *General Equilibrium of International Discrimination: The Case of Customs Unions* (Cambridge: Harvard University Press, 1965); Murray C. Kemp, *A Contribution to the General Equilibrium Theory of Preferential Trading* (Amsterdam: North-Holland Publishing Company, 1969).

7. Vanek points out that most of his 107 summarized conclusions concerning international discrimination were derived from a very simplified 2-product and 3-country model. Only about half of these are shown to hold true for any number of products and for any arbitrary number of areas. *International Discrimination*, pp. 211-31.

8. For a nonmathematical descriptive summary of the possible effects of preferences to developing countries under various assumptions as to the elasticities, standardization or heterogeneity of goods, etc., see Harry G. Johnson, *Economic Policies Toward Less-Developed Countries* (New York: Frederick A. Praeger, 1967), pp. 185-95.

9. Johnson, *Economic Policies*, pp. 199-204, and his classic article, "An Economic Theory of Protectionism, Tariff Bargaining, and the Formation of Customs Unions," *Journal of Political Economy*, 73, (June 1965), pp. 256-83.

10. See Balassa, *Structure of Protection*, pp. 155-56, 209, 303-304.

11. Johnson, *Economic Policies*, pp. 185-86.

12. Gardner Patterson, "Would Tariff Preferences Help Economic Development?" *Lloyds Bank Review*, no. 76 (April 1965), p. 27.

13. The post-Kennedy Round U.S. nominal tariff rate of about 20 percent on cotton clothing has been estimated to yield an effective rate of about 35 percent for the apparel industry. Similarly, the nominal and effective rates for woven jute fabrics are 20 and 53 percent, respectively, and corresponding figures for refined coconut oil are 15 and 186 percent. Source: Table A, Bela Balassa, "The Structure of Protection in Industrial Countries and its Effects on the Exports of Processed Goods from Developing Countries," UNCTAD, *The Kennedy Round: Estimated Effects on Tariff Barriers* (New York: United Nations document TD/6/Rev. 1, 1968), pp. 210, 212.

14. As quoted by Gerard Curzon, *Multilateral Commercial Diplomacy: The General Agreement on Tariffs and Trade and its Impact on National Commercial Policies and Techniques* (New York: Frederick A. Praeger, 1965), p. 60.

15. See UNCTAD document TD/B/C.2/103 of 21 December 1970.

16. On the correlation between labor-intensity and U.S. tariff rates, see J.E. Anderson, "Effective Protection in the United States," *Journal of International Economics*, 2., no. 1 (February 1972), p. 66.

17. UNCTAD, TD/6/Rev. 1, pp. 13-15, 17-18, 68-73, 204. See also G. Yadav, "Discriminatory Aspects of Canada's Imports of Manufactured Goods from the Less Developed Countries," *Canadian Journal of Economics*, 5, no. 1 (February 1972), p. 71.

18. UNCTAD, *Review of Trade in Manufactures of the Developing Countries, 1960-70* (TD/111 of 10 December 1971), p. 15. Developing countries have improved their share in all major industrial countries except France and the United Kingdom.

19. UNCTAD, *Special Measures for the Least Developed among the Developing Countries: Action Programme Submitted by the Secretary-General of UNCTAD* (TD/135 of 9 March 1972), para. 42.

20. A useful roundup of these developments is given by Gy. Adam, "New Trends in International Business: Worldwide Sourcing and Redomiciling," *Acta Oeconomica* 7, nos. 3-4 (Budapest, 1971), pp. 349-67. See also Sanford Rose, "The Poor Countries Turn from Buy-Less to Sell-More," *Fortune* (April 1970), pp. 91 ff.

21. George C. Reeves, *Tariff Preferences for Developing Countries: Existing and Proposed Arrangements* (U.S. Tariff Commission, 1971), p. 48.

22. Anderson, "Effective Protection," p. 63.

23. Corden, *Theory of Protection*, pp. 180-98.

24. Ian Little, Tibor Scitovsky, and Maurice Scott, *Industry and Trade in Some Developing Countries* (London: The Oxford University Press, 1970), pp. 158-59; Balassa, *Structure of Protection*, pp. 88-89.

25. See Santiago Macario, "Protectionism and Industrialization in Latin America," *Economic Bulletin for Latin America*, 9, no. 1, (March 1964), pp. 61-101; Harry H. Bell, *Tariff Profiles in Latin America: Implications for Pricing Structures and Economic Integration* (New York: Praeger Publishers 1971), Chapters 1, 2, and 4.

26. Source: Bell, *Tariff Profiles*, pp. 65-66, based on data from Macario.

27. Based on 1969 figures in UNCTAD, *Trade in Manufactures of Developing Countries: 1970 Review* (TD/B/C.2/102/Rev.1, New York, 1971), p. 20. The definition of manufactures here includes processed foodstuffs and excludes petroleum products and unworked nonferrous metals.

28. William P. Travis, *The Theory of Trade and Protection* (Cambridge: Harvard University Press, 1964), p. 248.

29. See Curzon, *Multilateral Commercial Diplomacy*, Chapter 3; Richard Snyder, *The Most-Favored-Nation Clause* (New York: King's Brown Press), Chapter 10.

30. See UNCTAD, *Main Problems of Trade Expansion and Economic Integration among Developing Countries* (U.N. document TD/110 of 29 February 1972), passim.

31. Johnson, *Economic Policies*, p. 211.

32. United States Tariff Commission, *Colonial Tariff Policies*, (Washington, D.C.: GPO, 1922), p. 42.

33. Ibid., pp. 1-5.

34. Ibid., pp. 32-43.

35. Sir Donald MacDougall and Rosemary Hutt, "Imperial Preference: A Quantitative Analysis," *Economic Journal*, 64, no. 254 (June 1954), pp. 233-57.

36. The U.S. ideological crusade—with its tendency toward allegedly excessive "Legalism, Universalism, and Economism"—has been vividly depicted in Richard N. Gardner, *Sterling-Dollar Diplomacy* (Oxford: Clarendon Press, 1956).

37. R.W. Green, "Commonwealth Preference: United Kingdom Customs Duties and Tariff Preferences on Imports from the Preference Area," *Board of Trade Journal* (December 31, 1965.

38. R.W. Green, "Commonwealth Preference: Tariff Duties and Preferences on United Kingdom Exports to the Preference Area," *Board of Trade Journal* (June 11, 1965).

39. For details of the U.K. scheme of GSP, see UNCTAD document TD/373/Add.8/III (United Kingdom) of 12 January 1972.

40. UNCTAD Document TD/124/Add.1, 9 March 1972, para. 52.

41. The items were chosen from the "UNCTAD tariff sample, "described in Annex I of UNCTAD document TD/6/Rev. 1. The list of "products of interest to developing countries" used therein has been brought up to date, however, on the basis of trade trends subsequent to those taken into account in the UNCTAD study. Certain corrections have also been made in the tariff data.

42. James R. Melvin, "The Effects of Tariff Preferences on Canadian Imports: An Empirical Analysis," *Canadian Journal of Economics*, 5, no. 1 (February 1972), pp. 48-69.

43. Melvin's coefficients of multiple regression (r^2) indicated, however, that the preferences themselves accounted for only about 10 to 20 percent of the total variance in the share of preferential trade, as compared to total imports of the respective commodity groupings examined. See ibid.

44. David Wall, *The Commonwealth Preference System and its Effects on the United Kingdom's Imports from Latin America*, Center Discussion Paper no. 21 (University of Wisconsin, Milwaukee, Latin American Center, September 5, 1969).

45. Source of trade data: United Nations Statistical Office, *Commodity Imports, 1967* (New York: United Nations Statistical Papers, series L, no. 2, vols. 1-5, 1969).

46. See discussion of nominal vs. effective tariffs above. According to Wall, *Commonwealth Preference System*, "There is, however, no *a priori* reason for expecting a relationship to exist between the size of the tariff preference and its '*degree of bias*'—we know from the theory of effective protection that the degree of protection afforded by a tariff to a preferred trade flow is not proportional to the size of the tariff (or preference margin in this case). . . ." This statement is too strong, however. Nominal tariffs are highly correlated with effective tariffs. See Benjamin Cohen, "The Use of Effective Tariffs," Discussion Paper no. 62, Economic Growth Center, Yale University (February 1969), and Chapter 3 above.

47. Regressions A.1 and A.2 made use of the UNCTAD tariff-sample averages for U.K. MFN and Commonwealth preferential tariffs before the Kennedy Round, averaged at the SITC 2-digit level. (See UNCTAD document TD/6/Rev.1.) Both the full sample and the subsample of "products of interest to developing countries" (PI) were tried. The former gave better results in the regression for India (A.2) and the latter for the ensemble of developing Commonwealth countries. The B. series of regressions use trade date at the "item" level of SITC (4 or 5 digits), which also corresponds to the BYN "heading" level. Tariffs were based on the U.K. tariff schedule as of May 1964, as published by the *Bulletin International des Douanes* (Brussels: International Customs Tariffs Bureau, Year 1964-1965, no. 2, 23rd edition), ad valorem conversions being based on information made available by the Board of Trade during the Kennedy Round. The MFN and CP duties then had to be averaged to correspond to the trade classifications. The averages were sometimes unweighted and sometimes weighted, in the light of available trade information or the analyst's judgment.

13 Trade Relations with the Third World: Emerging Patterns of Trade Preferences

Harry H. Bell

The foregoing chapter has considered the evolution of preferential trading arrangements within the broad context of discrimination in international trade, concluding with an assessment of the impact of perhaps the most distinguished colonial and postcolonial North-South trading complex—the Commonwealth Preference System. This chapter proceeds by analyzing in depth the development of the colonial preference systems of the charter EEC member-states, particularly France, into an extensive and expanding trading bloc focused on the European Community. What is happening to the Mediterranean states, and what will happen to the Commonwealth developing countries with the United Kingdom entry into the EEC? How are the commercial positions of the Latin American and Asian developing countries not parties to the EEC bloc affected, and what options do they have? What are the interests, rights, and obligations of the United States, Japan, and other outsiders in the face of these EEC-centered developments? Finally, what are the origins of the Generalized System of Preferences (GSP) and what impact will it have both on developed and developing countries? Each of these questions will be examined in turn, with particular reference to the position of the United States, which for the moment appears to have abdicated any significant role in these major questions which have important implications for its own international trade strategy in the decades to come.

Postcolonial Preferences: The EEC Complex

From the Franc Zone to the Tropical Associations

When the six member states of the European Coal and Steel Community agreed in principle—at the Messina Conference of 1955—to establish a full customs union, no consideration had been given to the implications for relationships with what were then the colonial empires of France, Belgium, Italy, and the Netherlands. Subsequently, however, the French government refused to consider participation in the Common Market unless the economic and commercial interests of its overseas "partners" in the French Union were assured, and succeeded in imposing its point of view over the opposition of Germany and the

335

lack of enthusiasm of the Netherlands and Italy. As a result, the Treaty of Rome contained a section recognizing the special commercial-policy regimes in effect between the extra-European dependencies and the respective colonial powers, but providing that they would gradually be multilateralized among the six. The member states would eliminate their duties on imports from the "associated countries and territories," and the latter would progressively remove their duties on goods from member states. Residual duties retained for purposes of revenue or development and industrialization had to be nondiscriminatory among the six. Out of these developments has evolved an elaborate system of interlocking association arrangements, not only with the eighteen African and Malagasy signatories of the Yaoundé Convention—those former territories which acceded to independence in the early sixties—and with those territories that remained politically dependent, but also with several tropical countries of the British Commonwealth, to be joined by other such applicants between 1972 and 1975.

The fundamental *raison d'etre* of the overall association process is to be found in the historical policy of France toward its colonies and is only partly a matter of customs preferences. The French colonial system traditionally involved a variety of tariff regimes, ranging from full customs assimilation to application of open-door treatment where this was required under international conventions. Beginning in 1928, the preferential policy was consciously strengthened and quantitative import restrictions were imposed against outsiders. The objective of maximum self-sufficiency in the empire was further reinforced following the outbreak of the Depression of the 1930s.

After World War II it was, however, the Franc Zone's exchange-control arrangements that formed the real basis of the French preferential area, with extreme discrimination against nonmember countries. This was only partly attributable to traditional colonial exclusivity, and it should be viewed mainly in the context of the chronic French domestic inflation, overvaluation of the franc, and balance-of-payments deficits that prevailed from 1945 until the reforms of 1958. Foreign-currency reserves of members of the zone were (and still are) pooled and administered in Paris. The severity of the rationing of allocations for imports from outside the zone contrasted markedly with the freedom of transfer and interconvertibility between the "metropolitan franc" and the satellite currencies—notably the "CFA franc"[1]—for both visible and invisible payments.[2]

In such a strictly closed system, in which the French inflation was automatically transmitted to the overseas territories, it was inevitable that trade flows were bilaterally concentrated. Until about 1955, some 80 percent of the overseas zone's trade in each direction was with metropolitan France. The zone provided an easy market for French exporters and had the effect of making them still less competitive internationally, but at the same time, the "reverse" currency preferences imposed on the territories sharply raised the prices of essential imports and capital equipment, thereby simultaneously rendering their exports of colonial products increasingly uncompetitive—except in the captive French market.[3]

From the French standpoint, to be sure, higher prices on colonial products was viewed not so much as a cost of the preferences, but as a cost of "France's deliberate wish to maintain the level of income of these countries' producers, which would otherwise have deteriorated seriously because of the fall of world-market prices."[4] Moreover, the mechanism whereby the excess prices were guaranteed was an integral part of the domestic French system of organization of markets.[5] When it became clear during negotiation of the EEC Yaoundé Convention that France's Common Market partners would insist on phasing out the preferentially higher price, the French negotiators had a strong argument for substituting outright multilateral financial aid from the European Development Fund.

The U.S. position on the commercially discriminatory aspects of the Franc Zone arrangements during the 1940s and 1950s was ambiguous. France was a major recipient of Marshall Aid and an important—though a very touchy—member of the Atlantic Alliance. While French efforts to reduce dollar expenditures aroused sympathy, energetic lobbying by certain U.S. business interests persuaded Congress that use of exchange-control techniques to circumvent the open-door pledges was intolerable. Despite independence of most of the member countries and the improved financial position of France, the techniques of commercial discrimination in the Franc Zone remained intact, except insofar as they had to be modified to reduce discrimination against other member states in the EEC.

When in 1958-59 the GATT contracting parties examined the Treaty of Rome for its compatibility with the criteria laid down for customs unions in Article XXIV, the association arrangements with the overseas territories came under critical scrutiny—since they involved a great expansion of the geographical scope of what had previously been mainly a French system of colonial preferences. The Community defended the scheme as a free-trade area in spite of the fact that a considerable sphere of trade (agricultural goods competitive with European production) was excluded from the preferential treatment envisaged, and that the complementary character of the economies meant that primarily trade-diverting effects were to be expected. The British—although they had their own comprehensive system of preferences—led the attack. The United States again took an ambivalent position, objecting to the extension of the scope of reverse preferences, but otherwise using its influence to head off any showdown, in view of its political commitment to the success of the Common Market. The debate was inconclusive, and it was decided to wait and see how the arrangements would work out. To this day, GATT has neither blessed nor damned the original convention of association or its successors.

Accession to independence by a number of the overseas dependencies of EEC members changed the entire constitutional basis of the association. Moreover, the non-French member states objected to the Franc Zone's system of preferentially high prices as a permanent feature. They also wanted to reduce the levels of tariff preference on tropical products for international diplomatic reasons.

Finally, simultaneously with the need to renew the original convention of association, the United Kingdom and other European candidates for EEC membership were increasingly active, and this necessarily posed the question of how the overseas Commonwealth countries would fare in the event that the applications were successful. The 1962 association negotiations were therefore complicated by the simultaneous confrontation of the six individual member states (plus the EEC Commission) with eighteen newly independent African states, while the British and their Commonwealth clients were participating indirectly at various levels. Other countries—notably the United States—were by no means passive onlookers.

The success of these Yaoundé negotiations at the end of 1962 was one among many examples of the Community's ability to resolve its crises by carefully balanced package deals.[6] In this case, agreement with the overseas countries was facilitated by French skill in persuading the other member states to provide a remarkably generous commitment of financial aid, an $800 million five-year package. A previously promised reduction of the common external tariff on coffee, cocoa, and several other tropical products was confirmed. The principles of nondiscriminatory application of reverse preferences (as among the EEC member states only) and of equal access by all the member states to project adjudications under the Community's tied-aid programs were reaffirmed.

A significant feature of the first Yaoundé Convention, further elaborated in the Yaoundé II Convention signed in 1969, was recognition by the Community of the associates' right to establish subregional integration groupings among themselves, or even with nonassociated countries of the region, provided the EEC member states continued to receive most-favored-nation treatment (in the literal sense of the term) and provided there was no abuse of the origin rules. Thus there now exist two subregional customs unions—the Central African Customs and Economic Union and the West African Economic Union—that cut across the eighteen separate free-trade areas between the community and the individual associated countries. Each customs union has a three-column tariff: (a) revenue tariff rates are applied to all foreign countries; (b) the general tariff is applied to most third countries, but not to EEC or the union partners; and (c) an extra-high tariff is reserved for such especially feared countries as Japan and Hong Kong. As of about 1966 the general tariffs, which determine the margin of reverse preference enjoyed by the European Community, averaged about 21 percentage points in the Central African Union (UDEAC) and about 13 percentage points in the West African Union (UDEAO).[7] In 1970, however, UDEAC announced a percentage reduction in most rates of its common external tariff, reducing the margins of reverse preference accordingly.

Nine of the Yaoundé associated states formerly had nondiscriminatory tariffs under international treaties. All except Zaïre subsequently introduced preferential tariffs, and that country promised to give the EEC reverse preferences within three years. Most of the Yaoundé countries appear to take satisfaction in the fact that their preferences are reciprocal, quite possibly because they feel that this contributes to a status of equality with the countries of the Community and possibly also because of a feeling that financial aid from the European Development Fund—or from the French bilateral aid program—would be reduced or terminated in the absence of the only *quid pro quo* they can reasonably be expected to give.

A protocol to the second Yaoundé Convention states that there is no conflict between the association and GSP, and that the Associated States may participate in the broader scheme. They are suspicious of any generalization of preferences to all developing countries, however, and have shown some resentment that the expected benefits of GSP will be obtained by other developing nations for nothing, while they have had to pay for theirs. However, the question would obviously be much more acute if tropical products were covered by GSP.

On the EEC side, the member states have had different views as to the desirability of insisting on reverse preferences from the African-Malagasy associates. During consultations prior to renewal of the Yaoundé Convention, the Netherlands wanted to eliminate them entirely. Germany preferred to leave the decision as to the degree of reciprocity up to the individual African states. France successfully insisted on full retention of reverse preferences, since two-way free trade is a requirement of the free-trade-area concept on which the association was justified internationally.[8]

Accompanying the multilateralization of reverse preferences, as among imports from the six, the other EEC member states have substantially increased their shares of the import market of the African Franc Zone countries at the expense of the French historical position. There has also been some increase in import shares of non-EEC countries.

Table 13-1
Percentage Shares in Imports of Yaoundé Associated States Belonging to the Franc Zone[a]

Year	France	Other EEC	Total EEC	U.S.	Other Africa	Communist Countries	Other Third Countries
1956	65.0	7.8	72.8	6.1		21.1	
1960	65.0	8.9	73.9	3.9		22.2	
1963	59.9	10.3	70.2	5.1	6.8	1.2	16.7
1966	54.1	13.8	67.8	6.2	7.4	2.9	15.7
1969	46.5	18.3	64.8	7.1	7.8	1.9	18.3

[a]Cameroon, Central African Republic, Chad, Congo (Brazzaville), Dahomey, Gabon, Ivory Coast, Madagascar, Mali, Mauretania, Niger, Senegal, Togo, Upper Volta.

Sources of Data: 1956-60: "The CFA Franc System" IMF *Staff Papers*, 10 (November 1963), p. 387. 1963-69: *Annuaire Statistique des Associés d'Outre-Mer* (Luxembourg: Statistical Office of the European Communities, 1970), pp. 113-23.

Although France is still the predominant supplier, the removal of all the customs discrimination and of most of the nontariff discrimination against the other EEC member states in those associated countries that also belong to the Franc Zone has probably greatly mitigated the major previous disadvantage of reverse preferences to the latter by reducing the price disparities on their manufactured imports in comparison with world-market prices. It has been argued, to be sure, that the cost of reverse preferences in terms of revenue foregone—estimated at $50 to $100 million per year—outweighs the advantages received through higher export proceeds for tropical products in the EEC market—about $30 million.[9] Such calculations would hardly be convincing to most of the associated states, which have been given to understand that the volume of EEC and bilateral member-country aid they receive is linked politically to maintenance of a closer trade relationship.

Since non-EEC countries never acquired a substantial vested interest in the import trade of the Franc Zone countries, they have had little to lose by the operation of Community reverse preferences in this particular area. From the standpoint of other developing countries, it is more serious that the Yaoundé system rules out future development of their trade with the associated LDCs in goods for which any of the EEC Member States are reasonably competitive, especially when supertariffs and prohibitive nontariff barriers are applied to potential imports from competitive Asian suppliers. Although the Yaoundé Convention permits the associates to form or join free-trade areas or customs unions that include other developing countries, they must first "consult" with the EEC through the Council of Association. EEC's system of reciprocal preferential associations with the present and former dependencies of member states is being expanded by stages to include a number of British Commonwealth countries. It had already been provisionally agreed in the 1961-63 Yaoundé negotiations that, when and if the United Kingdom entered the Community, similar association status would be offered to those African and Caribbean members of the Commonwealth "which accepted the reciprocal rights and obligations entailed in association arrangements with the EEC: if any of them were unwilling to accept these terms, they could have nothing beyond a trade agreement with the Community. The benefits they could enjoy under such agreements could not be equivalent to those deriving from association agreements."[10] South Asian Commonwealth countries would, in any case, only be offered trade agreements; Hong Kong was considered to pose very special problems.

Collapse of the first series of U.K. negotiations in the de Gaulle era did not long interrupt the process of absorbing "associable" Commonwealth countries into the EEC system. Certain member states—especially the Netherlands—were disturbed lest the developing Commonwealth suffer economically from continued discrimination by EEC in favor of the Francophone countries. Political pressures (including a long hesitation by the Dutch parliament before ratifying the first Yaoundé Convention) were applied until the French reluctantly agreed to join in a "declaration of intent" whereby the member states offered to examine in a favorable spirit applications by Commonwealth countries having economic characteristics similar to those of the EEC associates for closer trade relations with the Community. These might be: (a) accession to the Yaoundé Convention itself, (b) separate association agreements involving "reciprocal rights and obligations," or (c) mere trade agreements to reduce tariffs. It was not specified whether the tariff reductions would be preferential or MFN.

Nigeria was the first candidate. Because it had already rejected accession to the Yaoundé group on grounds that it was "neo-colonial," it chose the second formula, with the United Kingdom and the United States quietly but firmly lobbying against the reverse-preference feature. In any event, the convention signed at Lagos in 1966 was not ratified by the French and, after the outbreak of the Biafran crisis, was quietly forgotten. The terms of the abortive convention were modest on both sides; with respect to four of Nigeria's major tropical products, the free-entry privileges in the EEC were limited by tariff quotas in order to protect the prior claims of the Yaoundé associates, and the Nigerians themselves were extremely parsimonious with reverse preferences—only 26 customs positions were covered, with narrow margins of preference of only 2 to 5 percent.

The three East African States—Kenya, Tanzania, and Uganda—were the next candidates. Preliminary conversations began in June 1964, but the agreement was not signed until four years later. It too never took effect, this time because ratification formalities were overtaken by renegotiation of the Yaoundé Convention, and a somewhat revised Arusha Convention was signed in September 1969, taking effect at the beginning of 1971. It is scheduled to expire on January 31, 1975, at the same time as Yaoundé II. Following the precedent of the Lagos agreement, free entry into EEC for major East African products is subject to tariff quotas to protect the Yaoundé associates; no preference is given for agricultural products competing with European production; reverse preferences are limited to 59 positions of the East African tariff, and the margins, ranging from 2 to 9 percent, are quite narrow since they are added to revenue duties (from 25 to 70 percent) applied to all outside countries including EEC. However, the East Africans committed themselves not to reduce the advantages given to EEC vis-à-vis third countries for the duration of the accord. This seemed to indicate a stiffening of the EEC attitude on reverse preferences as compared with what it had accepted earlier from Nigeria.[1][2]

Following successful conclusion of the second series of U.K.-EEC negotiations, Mauritius was the first of the 21 independent Commonwealth developing countries to opt for entry into the Yaoundé association itself. The convention, signed in May 1972 is scheduled to take effect in early 1973. The agreed transitional provisions cover the period until expiration of Yaoundé II. The major Mauritian export product will continue to be marketed under the

Commonwealth Sugar Agreement until a conference among all association partners works out a comprehensive solution to the sugar problems of the entire enlarged Community, and Mauritius has already been allocated its interim quota of Community development aid. The Mauritian reciprocity, during this first period, is an initial adjustment of its duties toward EEC to the level of its Commonwealth preferential tariff.[13]

Whether the postcolonial EEC regime will cease to follow the principles of the "pacte colonial" with respect to reverse preferences after the expiration of Yaoundé II in 1975 will not depend on the tropical countries' bargaining power, which is very limited. They have little to lose from acceding to EEC demands in this respect, as long as the enlarged community can supply their manufactured imports at prices near the lowest world-market levels and continues to give them priority for development aid. Moreover, the generalized system of preferences is no alternative, since it will not cover commodities like sugar, cocoa, or vegetable oils, and none of the tropical countries concerned can yet benefit substantially from preferences on manufactures. If, as some propose, sanctions were aimed by the United States against such a large number of small, predominantly black, and generally poor countries, simply on grounds that they gave trade reciprocity to the European bloc, the resulting political disaster would be completely disproportionate to the U.S. trade stake, quite apart from any moral considerations.

As for the EEC, although it will continue to feel a special obligation to "its" Africans, and may now extend this obligation to other Africans and to the smaller countries of the Indian Ocean and the Caribbean, it is still only keeping its options open with respect to reverse preference from the tropical associates. It is increasingly looking to the developing world outside the African complex, first to the Mediterranean Basin, then to Latin America, and possibly—after the United Kingdom achieves its full role in community decision-making—even to the South Asian continent. It is in this wider context that an accommodation between economic regionalism and globalism will have to be sought. Nonreciprocal generalized preferences in favor of developing countries, if implemented in good faith, could contribute to such an accommodation and help avoid the formation of more seriously discriminatory trading blocs.

The Mediterranean: Mare Nostrum?

If EEC's system of associations with black African and other developing states evolved out of a decision to assume members' residual colonial rights and responsibilities, the remainder of the EEC regional preferential system involving developing countries—the network of associations and other bilateral agreements with most of the countries of the Mediterranean Basin—have grown haphazardly by comparison. The individual agreements are of different form and scope, with different historical and juridical justifications. On the surface, the main common elements in the agreements seem to be the preoccupation of the EEC partner countries with a few commodities of special interest: citrus fruit, olive oil, raisins, tobacco, and so forth. But other factors increasingly supplement and supersede trade pressures, notably Europe's recourse to Southern Europe and North Africa as a source of unskilled labor, the growth of tourism, and petroleum supplies with their associated investment infrastructure. Indeed, since about 1969-70, the European Commission has begun to rationalize the emerging Mediterranean system in outright geopolitical terms, and it has begun to advocate more comprehensive programs of technical, financial, and social cooperation.

Whether and how the Common Market was to be opened up to free access by the rest of Western Europe has been a dominant political issue for well over a decade. Because not all potential participants could or would accept full membership, the intermediate device of "association" was foreseen under Art. 238 of the Rome Treaty, providing that "the Community may conclude with a third state, a union of states, or an international organization, agreements creating an association characterized by reciprocal rights and obligations, actions in common, and particular procedures." It is generally agreed—not without debate—that the notion of "association" has a political and institutional content going beyond mere mutual trade concessions which can be negotiated under Arts. 111 and 113. Both forms of bilateral agreements have been used as the basis for the preferences with the Mediterranean countries.

When the complex of association arrangements with the EFTA members is completed, all of the industrialized states of Western Europe will be giving each other zero-duty preferential treatment for most industrial products, some within the framework of the inner customs union and others by means of bilateral free-trade-area agreements with the EEC, cross-linked together by what remains of the intra-EFTA arrangements. This fact must be kept in mind when evaluating the "discriminatory" character of the relationships with the Mediterranean countries, which are characterized by a general level of industrial development well below the EEC-EFTA complex. On the one hand, it is understandable that the United States and other "outsiders" are dismayed at the proliferation of arrangements expanding the area in which Western European products have privileged access through reverse preferences.

On the other hand, it is anomalous that GATT legalism has not effectively challenged the legitimacy of a system whereby the rich part of Europe can form a free-trading club, but had tended to condemn as "discriminatory" the efforts by the adjoining less-industrialized countries to obtain similar access to the same trading bloc by such association and trade agreements as they are able to negotiate.

The first Mediterranean association agreement—and the only one that has not been seriously challenged in GATT—was signed with Greece in 1961, and provided for complete customs union with the Community including ultimate harmonization of agricultural policies. Greece thus has aspired to eventual full membership. All Greek industrial goods except oil, cork, and those steel products controlled by the European Coal and Steel Community (ECSC) have free entry into EEC, and many agricultural goods already enjoy preferential reductions from the common external tariff. Greece has been adapting its own external tariff over a transitional period, and reverse preferences for imports from EEC into Greece will ultimately involve complete free entry; the duty reductions are being staged on a very gradual twenty-two-year schedule. The association agreement also provided for financial aid in the amount of $125 million in subsidized loans from the European Investment Bank. Drawings against this facility were interrupted for political reasons in 1968, the financial protocol has since expired, and the future of the Greek association is now in doubt.

Traditional parallelism in relations with Greece and Turkey ensured that the Athens Convention would have to be balanced by an Ankara Convention, and this was signed in 1963. The level of economic development in Turkey was such that it was not considered practicable to proceed at once towards full customs union, even on a gradual schedule, and the Ankara Convention therefore provided for three stages: (a) a "preparatory" period of at least five years, during which emphasis would be on strengthening Turkey's economy with the aid of low-interest loans provided from budgetary funds of the member states; (b) a twelve-year "transitional" period for gradual alignment of duties on both sides to form the customs union; and (c) a "definitive" phase of indeterminate length for establishment of the customs union and coordination of policies aiming at the final goal of membership in the EEC.

A protocol provided for immediate application of reduced-duty tariff quotas covering four nonindustrial products accounting for almost half of Turkish exports, and during the remainder of the preparatory period the EEC extended preferential concessions to other products including some textiles. The commercial-policy provisions of the Ankara Protocol were given advance implementation in September 1971, and all Turkish industrial goods except petroleum products and certain textiles obtained free entry into the EEC market. Turkey has also begun to give reverse preferences to the EEC on industrial goods.

An entirely different juridical basis underlay subsequent association conventions with Tunisia and Morocco which, as extra-European countries, are not considered to be candidates for eventual full membership in the EEC. Although formerly under French suzerainty, both achieved pre-EEC independence and hence were not covered by the Community's special association system. The Six did make a declaration of intent at the time the Rome Treaty was signed which foresaw that already-independent Franc Zone countries might wish to conclude association conventions at some point. Meanwhile, they continued to obtain preferences in the French market under bilateral arrangements.

The 1969 conventions with both countries covered only commercial-policy questions and are limited to five years. Duty-free entry to the EEC market was granted without quantitative restrictions for most industrial and some agricultural products. Other foodstuffs benefit from 50 percent, 40 percent, or 20 percent reductions of the common external tariff, but coal and steel (ECSC) products are excluded from the preferences, and petroleum products are subject to tariff quotas.

The two agreements differ with respect to reciprocity. Whereas Morocco does not give reverse tariff preferences to the EEC,[a] Tunisia did grant preferential duty reductions on a variety of goods. Both countries also made special concessions to the EEC in the form of preferential liberalization of existing quantitative restrictions. The United States has bitterly attacked both arrangements in GATT on the grounds that they do not legally qualify as free-trade areas, since there is no schedule for ultimate achievement of reciprocal free entry covering a substantial part of total trade.

Algeria, which unsuccessfully requested association on several occasions, is an anomalous case. Products covered by ECSC are admitted duty-free into the EEC, and Algerian goods other than wine have free access to the French market under the special relationship established when Algerian independence was recognized in 1962. The other five-member states "froze" their tariffs toward Algeria at the levels they had reached in their respective stages of intra-EEC dismantlement as of the time Algeria began to be treated as an independent third country, and this resulted in a rather incoherent preference situation on the EEC side, while dutiable items from EEC receive reverse preferences in Algeria, but not free entry. The other Maghreb country, Libya, still has no preferential agreement with EEC, although an association had been envisaged under the same understanding as for Morocco and Tunisia.

The next two bilateral preference arrangements, with Spain and Israel, were both signed in Luxembourg in June 1970 and took effect in October 1970. Both were negotiated as Community trade agreements rather than as association conventions. Both provide only for partial preferential reductions and not for free entry, do not aim explicitly at establishment of either a customs union or free-trade area with the EEC, and are consequently vulnerable with respect to nondiscrimination provisions of the GATT. Aside from these points and the role played by citrus fruit in both accords, their backgrounds and objectives are quite different.

Spain has sought association status with a view toward ultimate accession to the Rome Treaty since 1962, but political opposition repeatedly frustrated these efforts. Negotiating strategy was, therefore, to achieve as much commercial integration with the community as possible without unnecessarily specifying the ultimate objective until such time as the political obstacles might be overcome.[15] Thus Spain would be safely in the "antechamber of the Community" and could build up its vested interest—preferably for full membership, but at

[a]Under the provisions of the Act of Algeria, mentioned earlier.

least for status as favorable as that to be enjoyed by the "other-EFTA non-candidates." Only the details of the first stage—to be in effect for at least six years—were spelled out in the agreement and involve a reduction of 60 or 70 percent in the EEC external tariff on most Spanish industrial products to be staged over a twenty-seven-month period ending January 1, 1973. The preferences for cotton fabrics and petroleum products are limited by tariff quotas, while lead and zinc, footwear, refractory bricks, and products covered by ECSC are excluded. Particularly significant, in the context of the EEC's relations with its other Mediterranean partners and with the United States, are the citrus-fruit and other agricultural concessions. As reciprocity, Spain accords EEC reverse preferences in the form of tariff reductions of 25 to 60 percent and liberalized quotas, for various product lists, to be phased in at a gradual cadence extending through January 1, 1977.

Unlike Spain, Israel had no announced intention of joining the Common Market. In view of the fact that two-thirds of its export trade was then concentrated in Western Europe, its efforts to obtain some sort of preferential EEC link date back to pre-1957, and an application for association was approved in 1966-67 by the commission. This was blocked by France following the Six-Day War. But following the agreements with Tunisia and Morocco, the EEC attempted to balance the 80-percent preferential reduction on citrus fruit given to those countries by 40-percent reductions for Spain and Israel. However, when strong opposition to these citrus preferences emerged in GATT in late 1969, the EEC voluntarily withdrew them and replaced them with the comprehensive bilateral agreements taking effect in October 1970.[16]

Israel's present agreement covers only five years, but foresees a renegotiation "on broader foundations." EEC industrial tariffs toward Israel are reduced by 50 percent, phased over three years, and tariffs on Israel's main agricultural exports by 30 or 40 percent. Cotton fabrics are subject to a tariff quota. As reverse preferences, Israel grants tariff reductions to the EEC of 10, 15, 25, and 30 percent, respectively, on four lists of industrial and agricultural exports. By the time the agreement was finally concluded, Israel's industrial and export structure had so altered that the need for the EEC preferences had substantially diminished, and the arrangement was welcomed mainly as a political victory over Arab boycott attempts.

Just as the Greek association had to be balanced by association with Turkey, so the trade agreement with Israel had to have its counterparts in Arab countries. Parallel negotiations began with Egypt and Lebanon in 1970.[b] By spring 1972, the Egyptian agreement was close to signature, after a pragmatic solution was reached for certain political difficulties connected with the Arab boycott. The Egyptian and Lebanese preferential agreements are expected to take effect simultaneously for a five-year duration.

Malta—geographically a European country—was considered eligible for an

[b]Lebanon already had a nonpreferential trade agreement with EEC.

association agreement, rather than a simple preferential trade agreement. Immediately on taking effect, as from March 1971, the Valetta Convention brought about a 70-percent reduction of the EEC industrial tariffs for the duration of the association's first stage, subject to exceptions with respect to certain textiles, petroleum products, and ECSC products. At the same time, an initial 15-percent reduction of Maltese duties was introduced in favor of EEC. A year later, the Community was called upon to provide an aid package in addition to preferences, and Malta also demanded inclusion in the list of beneficiaries of the EEC generalized preference scheme, since this would give free entry for industrial products instead of the partial preference available under the association.[17]

As of spring 1972, negotiations were still going forward between the EEC and Cyprus. The EEC envisaged concessions parallel to those given to Malta. The Cypriot delegation sought an 80-percent tariff reduction for citrus fruit and relatively far-reaching concessions for a number of agricultural products to compensate for prospective loss or dilution of Commonwealth preference, although Cyprus already participates in EEC's generalized preference scheme.

Finally, it may be noted that Yugoslavia is also a Mediterranean country that has sought closer relations with the Community. A nonpreferential trade agreement was concluded in early 1970, mainly of political significance on both sides. However, Yugoslavia succeeded in obtaining reduction of the variable import levy applied on baby beef (a Yugoslav specialty) under the Community's common agricultural policy, subject to the condition that Yugoslavia maintain minimum export prices. Although this apparently violated no formal MFN commitments on this point—since the levies are not fixed tariffs and the EEC's agricultural policy has never followed GATT rules—it is an interesting form of *de facto* preference. By maintaining minimum prices through its own export control, Yugoslavia is thus able to "capture" part of the levy that would otherwise go to the Community's agricultural fund and thereby improve its terms of trade. Yugoslavia is also a GSP beneficiary, and recently requested a bilateral arrangement for "voluntary" quotas on its cotton-textiles exports to EEC whereby it would become eligible for duty-free entry on these products under the EEC rules described below. Given its ability to control its export prices, this would also ensure its "capture" of the duty, whether or not this resulted in increased market access.

It is clear from the foregoing that the EEC appears to be feeling its way into a Mediterranean policy; it announced the intention of applying this policy more consistently in the future. But for the moment—as with the tropical associ-ations—it is still keeping options open, and thus far it has demanded much less than full and immediate reciprocity from the partner countries. Reverse preferences are required in principle, but in all cases they are scheduled for more gradual implementation than the direct preferences given by the community.

The U.S. position has been inconsistent with respect to the reciprocity principle in the EEC Mediterranean arrangements. On the one hand, it fears the effects on its world-wide competitive position that would result from continued proliferation of preferences and reverse preferences in one market after another. It has been estimated that the operation of the bilateral preferential EEC agreements between the EEC and Spain, Israel, and Morocco would, by the mid-70s, displace U.S. exports to those areas by about 10 percent, 6 percent, and 9 percent, respectively.[18] These are not negligible proportions, especially when it is considered that the reverse preferences are only beginning to be applied under the present agreements. Taking the estimates at face value, none of these losses would in itself be disastrous to U.S. trade, but their logical progression would have far-reaching adverse consequences.

On the other hand, the only juridical ground on which the United States can challenge the EEC's bilateral preference arrangements in the Mediterranean is that they do not comply sufficiently with the GATT criteria for customs-union and free-trade-area exceptions to the principle of nondiscrimination. To meet these criteria, the EEC would have to demand more complete reciprocity, which would be even more damaging to U.S. trade. To be sure, the United States has been disturbed not only by the reverse preferences, but also by the direct preferences being acquired by the Mediterranean partners in the Common Market.[19] These will affect particularly such American agricultural exports as citrus fruit, dried fruit, nuts, and tobacco, which compete both with domestic EEC production and with major exports of the Mediterranean countries. While large-scale displacement of U.S. exports in these categories would indeed be disruptive to the industries concerned, some displacement is inevitable for reasons other than discrimination, and in the case of citrus the United States still has an inherent advantage during certain seasons. Moreover, when the chips are down, it is politically implausible that the United States will engage in the outright trade war that would be necessary to eliminate the citrus preferences now enjoyed by Spain, Morocco, and Israel for the sake of a trade stake that amounted to only $15 million in 1970.

If it is decided that the reverse preferences given to developed countries by developing countries indeed represent greater danger than the direct preferences for developing countries in developed-country markets, then nonreciprocal generalized preferences in favor of the developing countries appear to offer a unique way out of this dilemma. Whether this is feasible depends, of course, on whether the access afforded by the generalized preferences is a credible alternative to that negotiable under special EEC arrangement involving reciprocal preferences. In the case of the Mediterranean countries, a special problem arises because several of them are not classified as "developing" and hence are excluded from the UNCTAD generalized preferences—although all of these countries *claim* to be "developing." On the other hand Yugoslavia, which is by any criterion more industrialized than Turkey or even Greece, has succeeded in being recognized as a generalized preferences recipient.

Another problem has to do with GSP product-coverage, which is mainly limited to manufactures and semimanufactures and is hardly likely to be extended to oranges, raisins, wine, or olive oil. Although the Mediterranean countries differ widely in levels of industrialization, all have a more realistic interest in developing their manufactured exports than do, for example, the Yaoundé countries. To the extent that GSP coverage could be extended to more processed agricultural products, this might substantially improve the attraction of generalized preferences relative to special EEC preferences.

Precisely because the Mediterranean group includes countries on the borderline between developed and "developing" countries,[c] there is much room for maneuver in using generalized preferences to eliminate or reduce the role of reverse preferences in those countries with little prospect of full integration with the enlarged Community. This is not a question of applying "sanctions" against EEC associates, but rather of recognizing that the preference-donors must judge for themselves whether a given country's participation in an integration grouping of developed countries is incompatible with receipt of generalized preferences—justified on grounds of assisting development—from third countries. Such an approach, based on reducing the incentive for developing countries to "buy" access to the Community with reciprocal preferences unless they are bona fide prospective members, would strengthen their bargaining power when it comes to renewing the present bilateral agreements in the Mediterranean area. It would also strengthen the hand of those elements in the EEC Commission and the member states that do not want to use bilateralism as a form of aggressive export promotion, either in the Mediterranean or in other areas of the world. But this strategy does require that the United States have a meaningful GSP system of its own to provide a constructive alternative to proliferating bilateralism and commercial warfare between North-South trading blocs.

The Latin American Dilemma

Orphans of the Trading World

The Latin American countries and their regional organizations have been, from the beginning, the most bitter critics of the EEC commercial policies, especially on agriculture and association-arrangements with the tropical countries. While they are somewhat less concerned over the Mediterranean bilateral agreements—which affect relatively few Latin American interests—the prospect of merger of Commonwealth with EEC preferences has again aroused their alarm.

The EEC was aware of Latin American fears from the outset, but affirmative action has not been forthcoming. Because of internal difficulties over the

---

[c]The rule of "self-election" is subject to the veto of the preference-giving countries with respect to individual applicants.

Commission's competence to elaborate and execute trade policies, and because of the zealous French guardianship of the priority of the African associates' interests, Latin American envoys and visiting missions often received brusque treatment. And it was not until the 1970 Declaration of Buenos Aires, on the need for closer cooperation between Latin America and Europe, that the EEC Commission finally succeeded in convincing the member states that something concrete would have to be done to improve relations with the area. In June 1971 a mechanism was established for permanent "dialogue" between the continents.[21]

The community's long delay in responding to Latin America's preoccupations contributed to an exaggeration of the damage actually incurred as a result of multilateralization among the Six of the preferences for the African Franc Zone. The major commodities affected were coffee, cocoa, and bananas. The EEC common external tariffs on coffee and cocoa were reduced twice, and the relatively moderate EEC discrimination on these products was not the reason behind the advance in the African shares in world production of both commodities.

Bananas were another matter. The external tariff was set at 20 percent and, more important, strict quantitative restrictions and special marketing arrangements reserved the French market by priority to the Antillean departments and residually to African Franc Zone countries. Italy arranged to absorb the entire population of Somalia before importing residual requirements from the Western Hemisphere. However, a special protocol to the Yaoundé Convention gave Germany a tariff-free quota adequate to cover its annual consumption, and this was used entirely for imports from the low-cost Latin American producers in Ecuador, Colombia, and Central America. The Community's support of high-cost preferential suppliers of bananas is not nearly as discriminatory as the policy of the United Kingdom, which allocates a quota of barely 4,000 tons a year to Latin American countries as compared with total imports averaging 350,000 tons, mainly from the Caribbean Commonwealth areas.[22] Impartial observers agree that sudden removal of the special preferences for bananas would have unacceptably serious economic and human repercussions for the African and Caribbean producers concerned.[23]

Proposals for Special Hemispheric Preferences

Although Brazil and Portugal retained their preferential ties with each other until well into this century, the resentment of most Latin American countries against Europe's colonial-type preferences long antedated the Common Market, but was accompanied—perhaps paradoxically—by intermittent sentiment in favor of special trading relationships with the United States. At the first inter-American conference, in 1889-90, the Americans proposed a pan-American customs union, in reality a free-trade area, apparently motivated by a desire for preferential access for U.S. manufactures to the emerging Latin American markets. Argentina and Chile rejected the idea, pointing out the loss of sovereignty involved and the need to retain trade links with Europe to balance U.S. influence, and many of the countries involved cited the loss of revenue and their doubts that the United States would really give up its own protective tariffs on manufactures. They felt that regional free trade, let alone a North-South customs union, was premature at that time. Instead, they recommended negotiation of bilateral "partial reciprocity" agreements within the hemisphere.[24]

The idea of a hemisphere free-trade area was revived during the mid-1960s, within the context of the Alliance for Progress, by various influential personalities on the American side, and by pro-American Brazilians, Colombians, and Mexican, on the Latin American side.[25]

Although the concept had some congressional support and was examined in depth in the U.S. executive branch, the "GATT-universalists" in the State Department won the day, partly because such discriminatory arrangements were counter to long-standing U.S. doctrine and partly because of the potential damage to U.S. political relationships with both developed and developing countries outside the hemisphere that might result. The neocolonial and paternalistic aspects of "vertical" or "North-South" preferences were stressed.[26] But on other occasions, even the State Department revived the notion of a special U.S. trade relationship with Latin America, presumably to dramatize U.S. displeasure over the EEC's sphere-of-influence policies.[27]

Regardless of questions of principle, it would not take much country-by-country and product-by-product analysis to demonstrate that a "vertical" preferential system linking the United States with Latin America would have made little economic sense. The United States had little to give and little to gain. Unlike the situation in the EEC, which started from a position of preferential support prices for tropical products, major Latin American primary products already had largely duty-free access to the U.S. market. To create a preference it would have been necessary to establish new discriminatory barriers toward nonhemispheric developing countries. Although regional preferences might have conceivably been granted on manufactures, it is doubtful that these would have been easier to get through Congress than similar preferences generalized worldwide.

It was earlier pointed out that only in the last several years have any Latin American countries been able to develop their sales of manufactured goods in world markets, with or without preferences. Moreover, for the United States to demand reverse preferences in Latin American markets would not only have been undignified in the light of past U.S. pronouncements; it would also have been dangerous in that EEC—and *a fortiori* an expanded EEC—could play the same game with more bargaining power. This is because Western Europe has a structural excess of imports over exports with both Latin America as a whole and with the major individual trading countries of the area.

For their part, the Latin American republics have also had strong grounds of principle for not entering into a free-trade-area arrangement with the United States. The intellectual leadership of the Economic Commission for Latin America (ECLA), including Raúl Prebisch, has been strongly committed against all vertical preference schemes and in favor of generalized unilateral preferences on a worldwide basis. Throughout and following Prebisch's tenure as Secretary-General of UNCTAD, he consistently insisted on abolition of any preferential system that would discriminate as among different regional groups of developing countries and in favor of the industrialized countries. ECLA also remains oriented toward import-substitution policies, albeit now at the regional rather than the national level and with more emphasis on export promotion than formerly.

Reverse preferences in favor of the United States are thus inconceivable in the Latin American political climate. Countries that already have a high geographic concentration of their trade with the United States—e.g., Mexico, Colombia, Venezuela—are trying to diversify both their export markets and import sources. Others, including Argentina and Uruguay, are highly Europe-oriented in their import trade and even more dependent on Europe for their export markets, and they would not dare discriminate in favor of the United States even if this were ideologically thinkable.

Future Relationships between EEC and Latin America

If a U.S.-Latin American preferential area is not in the cards, what are the possibilities that the EEC system of preferential bilateral agreements might at some future time be extended to individual Latin American countries, or to a regional organization like the Andean Group? There is no indication at present that either the Europeans or Latin Americans are thinking in such terms. On the contrary, it has been stressed on both sides that they are considering only *nonpreferential formulas* that would coexist with generalized preferences.

The first of these was the nonpreferential commercial agreement signed between EEC and Argentina in November 1971, to be effective for a three-year period from January 1972. It has been described as the model for EEC's future agreements with Latin American countries, and negotiations for similar arrangements are already underway with Uruguay and Brazil. The Argentine agreement provides for the removal of quantitative import restrictions in each direction, gradual elimination of the Argentine advance-deposit requirement on products of special interest to the community, and related issues. The most significant provisions concern imports into EEC of frozen beef for processing, a category of meat that is mainly exported by Argentina. Subject to certain safeguards and exchange of information with respect to such questions as offer prices and timing, the variable import levy on Argentine beef under the common agricultural policy could be suspended. In addition the tariff-free quota on the beef could be increased on a technically nondiscriminatory basis.

Together with the eventual agreements with Uruguay, Brazil, and perhaps other countries, this arrangement may go far to alleviate the Latin American complaints about the CAP as it affects their particular export specialties. At the same time, generalized preferences for manufactures and semimanufactures under the EEC GSP program are implicitly part of the total package of advantages received without reciprocity in the form of reverse preferences. At least for the time being, therefore, the existence of GSP, in conjunction with the community's greater interest in coming to terms with Latin America, has made it easier for both sides to reach a *modus vivendi* not involving special preferences, albeit with the U.S. relegated to a back-seat role.

There are some potentially disturbing aspects to be considered. One is the very fact that it was considered necessary to negotiate such agreements separately, in the framework of bilateral bargaining. Second, the major concessions on access of meat under the CAP are based on product discrimination and may also involve a certain amount of voluntary restraint; they may not be as liberal or nonpreferential as they purport to be. A third and more important question arises because of the shortcomings of the EEC generalized preference system and the fact that it is subject to revocation on short notice, e.g., possibly because of failure of the United States to "share the burden" by implementing its own preferential scheme in favor of the developing countries. If the GSP were suddenly withdrawn, might the Latin Americans not have a strong incentive to seek a more stable special relationship at the price of reverse preferences? How long would the EEC resist the temptation to use its barbaining power in that situation? Thus, in the event of a collapse of expectations with regard to the GSP, one can imagine a scenario whereby the intentions of both sides to avoid extension of the special-preference system to Latin America might be overcome.

Negotiating the Generalized System of Preferences (GSP): The Main Issues

Two essential innovations were involved in the concept of generalized preferences; (1) the conscious use of nonreciprocal trade preferences in all major industrial markets as a specific strategy to assist developing countries; (2) the use of across-the-board rules and procedures to minimize the politically disruptive effects resulting from the exponentially-increasing complexity of international trade relationships.[28] A brief review of the evolution of the GSP approach may help put these points in perspective.

The Origins of Generalized Preferences

The GATT has long permitted the application of a double standard in trade policy with respect to infant-industry protection and use of quantitative import restrictions in developing countries. In 1958, the report of a GATT panel of experts ("the Haberler Report") called attention to the special sensitivity of developing countries' material progress to the domestic and international economic policies of industrial nations. This led in 1959 to a special mandate to open up a comprehensive dialogue with the less-developed contracting parties to the GATT. After five years of increasingly spirited debate, a new provision in the GATT added the significant concession that "the developed contracting parties do not expect reciprocity for commitments made by them in trade negotiations to reduce or remove tariffs and other barriers to the trade of less-developed contracting parties."[29] But by the time it was adopted, the GATT initiative was already on the way to being superseded by events.

The preferences issue was precipitated in 1961, when Nigeria proposed immediate dismantlement of tariffs on tropical products, thereby challenging EEC head-on just as the Six were beginning their multifaceted negotiations for renewal of the association with the African-Malagasy states. At the same time the EEC tropical preferences were undergoing critical analysis in U.N. bodies—especially in the Economic Commission for Latin America, at that time headed by Dr. Prebisch who was about to bring forward the "trade-gap" interpretation of the development problems of "peripheral countries." This stressed not only the need for greater capital assistance to development, but also improved access to the industrial countries' markets by developing countries' exports of both manufactures and primary products. In mid-1962 the developing countries, in a very impatient and militant mood, joined forces in the U.N. with the Soviet Bloc to call for the convening of a United Nations Conference on Trade and Development (UNCTAD) in 1964.

This new external challenge greatly accelerated the evolution of ideas in preferences in GATT. In late 1962, a proposal was made by a group of developing countries that, among other things, the industrialized nations schedule over a three-year period a 50-percent reduction of duties on semiprocessed and processed imports from developing countries. This implied generalized preferences and was adopted in principle the following year, albeit with many qualifications and with the EEC countries and their African associates abstaining.

"Selective" vs. "Generalized" Preferences

Parallel studies were meanwhile being launched on the same questions in U.N. bodies in preparation for UNCTAD. The EEC countries—and particularly

France—were at first embarrassed by the attacks on the tropical preferences, which were still controversial among the Six. Nevertheless, it was the Belgian Minister of Foreign Trade and Technical Assistance, Maurice Brasseur, who in May 1963 proposed a detailed scheme whereby the developed countries might individually give selective, temporary, and degressive preferences for those products of industries in developing countries that were not yet competitive.[30] These preferences might involve total or partial suspension of duties and would be quantitatively limited by tariff quotas. They would be negotiated bilaterally between the individual developed and developing countries, and there would be no reciprocity in the form of reverse preferences.[31] On the other hand, the scheme provided for strict measures against "market disruption," under which developing countries selling at exceptionally low prices would be subject to a system of compensatory rates of duty—in effect, *negative* preferences. The revenue proceeds of such compensatory duties would however be allocated to the developing countries affected.

The Brasseur Plan had the virtue of "breaking the ice" on the preferences issue, although it had numerous disadvantages.[32] Perhaps most important was its complexity and the fact that, since the preferences would be strictly temporary, degressive, and closely circumscribed on a product-by-product and country-by-country basis, they would be too uncertain in duration and scope to accomplish the purpose of establishing trade beach-heads and fostering new investment and scale economies in the developing countries.

Instead, considerable support at the 1964 UNCTAD was received for the generalized and automatic approach, not only for a number of developing countries but also from the United Kingdom and Germany, which were attracted by the relative simplicity of the concept. It was pointed out that, instead of increasing deviations from MFN treatment, "if the preferential arrangements to be worked out also consolidated the existing preferences, the exceptions to the most-favored-nation principle might become even less numerous and complicated than the existing ones."[33] For Commonwealth countries like India and Pakistan not linked into the EEC complex, generalized preferences promised to ease the problems posed by eventual U.K. entry into the Community. Loss or dilution of their Commonwealth preference would be compensated for by the opening of new preferences in other areas. While the principle of generalized preferences clearly prevailed over the selective version, rules and procedures eventually applied in some of the GSP schemes—especially that of EEC—are turning out in practice to be so complicated and differentiated that they have more features of the Brasseur Plan than of a real system of generalized preferences.

The first scheme of nonreciprocal preferences for development purposes was that introduced by Australia in 1966, under a special GATT waiver. It was highly selective with respect to products, margins of preference granted, and beneficiary countries—on the basis of the "competitive need" principle. Preferences were limited by tariff quotas arbitrarily set and "so designed as to provide a safeguard for Australian domestic industry and to avoid substantial injury to the established trade of third countries in the products concerned."[34] All the products covered were "nominated by developing countries, or by importers in Australia, as being of present or future interest."[35] In point of fact, total preferential imports under the scheme after three years of operation were still less than 2 percent of total developing-country exports to Australia. It has been estimated, however, that within the quota limitations the Australian scheme did significantly increase the exports of the products concerned, accounting for about nine-tenths of their increase in value over the first three years, but without significant complaints of resultant market disruption.[36]

"Burden-Sharing" among Preference-Giving Countries

As used in the GSP exercise, the term "general preferences," being distinguished from "special preferences," implies that preferences will be given by "all" developed countries to "all" developing countries. There is, of course, no precise boundary between the two categories except, pragmatically, in accordance with the principle of self-election as modified by political realities. For most purposes, it is sufficient to consider as preference-donors the eighteen countries that adopted common positions on this issue in an OECD caucus in October 1970.[d]

Since each preference country's offer is *sui generis* for institutional, structural, or political reasons, it is difficult to apply common standards of comparative evaluation. Nevertheless, the concept of "burden-sharing"—undefined and perhaps undefinable—is insisted upon by all of the major participants. For example, the EEC insisted on equitable burden-sharing from the start and, when implementing the offer in July of 1971, the commission noted that the Community might reconsider "in case other donor countries did not implement their offers in reasonable periods of time."[37] Community spokesmen have subsequently called attention to the failure of the United States even to submit legislation to Congress to implement its preferences offer.

The question of equity is not a matter of giving donor countries an excuse to renege, since the legal position is already clear that GSP (a) is temporary in nature, (b) does not constitute a binding commitment, (c) can be withdrawn in whole or in part, (d) does not prevent subsequent MFN tariff reductions, and (e) is conditional on waivers of existing GATT or other international obligations.[38] Rather, the widest participation on the part of GSP is essential for two

---

[d]Austria, Canada, the EEC members, Ireland, Japan, New Zealand, four Nordic countries, Switzerland, the United Kingdom and the United States. Australia already had the preference scheme described above, and Bulgaria, Czechoslovakia, Hungary, Poland and the USSR also considered themselves as giving trade advantages to developing countries.

substantive reasons. First, extension of general-preferential access to a broader market is the main compensation offered to those developing countries of the Commonwealth and of the EEC sphere of influence that now face dilution of their special-preferential positions because these have to be shared with additional developing-country competitors. Second, the theory of preferences clearly demonstrates that after preferences have been introduced by a group of industrial countries, developing-country exports to the nonpreference-giving developed countries will tend to decline, thereby giving the latters' import-competing producers a "free ride." Conversely, if other developed countries join in the preference scheme, there will tend to be less of an increase in the imports of a particular preference-giving country than if it alone implemented preferences.[39]

Discrimination among Developing Countries and Reverse Preferences

The UNCTAD system of generalized preferences is supposed to be nondiscriminatory, and this means that all developing countries are to be treated alike—regardless of whether or not they are otherwise affiliated with the donor countries. Various lists of countries considered to be "less-developed" or "developing" have been used by international organizations for different purposes. The best-known list of developing countries is the "Group of 77," a strictly political coalition which grew out of the first UNCTAD in 1964 and now includes ninety-six independent states. For political reasons, neither Israel or Taiwan is a member, Cuba joined recently, and only one European country—Yugoslavia—is a member. The members of the "77" stated that they are all candidates for GSP beneficiary status under the self-election rule. Announced candidates not belonging to the "77," as of March 1972, were Bulgaria, Greece, Israel, Malta, Romania, Spain, Taiwan, Turkey, and the United Arab Emirates. The exclusion from the outset of particular countries was not supposed to be based on competitive considerations. Yet it is difficult to view as motivated otherwise the tendency of several GSP donors to exclude Hong Kong, Taiwan, Macao, and the Republic of Korea, either completely or for specific groups of products.

For example, the EEC scheme systematically discriminates among different categories of countries listed as its GSP beneficiaries. Those—such as the Yaoundé and Arusha groups and Tunisia and Morocco—which enjoy both association relationships and GSP status with the community, continue to obtain the greater advantages of the special preferences and are not subjected to complicated tariff-quota limitations on GSP. Moreover, only those few developing countries that have adhered to the Long Term Arrangement on Textiles (LTA) or have undertaken similar voluntary-restraint commitments are eligible for free entry under GSP with respect to cotton textiles and assimilated noncotton textiles. Dependent territories or third countries (including notably Hong Kong and Macao) are ineligible for GSP treatment for textiles and footwear. Finally, it will also be noted below that the "buffer" feature of the tariff-quota system applied by the community tends to limit preferential imports from Hong Kong and Yugoslavia of a number of industrial products. Since especially favorable application of the GSP in favor of the least developed among the developing countries is generally recognized as desirable, the EEC frequently justifies its policy of giving precedence to the interests of the Yaoundé group in these terms.

The United States threatened to exclude from its eventual GSP program those developing countries which receive special preferences in developed-country markets for products covered by the scheme and/or which grant reverse preference to developed countries—unless adequate assurances are given that the special or reverse preferences are phased out within a reasonable period of time.[40] The question of reverse preferences is probably the most critical political issue in the whole GSP exercise, and the diplomacy with which it is handled may be of crucial importance as to whether GSP operates to moderate or accelerate tendencies toward exclusive trading blocs. Since the United States has done nothing to implement its GSP offer, it remains a hypothetical question whether it could really apply the ban on special and reverse preferences in full rigor, or would find a more flexible formula. It is hardly conceivable that no distinction at all would be drawn between enjoyment of special preferences, on the one hand, and the giving of reverse preferences, on the other hand. It should also be noted that the leverage available to the United States for eventual elimination of reverse preferences depends on the amount of real advantage offered to beneficiaries of the American GSP scheme when eventually implemented.

The Japanese tactics with respect to this problem appear much more realistic, to the effect than those countries

. . . which discriminate in trade or tariffs against Japan, will in principle lose their beneficiary status after three years from the entry into force of the Scheme if they have not discarded the discriminatory measures during the intervening period.[41]

Product Coverage

From the beginning, the GSP was intended to apply mainly to manufactures and semimanufactures. This reflected partly the special importance attributed to the diversification of developing economies away from dependence on primary exports. It was also a pragmatic recognition of the facts of life with respect to the strength of agricultural protectionism and the prevalence of variable levies, subsidies, and other nontariff measures not susceptible of across-the-board treatment in trade negotiations. Tropical agriculture was also left out, in principle, because its inclusion would have split the developing countries even more seriously as between those dependent on special preferences and outsiders like the Latin American countries.

In the course of negotiations, general agreement was reached whereby most countries would apply the GSP automatically—using *negative lists* for exceptions—to semimanufactured and manufactured products.[e] The number and scope of exceptions invoked by donor countries depended partly on the type of safeguard systems they used. The main exceptions covered by the negative lists were usually in the textiles, petroleum, and leather sectors. EEC took pride in being the only donor area with no exceptions list for industrial manufactures and semimanufactures. This was a rather empty claim, given the restrictiveness of the EEC's system of multiple safeguards based on tariff-quota mechanisms, as outlined below.

There are a large number of processed and semiprocessed agricultural products of considerable potential interest to developing countries—including even the "least-developed"—which the preference-donors considered particularly sensitive, either because the domestic industries were dependent on high-cost inputs or simply because it was traditional to be highly protective of anything agricultural. As a result, agricultural commodities are covered under the GSP by a *positive-list* procedure; small concessions were made on what looked like many individual items, but these were generally so narrowly defined that the potential trade coverage was relatively negligible.

Margins and Duration of Preferences

The first proposals for the GSP demanded at least a 50-percent preferential cut from MFN tariff levels. But by the time of 1964 UNCTAD session the developing countries had raised their sights and were asking for full duty-free entry. In any case, the successful conclusion of the Kennedy Round in 1967 substantially reduced the potential margins of preference available on most industrial products other than textiles. If simplification of the pattern of discriminatory systems was one of the advantages claimed for GSP, there were strong arguments for duty-free treatment instead of partial cuts. Exemption from duty symbolizes equalization of conditions of access by all beneficiary developing countries—not only with those enjoyed by domestic producers, but

---

[e]Most of the primary industrial products either had zero or low duties anyway and were of little interest for preferences. Individual preference-giving countries followed different policies as to whether or not to include in their offers such of these products as were dutiable.

also with those applicable to the ever-increasing number of producers in other developed countries who obtain free entry through the expansion of customs unions and free-trade areas.[42]

Viewed in this sense, generalized preferences would reduce total discriminatory differentiation of protection. Developing-country producers would simply be assimilated with home producers, thus emphasizing the trade-creation aspect relative to the trade-diversion aspect of preferences. Another psychological advantage of the free-entry rule is that a zero duty places a natural limit on margins of preference, which therefore have to be degressive over time if MFN duties are still subject to downward negotiation in the GATT framework. The infant-industry argument logically implies gradual elimination of special customs advantages as the industries become visible, and this was recognized in the original argumentation for preferences through the explicit acceptance of degressive margins of preference within an overall limitation on the duration of the scheme.[43]

There is an inevitable danger that beneficiary countries will seek to "bind" their margins of preference at some percentage level, thereby implying a permanent vested interest in artificial trade advantages as well as inhibiting progress toward worldwide reduction of trade barriers on an MFN basis. This tendency was evidenced by a number of developing-country delegates at the Santiago session of UNCTAD in 1972, who expressed the fear that the new GATT negotiations planned for 1973-74 would result in a general trade liberalization that might cancel out the effect of GSP before it had really been implemented.[44] Such statements have almost certainly been counterproductive.

With regard to industrial products, the general principle of duty-free treatment has been accepted by EEC, the United Kingdom, the Nordic countries, and Japan (although Japan applied only a 50-percent reduction for selected products). The United States offer, still not implemented, also envisaged zero duties for the items covered. On the other hand, Austria, Canada, Ireland, and Switzerland provided for linear tariff reductions falling short of duty-free entry, and New Zealand's scheme involves only miscellaneous reductions in the relatively few concessions made.

For agricultural products, the EEC and Japan provided mainly for partial tariff cuts, and the United Kingdom made a few exceptions from its normal duty-free rule. The EEC's practice reflects in part its two-element system of protection with respect to a number of processed agricultural items. The element corresponding to the raw-material component is subject to the agricultural levy and is unaffected by preferences; any preferential cut applies only to the tariff element corresponding to value added as a result of processing.

The 1970 UNCTAD agreement on the GSP envisages an initial duration of ten years. A comprehensive review before the end of the period will determine whether it should be continued.

Safeguard Mechanisms: Escape Clause vs.
Tariff Quotas

It was envisaged from the beginning that some kind of safeguard would be required to limit the risks of "excessive" imports and "market disruption" as a result of the GSP, especially since the preferences were to be bestowed unilaterally and without commitment as to permanence, thus at the mercy of public opinion in the preference-granting countries. The Brasseur Plan had envisaged a tariff-quota mechanism, and the initial report of the Secretary-General to the 1964 UNCTAD contemplated an overall ceiling on preferential imports into all the developed countries taken as a group, the ceiling to be divided among importing countries according to a formula based on total consumption and/or total imports. Individual importing countries could also withhold from preferences a reasonable percentage of their aggregate consumption or imports, or they could limit their preferential imports of each item to national ceilings, to be fixed in advance, based on domestic consumption.[45] All such ceilings had specific conceptual or implementational weaknesses.

An early draft scheme proposed by the EEC, based on a rigid tariff-quota mechanism, alarmed both the UNCTAD Secretariat and the representatives of countries—like the United States—which had a traditional distaste of any kind of fixed quantitative limitations, but which were accustomed to occasional recourse to an escape-clause mechanism. In any case, there was no a priori reason to assume that one system would necessarily be more restrictive than the other. Therefore, the preparatory work for the 1968 session of UNCTAD was equally receptive to three approaches to the safeguard mechanism: (1) an escape-clause system with no advance limitations but in which certain products might be excluded from preferences entirely; (2) a tariff-quota type of system with ceilings based on a percentage of consumption, production, or total imports of particular items, and (3) a system based on the escape clause but providing for a partial reduction of duties rather than free entry. It was also recognized that combinations of the three approaches were conceivable.[46]

Long debate within OECD and UNCTAD during the time between the 1968 conference and the final decision to implement the GSP in 1970 failed to achieve agreement on a unified approach. Austria, EEC, and Japan adopted *a priori* limitation formulas of varying degrees of complexity, which not only took into account the level of imports in reference years, but also limited the amount of the quotas or ceilings available to the major suppliers of the products concerned. The latter provisions, reflecting the "competitive need" principle, were intended to ensure that the most competitive developing countries would not preempt the preferences. The other preference-giving countries chose to depend mainly on the escape clause together with product exclusions and/or preferential rate reduction falling short of free entry.

It is important to remember that when a maximum limit (tariff-quota or ceiling) is exhausted or an escape clause is invoked under a preference scheme, imports may still enter but are then subject to the normal (MFN) customs duty. From that point on, and until a new quota period is opened or the escape clause is suspended, there is presumably no incentive at the margin to expand trade. From this standpoint either system may be applied liberally or restrictively. The test is not whether there is an absolute increase in trade but whether the incentive operates to induce an increment over the trade flow that would have occurred in the absence of preferences. In the case of the tariff-quota system, this might be determined in advance by comparing the size of the quota with a projection of the expected trade trend. In the case of the escape clause, it can only be determined after the fact. Either the importing country's limit of tolerance is reached or it is not. In either case, however, expectations play a key role.[f]

Implementation of Generalized Preferences
in the Common Market

The 1970 consensus reached in UNCTAD established only a very loose multilateral framework for GSP, leaving to the preference-giving countries wide latitude not only with respect to administrative and institutional adaptations, but also with respect to substantive questions. What GSP means in practice therefore depends on the details of the separate schemes. The EEC scheme provides a good example. Introduced for a provisional six-month period in July 1971 and renewed with certain modifications at the beginning of 1972, it has yielded a certain amount of operational experience—although it will be some time before any meaningful statistics are available for *ex post* evaluation.

The main lines of EEC's quota-type safeguard system furnished the model for the Japanese scheme, also already implemented, and it will presumably supplant the escape-clause-type British safeguards when that is phased out over the next several years. It now also seems likely that any eventual U.S. legislation on preferences will have to embody some quantitative import limitations and more selectivity with respect to products and beneficiaries than was envisaged in the provisional U.S. offers tabled in 1969 and 1970. Finally, regardless of the intrinsic importance to developing countries of U.S. action on preferences, the geopolitical significance of the whole GSP exercise hinges primarily on the type of arrangements governing access of developing countries, whether or not

---

[f]It might appear that the tariff-quota system gives greater certainty, at least within the specified limit. But if the limit is clearly too small, then there may still be no certainty that individual marginal shipments will "get in under the wire" or, if they do, that the benefit of nonpayment of duty will be captured by the developing-country exporter in the form of a higher export price. Much depends on the manner in which the maximum limits are administered.

associated with the Community, to the expanding preferential European market.

The EEC GSP system is not only a political challenge. In its present form it is also an analytical challenge, defying simplification—an oversimplified description would fail to bring out the extent to which it is a *curiosum*—some have said a horrible example—of complexity. One can legitimately question whether it is a "generalized" system at all. The conceptual dichotomy between a selective *ad hoc* system (exemplified by the Brasseur Plan and the Australian scheme) and a system based on generalized across-the-board rules becomes more and more blurred as the number of "automatic" formulas and exceptions increases.

*Productwise and Areawise Differentiation
in the EEC Scheme*

In what follows, we consider only "industrial" goods (BTN Chapters 25-99), excluding those considered by the EEC as primary products.[g] The three automatic formulas for limiting preferential duty-free imports into the EEC are applied on a product-by-product basis. Since the formulas are calculated from trade statistics, the level of aggregation is important. Many "products" are defined for convenience at the BTN four-digit ("heading") level, but there are numerous cases involving more minutely-defined subitems or combinations of subitems for which statistics have not been publicly available on a continuing basis. This makes it extremely difficult (in some cases impossible) for those outside the EEC Commission, and especially the concerned potential exporters in developing countries, to evaluate the economic significance of the particular concessions. In general, such EEC *ad hoc* product definitions below the four-digit level are more frequent among the relatively "sensitive" goods. On the other hand, some products are defined much more broadly, at the two-digit or "chapter" level of the BTN.

Treatment accorded to products thus defined is differentiated according to *lists*. Major distinctions are made with respect to: (a) cotton (and assimilated) textiles subject to the GATT Long Term Arrangement on Cotton Textiles; (b) most other textiles and footwear; (c) products subject to the jurisdiction of the European Coal and Steel Community (ECSC); and (d) other products. Each of these categories is then cross-classified as between "sensitive" and "other" products, but the latter category really contains two subcategories: (a) "quasi-sensitive" and (b) "nonsensitive." The EEC has retained the option to switch

---

[g]Although most industrial raw materials are already duty-free and irrelevant to preferences, the EEC has unilaterally chosen to class as primary products—excluded from preferences—a number of unwrought metals *through the ingot stage* that bear duties. These are important in developing-country trade, and are usually designated as semimanufactures in statistical classifications.

products from one list to another; this is normally done only at the beginning of a new quota period and occurred for some products at the beginning of 1972.

We noted earlier that the EEC's "nondiscriminatory" system of generalized preferences is considerably differentiated in the geographical dimension. Some confusion results from the use of the term "beneficiary country" in several senses. Those beneficiaries—such as the Yaoundé and Arusha countries, the remaining dependent overseas territories of the EEC member states, and Tunisia and Morocco, which already enjoy free-entry privileges for manufactures and semimanufactures under association arrangements—are not subject to the GSP safeguard limitations. Also, certain countries that have not subscribed to self-restraint commitments are excluded from GSP for cotton textiles, and Hong Kong and other dependencies of non-EEC countries are entirely excluded with respect to the textiles-and-footwear special lists. The remaining developing countries, to which the ceilings, tariff quotas, and so forth do apply for a given product list, can be described for present purposes as *narrow-sense beneficiaries* with respect to that particular list. Conversely, the term *nonbeneficiary* countries as used in the formulas denotes all "third" (i.e., non-EEC) countries except the narrow-sense beneficiaries.

To see what the preference-ceilings mean in particular cases involves a discouraging task of aggregating and disaggregating published trade statistics for the special country-groupings and for hundreds of product definitions that are themselves frequently difficult to piece together.

Ceilings, Buffers, and Subquotas

Three logically distinct but interacting tariff-quota mechanisms are applied under the EEC scheme. The most fundamental concept is the "ceiling" (*plafond*). For a given annual or (in the case of the second-half 1971) prorated period, and for a given product and subset of narrow-sense beneficiaries, the ceiling normally consists of a *basic element*—equal to EEC imports from the beneficiaries in 1968—plus a *supplementary element*—equal to 5 percent of the imports from nonbeneficiaries in 1968 (or a more recent year designated by the EEC), whichever gives the greater amount.[h]

When it came to establishing the rules for 1972, the reference year used in calculating the supplementary ceilings was changed from 1968 to 1969 (except for textiles and ECSC products). If one assumes that 1968 will continue to be the reference year for the basic element and that the reference year for the supplementary element continues to be shifted annually by one year, one can write the general formula for total annual ceilings (C_t) as follows:

[h]For some products, to be sure, no supplementary element is provided, or it is reduced to only 1 percent of imports from nonbeneficiaries, or other special exceptions are made.

Total = basic element + supplementing element;

$$C_t = m_{1968} + 0.05\,(M_{t-3} - m_{t-3}),$$

where m = EEC imports from narrow-sense beneficiaries and

M = EEC imports from all non-EEC countries.

For reasons that will subsequently be apparent, let us consider the total ceiling to be "open-ended" if:

$$C_t > m_t$$

and "closed-ended" if:

$$C_t \leqslant m_t.$$

The general formula can be rearranged so as to bring out the fact that the size of the total ceilings depends on the share of the beneficiaries in total imports in the base year (1968) and on the *growth* both in total EEC imports from third countries and in EEC imports from beneficiaries between the base year and the reference year for calculating supplementary ceilings.[47] However, the adequacy or "open-endedness" of the ceilings also depends on the growth of imports from beneficiaries through the *current* year, indicated by the subscript t.

Total ceilings of those products for which the beneficiaries had initially a large relative share and/or show a rapid growth rate as compared to total imports from third countries will be quickly overtaken and therefore become "closed-ended." In a remarkably large number of cases, they have already been overtaken. On the other hand, the ceilings may continue to be "open-ended" for a long or indefinite period if only a small share of total imports was initially accounted for by beneficiaries and/or if imports from beneficiaries have been growing less rapidly than imports from nonbeneficiaries. Moreover, the longer the time-lags built into the formula, the more total ceilings are likely to be "closed-ended."

Although the Community heralded the shift in reference years for the supplementary ceilings from 1968 to 1969 as a substantial liberalization, it is clear that the time-lag with respect to the *basic* element was really lengthened from three to four years, and that the supplementary element merely remained at three years—except, of course, for textiles and ECSC products on which the lag lengthened to four years.

The ceilings are not applied with uniform rigor, however. For goods on the "sensitive" lists, strict tariff-quota control procedures are used at the borders of the member states to limit the imports receiving duty-free treatment. Other goods are subject to more flexible procedures with controls based on statistical information and with varying degrees of uncertainty as to whether the ceilings are to be taken seriously. For those classed as "quasi-sensitive," special surveillance is maintained. When the limit is approached for a given category, the EEC Commission urgently consults with representatives of the member states, the presumption being that measures will be taken promptly to withdraw preferences and reinstate MFN duties for the remainder of the year. With respect to "nonsensitive" goods on the other hand, import trends are followed with little or no concern; it is presumed (but not certain) that total imports from beneficiaries will be allowed to exceed the ceiling.

The ceiling formula described above, modified by its probabilistic features for goods not on the sensitive lists, produces a reasonably consistent application of the "competitive need" principle with respect to individual products. However, the principle is also applied with respect to individual developing countries of origin, and it is here that the EEC scheme—and, for that matter, the analogous Japanese scheme—becomes somewhat complicated. The overall ceilings are subdivided by another type of limitation, referred to in the legal texts as the "maximum amount," more commonly called the "buffer" (*butoir*), and intended to prevent the *most competitive* developing-country beneficiaries from preempting the entire amount within the ceiling. The buffer limit is in principle set at 50 percent of the ceiling, but for most sensitive, many quasi-sensitive, and some nonsensitive goods it is only 20 or 30 percent. From the standpoint of the major suppliers (most frequently Yugoslavia or Hong Kong) this is an important restrictive factor, but it greatly liberalizes the scheme for all the other countries. When a major supplier runs into the buffer and his preference is withdrawn, the minor suppliers may well find themselves enjoying an open-ended situation, i.e., they may be able to obtain the benefit of the preference for all the exports they can reasonably expect to supply, depending in part on the amount of the trade historically accounted for by the major suppliers.

If one accepts the competitive-need criterion, the ceiling-*cum*-buffer combination of constraints has reasonable justification, although it significantly reduces the real scope of GSP as compared with the preferential access obtainable by countries having special-preference arrangements. However, the EEC Council—acting against the strong recommendations of the commission—chose to superimpose yet a third automatic safeguard. Allegedly based on the principle of equitable "burden-sharing" among member states, this action further increased the complexity, restrictiveness, and especially the uncertainty of the system.

Recall that the ceilings on sensitive-list goods are enforced by formal tariff-quota procedures. Customarily, tariff quotas are allocated to the EEC member states according to estimated import needs, but a special community reserve is kept available to balance out shortfalls and surpluses and thereby equalize conditions of access throughout the Common Market. In the case of

GSP, however, an arbitrary allocation was made for each product according to the following percentage "key": Germany 37.5 percent; France 27.1; Italy 20.3; and Benelux 15.1. No provision was made for a Community reserve, although the foregoing allocations bear no relationship either to historic import shares or to prospective demand for the specific sensitive-list products.[1] Moreover, the direct-consignment provision in the rules of origin applied by the Community—if literally enforced—would inhibit the diversion of particular shipments from one member state to another whereby surpluses and deficits in particular destination countries could be offset through operation of market forces within the Community.

It might be expected that this additional set of constraints would waste a major part of any "slack" remaining in the ceilings after application of the buffer rule. However, there is considerable overlap between the subquota wastage, and the buffer wastage. For example, exclusion from free entry of an excess of imports from Yugoslavia over a 30-percent buffer limit would probably in itself eliminate all or most of an excess of imports into Germany over the latter's subquota allocation. A more serious problem is the increased uncertainty facing individual developing-country exporters, who do not know which of the three automatic constraints will be triggered first: ceiling, buffer, or subquota.

Still more uncertainty has resulted from the procedures followed by EEC member states in administering their subquota allocations. Where, as in the Netherlands, a first-come-first-served procedure is traditionally followed, the race to get goods to the border in time introduces still more complexity. Where, as in Germany, the subquotas are largely allocated to established domestic traders according to their historical import requirements, there may be less uncertainty but the tariff quotas are, in effect, further compartmentalized.

Quantitative Restrictions (QRs) and the GSP

The three-way tariff-quota mechanism described above does not itself involve any nontariff barriers (NTBs). But for a number of items (mainly textiles and petroleum products), account must be taken of the way it interacts with—or is overriden by—more absolute quantitative limitations on imports. These may be either those relatively few formal QRs still imposed unilaterally by EEC member states, or the so-called voluntary quotas agreed to bilaterally under self-restraint agreements (see Chapter 5).

Reservation of the GSP free-entry privilege for cotton textiles to signatories of the GATT Long-Term Arrangement operates as an incentive for other developing countries to subscribe to similar commitments with respect to export

---

[1] Indeed, in a number of cases there was a substantial underallocation to Germany and Benelux and overallocation to France and Italy—countries that could be expected to show particular reluctance to admit incremental competitive imports.

quantities and prices. Moreover, GSP treatment of jute and coir products has been withheld by the EEC in an effort to induce India and Pakistan to conclude new bilateral agreements regulating these fibers at the processed level. Such carrot-and-stick manipulation of the GSP to extend the scope of NTBs is clearly a perverse effect of the preferences from the standpoint of a liberal world trade order in general, and of the broad interests of developing countries in particular. However, despite the inherent contradiction between use of NTBs and the trade-expanding objective of generalized preferences, those individual developing countries (such as India) which are uncompetitive in cotton textiles and clothing relative to such suppliers as Hong Kong and Taiwan and benefit from remission of tariffs because this permits them to utilize their bilateral quotas more fully, provided that they have the institutional capability (through export cartelization) to "capture" the price advantage.

Open-Ended vs. Closed-Ended Tariff Quotas

It has been shown that the available opportunities for duty-free access for a given product during a given period of time under the EEC GSP scheme may be limited in four different ways: by the overall ceiling, by the operation of the buffer rule, by the allocation of subquotas to the member states, and by existing and emerging NTBs. The net tariff-quota availability, after taking account of these four potential constraints, may be larger or smaller than the trade flow that would be expected to occur subject to regular MFN duties. For convenience, we describe the *net* tariff quotas as "open-ended" or "closed-ended."

If the main purpose of GSP is considered to be the provision of an incentive for incremental expansion of trade, we are mainly concerned with the existence or nonexistence of a price incentive at the margin. With open-ended quotas there is room for trade expansion. The usual analysis of preference effects, based on the size of the margin of preference and on the price elasticity of import demand and of export supply, is applicable. On the other hand, many tariff quotas are clearly closed-ended and there is no marginal slack for a GSP-induced expansion of trade.

Even if there is no marginal incentive for expansion of trade, the fact that no tariff is collected within a closed-end quota may still be advantageous to the beneficiary supplying countries, if the foregone tariff is transferred through higher export proceeds that are effectively repatriated. The extent to which this will occur would appear to depend on the respective bargaining power and expectations of the EEC importing firms. On the other hand, if the importers are in an oligopolistic position and the exporters are competing with each other (which in many instances is the likely configuration), there appears to be little scope for effective transfer of the foregone tariff and considerable likelihood that it will be captured as windfall profit by the importers—especially when it is uncertain whether particular shipments will in fact benefit from free entry.

With respect to sensitive goods, which are subject to strict tariff-quota procedures applied separately by the member states and to the additional uncertainty as to the triggering of the subquota constraint, it is quite dubious whether any benefit will in fact accrue to the beneficiaries. The special documentation requirements with respect to rules of origin, especially the direct-consignment rule, make it still more difficult for the developing countries to obtain the margin of preference. It may also be noted that both the German system, whereby GSP subquotas are allocated largely on the basis of historical shares of established importers, and the Dutch system, based on the first come-first served "greyhound" procedure, appear to contribute to this result: the former by directly encouraging oligopsonistic market power for the importers and the latter by augmenting uncertainty and perhaps also by favoring large firms holding stocks in bond or en route. The importers might conceivably divide their windfall profit with the overseas exporters, who in turn might repatriate it, but such an outcome would depend more on altruism than on economic incentives.

We thus conclude that, both from the standpoint of encouraging incremental imports from beneficiary countries and from the standpoint of transferring the foregone tariffs, it is important the quotas be open-ended. To calculate which products and which countries of origin will enjoy open-ended opportunities involves case-by-case analysis, but certain generalizations are possible. Sensitive goods from traditional suppliers usually face a closed-end situation, and their margins of preference offer little if any benefit to the supplying countries. Nonsensitive goods from nontraditional suppliers will probably obtain a real advantage. Depending on the margin of preference and the elasticities, the price differential may be sufficient to justify export-promotion efforts and even induce investment in the developing countries for manufacture of the affected products.

The Scheme in Perspective

We have emphasized the obviously negative aspects of the EEC GSP scheme: the complexity, the uncertainty, and the way in which the multiple system of safeguards has rendered the preferences meaningless for many if not most of the existing dutiable products from the beneficiaries. Indeed, the worst feature of the scheme is that it gives the impression of being an ingenious exercise in bad faith. The Community has tried to show generosity by avoiding an explicit exceptions list for industrial goods, but political pressures forced it to overcompensate, in effect preventing the preferences from stimulating *any* imports of goods already competitive enough to be considered sensitive by domestic pressure groups in a given member state. Similarly, it has tried to avoid excluding a priori such strong exporters as Hong Kong and Yugoslavia, but at the same time has kept them from using their preferences where their most characteristic export products are concerned.

Nevertheless, there *are* a large number of potential exports that are not at present considered sensitive and for which the system, even as now operated, can give substantial incentives for new market penetration and diversification by developing countries. For these incentives to be effective, they first have to be recognized, then the potential suppliers will have to be identified, and finally the potential suppliers will have to take positive complementary measures on their side. Many of the quotas likely to be open-ended are in such categories as chemicals and machinery and transport equipment where trade has heretofore been predominant among industrial countries. Developing countries already possessing a substantial industrial base (e.g., Mexico, Brazil, and India) can find a large market for subcontracted components and labor-intensive processing for the engineering industries—e.g., auto and cycle parts, pumps and gauges, machine tools, business machines, and so forth. In most cases, this requires close collaboration with firms already having established market positions in Europe. The latter, for their part, may have to liberalize their own restrictive business arrangements. In the context of continued scarcity of manpower in Europe and recent trends toward "worldwide-sourcing" activities of multinational firms, the available margins of preference—of the order of 8 to 15 percent—appear to be sufficient to offset transport costs and to stimulate important new trade flows.

However, the EEC GSP scheme will have to be substantially liberalized in the future to forestall the disappointment and recrimination that seem inevitable once the developing countries fully appreciate the extent of its present shortcomings. Much improvement is possible, even within the framework of the existing scheme, if measures such as the following are taken: (1) abolition of the arbitrary and large-redundant suballocation of tariff quotas as among the member states; (2) more flexible application of the rules of origin; (3) elimination from the sensitive and quasi-sensitive lists of a number of items that appear to have been so classed mainly for reasons of restrictive business practices rather than because of the impact of imports on local employment; and (4) raising the total ceilings by updating the reference year for the basic element of the ceiling and by reducing the present three-year time-lag for calculation of the supplementary element.

Meaningful U.S. implementation of generalized preferences would make it easier for the Community to make such reforms and thereby—hopefully—prevent the whole GSP experiment from falling into disrepute. The most likely alternative to GSP is not a "return" to a mythical state of universal nondiscrimination in trade, but rather an intensification of tendencies toward preferential systems of the spheres-of-influence type. The United States has perhaps the most to lose and the least to gain from a process of bilateral bargaining of reciprocal preferences. Countries to the South will not forever be inhibited from using access to their own markets as leverage in playing off the rival blocs of the industrialized countries. The United States, particularly, cannot afford to relinquish its share of the joint responsibility for the viability of the broader approach embodied in the GSP.

Notes

1. "Communauté Financière Africaine." Formerly "Colonies Françaises d'Afrique."

2. For descriptions of the Franc Zone arrangements, see: "The CFA Franc System," International Monetary Fund *Staff Papers*, 10 (November 1963), pp. 345-96; André De Lattre, *Politique Economique de la France depuis 1945* (Paris: Sirey, 1966), pp. 406-32; annual reports on *La Zone Franc* published by the Comité Monétaire de la Zone Franc; and Secretariat of the UN Economic Commission for Europe, *Implications for Trade and Development of Developing Countries of Economic Groupings of Developed Countries and/or Preferential Trading Arrangements* (UNCTAD document E/Conf. 46/31, 3 February 1964), paras. 53-68.

3. De Lattre, *Politique Economique*, p. 409; J.P. Agarwal, *Die Assoziierung der Uberseeischen Staaten und Gebiete mit der EWG und die Auswirkung dieser Assoziierung auf die Ausfuhr der nicht assoziierten Entwicklungsländer in dieser Gemeinschaft*, Kieler Studie Nr. 77 (Tubingen: Mohr, 1966), p. 10, Table 5.

4. De Lattre, *Politique Economique*, p. 408.

5. For an analysis of the market-organization measures affecting major tropical products, see E/Conf. 46/31, 3 February 1964, Annex I.

6. See Gerard Curzon, *Multilateral Commercial Diplomacy*: The General Agreement on Tariffs and Trade and Its Impact on National Commercial Policies and Techniques (New York: Frederick A. Praeger, 1965), p. 280; and Gardner Patterson, "Would Tariff Preferences Help Economic Development?" *Lloyds Bank Review*, no. 76 (April 1965), p. 238.

7. Based on an UNCTAD memorandum cited by Richard Senti, "Africkanische Präferezen zugunsten der EWG," *Aussenwirtschaft* (December 1970), p. 249.

8. Ibid., p. 432 fn.

9. Ibid., pp. 441-442.

10. *Opinion on the Applications for Membership received from the United Kingdom, Ireland, Denmark, and Norway* (EEC Commission document COM (67) 750, 29 September 1967), para. 165.

11. For a full account, see J. Costonis, "The Association with Nigeria," in *L'Association a la Communauté Economique Européenne* (Brussels: Institute d'Etudes Européennes, 1970), pp. 215-317.

12. See Horst Schmidt-Ohlendorf, "L'Association avec les Etats de l'Afrique de L'Est," in ibid., pp. 319-52.

13. "Mauritius auf dem Weg zur EWG-Assoziierung," *Neue Zürcher Zeitung* (13 March 1972).

14. SEC (71) 2700 Final, 27 July 1971, section 2.

15. See Antonio Alonso and Camilo Barcia, *El Acuerdo España-Mercado Comun* (Madrid: Asociacion para el Progreso de la Direccion, 1970), pp. 5-79.

16. *Neue Zürcher Zeitung*, 31 July 1970.

17. Ibid., 24 April 1972.

18. Gunther Ruff and Associates, *The Preferential Agreements between the European Economic Community and Tunisia, Morocco, Spain, and Israel: Implications for U.S. Commodity Exports* (Unclassified study, U.S. Department of State, Bureau of Intelligence and Research, RECS-12, July 19, 1971), p. 1.

19. Ruff and Associates (ibid.) estimate the maximum U.S. trade displacement in the EEC market as a result of the four agreements, as of the mid-70s to be about 1 to 2 percent.

20. *Possible Lines of Action for Latin America in Its Trade Relations with the Developed Areas* (ECLA document E/CN.12/910, 2 April 1971), p. 7. Six addressed a memorandum to the Latin American governments.

21. EEC Commission, *Cinquème Raport Genéral* (Brussels: EEC, 1972), para. 473. It would, *inter alia* "seek non-preferential formulas with a view to increasing and diversifying their trade, without prejudice to the advantages the Communities will give in the framework of generalized preferences."

22. Economic Commission for Latin America, *Latin America and the Third Session of UNCTAD* (UN ECOSOC document E/CN.12/932, 13 April 1972), p. 30, English text.

23. See David Wall, "The International Banana Market," *Journal of Economic Studies*, 3 no. 3/4 (December 1968), pp. 45-61. Similar conclusions were reached in unpublished studies by the UNCTAD Secretariat, *which could not be accused* of bias favoring special preferences.

24. Sidney Weintraub, *Trade Preferences for Less-Developed Countries* (New York: Frederick A. Praeger, 1967), pp. 39-41.

25. See *Latin American Development and Western Hemisphere Trade* (Hearings before the Subcommittee on Inter-American Relationships of the Joint Economic Committee of the United States Congress, September 8-10, 1965), pp. 170, 211-19, 220-28, cited and discussed by Weintraub, *Trade Preferences* pp. 44-46, 160-64; Carlos Lleras Restropo, *Comercio Internacional* (Medellin: Editorial Bedout, 1965), pp. 278-79. The personalities involved included Jacob Javitz, Will Clayton, Thomas Mann, and Roberto Campos.

26. See George W. Ball, "The Open System in North-South Relations," Department of State Press Release no. 156, April 9, 1964.

27. George W. Ball, *The Discipline of Power* (Boston: Little Brown & Co., 1968), pp. 240-42.

28. "The capacity to manage through negotiation of each specific economic issue which arises must be limited. There has to be some means of cutting through the complexity. This puts a high priority on finding generalized procedures and rules which can be internationally defended, not just to satisfy other nations but also to help manage affairs internally." Harald B. Malmgren, "Managing International Economic Conflicts," in *Annals of International Studies*, vol. 3 (Geneva: Association des anciens etudiants de l'Institut Universitaire de Hautes Etudes Internationales, 1972), p. 194.

29. Article XXXVI, 8 of the General Agreement, added in 1964.

30. Brasseur was speaking as a Belgian delegate, but his proposal closely coincided with French views and with the dominant views in the EEC Commission. Other member states had not yet concerted their positions. See Weintraub, *Trade Preferences*, p. 152; Patterson, "World Tariff Preferences," pp. 361-62.

31. Although the French supported the main lines of the Brasseur proposal, in their view "the negotiation of a preference system should involve the granting of reciprocal concessions." Quoted by Weintraub, *Trade Preferences*, p. 148.

32. See Harry G. Johnson, *Economic Policies toward Developing Countries*.

33. Report of the Second Committee, in *Trade and Development: Final Act and Report, Proceedings*, vol. I (1964), para. 56.

34. *The Australian System of Tariff Preferences for Developing Countries* (Canberra: Department of Trade and Industry, 1969), p. 2.

35. Ibid.

36. P.J. Lloyd, "The Value of Tariff Preferences for the Developing Countries: Australian Experience," *Economic Record* (March 1971), pp. 1-16.

37. See UNCTAD document TD/B/AC.5/24.Add. 1 (10 November 1969), and EEC Commission document SEC (71) 1000 final (15 March 1971), sec. A. 3.

38. "Agreed conclusions of the Special Committee on Preferences," in *Report of the Special Committee on Preferences on the Second Part of its Fourth Session*, 21 September-12 October 1970.

39. See Christopher K. Clague, "The Trade Effects of Tariff Preferences," *Southern Economic Journal*, 38 no. 3 (January 1972), p. 389.

40. See U.S. Submission in UNCTAD document TD/B/AC.5/34/Add.5/Rev. 1, 24 September 1970.

41. See Japanese Submission in UNCTAD document TD/B/373/Add. 7/Annex (Japan), 12 August 1971.

42. See *A System of Preferences for Exports of Manufactures and Semimanufactures from Developing to Developed Countries*; Report by the UNCTAD Secretariat (TD/B/C.2/AC. 1/7, of 31 May 1967), para. 63.

43. See "Report by the Secretary-General of the Conference," in *Trade and Development: Policy Statements* (UNCTAD Proceedings, vol. II, 1964), pp. 37-38; TD/B/C.2/AC.1/7, 31 May 1967, paras. 113-22.

44. Statements of the delegates of Chile, Pakistan, and Mexico in the third meeting of the Second Committee, UNCTAD III, Santiago, 20 April 1972.

45. "Report of the Secretary-General," pp. 38-39.

46. *The Question of the Granting and Extension of Preferences in Favour of Developing Countries* (TD/12, 1 November 1967, pp. 2-3).

47. Richard N. Cooper, "The European Community's System of Generalized Preferences: A Critique," *Center Discussion Paper no. 132* (New Haven: Economic Growth Center, Yale University, November 1971), p. 3.

14 The Evolving Policy on East-West Trade

Thomas A. Wolf and
Robert G. Hawkins

As a result of the hardening of cold war attitudes and the imposition by the United States of severe controls on East-West trade in the late 1940s and early 1950s, American trade with the Socialist countries of Eastern Europe and Asia fell dramatically from its prewar and immediate postwar levels.[a] From prewar trade turnover (exports plus imports) of $310 million (1938) and immediate postwar annual turnover of $622 million (1947-49), U.S. trade with these countries fell to a postwar low of $48 million in 1953. While gradual relaxation of some of these restrictions and a thawing of cold war attitudes helped to raise this trade to $225 million annually by 1959-61 and further to $547 million annually in 1969-71, the level of U.S. commerce with the East still remained below that of the early postwar period.

The very minor role of the United States in East-West trade has until recently been a neglected subject of research. The purpose of this study is to help rectify this neglect by summarizing and elucidating the major trends and economic policy issues concerning U.S. participation in East-West commerce, and attempting to establish some useful guidelines for future East-West trade policy-making. In the following section the evolution of U.S. East-West trade policies over the past twenty-five years is outlined, indicating some of the changing political and economic factors influencing these policies. In the second section we briefly describe the basic structure of and trends in East-West commerce, in which the United States is still such a minor participant. In the third part the available empirical evidence on the economic impact of U.S. restrictions on trade with the Socialist countries is summarized. Finally, in a concluding section, we examine the basic alternatives facing East-West trade policy makers in the 1970s in the light of our earlier discussion.

The authors gratefully acknowledge the helpful comments of Ingo Walter on earlier versions, and the research assistance of Sita Ram Mohan.

[a]For purposes of this chapter the Socialist countries of Eastern Europe and Asia consist of Albania, Bulgaria, Czechoslovakia, East Germany, Hungary, Poland, Rumania, and the Soviet Union (Eastern Europe) and North Korea, the People's Republic of China, and North Vietnam (Asia). Cuba is consistently excluded from our discussion, as is Yugoslavia, which has been treated by U.S. trade policy basically as a "Western" country since the late 1940s. Unless otherwise specified, the terms "Socialist countries," "Eastern countries" and "the East" are interchangeable in meaning throughout this study.

Evolution of U.S. East-West Trade Policies

The National Security Context

The postwar policy of the "containment" of communism was in direct response to perceived belligerence and expansionist tendencies of the Soviet Union and the Communist movement in general, exemplified by the Berlin Blockade of 1948-49, the Communist takeovers in Czechoslovakia in 1948 and China in 1949 and the outbreak of the Korean War in 1950. Increasingly the Socialist countries came to be characterized in the West as an aggressive and monolithic "Sino-Soviet bloc." As a complement to military containment, the system of U.S. trade controls which began to evolve in the 1948-51 period had as their purpose (a) to deprive the Socialist world of military and strategic economic goods, thereby hindering Communist expansionism, and (b) to attempt, by various means, to keep the Eastern countries as economically weak and vulnerable as possible, in the hope that this would encourage internal rebellion and independence of the presumed "satellite" countries from the Soviet Union.[1]

Given the basic assumptions underlying the policy of containment, the evolving heavy blanket of restrictions on trade with the East made eminent sense in theory. The United States emerged from the War with the greatest intact productive capacity in the world, while many of the other nations, both East and West, had suffered grievous damage to their economies. Furthermore, the Western Allies of the United States desperately needed protection against the threats of Communist aggression, and also required massive economic aid in the reconstruction of their economies. There was, therefore, a certain willingness of the Western Allies to cooperate with the restrictive trade policies of the United States. In addition, there seemed to be evidence that the war-torn Eastern economies could not withstand massive economic sanctions imposed by the West. A glimpse at the map and at present day international power realities, however, should serve to dispel any illusions that these necessary preconditions in the East were in fact met.[2]

Maximum Economic Warfare, 1948-60

The United States had left intact many of its World War II trade controls after the fighting ended, principally for "short supply" and various foreign policy reasons. As the cold war intensified in 1948-49, these controls were broadened in relation to the Socialist world, first under authority of amended World War II legislation, and later with the adoption of the Export Control Act of 1949. In addition to the "short supply" and "foreign policy" rationales for export controls, this act directed the president to "exercise the necessary vigilance over exports from the standpoint of their significance to national security."[3] Actual administration of the act was delegated to a division of the Commerce Department, now the Office of Export Control, although a continuing system of consultation was established with other interested federal agencies and departments. The control authorities established a compendium of export regulations which effectively separated all goods into two categories. Products deemed clearly nonstrategic were allowed to be exported under open general license; no application for official approval was necessary. All other products and technical information of a strategic nature required a validated license for export. Furthermore, the export of technical data and reexports of certain products from other non-Socialist countries were also brought under control. In this way the number of leakages in the control system were at least theoretically minimized.

The other basic means by which the economic isolation of the Eastern countries could be assured was to press for multilateral Western controls over trade in strategic products and technical data. Early U.S. efforts to negotiate this isolation of the Communist world led to the formation of COCOM (Coordinating Committee of the Consultative Group) in 1950. This group is now composed of fourteen of the fifteen NATO countries (Iceland excluded) and Japan. Each item on the COCOM list of embargoed exports to the Socialist countries must be agreed to unanimously by the COCOM members, and exceptions to the embargo likewise must receive unanimous approval.

While the basic thrust of this cooperative embargo was in military goods, nonmilitary products of strategic importance were also included. The "Battle Act" of 1951, the U.S. legislative underpinning for American participation in COCOM, specifically provided for the embargo of strategic nonmilitary goods. The Battle Act also contained a provision which required termination of all "military, economic or financial assistance to any nation" which "knowingly permits" the shipment to the Communist countries of any of the goods subject to embargo under authority of this act.[4]

The United States also supplemented the multilateral control procedures established under COCOM through issuance of the Transaction Control Regulations in 1953. These regulations prohibit, except under specific license, any person within the United States, and foreign firms controlled by such persons, from purchasing or selling or arranging the purchase or sale of COCOM-controlled goods located outside the U.S. for ultimate delivery to the Socialist world. Obtaining credit in connection with such a transaction is also forbidden. These regulations are enforced by the Treasury Department, Office of Foreign Assets Control, and are issued under the authority of the Trading with the Enemy Act (1917), as amended in 1933.[5]

As a result of the COCOM arrangement, the Transactions Control Regulations and the sanctions threatened under the Battle Act, the United States was at least in principal able to totally isolate the Socialist countries with respect to an inner core of military and strategic nonmilitary goods. Furthermore, the United States maintained unilateral control over an additional list of products for which it was not able to obtain the unanimous consent of its COCOM allies to control on a multilateral basis.

Consistent with such a massive policy of economic warfare on the export side would have been an import policy designed to minimize foreign exchange earnings of the Socialist countries. Presumably a general embargo on imports from this region, with the exception of goods sorely needed by the West and only available in the East, would have satisfied this objective. Instead, a section was added to the Trade Agreements Extension Act of 1951 (which incidentally was an important legislative step in the participation of the United States in the postwar multilateral trade liberalization negotiations under the aegis of GATT), which had the effect of withdrawing most-favored-nation (MFN) treatment from U.S. imports from the Socialist countries. Section 5 of this act directed the president to "suspend, withdraw or prevent the application" of MFN treatment to "imports from the Union of Soviet Socialist Republics and to imports from any nation or area dominated or controlled by the foreign government or foreign organization controlling the world Communist movement."[6] The motivations for this particular legislation were not simple national security considerations; they appeared to also include protectionist and ideological motivations, and reflected as well the historic congressional preoccupation with *tariff rates* on imports.[7]

Revoking MFN treatment for the target socialist countries meant that they were to be denied the tariff concessions agreed to by the United States in reciprocal trade agreements negotiated over the period since enactment of the Reciprocal Trade Agreements Act in 1934. The new tariff rates for these countries, referred to as the "Column 2" duties, approximated the generally higher duties prescribed by the Hawley-Smoot Tariff Act of 1930.

Other restrictions were also placed upon U.S. commerce with the East in this early period. Private capital and credit flows to the East were implicitly prohibited by the Johnson Act, enacted in 1934 to protect American investors against aggressive peddling in the United States of uncreditworthy foreign securities. The act prohibited new loans or any type of credit extension to governments still in default on obligations to U.S. citizens.[8] This implicitly meant an embargo on anything but very short-term export credit to all the Communist countries, with the exception of Yugoslavia, which is a member of the IMF and the World Bank (which earns exemption from Johnson Act coverage), and Albania and Bulgaria, which had no outstanding defaulted debt to the United States.

From an early point there was some discrimination among the communist-controlled countries by U.S. foreign economic policy. With the onset of the Korean War in 1950, the United States slapped a virtual embargo on all trade, both exports and imports, with North Korea and the People's Republic of China. This embargo was implemented by issuance in 1950 of the Foreign Assets

Control Regulations under the authority of the Trading with the Enemy Act mentioned earlier.[9]

Emerging Policy Differentiation, 1960-64

After a full decade of East-West trade restrictions, small steps towards greater U.S. differentiation among the Eastern countries began to occur. They were distinguished from the foregoing discrimination against China and North Korea by virtue of the fact that they were trade *liberalizing* actions. The basis for this more flexible policy stance seems at least two-fold. First, several of the Eastern European Soviet "satellites" were beginning to strike foreign policy postures which ever so slightly deviated from the Soviet line. Secondly, the abortive Hungarian revolution in 1956 and the change of regimes in Poland the same year hinted at a need for the Eastern Europeans to undertake internal economic reforms. In the West a new way of thinking began to develop. It was now believed that preferential economic treatment and increased economic ties with the Eastern European "satellite" countries might encourage them to pursue more independent foreign policies ("polycentrism"), as well as to stimulate internal economic reforms which, it was believed, would inevitably affect the internal political system as well.[b] Indiscriminate "containment" was now to be replaced with a cautious, delicate policy of "building bridges" to the East.[10]

Poland, which had been allowed to purchase U.S. cereal grains in a limited measure under the PL 480 program in the late fifties, was the first beneficiary of this more discriminating policy. While Congress had proscribed denial of MFN in the 1951 legislation to all nations "dominated or controlled by the foreign government or foreign organization controlling the world Communist movement," it left with the president the discretion as to determining which such countries were in fact so dominated. The president made the determination in late 1960 that Poland was not Soviet-dominated within the meaning of the 1951 legislation.

On the export side, selective "decontrolling" of various exports to Poland was begun as early as 1958. This practice was extended to Rumania in 1964, when that country began to pursue a more independent foreign policy.[11] Although there was a very definite Sino-Soviet split in 1960-61, with the Soviet Union drastically reducing its trade and aid to China, no such preferential treatment was extended to the People's Republic of China. In fact, the harsher controls applying to the Asiatic Communist countries remained, and were extended to North Vietnam during the period 1961-64.[12]

---

[b]The earliest case of policy-making predicted upon the "polycentrism" concept related to Yugoslavia, which began to show her independence from the dominant bloc country, the Soviet Union, as early as 1948, as a result of which she was expelled from the Cominform. U.S. policy makers made the decision at that time to treat Yugoslavia more or less as a "Western" country as far as trade relations were concerned.

Another important sign of the increased flexibility of the executive branch was the negotiation of the massive U.S. wheat exports to the Soviet Union in late 1963 and 1964. Unfortunately, however, this transaction was only made possible by virtue of a presidential concession to vocal anti-Communist groups on the "cargo preference" issue. Arguing out of a mixture of national security, protectionist and ideological motives, the dockworkers unions were unwilling to load the scheduled wheat shipments to the Soviet Union unless a provision was made that at least 50 percent of all such cargoes were carried by uncompetitive U.S. flag carriers. Anxious to complete the transaction, President Kennedy authorized a modification to the export control regulations to that effect, which became the rule for all future potential grain deals.

Ironically, just at the time that the administration was taking small steps towards selectively reducing the barriers to U.S. trade with the East, Congress was passing legislation which was meant to limit presidential discretion in this regard. In the course of the 1950s the Soviet Union and its presumed satellites had narrowed the margin of military superiority enjoyed by the United States and its NATO allies. At the same time, these Socialist countries were also demonstrating an ability to realize rapid economic growth, and Soviet spokesmen were beginning to put forth the prediction that they would in a short time surpass the United States as the preeminent world economic power. These developments within the Socialist world contrasted with a period of relatively sluggish economic growth for the United States, which experienced three recessions within seven years. As the decade of the sixties opened, the Soviet boasts of future economic supremacy became more credible. Against this background, combined with growing U.S. balance of payments deficits and the heightened military-political tension between the United States and the Soviet Union in the early 1960s, Congress passed several important trade restrictive measures.

With respect to exports, Congress in a 1962 amendment to the Export Control Act of 1949 determined that the president should embargo the export not only of products having direct military significance, but also exports which might make "a significant contribution to the . . . *economic* potential of such nation or nations which would prove detrimental to the national security and welfare of the United States.[13] Although the Commerce Department, as the implementing body, claimed to take foreign availability of goods into consideration when making determinations on applications for validated licenses, it also made clear that the burden of proof was on the exporter, who must successfully argue that a product contributing significantly to the economic potential of one of the Communist countries was not detrimental to U.S. national security.[14]

The new congressional legislation on imports from the East was to have a more enduring impact on U.S. policy. The president's message accompanying the introduction of the proposed Trade Expansion Act of 1962, which authorized U.S. participation in the Kennedy Round trade negotiations, asked for continued discretionary authority with respect to the determinations under the 1951 legislation.[15] Despite this request, Congress proceeded to enact subsection 231(a) of the Trade Expansion Act, which removed the discretion of the president in the matter of MFN treatment, and required denial of MFN to "products whether imported directly or indirectly, of any country or areas dominated or controlled by Communism."[16] The administration urged Congress to permit Yugoslavia and Poland to continue to receive MFN treatment, however, and was finally successful in having Congress make an amendment (subsection 231(b)) to this act in 1963 which preserved MFN for just these two countries.[17]

Pressures for Change 1964-1971

Pressures for liberalization of the battery of U.S. East-West trade controls continued, however, in the second half of the 1960s, and in fact intensified. Nevertheless, as we shall see, trade-biased interests were not always in the ascendant. The question of an optimal trade policy for the Socialist countries became increasingly complicated by the escalation of the war in Vietnam.

The mounting liberalizing pressures were only in part caused by the continuing awareness of the possibilities for stimulating "polycentric" forces and internal reforms within Eastern Europe as a result of positive trade measures. Perhaps of greater importance were the increasing economic problems faced by the United States in the course of the 1960s, and a growing awareness that there is in fact a trade-off between national security and shortrun economic welfare considerations, and that perhaps the latter had been receiving all too little attention. Not only were government policy makers more interested in stimulating export expansion than ever before in the postwar period, because of continuing and growing balance of payments deficits. There was now a groundswell of opposition among exporters to the unilateral, extra-COCOM export controls and credit restrictions of the U.S. government. As we shall see in the third section, these unilateral restrictions effectively embargoed or severely curtailed large volumes of potential U.S. exports to the East over a twenty-year period. Furthermore, there existed the possibility that significant market footholds in rapidly growing Eastern markets were being given by default to competitors in allied countries. Indeed, throughout the period of Western economic warfare directed towards the East, but particularly in recent years as reconstruction was completed and the Allies looked more and more to export markets, most of the other Western industrialized countries were much more aggressive in pursuing economic relations with the East.

While there were periodical congressional hearings on East-West trade throughout the 1960s, as control legislation came up for extension or amendment, liberalization pressure from business groups and others interested in relaxed East-West trade controls really came to a climax in the 1968 and 1969 hearings concerned with the extension and modification of the Export Control Act of 1949 (as already amended). As a direct outcome of this congressional attention, the Export Administration Act of 1969 was enacted with the objective of replacing the emphasis on control with a stress on trade expansion.

While noting the need for export controls with respect to goods contributing to the military potential (the economic potential phrase was dropped) of certain foreign nations, this act explicitly warned that "the unwarranted restriction of exports from the United States has a serious adverse effect on our balance of payments," and that the uncertainty of the control procedures had discouraged exporters and thereby worked against the national objective of improving the balance of payments. Furthermore, the act stated that it should be an objective of trade policy to improve the U.S. market share in trade with the East, particularly vis-à-vis the share in this trade of other allied nations. The act directed the Commerce Department to make an early review of the commodity control list with a view to eliminating items which could no longer be deemed critical to the national security, to streamline its control procedures so as to minimize delays and uncertainty connected with the license approval process, and to maintain closer contact with the business community as to changes in control procedures. Finally, the executive was instructed to take into account foreign (Western) availability of the goods in question. Whenever "considerations of national security override considerations of foreign availability, the reasons for so doing shall be reported to the Congress in the quarterly report following the decision to require such licenses on that ground to the extent that considerations of national security and foreign policy permit. . . "[18]

In the meantime, however, and as a direct result of the then increasing involvement of the United States in the Vietnam conflict, Congress chose to apply certain economic sanctions against those nations aiding the North Vietnamese, which of course involved practically all of the Socialist countries in Eastern Europe and Asia. One of these actions was to remove presidential discretion with respect to PL 480 exports to the East. The new congressional restriction was contained in a section of the Food for Peace Act of 1966 as it amends PL 480. Section 103 of the latter act as amended now forbids PL 480 exports to any country trading with or transporting goods to North Vietnam or Cuba, with certain exceptions.[19] As a result, Poland and Yugoslavia, both of which trade with North Vietnam, are now ineligible for PL 480 sales.

The second congressional action hindering East-West trade dealt with the Export-Import Bank and its role in financing U.S. exports to the Socialist world. Legislation specifically embodying restrictions on Eximbank support of exports to the East actually dates from 1964, as a direct result of negotiations surrounding the massive wheat purchases from the United States in 1963-64. Following lengthy congressional debate, legislation was enacted which authorized Eximbank support (but not direct credits) to "any Communist country" *only* when the "President determines that such guarantees would be in the national interest and reports each such determination" to Congress within thirty days.[20] After passage of this legislation the president issued four such determinations permitting Eximbank support of exports of all "peaceful" products and services to Bulgaria, Czechoslovakia, Hungary, Poland, Rumania, and Yugoslavia, and exports of agricultural products to the Soviet Union. Between 1964 and 1968 about $145 million of export credit to these countries was supported by the Eximbank, over one-half involving exports to Yugoslavia.[21]

Early in 1968, Congress decided to impose a stricter series of restrictions on Eximbank's role in East-West trade; indeed the bank's activities were now to be effectively prohibited. The restrictions were incorporated in PL 90-267, which was an amendment to the Export-Import Bank Act of 1945 (as amended). Basically, this legislation removed presidential discretion in this area by prohibiting Eximbank support to any nation (a) engaged in "armed conflict" with the United States; (b) which furnishes "by direct government action" economic or military assistance to such a belligerent; and also in connection with the purchase by any nation of products or technical data "which is to be used principally by or in" nations falling within either (a) or (b).[22]

Accelerated interest in the deteriorating U.S. balance of payments situation in 1970-71, together with the winding down of the American involvement in Vietnam, made Congress increasingly receptive to proposals for returning to the president his basic discretion with regard to Eximbank credit support for exports to the East. This movement finally bore fruit in August 1971, in the Export Expansion Finance Act of 1971. The statute, aimed at stimulating the Eximbank's export-promoting role on many fronts, included a new amendment to the Export-Import Bank Act of 1945 which effectively prohibited presidential discretion only in the case of exports going directly or indirectly to a nation engaged in armed conflict with the United States.[23] In effect, this allows the president to make favorable determinations now with respect to all the nonbelligerent Eastern countries.

Greater awareness of the interdependence of export and import liberalization measures, particularly in the case of the Eastern countries which are short of convertible currencies, has led to renewed attempts by the executive and some congressmen to get Congress to return presidential discretion with respect to import barriers.[24] This fight has been made particularly difficult by the same economic forces which have facilitated more liberal export legislation; that is, the deteriorating U.S. balance-of-trade situation together with the highest unemployment figures in a decade have stirred up *protectionist* pressures on the import side as well as the trade-biased interests on the export side.

Trade Policy as a Signal

The decision in the late 1950s and early sixties to selectively liberalize trade restrictions for certain Eastern European countries may be interpreted as "signals" to these countries of the goodwill of the United States, and hints of future liberalizing actions which might follow upon foreign policy and/or internal reform initiatives undertaken by the other side. The expected "political" *quid pro quos* were never really clearly delineated, however, at least not publicly.

The Nixon administration's evolving economic policy vis-à-vis the People's Republic of China would seem, on the other hand, to have had a much more basic role as a "signalling" device; a means by which to indicate to that country, through small but tangible steps, that the United States wished to move away from the cold war confrontation of over twenty years and towards a "normalization" of relations with China.

Beginning with some minor measures relating to travelling to China and bringing back small quantities of Chinese goods in mid-1969, the administration proceeded to announce more and more significant liberalizations. Partial relaxation of the export embargo and a complete lifting of the import embargo were announced in June 1971. Just before his visit to Peking in February 1972, President Nixon authorized further "decontrolling" with respect to exports to the People's Republic of China, together with other changes in regulations. This meant that henceforth China would be treated on a par with the Soviet Union and most of the other Eastern European countries (Group Y for export control purposes; denial of MFN for imports).[25] Preferential treatment continued to be granted to Poland and Rumania, but in an inconsistent fashion. Rumania received more liberal export control supervision (Rumania–Group Q; Poland–Group W), while only Poland was accorded MFN. All trade with Cuba,[c] North Korea, and North Vietnam continued to be virtually embargoed.

Structure and Trends in East-West Trade

Of the five principal Western industrialized trading regions (the United States, the EEC, EFTA, Japan, and Canada), the United States ranks fourth in trade volume with the Socialist countries, just above Canada. Although the gross national product of the United States was over twice as high as the combined GNP of the six-member European Economic Community in 1969, total U.S. trade with the East amounted to less than 7 percent of EEC turnover with the East in that year.[26]

This result is not solely due to the traditionally higher reliance on trade of the European countries. The Eastern trade is much larger for these nations also as a proportion of all their foreign trade. In the 1967-9 period, trade with the Socialist countries amounted to only 0.6 percent of the total foreign trade of the United States. The other NATO countries as a group, however, transacted 4.3

---

[c]The Cuban embargo is implemented by means of the Cuban Assets Control Regulations (31 CFR 515.101-515.808), issued in 1963.

percent of their foreign trade with the East.[27] While there are obvious geographical and longstanding cultural and political reasons for Western Europe and Japan to have closer trading ties than the United States with the East, the fact remains that the relative position of the United States in this trade has on balance deteriorated in the postwar period. (This point will be covered in more detail in the next section.)

The geographical distribution of U.S. trade with the Socialist countries of Eastern Europe and Asia is summarized in Table 14-1. The almost nonexistent trade with the Socialist countries of Asia reflects the virtual embargo policy followed by the United States with respect to these countries since the Korean War. Poland and the Soviet Union are the principal Socialist trading partners of the United States. In the 1969-71 period Poland supplied almost one-half of U.S. imports from these countries, and purchased about one-fifth of U.S. exports to the East. The Soviet Union supplied one-quarter of U.S. imports and accounted for practically 40 percent of all American exports to this region. Rumania of late has also become a major U.S. export market in the East, taking about 15 percent of total U.S. exports. While the United States has a trade surplus with most Socialist countries, the trade balance with Poland has recently been consistently in deficit.

Table 14-1
U.S. Merchandise Trade with Individual Socialist Countries, 1969-71

	U.S. Exports		U.S. Imports		Trade Balance
	($ Millions)	%	($ Millions)	%	($ Millions)
Albania	a	–	0.3	0.1	(0.3)
Bulgaria	8.1	2.5	2.5	1.2	5.6
Czechoslovakia	25.2	7.7	23.9	11.0	1.3
East Germany	30.1	9.1	9.2	4.2	20.9
Hungary	21.2	6.4	6.0	2.8	15.2
Poland	65.3	19.7	101.0	46.5	(35.7)
Rumania	50.4	15.3	11.7	5.4	38.7
U.S.S.R.[b]	128.6	39.1	60.2	27.7	68.4
P. Rep. China	a	–	1.6	0.7	(1.6)
Outer Mongolia	a	–	1.2	0.6	(1.2)
North Korea	a	–	a	–	a
North Vietnam	a	–	a	–	a
Total[c]	328.9	100.0%	217.6	100.0%	111.3

aNegligible.
bIncludes Estonia and Latvia.
cColumns may not always add to exactly 100.0% because of rounding.
Source: Compiled from Secretary of Commerce, *Export Control* (Ninety-seventh Quarterly Report), Washington, D.C., 1971, p. 29.

American trade has played far too minor a role to be considered as representative of the major trends in East-West commerce. To obtain a satisfactory picture of the basic commodity composition of East-West trade and recent changes in this pattern, it is necessary to examine a broader group of countries. The East-West trade commodity structure of the OECD countries as a group is summarized in Table 14-2.[d] Exports and imports for each major product group are shown as a percentage of total exports to and imports from the Socialist countries of Eastern Europe (including the Soviet Union). The periods shown are 1963-4 and 1967-9, and the change between these periods is also indicated.

While OECD exports of food and live animals (SITC Division O) represented the second most important category in the earlier period (25.5 percent of total exports to the East), these products had slipped to fourth place (9.0 percent) by the late sixties.[e] On the other hand exports of various manufactured goods classified by materials (SITC 6), particularly paper, paperboard, textile yarn and fabrics, iron and steel, nonferrous metals and other metals manufactures, grew in importance in the second half of the 1960s, reaching 22.2 percent of total exports by the end of the period. Exports of miscellaneous manufactured articles (SITC 8), particularly clothing, footwear, and professional and scientific instruments, also grew significantly over this period, rising from 3.2 to 6.9 percent of total OECD exports to Eastern Europe. Most dramatic, however, was the increasing importance of machinery and transport equipment exports, particularly nonelectrical machinery of various types. While this category (SITC 7) accounted for 28.4 percent of total exports in 1963-4, its share by 1967-9 had risen to 38.9 percent; by far the most important export product of the OECD countries in trade with the East.

The pattern of OECD imports from Eastern Europe presents a quite different picture, which basically reflects the lower level of economic development and the greater raw material resources of the Eastern countries as a group. While the lower-numbered SITC divisions (0-3) became relatively less important in the Eastern export structure in the late 1960s, they continued to account for well over one-half of OECD imports from the East. Most important were the export of live animals, meat preparations, cereals and cereal preparations and fruit and vegetables among agricultural products (SITC O); wood, lumber, cork, textile fibers, crude fertilizers and metalliferous ores among crude materials (SITC 2); and coal, coke and petroleum and petroleum products among mineral fuels (SITC 3).

Manufactured goods classified by materials (SITC 6) increased in relative

---

[d]Actually these OECD calculations exclude trade figures for Japan. OECD statistics for that country were not published prior to 1964.

[e]The relative importance of agricultural products in OECD exports to Eastern Europe may be somewhat exaggerated for 1963-4, however, because of the large wheat sales by the U.S. to the Soviet Union in those two years.

importance in Eastern exports during this period, becoming the single most important category by 1967-9 (21.4 percent). Most significant in this group were exports of textile yarn and fabrics, nonmetallic mineral manufactures, iron and steel and nonferrous metals. While Eastern exports of machinery increased as a proportion of total exports in the late sixties (from 7.8 percent to 8.7 percent), they still represented a minor segment of the westward flow of trade to the industrialized countries.

Table 14-2

Commodity Structure of OECD[b] Trade with the Socialist Countries of Eastern Europe (Percentage of Total Trade)

SITC Commodity Division	Exports			Imports		
	(1963/64)	(1967/69)	Change	(1963/64)	(1967/69)	Change
0 Food and live animals	25.5%	9.0%	(16.5)%	20.8%	19.2%	(1.6)%
1 Beverages and tobacco	2.3	1.7	(0.6)	1.0	0.8	(0.2)
2 Crude materials except fuels	9.8	7.9	(1.9)	22.3	19.3	(3.0)
3 Petroleum and other mineral fuels	0.5	0.5	–	18.7	17.3	(1.4)
4 Organic oils and fats	1.1	0.4	(0.7)	1.0	1.9	0.9
5 Chemicals	10.3	12.5	2.2	5.4	5.8	0.4
6 Mfgd. goods, classified by material	19.4	22.2	2.8	17.9	21.4	3.5
7 Machinery and equipment	28.4	38.9	10.5	7.8	8.7	0.9
71 Nonelectrical	18.1	26.7	8.6	4.7	4.6	(0.1)
72 Electrical	4.8	6.3	1.5	1.2	1.6	0.4
73 Transport equipment	5.4	5.9	0.4	1.9	2.5	0.6
8 Misc. Mfgd. goods	3.2	6.9	3.7	5.3	5.7	0.4
Total excluding SITC 9)[a]	100.0%	100.0%	–	100.0%	100.0%	–

[a]Columns may not always add to 100.0% because of rounding.

[b]Japan's trade is excluded from this presentation because OECD trade statistics for Japan are not available prior to 1964.

Source: Compiled from OECD *Commodity Trade Statistics* (Series C), Paris. Various Issues, 1963-69.

Although the different structures of OECD exports to and imports from Eastern Europe have been changing, with agricultural products and crude materials becoming relatively less important on both sides, the general pattern persists. This may be characterized as a large two-way trade in various semimanufactured materials, ranging from textile yarns to various metals; a very large Western export market for machinery; and the typical pattern of exports from less developed to the more developed areas, namely, sizable Eastern exports of agricultural products and various crude materials, including fuel, to the industrialized West.

One would not expect the structure of United States trade with the Socialist countries to be necessarily similar, particularly given the distorting effect of the wide array of restrictions placed upon trade with the East. For comparability with the results of Table 14-2, a profile of U.S. trade with the East in one year, 1968, is provided in Table 14-3.

The pattern of U.S. exports to Eastern Europe was weighted much more heavily towards agricultural and various crude materials (particularly hides, skins and furskins, pulp and waste paper, and textile fibers), than were OECD exports.

Table 14-3
Commodity Structure of U.S. Trade with the Socialist Countries of Eastern Europe, 1968

SITC Commodity Division	Exports		Imports	
	($ Millions)	%	($ Millions)	%
0 Food and live animals	78.5	36.8	52.2	26.5
1 Beverages and tobacco	3.8	1.8	0.8	0.4
2 Crude materials except fuels	53.0	24.7	23.7	12.0
3 Petroleum and other mineral fuels	2.2	1.0	1.6	0.8
4 Organic oils and fats	4.2	2.0	0.1	—
5 Chemicals	25.8	12.0	8.4	4.3
6 Mfgd. goods, classified by material	7.0	3.3	81.0	41.1
7 Machinery and equipment	33.0	15.4	9.1	4.6
71 Nonelectrical	26.0	12.1	6.8	3.5
72 Electrical	6.2	2.9	0.5	0.3
73 Transport equipment	0.8	0.4	1.9	1.0
8 Misc. mfgd. goods	7.8	3.6	20.2	10.2
Total (excluding SITC 9)[a]	215.3	100.0	197.1	100.0

[a]Columns may not always add to 100.0% because of rounding.

Source: Compiled from OECD, *Commodity Trade Statistics*, (Series C), Paris, 1968.

Machinery and transport equipment sales, normally a very important part of U.S. exports, represented only 15.4 percent of U.S. sales to Eastern Europe. As will be argued later, this principally reflects the very serious impact which unilateral U.S. export controls have had on an historically important area of American competitive advantage, machinery and equipment.

On the import side, the United States purchased over two-thirds of its imports from Eastern Europe in two product groupings: agricultural products (SITC 0) and manufactured goods classified by material (SITC 6). Particularly significant were various meat and meat preparations (Polish hams being a perennial U.S. favorite), and iron and steel, nonferrous metals and various nonmetallic manufactures. Also important relative to the pattern of OECD imports were imports of various manufactured articles such as furniture, footwear, and other finished goods, often from the smaller countries of Eastern Europe (SITC 8: 10.2 percent versus 5.7 percent for the OECD as a group).

A statistical profile of commodity trade between East and West is probably becoming less and less reliable, however, as the sole guide to changing patterns of East-West commerce. This is because of the increasing role of "technology transfer" in East-West commerce, which is not always directly tied to the export of specific materials or machinery. While this in one sense is merely a reflection of the general phenomenon of technology transfer to be found on a worldwide basis, it is attaining special importance in East-West trade because of the Eastern countries' massive need for new technology to boost lagging productivity and to improve their export competitiveness, while at the same time having to deal with severe shortages of foreign exchange brought on by the inconvertibility of their currencies. At the same time, Western governments and businessmen are gradually obtaining more expertise in the various forms of technology transfer to the East, and in many cases are finding it to be a definite complement to, substitute for, and in some cases a prerequisite for, increased exports of machinery and other products embodying the latest technological advances.

Often technology transfer is embedded in so-called industrial cooperation agreements between East and West. While little systematic empirical evidence is available with respect to these agreements, it is already clear that they vary tremendously in terms of magnitudes of capital and credit involved, resulting trade, transacting parties, and the degree of government intervention on both sides. In some cases such "cooperation" is nothing more than a straightforward licensing of a plant design, process or product to an Eastern country. In other instances it involves an agreement to exchange technological information, the co-production of an article for sale in the Western market, or a joint marketing agreement which may involve a sharing of marketing responsibilities in third countries. In still other (and the most publicized) cases, the nature of the transaction is less a "cooperation" agreement than a massive export of a system of complete plants, which involves the participation of consortiums of Western industrial firms and banks, and requires the export of capital equipment, materials, technical data, and credits in return for a payment stream over many years in hard currencies or perhaps Western purchase of a part of the plant's output.[28]

It is generally believed that these more complex transactions involving goods, technology and medium-term or long-term credit in East-West commerce have been more important for Western Europe, Canada and Japan than for the United States.[29] As will be argued in the next section, this is largely because of the more restrictive U.S. posture towards commodity exports, the extension of credit and the export of technical data to the Socialist world. The product structure of OECD exports to and imports from the East suggests further that these complicated commercial "packages" are much more characteristic of exports to the East than for the reverse. This is supported by the journalistic and other popular accounts of East-West trade, which seldom mention large transactions involving technology transfer to the West.

Despite the more restrictive nature of United States policies, there is some evidence that even U.S. commerce with the Eastern countries has become relatively less dependent on the simple exchange of goods. United States fees, royalties, and income from other services (excluding transport and tourist services) earned in Eastern Europe have risen as a percentage of U.S. merchandise exports to this region from five percent in 1960-61 to seven percent in the 1968-70 period. A similar grouping of service income accruing to the Eastern European countries in dealings with the United States has not grown in relative importance over this period, however, remaining at about 4 percent of total merchandise exports to the United States.[30]

Impact of U.S. Restrictions on East-West Trade

The relative deterioration of the U.S. role in East-West trade in the postwar period is perhaps best captured by Table 14-4, in which the relative volumes of trade with the East for the United States and its COCOM partners as a group are illustrated. Between 1948, when the United States began to implement its system of postwar "national security"-oriented controls, and 1957-9, U.S. trade with the Socialist countries fell dramatically while the other COCOM countries increased their Eastern trade at rates approximating ten percent annually. The U.S. decline was particularly spectacular, of course, with respect to trade with the Socialist countries of Asia, for which trade was virtually embargoed from 1950 onwards.

As we have seen, U.S. trade restrictions began to be liberalized gradually in the late 1950s, and there would appear to have been a turn away from autarky in the East as well, particularly after Stalin's death in 1953. Yet, in spite of the very low level to which U.S. trade had declined by the mid-1950s, the rate of growth of U.S. trade in the second period, 1957-9 to 1967-9, still failed to match that of its COCOM partners, who were not faced with the cumbersome extra-COCOM restrictions on trade with the East.

Nevertheless, there are many who doubt that unilateral U.S. restrictions have really worked to diminish trade significantly, and who remain extremely skeptical that unilateral U.S. trade liberalizations could really result in much trade expansion. Other obstacles exist to expanded U.S. trade with the East, it is argued, which tend to result in only marginal meaning, if any, for unilateral liberalization measures. These other barriers may be classified into three types: structural, ideological, and policy. The structural obstacles are most frequently cited. These include the relative U.S. lack of historic trading ties with the Eastern countries; the greater geographical distance (and hence higher transport costs) between the Eastern countries and the United States, relative to the other Western industrialized countries; and the continuing inconvertibility of the

Table 14-4

Total Trade with the Socialist Countries—U.S. and Other COCOM Countries

Trade with Socialist Countries of Eastern Europe	1948	(1957/59)	(1967/69)	Average Annual	Growth Rates
		(In $ Millions)		(1948-1957/9)	(1957/9-1967/9)
Exports:					
U.S.	123.1	95.8	219.9	Negative	8.7%
Other COCOM	453.1	1,294.6	4,064.1	11.1%	12.1%
Imports:					
U.S.	113.1	68.5	190.3	Negative	10.8%
Other COCOM	697.0	1,455.7	4,345.8	7.7%	11.5
Trade with Socialist Countries of Asia					
Exports:					
U.S.	273.4	a	a	Negative	–
Other COCOM	91.3	331.2	972.9	13.8%	11.4%
Imports:					
U.S.	120.3	5.4	2.4	Negative	Negative
Other COCOM	84.3	213.2	656.1	9.7%	11.9%

aNegligible.

Source: Compiled from U.S. Department of State, *Battle Act Report*, Washington, D.C., Various Issues.

Eastern currencies combined with their generally uncompetitive export sectors, which together have the effect of restricting the import potential of the Socialist countries and hence the export potential for the United States.

The principal ideological obstacle, according to the skeptics, is the unwillingness of U.S. businessmen, on moral or ideological grounds, to trade with Socialist countries. The basic policy obstacle which is cited is the lack of U.S. bilateral agreements with these countries, which is assumed to be a prerequisite for significant expansion of trade with the East.

Obviously all these barriers exist, together with others, and undoubtedly do work to keep trade with the East at lower levels than it otherwise would be. Nevertheless, existing empirical studies, and they are rare, for the most part suggest that the impact of unilateral U.S. export controls and the (until very recent) prohibition of Eximbank support for exports to these countries has had a significant impact on U.S. exports to this region. While the evidence with respect to imports is more tentative, it too suggests that the denial of MFN treatment to imports from most Socialist countries has an important trade restricting effect, in spite of the more general obstacles mentioned earlier.

Evidence of the significant restrictive effect of U.S. unilateral export controls is available at both the "micro" and "macro" levels. At least one American company has undertaken a survey of its own products with a view to obtaining perspective on this question. The Hewlett-Packard Co., a diversified corporation concentrating in electronic components and equipment, determined that in 1968, 44 percent of its worldwide sales were in products on the COCOM list. But an additional 53 percent of worldwide sales were composed of products which would have been subject to unilateral (extra-COCOM) control had the company attempted to export to the Socialist countries. In every instance investigated, the company found that competitive suppliers in other industrial countries could supply those goods to the Eastern countries.[31] This implied that (a) unilateral U.S. control was generally ineffective in denying these goods to the East, and (b) such unilateral control adversely affected the export potential of U.S. companies.

At a more macro level, a recent study which compares the U.S. share of Western industrialized countries' exports to the East, for both unilaterally-controlled products on the one hand, and multilaterally (COCOM) or uncontrolled articles on the other, concludes that over $300 million in potential exports to Eastern Europe (including the Soviet Union) were foregone in 1968 as a result of the unilateral control procedures. This compares with actual U.S. exports to the Socialist countries of Europe in 1968 of $217 million. Moreover, this study tentatively concluded that in that year this restrictive effect of unilateral export controls was roughly equivalent to the combined inhibiting impact of the various "structural" factors mentioned earlier.[32]

A more comprehensive study also attempted to estimate roughly the separate restrictive effects of the former prohibitions on Eximbank facilities to Eastern

Europe, and the impact of denying most of these countries MFN accommodation.[33] Table 14-5 presents the principal results of this study under the conservative assumption that total Western exports to the East would only grow at about half the rate between 1968 and 1975 as they did for the previous five-year period.

If anything, the various export estimates may be significantly underestimated, at least if actual 1969-71 export performance is any guide. U.S. exports to these same countries rose to $249 million in 1969, $354 million in 1970, and $384 million in 1971.[34] It is probable, of course, that some of this expansion reflects "decontrolling" which has already taken place since passage of the Export Administration Act in December 1969. The study shows that the greatest impact from liberalizing both the export control and Eximbank provisions would occur in the export of various types of machinery and transport equipment, various chemicals and chemical-based products such as plastics, and cereals and cereal preparations. This latter result is corroborated by the negotiation of a $136 million feed grain transaction in late 1971 between the United States and the Soviet Union, which was made possible by the administration's deletion of the "cargo preference" requirement in June 1971. Further confirmation is given by the $500 million deal in agricultural commodity exports negotiated in the summer, 1972 with the same country.

Montias has also presented evidence that the unilateral export restrictions

Table 14-5
Estimates of U.S. Trade with the Socialist Countries of Eastern Europe after Trade Liberalization (in $ millions)

| | 1968 | | 1975 | |
	U.S. Exports	U.S. Imports	U.S. Exports	U.S. Imports
Before Liberalization (1968: Actual Trade Volumes)	217	198	320	457
1–Elimination of Unilateral Export Controls	+342	–	+585	–
2–Elimination of Prohibition on Eximbank Support	+ 48	–	+ 85	–
3–1 and 2[a]	+589	–	+1,000	–
4–Granting of MFN	–	+220	–	+473

[a]The impact on trade volumes of alternative (3) would be more than the simple sum of the impact for alternatives (1) and (2) separately. For explanation see source.

Source: Thomas A. Wolf, "The Quantitative Impact of Liberalization of United States Unilateral Restrictions on Trade with the Socialist Countries of Eastern Europe," *External Research Study* XR/RECS-3, Washington, D.C., 1972.

have a significant trade restrictive impact. Employing comparative East-West trade statistics for 1928 and 1969, he demonstrates that the U.S. position in the Eastern European markets has sorely deteriorated since that time, and this decline is particularly noticeable in the case of machinery exports. In fact, if the U.S. had had the same share of the machinery export market in Eastern Europe in 1969 as in 1928, these exports alone would have been almost $550 million greater than actually recorded. While willing to attribute much of this decline to some of the structural factors mentioned above, he concludes that the major impediment rested with the unilateral export restrictions.[35]

The import estimates reported in Table 14-5 are more tentative. In any event the trade surplus which emerges with full liberalization by 1975 (alternative 3 plus 4 in Table 14-5) is probably unrealistically large. It is doubtful whether the Eastern European countries together could afford to run roughly a one-half billion dollar trade deficit with the U.S. alone, although it is interesting to note that this trade deficit amounted to as much as $161 million in 1971, before many of the liberalization measures already announced have their full effect. But the basic point is clear; while enormous U.S. export potential exists, only a portion of that business will be realized unless the westward flow of trade from the Eastern countries can be significantly augmented.

In theory U.S. imports from the Socialist countries should increase as a result of extension to these countries of MFN treatment. This is basically because of two effects—the substitution of lower-cost Eastern products for higher cost import-competing goods in the United States, and the substitution of lower-cost Eastern products for higher-cost imports from other foreign countries which are favored by the U.S. discrimination against imports from the Socialist world. The differences between the tariff rates applicable to the Socialist countries, with the exception of Poland, (column 2 rates) and the column 1 rates are in most cases appreciable. One study has tentatively calculated that for fifty-five 2-digit SITC product groups, the average non-MFN tariff rates are more than two times the MFN rate for thirty-eight of these groups, and more than three times as high for fourteen groups.[36]

Despite the very dramatic tariff differentials, it is not at all clear that the Socialist countries have the plant capacities, product quality or marketing skills to take advantage of the opportunities opened up once MFN is granted. As mentioned, this is one of the arguments of those who are skeptical about any significant expansion of East-West trade. Unfortunately, the available evidence on the one Socialist country to which MFN has been accorded is ambiguous. As noted earlier, Poland is the largest Eastern supplier to the U.S. market, accounting for an average of $101 million, or 46.5 percent of total Eastern exports to the United States in 1969-71. Yet this compares with a 45.2 percent share of the market in the 1956-60 period, the last five years before the granting of MFN. Polish exports to the United States have grown significantly in this period, from an average of $31.6 million in the 1956-60 period. But the growth of the other Socialist countries' exports has kept pace. If Poland was not able to increase its U.S. export-market share at the expense of the other Socialist countries after being accorded MFN, it is at least open to question whether these countries as a whole could significantly expand their exports to the United States at the expense of the competitive Western suppliers of the United States.[37]

Alternative East-West Trade Policies for the 1970s and their Implications

United States trade policies can only be reasonably evaluated within a framework which explicitly recognizes the tradeoff between economic welfare and national security-motivated, economic warfare. Generally speaking, freer trade means greater world productive efficiency and higher consumer welfare through lower prices brought about by international competition. Trade restrictions, whether for protectionist or national security reasons, reduce a country's exposure to international competition, and tend to diminish economic welfare as conventionally described. On balance there is not necessarily a welfare loss, however, if it can be demonstrated that in some sense the welfare of consumers and producers has been increased through the greater protection, whether from unemployment or from foreign attack, resulting from these trade barriers.

There exist two very basic alternative strategies with respect to trading with the Socialist world. One is to essentially ignore the national security-economic welfare tradeoff, and to pursue a more or less maximal strategy of *offensive* economic warfare.[38] That is to say, ignore the possibility that the economic losses following on a strategy of aggressive economic warfare might be significant, and adopt the posture that perhaps any economic cost is worth it if national security can be assured. This strategy comes close to that pursued by the United States in the early postwar period, when the number one priority appeared to be to stop Communist expansionism "at any cost." Needless to say, the influence of this type of thinking has greatly declined, even if it has not quite disappeared. As a strategy it undoubtedly makes eminent sense in the midst of a war or national crisis, providing the war or crisis is not too prolonged. But should the crisis situation seem to endure, one may legitimately question whether the crisis really continues to exist, or if it does, whether it still calls for a continued high level of economic sacrifice.

The other basic strategy, which involves a recognition of the inevitable national security-economic welfare tradeoff, has slowly come to influence and finally perhaps to dominate U.S. policy-making in regard to East-West trade. While there continue to be signs of Communist expansionism, little evidence has accumulated over the past quarter century that anything but the COCOM-coordinated control of an inner core of strategic goods has really made any difference in curbing Communist aggression. The Socialist countries as a group have been able to call upon enormous resources among themselves to foster their military and economic development. Furthermore, the attempt by the United States to deprive the Eastern countries of an even wider array of products than proscribed by the COCOM list has failed increasingly over the past twenty-five years. In the course of the postwar period the COCOM allies have narrowed the competitive edge of the United States and have looked more and more ambitiously for new export markets, often in the East. True, the withholding of U.S. supplies from the Eastern market has in general had the effect of raising the cost to those countries of economic development and expansion. But rapid economic growth has occurred anyway, and the hoped-for signs of internal rebellion are infrequent, and typically without much conse-quence in any event. Moreover, the apparent ineffectiveness of the strategy of unilateral offensive economic warfare has been matched, apparently, by real economic losses for the United States, as discussed in the preceding section.

It would seem, therefore, that the really interesting policy alternatives fall within the latter framework, in which the tradeoff between national security and economic welfare is clearly understood. These policy alternatives are essentially four-fold. One approach is to use trade liberalization vis-à-vis the East as a *quid pro quo* for political concessions. The intention could be either to reward recent reform or foreign policy initiatives favorable to the United States, to encourage future policy changes of this nature within these countries, or to actually link the U.S. economic concession and Eastern "political" concession in some form of formal or informal agreement. The latter course would seem to be out of the question with all the smaller Eastern European countries save the USSR, because such an agreement would presumably not be tolerated by the Soviet Union. A policy of weak linkage of U.S. economic and Eastern political policy changes would appear to have been pursued for some time in relation to the Rumanian government. Certainly it is no accident that Rumania, which consistently has had the most independent foreign policy in Eastern Europe, receives the most preferential export control treatment. As pointed out by Montias, however, this basic approach may not yield any enduring political advantages. The hopes that Poland would make far-reaching reforms after the ascendancy of the Gomulka regime in 1956 encouraged the U.S. to unilaterally grant MFN treatment to that country. Such hopes were soon disappointed.[39]

A second alternative is to negotiate a mutual reduction in economic barriers with the Socialist countries. This of course has been a common practice among the Allies in the postwar period, typically within the context of formal bilateral agreements. At stake here is the native American determination to minimize government intervention in business matters, and an historical unfamiliarity with and dislike for formal governmental bilateral trade agreements. Needless to say, these propensities are changing; witness the agreements with certain foreign governments to limit their exports to the American market of textiles, steel and footwear. Furthermore, the government increasingly is taking on an active role in promoting exports (for example, expansion of the Eximbank charter, OPIC, DISC). An important question here is what real concessions could the Socialist countries offer, and how can they be evaluated in terms of the concessions the United States is willing to make. Certainly guaranteeing U.S. exporters access to Eastern markets which is in some sense equivalent to that of other Western countries is an important consideration. This would include equivalent rights to exhibit and other forms of trade promotion, to hire sales representatives, and so forth. Questions concerning patent rights, licensing and arbitration of disputes could also be covered in such an agreement.[40] Obviously the United States would want its exports to receive MFN treatment in those Eastern countries which maintain retaliatory two or three-column tariff schedules, although it is not at all clear that these tariff schedules have a very significant bearing on the competitiveness of U.S. exports in these markets.

A third approach is to initiate unilateral measures of trade liberalization. Such steps would be taken perhaps with no specific political or economic *quid pro quo* in mind, but rather with a view to improving the overall atmosphere for cooperation with the Socialist countries, and with the objective too of achieving economic gains for the United States, either in the form of lower consumer prices through a lowering of import barriers, or an expansion of exports by eliminating various unilateral restrictions on these exports. There are several recent examples of this type of strategy: passage of the Export Administration Act of 1969, the Export Expansion Finance Act of 1971, the removal of embargoes on the substantial list of commodities for trade with mainland China as well as "decontrolling" various commodities for export to the USSR in the 1971-72 period, indicating the administration's willingness to make limited use of unilateral concessions.

A fourth alternative is simply a "mixed strategy" which seeks to use that particular type of policy change in any given situation which appears to jointly maximize some function composed of both national security and conventional economic considerations. Although reservations were voiced above about the first of the foregoing alternatives if utilized alone, the policy maker adopting this fourth approach would at least be choosing to retain maximum flexibility.

We have already discussed the inadequacy of an offensive economic warfare policy directed against the Socialist nations which seeks to stimulate internal rebellion in these countries. And hopes placed on "polycentric" foreign policy movements encouraged and rewarded by U.S. economic concessions have only in part been realized, Rumania being the sole example of real "polycentrism" in Eastern Europe. Yet it is not at all clear that the preferential treatment accorded Rumania by U.S. foreign economic policy has influenced the Rumanian policy. Presumably Rumania has followed this tack for both political and economic reasons primarily having to do with its relationship with the Soviet Union and integration within COMECON. We have little tangible evidence that the ability to purchase a wider array of products in the U.S. has been a central consideration for the Rumanians.

Likewise, the hopes placed on "internal reform" (first economic, induced by more trade with the West, then political, supposedly following naturally from the economic changes) encouraged by liberalized U.S. trade with the East have not been fulfilled. As mentioned earlier, such hopes with respect to Poland in the late 1950s and early 1960s were soon dashed. Rumania apparently is one of the least flexible regimes, internally; and Hungary, which is now boldly experimenting with some quite sweeping reforms, has never received any special economic advantages from the United States.

We conclude that an aggressive policy of unilateral economic warfare designed to achieve "containment," "rebellion," "polycentrism" or "reform" cannot be expected to yield any calculable results. The currents of international and internal politics are too swift and devious, and the combined resources of the Eastern countries too great, to be able to predict with any degree of success that political objectives of this kind can be achieved within the Socialist world. Given this assessment, and yet a continued concern with the problem of U.S. national security, an optimal policy might be characterized as a *defensive* policy of containment. Such a policy would view trade policy instruments not as a means for attaining specific political objectives. Rather, this approach would use these policy tools to protect the United States from economic or military developments which could be said to directly affect U.S. national security. Given such a general posture, a "mixed strategy" approach similar to that described above might be warranted. This policy would attempt to carefully differentiate between these situations which suggest seeking a political *quid pro quo*, those where mutual economic bargaining would be advantageous, and those in which unilateral trade concessions are in order.

It is altogether possible that mixing economic and political *quid pro quos* might make sense in the case of U.S. relations with the Soviet Union. But the burden of proof should be on those who argue that such a policy approach is reasonable. Given the fact that many U.S. policies are still way out of line with those of its Western allies, priority should probably continue to be given to unilateral trade liberalization, with the pros and cons of negotiating further mutual economic concessions continuing to be carefully examined.

Priorities remaining with respect to unilateral liberalization include: (a) Further decontrolling of the extraCOCOM commodity control list, so as to bring it closer in line with the multilaterally-agreed list; (b) active involvement of the Eximbank in supporting export credits extended to the Socialist countries, providing that there is satisfactory evidence that eventual repayment can be made (this would constitute a parallel move to recent announced intentions to involve the Overseas Private Investment Corporation (OPIC) in underwriting investments in certain Eastern countries);[41] (c) congressional action which would return to presidential discretion extension of MFN treatment to the

Socialist countries; and (d) amendment of the Johnson Act so as to terminate this archaic restriction on private capital outflows to the Eastern countries.

With regard to negotiation of mutual economic concessions with the Socialist countries, agreements should be concluded with these countries to end any discrimination practiced against U.S. exports. Furthermore, significant opportunities may well exist for assisting the Russians and also the Chinese in the development of their vast mineral resources, in return for long-run deliveries of various metals and fuels in which the United States is faced with rapidly deteriorating domestic reserves. In this connection, more thought needs to be given to defensive economic warfare considerations, including the careful delineation of acceptable ranges for the import of raw materials from the East.[42]

While the empirical evidence summarized in the previous section is only fragmentary and tentative,[f] it does suggest that such a positive strategy as outlined above would lead to a significant increase in U.S. economic intercourse with the East, and that aside from the favorable effects on domestic consumer prices and the expansion of certain industries (particularly those in the machinery and equipment sector), it would also help alleviate the problem of farm surpluses for certain commodities, and at least in the short run, would improve the overall merchandise balance of trade. It is impossible to precisely calculate all the economic benefits, but it is clear that they would be positive. The political and national security risks seem minimal. What is really at issue is the need to give up the old myth that the United States can engage in a policy of active unilateral economic warfare against the East with the expectation of gaining tangible political advantages that outweigh the economic sacrifices involved in such a policy.

Notes

1. For a fairly comprehensive history of the development of United States and other Western trade restrictions in the postwar period, see Gunnar Adler-Karlsson *Western Economic Warfare 1947-1967*, Stockholm, Almqvist and Wiksell, 1968.

2. See Thomas A. Wolf, "Optimum Tariff Theory and Differentiation Among Foreign Markets" (*Preprint Series*, International Institute of Management, Berlin, 1972) for a theoretical discussion of the general conditions which must be satisfied for a policy of offensive economic warfare to be successful.

3. Export Control Act of 1949, Section 2 (63 Stat. 7).

4. Mutual Defense Assistance Control Act of 1951 (65 Stat. 644) as amended by the Foreign Assistance Act of 1961 (75 Stat. 424).

[f]For example, the various estimates related only to possible expansion of trade with Eastern Europe and the Soviet Union. Lacking are similar tests for the Peoples' Republic of China and the other Socialist countries of Asia.

5. Transaction Control Regulations (31 CPR Part 505.10).

6. Trade Agreements Extension Act of 1951, Section 5 (65 Stat. 72).

7. For a more detailed discussion of this point, see Thomas A. Wolf, "Towards a Theory of Optimum Trade Policy in a National Security Context: The Case of United States Policies with Respect to East-West Trade" (unpublished dissertation, New York University Graduate School of Business Administration, 1971) pp. 191-97.

8. 19 U.S.C. 955 (1965).

9. Foreign Assets Control Regulations (31 CFR 500.101-500.808).

10. See President Kennedy's Inaugural Address, January 20, 1960; also President Johnson's State of the Union message, January 12, 1966.

11. See testimony of Laurence C. McQuade before 1968 Senate Committee on Banking and Currency hearings on *East-West Trade*, U.S. Government Printing Office, Washington, D.C., 1968, p. 221.

12. Foreign Assets Control Regulations (31 CFR 500.101-500.808). Actually the Commerce Department's Office of Export Control had established a virtual embargo on exports to North Vietnam at least as early as 1961 (see *Export Control*, Fifty-Fifth Quarterly Report, First Quarter 1961, Secretary of Commerce, Washington, D.C.).

13. Amendments to the Export Control Act of 1949, Section 3(a) (76 Stat. 127).

14. See *Export Control*, Sixty-First Quarterly Report, Third Quarter 1962, Secretary of Commerce, Washington, D.C., pp. 6-7.

15. President's Message submitted to the House Committee on Ways and Means, Hearings on the proposed *Trade Expansion Act of 1962*, 87th Congress, second session (U.S. GPO, Washington, D.C., 1962), p. 15.

16. Trade Expansion Act of 1962, section 231(a) (76 Stat. 872).

17. Foreign Assistance Act of 1963, section 402 (77 Stat. 379).

18. Export Administration Act of 1969, section 2 (PL 91-184).

19. "Legislative Provisions Relevant to Trade with Communist Countries," an information memorandum prepared by the Department of State.

20. Foreign Assistance and Related Agencies Appropriation Act of 1965, Title III (78 Stat. 1022). This act was actually passed in 1964.

21. Testimony of Harold F. Linder, President and Chairman, Export-Import Bank of the United States, and Warren W. Glick, Assistant General Counsel, Export-Import Bank, before 1968 Senate hearings on *East-West Trade*, pp. 130-34 and p. 147.

22. See section 2(b) of the Export-Import Act of 1945, as amended by PL 90-267.

23. Export Expansion Finance Act of 1971 (P1 92-126).

24. The *New York Times*, July 25, 1971; *International Herald Tribune*, October 2, 1971, and March 27, 1972.

25. *International Herald Tribune*, February 15, 1972.

26. Calculated from *Yearbook of International Trade Statistics*, New York, United Nations, 1971.

27. Calculated from "Trade of NATO Countries with Communist Countries, 1966 to 1969," *Research Study*, (unclassified) Bureau of Intelligence and Research, Department of State, December 17, 1970.

28. See Samuel Pisar *Coexistence and Commerce* (New York: McGraw-Hill, 1970), particularly Chapter 18.

29. Ibid. p. 76.

30. Compiled from various issues of the *Survey of Current Business*, Department of Commerce, Washington, D.C.

31. Statement submitted by Thomas A. Christiansen, Manager of International Planning, before 1969 Senate Committee on Banking and Currency hearings on *East-West Trade*, GPO, Washington, D.C., 1969.

32. Thomas A. Wolf "A Note on the Restrictive Effect of Unilateral United States Export Controls," *Journal of Political Economy*, forthcoming.

33. Thomas A. Wolf "The Quantitative Impact of Liberalization of United States Unilateral Restrictions on Trade with the Socialist Countries of Eastern Europe," *External Research Study* XP/RECS-3 (unclassified), U.S. Department of State, February 16, 1972.

34. *Export Control*, Ninety-Seventh Quarterly Report, Third Quarter 1971, Secretary of Commerce, Washington, D.C.; and *U.S. Foreign Trade: Highlights of Exports and Imports*, U.S. Department of Commerce, Washington, D.C., December 1971.

35. Statement of John M. Montias before the Joint Economic Committee hearings on *A Foreign Economic Policy for the 1970's*, 91st Cong., 2nd sess., GPO, Washington, D.C., 1971, pp. 1231-41.

36. Wolf, "Impact of Liberalization."

37. See also Stanislow Wasowski *East-West Trade and the Technology Gap*, New York, Praeger Publishers, 1970, p. 3.

38. The distinction between offensive and defensive economic warfare is developed at some length in Wolf, "Optimum Trade Policy," Pt. 1, Chapters 2 and 4.

39. Montias, hearings on *Foreign Economic Policy . . . 1970's*, p. 1253.

40. A bold outline for a new legal and institutional "charter" for East-West economic relations may be found in Pisar, *Coexistence and Commerce*, Chapter 25.

41. *International Herald Tribune*, March 22, 1972.

42. On this question see Wolf, "Optimum Tariff Theory."

15 Summary and Conclusions

The Editors

The intent of this volume has been to examine, in some depth, the major issues that confront United States commercial policy in the years ahead. The dominant theme is one of disunity: action and pressures for action will take place on a variety of fronts and will involve several different modalities. The United States frequently will have to *react* to the policy initiatives of others, but its ability to adopt a global perspective beyond its own short-run self-interest gives it a special challenge and responsibility. One possible thrust may develop in the direction of freer trade, focused on gradual elimination of some of the more traditional trade barriers—such as tariffs on industrial products—but even this will involve complex negotiations as nations attempt to assure themselves that their adjustment burden due to balance of payments and employment changes are tolerable. At the same time, however, there is the undeniable prospect of expanded governmental and intergovernmental involvement in the allocation of resources in a variety of sectors, and in the economy as a whole. The United States and Europe will be partners in the shaping of trade relations on a global scale, but they will be rivals on the issues of commercial regionalism and in competing for East-West trade.

One of the primary missions of the volume was to identify and analyze the growing tendency for national states to join with others in regional groups, to examine its implications for the United States and, in turn, to assess and evaluate the effects of alternative United States policy actions in the face of such regional segmentation of international commercial relations. At the same time, the volume was intended to bring out the increasing tendency for individual nations and regional groups of nations to control international trade in a discriminatory and frequently arbitrary manner by means other than tariffs. In the face of these dual policy thrusts, the argument was that the United States cannot maintain unequivocal adherence to admittedly laudable principles of nondiscrimination. If the United States is forced to abandon its historical position in this regard, what policy configurations would appear to make sense from the standpoint of the national interest? The volume sets out some of the alternatives in a number of spheres.

Overview

To summarize, this volume attempts to describe and analyze several of the major factors that will shape the future of U.S. commercial policy. The introductory chapter examined recent trends in international commercial policy and outlined the alternatives for the United States. It forms a unit with the second chapter on the domestic political dynamics of trade-policy formation and its expression in programs for multinational and regional liberalization of international commerce. An international comparison of tariff rates is presented for the industrial nations, both before and after the 1964-67 Kennedy Round of trade negotiations, the results of which have been fully implemented by the participating countries in 1972. The analysis included estimates of the effective rate of tariff protection accorded the specific economic sectors. The analysis was intended to provide a basis for estimates of the prospective impact on international trade flows of alternative commercial-policy options.

Coequal in importance was a major comprehensive analysis and classification of nontariff barriers to international trade for each of the industrial countries. The nature and operation of NTBs was discussed in detail with respect to their role as obstacles to international market access and tools of commercial policy. The frequency with which NTBs are applied was analyzed with reference to individual products and product groups as well as individual industrial countries applying them. The analysis paralleled the discussion of tariff obstacles, and the two studies together form an overall view of the principal governmental distortions of international trade in the 1970s.

Third, governmental distortions of international competitive relations must be seen in relation to barriers to effective market access applied by the private sector. This issue was analyzed, in a comparative context, as were the policies applied by the major industrial countries to promote effective competition and combat collusive business practices. Whether pursued globally or regionally, trade liberalization will fall short of its goals unless effective international competition is assured. This study brought out the importance of divergences in national competition policies and regulatory systems in achieving or inhibiting the goals of alternative commercial policy options and regional free-trade proposals.

Set against the extensive discussion of barriers to international competition and market access were a number of studies of the possible consequences of several trade-policy alternatives of relevance in the coming years. One empirical contribution addressed an issue that has received surprisingly little attention in the field of commercial policy and international economics generally: an assessment of the importance for trade flows and commercial policies of (a) similarities and dissimilarities in nations' respective industrial structures, (b) the relative size of national economies, (c) economic distance or proximity between individual national economies, (d) indications of relative costs, at existing exchange rates, of industries in various countries, (e) relative national tariff and nontariff structures, and (f) relative growth of individual industries. The analysis focused on the expected relative gains from the liberalization of trade among industrial countries based on these critical economic characteristics.

Another consideration is an analysis of the prospective impact of United States participation in broad-scale liberalization of tariffs on manufactures and semimanufactures among the industrial countries, which represents an important countervailing policy option to the prospect of intensified formation of regional trading blocs. This study was based on an adaptation of the International Monetary Fund world-trade econometric model to assess the impact of the indicated policy action after five years have elapsed.

Four additional contributions round out the substance of the volume by addressing specific issues of relevance to the liberalization of international trade, whether on a regional or global basis. One study considered the prospective indirect or "dynamic" effects of trade liberalization, with emphasis on potential economies of scale. In particular, the issue of economic size of markets was considered as a means of achieving the "economies of scale" by widening meaningful access to national economies by means of trade liberalization. A second study examined the critical area of agricultural trade and the implications of variations in national and regional farm-support programs—an area that already represents one of the principal obstacles to broad-gauge trade liberalization and a major area under administrative control in international commerce. The emphasis here was on the implications of the evolving agricultural policy in an enlarged EEC on United States trade and commercial-policy objectives. A third issue-oriented study deals with trade relations between developed and developing countries: the Commonwealth Preference System, the EEC-Yaoundé II arrangement in Africa and other bilateral preference schemes employed by the community, and the UNCTAD Generalized System of Preferences were examined within the overall context of trade discrimination. The implications of each of these issues were assessed both for the United States and the developing world. Finally, new trade policy options for the United States with respect to trade with the Socialist countries of Eastern Europe and Asia were examined, as was the effect of past U.S. policies.

Some Closing Thoughts

A principal unknown remains the configuration of economic and political pressures in the determination of the American trade policy position itself. Will the new protectionist sentiment of the late 1960s and early 1970s endure? The high unemployment, excess productive capacity, and an overvalued dollar of these years have not augered well for further liberalization of imports with a lack of dramatic evidence that the potential increase in export-centered jobs will more than offset the jobs lost from imports, and that the inevitable adjustment burdens will be substantially eased by government action; the environment of unemployment has fed and given credence lately to the protectionist sentiment. A widespread feeling that emerged is that the United States has given more than it has received in effective market-access to foreign goods (and investment), as a result of trade agreements in the postwar period.

But more than this, the economic structures of the United States and its trading partners will change markedly in the coming decades. Products in which the United States currently holds a competitive edge, or at least provides effective competition for imports, will gradually yield to foreign suppliers. Other products will emerge to bolster the overall U.S. trade position. Services, particularly the services of capital, will provide an increasing share of American earnings of foreign exchange. The basic question is whether such structural readjustments will be allowed to run their course and be reflected in the U.S. trade-policy position, or whether the protectionist pressures which would attempt to block them by additional governmental involvement will gain the upper hand.

Most striking on both fronts has been a U.S.-Japanese confrontation in 1970-71. With rapidly-expanding supply capabilities and liberal access to the American market, Japanese penetration reached massive proportions in a variety of products ranging from toys to automobiles to electronics. At the same time, the United States was effectively excluded from the Japanese markets for a wide variety of products by import controls and from viable direct investments in Japan. That the Japanese failed to see a confrontation emerging—or chose to ignore it—is an ominous sign. Asymetrical movements in technological and structural changes, in that one proceeds and the offsetting one is blocked, must inevitably give rise to a monetary disequilibrium. The danger is that the response to the monetary disequilibrium may be additional restrictive policies, attempting to shore up the defenses against both sides of the structural change, rather than the freeing of the one that was blocked in the first place. When this came in August 1971, on both the monetary and trade fronts, the Japanese and others were reported to have suffered "Nixon shock." But the results were a major revaluation of the Yen, the easing of Japanese import restrictions, and the liberalization of investment constraints, all of which tended to ease the problem in a liberalizing manner; whether this represents a permanent *modus vivendi* remains to be seen.

Certainly controls will remain for years to come and in some sectors may even be intensified, since "administrative guidance" is an integral part of the Japanese business system and a growing one in others. Pressure on U.S. markets from imports will ensure a continued bias toward "equitable" sharing of markets, which may continue to be handled through "voluntary" export quotas in the exporting countries or take on the more formal tone of multinational agreements. But a commercial détente has been temporarily achieved, and improvements in the world monetary system combined with a redefinition of Japanese economic goals may ensure a long-term commercial partnership. Both countries are outsiders with respect to European regionalism, and this may promote a common search for a long-term solution in the interests of both sides.

United States trade policy toward Western Europe likewise focuses on controls, most particularly related to agriculture. The EEC has adopted an agricultural policy that is probably the least favorable from the standpoint of U.S. interests, based on high internal support prices, variable import changes, and subsidized disposal of surpluses on world markets. Over the decade 1959-69, U.S. agricultural exports to the EEC increased by 78 percent in spite of the fact that the Common Agricultural Policy (CAP) was in the process of development. But in the latter half of that period (1964-69) the growth was only 6 percent, and the exports of most feed grains declined dramatically.

Here the United States and other efficient agricultural suppliers have a legitimate grievance, but one that is extremely sensitive politically. On the other hand the EEC insists on freer trade in industrial products—where it is competitive—and yet refuses to recognize that agricultural products—where it is not competitive—should be subject to similar terms of market access. On the other hand, agricultural products have been systematically excluded from past trade negotiations (and from generalized preferences for developing countries) partly because the United States was itself not prepared to accept more liberal trade in this sector. Being inexorably bound to domestic and regional income-maintenance and structural economic policies, it is virtually certain that strict controls will govern trade in farm products for the foreseeable future, although a certain degree of liberalization may be applied to trade in specific product groups.

The other point of friction in United States-EEC trade relations is the Common Market's aggressive preference and association policies with an expanding array of African and Mediterranean countries. These are clearly in violation of the spirit, if not the letter, of the GATT and are likely to expand significantly with the accession of the United Kingdom to the Community and with special bilateral arrangements for the non-EEC Western European countries. The EEC already accounts for 28 percent of world trade, and will account for almost 40 percent once enlargment is completed, representing over half of all trade among the industrial countries (compared with 14 percent for the United States).

The United States, Japan, and Canada are fast becoming the outsiders. There will be increasing pressure on Japan to reach an accommodation with the EEC, although its heavy dependence on the U.S. market and the community's fear of Japan's trade competitiveness will tend to counteract this. At the same time, it is clear that the community's preferential trade arrangements with the less-developed associated countries is far superior to its nonreciprocal generalized preferences for all developing nations. There will thus be a national tendency for LDCs in Latin America, Asia and elsewhere to seek special trade arrangements with the community, thereby tending further to isolate the United States and Japan. The final outcome could thus be be a global trading system based on terms and conditions set in Brussels, with which the United States and Japan would ultimately have to come to terms.

While this could be distasteful, it would hardly represent the worst possible outcome but it is also unlikely. More probable is that the United States and Japan will adopt defensive measures at an early stage, which could take one of two forms. Major new trade initiatives could further reduce tariffs and nontariff barriers on a multilateral basis and hence reduce or remove the margins of preference upon which the EEC-centered complex necessarily rests. Alternatively, each of the two poles could establish separate and defensive economic spheres based on trade preferences for a select group of countries in the Pacific Basin and Western Hemisphere, respectively. This would lead to a tripolarization of the international economy with a potential for increased, not decreased, commercial frictions and potential for crisis. Furthermore, while preferable to protected national economies, protected economic blocs would clearly be suboptimal from the standpoint of international resource allocation and production efficiency. So long as the margin of protection from outsiders is no higher than currently exists, this type of system would have definite advantages over the existing one based on a mixed bag of MFN policies and "bloc" exceptions for the European group. The real danger of blocs is that they become more exclusive via hidden NTBs, bilateral trade and payments agreements, and so on, with respect to nonmembers. The modern international economy forms an interdependent system, and a restrictive multipolar trading complex would clearly be out of harmony with that system.

Yet another question for American strategy concerns the developing countries, which have declined in terms of their share of world trade from 27 percent in 1953 to under 18 percent in 1970—compared with an increase from 63 to 72 percent for the developed market-economy countries and from 10.1 to 10.5 percent for the Socialist countries of Eastern Europe and Asia. The growth of trade in manufactures (in which the developing countries participate to a smaller extent) has been far more rapid than the growth of trade in primary products, where the LDCs have traditionally been important suppliers. In industrial raw materials, characterized by increasing competition from synthetics; in agricultural commodities, characterized by relatively low-income elasticity of demand and highly protected markets; and in labor-intensive manufactures, generally considered "sensitive" in most industrial countries; price, competitive, and protectionist trends have not favored the developing nations.

With the exception of oil, commodity agreements have not worked well and are conceptually unsound, partly due to an inherent tendency to fall apart, and partly because of the existence of substitute materials. "Standstills" on new trade restrictions on exports of developing countries are of little practical value, since government simply cannot preclude entirely the option to intervene in the case of market disruptions. Trade preferences have fallen far short of their goals, again because of the inability or unwillingness of the major markets to permit rapid market-penetration in sensitive product categories.

In part, a fundamental weakness lies with the developing countries themselves, in the form of prohibitive import controls which, in turn, impede satisfactory export performance. This has also prevented many developing countries—with the notable exceptions of Mexico, Brazil, South Korea, Taiwan, and Hong Kong—from harnessing the ability of multinational corporations to pursue global sourcing and intraindustry specialization on the basis of value added governed by national costs of production. What good is improved general or preferential access to world markets if the LDCs' own import barriers prevent effective supply? The problem should of course, be tackled *as a unit*, with developing and developed countries' trade barriers liberalized simultaneously— with the important side-benefit of ensuring export opportunities for the industrial nations. Trade negotiations to this point have not faced this issue, although in a perverse sort of way perhaps the EEC "reverse preferences" have (unintentionally) moved part of the way in this direction.

On the agricultural side, the developing countries should soon realize that significant liberalization will be long in coming, even if pursued by a coincidence of interest with such powerful allies as the United States. Export dependence on temperate-zone foodstuffs and on substitutable tropical commodities will provide little hope for optimism in the foreseeable future.

Lastly, the developing countries lack the leverage to exact significant trade concessions from the advanced countries. They must play by the rules that the rich countries set; they rarely get the opportunity to participate in setting those rules. Certainly in the area of market-sharing arrangements, the developing countries will be at a severe disadvantage since the resultant quantitative limits on trade growth will impede the achievement of viable economic size.

These issues, together with the increasingly close tie between international trade, foreign investment, and world monetary questions, will determine the shape of things to come. Their sorting out in the environment of multiple international negotiations will be slow and arduous, but surely the price of "muddling through" is lower than renewed protectionism in isolated national— or regional—enclaves.

Index

accounting: and cost approximation, 269
acreage limitation program, 289
advance deposits, 81
African Franc Zone, 339
African Malagary associates, 339
aggregation: and industry definitions, 200
agriculture: barriers as protection, 41; commodities, 11; gains in sector, 285; and NTB, 96, 119; policy formulation, 290
Algeria: and EEC, 345
Alliance for Progress, 351
allocation, of resources, 262
American Economic Association, 140
Andean Group, 41, 317, 352
Ankara Convention: strategy, 344
Ankara Protocol, 344
anticompetitive practices, 132
antidumping measures, 79
antitrust, 133
Arab-Israeli War, 140
Argentina: and EEC, 352
Arusha Convention, 341
assimilation policy, 317
Athens Convention, 344
Atlantic Alliance, 337
Atlantic Charter, 321
Australia: agricultural exports, 290; industrial efficiency, 275; industrial structure, 201; trade adjustment costs, 221
Austria: high tariffs, 54; industrial efficiency, 275; industrial structure, 200, 201; linear tariff reductions, 360
automobiles, 406
Automotive Products Act, 1965, 315

Bain, J.: comparative plant size, 271–273; plant concentration, 263
balance-of-payments, 6, 32; deficits, 336; and disunity, 403; and NTB, 65–69, 91
Balassa, B., 46
Baldwin, R.E., 116–118
bananas: external tariff, 350
barriers: trade and economic variables, 234. See restrictions.
"Battle Act," 377
Baumgartner-Pisani proposals, 292
Belgium: cartels, 156; colonial empire, 335; disclosure law, 134; industrial efficiency, 275
Berlin blockade, 376
bilateralism, 315
bonus voucher scheme, 313
border tax: adjustments, 80

boycotts, 128
Brasseur, Maurice, 355
Brasseur Plan: tariff quota, 361
Brazil: bias against exports, 313
British Corn Laws, 285
British Imperial Preference, 320
British Monopolies Act, 138
British Nylon Spinners, 136
BTN (Brussels Tariff Nomenclature), 310, 322
buffers: and tariff quota, 364–367
Bulgaria: cartels, 156
"burden-sharing," 356
Burke-Hartke bill, 163, 311
buy-domestic: extensions, 78

CACM (Central American Common Market), 312
Canada: agricultural liberalization, 119; agriculture exports, 290; bilateral negotiations, 210; disclosure laws, 134; NTB structure, 108; industry size, 274; linear tariff reductions, 360; NTB use, 92; paper products, 200; plant concentration, 263; plant size, 271; subcontracting, 264; world-trade model, 230
Canadian Act to Provide for the Investigation of Combines, Monopolies, Trusts and Mergers, 123
Canadian-U.S. Automotive Agreement, 3, 41, 166, 308
cartels, 12, 84, 126, 150; Philips case, 133–135, 155, 156. See Canada, Germany, etc.
cash assistance, 313
ceilings: tariff quota mechanism, 364–367
Central African customs, 338
Central American Common Market, 41
cereal grains: and Poland, 379
chemical industry: growth rate, 217
China: and normalization of relations, 384
citrus fruit: commodity and special interest, 343; U.S. competition with Spain, Israel, 348
COCOM (Coordinating Committee of the Consultative Group), 377
coffee: African Franc Zone, 350; common external tariff, 338
collective bonus, 147
collective exclusive dealing, 131
colonial background, 318–320
Commerce Dept. (U.S.): and commodity control list, 377–382

411

About the Authors

Harry H. Bell, formerly Director of the Research Division, United Nations Conference on Trade and Development, Geneva, is a private consultant on international economic and development affairs in Washington, D.C.

Corwin D. Edwards, prior to his retirement in 1971 was Professor of Economics at the University of Chicago and, subsequently, Professor of Economics at the University of Oregon.

Morris Goldstein is a Staff Economist in the Research Department of the International Monetary Fund, Washington, D.C.

Robert G. Hawkins is a Professor of Economics at the Graduate School of Business Administration, New York University.

Ernest H. Preeg, formerly a Foreign Affairs Fellow at the Council on Foreign Relations and a Guest Scholar at the Brookings Institution, is a member of the Planning and Coordination Staff of the Department of State in Washington, currently on leave to the National Planning Association for a study on the tripolarization of the world economy.

Rita M. Rodriguez is Assistant Professor at the Harvard Graduate School of Business Administration, Boston, Massachusetts.

Ingo Walter is Professor of Economics and Finance at the Graduate School of Business Administration and a Senior Fellow at the Center for International Studies, New York University.

Thomas A. Wolf is a Research Fellow at the International Institute of Management in Berlin, Germany.